PORTFOLIO / PENGUIN

ALL THE DEVILS ARE HERE

Bethany McLean is a writer for *Vanity Fair* and the coauthor of *The Smartest Guys in the Room: The Amazing Rise and Scandalous Fall of Enron*. Before joining *Vanity Fair*, she wrote for *Fortune* for thirteen years (most recently as an editor at large) and spent three years working in the investment banking division of Goldman Sachs. She lives in Chicago.

Joe Nocera is a columnist for *The New York Times*. He spent ten years at *Fortune* as a contributing writer, editor at large, executive editor, and editorial director. He has won three Gerald Loeb awards for excellence in business journalism and was a finalist for a Pulitzer Prize in 2006. He lives in New York.

ALL THE DEVILS ARE HERE

The Hidden History of the Financial Crisis

Bethany McLean and Joe Nocera

Portfolio / Penguin

PORTFOLIO / PENGUIN
Published by the Penguin Group
Penguin Group (USA) Inc., 375 Hudson Street, New York, New York 10014, U.S.A. • Penguin Group (Canada), 90 Eglinton Avenue East, Suite 700, Toronto, Ontario, Canada M4P 2Y3 (a division of Pearson Penguin Canada Inc.) • Penguin Books Ltd, 80 Strand, London WC2R 0RL, England • Penguin Ireland, 25 St Stephen's Green, Dublin 2, Ireland (a division of Penguin Books Ltd) • Penguin Books Australia Ltd, 250 Camberwell Road, Camberwell, Victoria 3124, Australia (a division of Pearson Australia Group Pty Ltd) • Penguin Books India Pvt Ltd, 11 Community Centre, Panchsheel Park, New Delhi – 110 017, India • Penguin Group (NZ), 67 Apollo Drive, Rosedale, Auckland 0632, New Zealand (a division of Pearson New Zealand Ltd) • Penguin Books (South Africa) (Pty) Ltd, 24 Sturdee Avenue, Rosebank, Johannesburg 2196, South Africa

Penguin Books Ltd, Registered Offices: 80 Strand, London WC2R 0RL, England

First published in the United States of America by Portfolio, a member of Penguin Group (USA) Inc. 2010
This paperback edition with a new afterword published 2011

THE LIBRARY OF CONGRESS HAS CATALOGED THE HARDCOVER EDITION AS FOLLOWS:
McLean, Bethany.
All the devils are here : the hidden history of the financial crisis / Bethany McLean and Joe Nocera.
p.   cm.
Includes index.
ISBN 978-1-59184-363-4 (hc.)
ISBN 978-1-59184-438-9 (pbk.)
1. Global Financial Crisis, 2008–2009   2. Financial crises—United States—History—21st century.
3. Mortgage-backed securities—United States.   4. Subprime mortgage loans—United States.
I. Nocera, Joseph.   II. Title.
HB3717.2008 .M35 2010
330.973'093—dc22   2010032893

Printed in the United States of America
Designed by Carla Bolte • Set in Adobe Garamond

For Sean, and Dawn

CONTENTS

CAST OF CHARACTERS

THE MORTGAGE MEN

Ameriquest

Roland Arnall Founder of ACC Capital Holdings, the parent company of Ameriquest. A subprime lending pioneer who became a billionaire. His first company, Long Beach Mortgage, spawned more than a dozen other subprime companies.

Aseem Mital Ameriquest veteran who became CEO in 2005.

Ed Parker Mortgage veteran hired in 2003 to investigate lending fraud in Ameriquest's branches.

Deval Patrick Assistant attorney general who led the government's charge against Long Beach in 1996, only to join Ameriquest's board in 2004.

Countrywide Financial

Stanford Kurland President and COO. Long seen as Mozilo's successor, he left the company in 2006.

David Loeb Co-founder, president, and chairman. Stepped down in 2000.

John McMurray Countrywide's chief risk officer.

Angelo Mozilo Co-founder and CEO until 2008. Dreamed of spreading homeownership to the masses. Became a billionaire in the process, but couldn't resist pressure to enter the subprime mortgage business.

David Sambol The head of Countrywide's sales force. Aggressively pushed Countrywide to keep up with subprime lenders.

Eric Sieracki Longtime Countrywide employee who was named CFO in 2005.

Primary Residential

Dave Zitting Old-school mortgage banker who steered clear of subprime lending.

Ownit

Bill Dallas Founder of Ownit, a subprime company in which Merrill Lynch held a 20 percent stake.

THE FINANCIAL INSTITUTIONS

American International Group (AIG)

Steve Bensinger CFO under Martin Sullivan from 2005 to 2008.

Joe Cassano CEO of AIG Financial Products from 2001 to 2008.

Andrew Forster One of Cassano's chief deputies in London.

Al Frost AIG-FP marketer at the center of the multisector CDO deals that put AIG on the hook for $60 billion of subprime exposure.

Maurice R. "Hank" Greenberg AIG's CEO from 1968 to 2005. Forced to resign by Eliot Spitzer.

Gene Park AIG-FP executive who noticed the early warning signs on multisector CDOs.

Tom Savage CEO of AIG-FP from 1994 to 2001.

Howard Sosin Founder of AIG-FP. Ran it from 1987 to 1993.

Martin Sullivan Succeeded Greenberg in 2005. Forced out by the board in 2008.

Robert Willumstad Sullivan's successor as CEO until the financial crisis hit four months later.

Bear Stearns

Ralph Cioffi Bear Stearns hedge fund manager. His two funds—originally worth $20 billion—went bankrupt in the summer of 2007 because of their subprime exposure.

Matthew Tannin Cioffi's partner. Cioffi and Tannin were tried for fraud and found not guilty.

Steve Van Solkema Analyst who worked for Cioffi and Tannin.

Fannie Mae

Jim Johnson CEO from 1991 to 1998. Perfected Fannie's take-no-prisoners approach to regulators and critics.

Daniel Mudd CEO from 2005 to 2008.

Franklin Raines CEO from 1999 to 2004. Forced to step down over an accounting scandal.

Goldman Sachs

Josh Birnbaum Star trader who specialized in the ABX index.

Lloyd Blankfein Current CEO.

Craig Broderick Current chief risk officer.

Gary Cohn Current president and COO.

Jon Corzine Senior partner who convinced the partnership to go public. Replaced by Hank Paulson within days of the IPO.

Steve Friedman Co-head of Goldman Sachs with Robert Rubin.

Dan Sparks Head of the Goldman mortgage desk from 2006 to 2008.

Michael Swenson Co-head of the structured products group under Sparks.

John Thain Co-COO under Paulson until 2003.

Fabrice Tourre Mortgage trader under Sparks. Later named as a defendant in the SEC's suit against the company.

David Viniar CFO.

J.P. Morgan

Mark Brickell Lobbyist who fought derivatives regulation on behalf of J.P. Morgan and the International Swaps and Derivatives Association. President of ISDA from 1988 to 1992.

Till Guldimann Executive who led the development of Value at Risk modeling and shared VaR with other banks.

Blythe Masters Derivatives saleswoman who put together J.P. Morgan's first credit default swap in 1994.

Sir Dennis Weatherstone Chairman and CEO from 1990 to 1994.

Merrill Lynch

Michael Blum Executive charged with purchasing a mortgage company, First Franklin, in 2006. Served on Ownit's board.

John Breit Longtime Merrill Lynch risk manager who specialized in evaluating derivatives risk.

Ahmass Fakahany Co-president and COO under CEO Stanley O'Neal.

Greg Fleming Co-president—with Fakahany—until O'Neal's resignation in 2007.

Dow Kim Head of trading and investment banking until 2007.

David Komansky O'Neal's predecessor as CEO.

Jeffrey Kronthal Oversaw Merrill's mortgage trading desk under Kim. Fired in 2006.

Dale Lattanzio Chris Ricciardi's successor as the leader of Merrill Lynch's CDO business.

Stan O'Neal CEO from 2002 to 2007. Created the culture that allowed the buildup of Merrill Lynch's massive exposure to securities backed by subprime mortgages.

Tom Patrick CFO under Komansky and executive vice chairman under O'Neal. Seen as O'Neal's ally until O'Neal fired him in 2003.

Chris Ricciardi Head of Merrill's CDO team from 2003 to 2006. While at Prudential Securities in the mid-1990s, worked on one of the first mortgage-backed CDOs.

Osman Semerci Installed as global head of fixed income, reporting to Kim, in 2006. Fired in 2007.

Arshad Zakaria Head of global markets and investment banking. Considered a close ally of O'Neal until forced out in August 2003.

Moody's

Mark Adelson Longtime Moody's analyst and co-head of the asset-backed securities group whose skepticism was at odds with Brian Clarkson's vision for the agency. Quit in 2000.

Brian Clarkson Co-head of the asset-backed securities group who aggressively pursued market share. Named president in 2007.

Eric Kolchinsky Managing director in charge of rating asset-backed CDOs. Oversaw the rating process for John Paulson's Abacus deal.

Raymond McDaniel CEO.

THE PIONEERS

Larry Fink Devised the idea of "tranching" mortgage-backed securities to parcel out risk. Underwrote some of the first mortgage-backed securities for First Boston in the 1980s. Later founded BlackRock and served as a key government adviser during the financial crisis.

David Maxwell Fannie Mae's CEO from 1981 to 1991. Important player in the early days of mortgage securitization.

Lew Ranieri Salomon Brothers bond trader who helped invent the mortgage-backed security in the 1980s.

THE REGULATORS

Attorneys General

Prentiss Cox Head of the consumer enforcement division in the Minnesota attorney general's office from 2001 to 2005.

Tom Miller Iowa attorney general who fought predatory lending.

Eliot Spitzer New York State attorney general from 1999 to 2006.

Commodity Futures Trading Commission

Brooksley Born Chair of the CFTC from 1996 to 1999. Attempted to increase oversight of derivatives dealers.

Wendy Gramm Chair of the CFTC from 1988 to 1993.

Michael Greenberger Director of the CFTC's division of trading and markets under Born.

United States Congress

Richard Baker Louisiana congressman who introduced a bill to reform Fannie Mae and Freddie Mac in 1999.

James Bothwell Author of two key General Accounting Office reports, one criticizing Fannie and Freddie and the other calling for regulation of derivatives.

Charles Bowsher Head of the GAO from 1981 to 1996. Bothwell's ally.

Phil Gramm Chairman of the Senate banking committee from 1989 to 2003. Opposed regulation of derivatives. The "Gramm" in Gramm-Leach-Bliley, the law that abolished the Glass-Steagall Act.

Jim Leach Chair of the House banking committee from 1995 to 2001. Criticized Fannie and Freddie. The "Leach" in Gramm-Leach-Bliley.

Department of Housing and Urban Development

Andrew Cuomo HUD secretary from 1997 to 2001. Crossed swords with Jim Johnson. Increased Fannie and Freddie's affordable housing goals.

Armando Falcon Jr. Director of the Office of Federal Housing Enterprise Oversight from 1999 to 2005. Outspoken critic of Fannie and Freddie, the two institutions his office was charged with regulating.

Jim Lockhart Director of OFHEO from 2006 to 2008.

Department of the Treasury

John Dugan Comptroller of the currency starting in 2004.

Gary Gensler Former Goldman executive who became assistant Treasury secretary under Robert Rubin. Testified in favor of Baker's bill. Current chairman of the U.S. Commodity Futures Trading Commission.

James Gilleran Director of the Office of Thrift Supervision from 2001 to 2005.

John "Jerry" Hawke Comptroller of the currency from 1998 to 2004.

Henry "Hank" Paulson Jr. Treasury secretary from 2006 to 2009. Previously chairman and CEO of Goldman Sachs.

John Reich Director of the OTS from 2005 to 2009.

Robert Rubin Treasury secretary from 1995 to 1999. Previously co-chairman of Goldman Sachs.

Bob Steel Undersecretary for domestic finance in 2006. Former Goldman vice chairman brought to Treasury by Paulson.

Larry Summers Treasury secretary from 1999 to 2001. Rubin's deputy before that. Along with Rubin and Alan Greenspan, the third member of "the Committee to Save the World."

Federal Deposit Insurance Corporation

Sheila Bair Current chair of the FDIC. Assistant Treasury secretary for financial institutions from 2001 to 2002.

Donna Tanoue Chair of the FDIC from 1998 to 2001.

Federal Reserve

Ben Bernanke Chairman of the Federal Reserve starting in 2006.

Timothy Geithner President of the New York Federal Reserve from 2003 to 2009.

Edward "Ned" Gramlich Federal Reserve governor from 1997 to 2005. Longtime head of the Fed's committee on consumer and community affairs under Alan Greenspan.

Alan Greenspan Chairman of the Federal Reserve from 1987 to 2006.

Securities and Exchange Commission

Christopher Cox Chairman from 2005 to 2009.

Arthur Levitt Chairman from 1993 to 2001.

THE SKEPTICS

Michael Burry California hedge fund manager who began shorting mortgage-backed securities in 2005.

Robert Gnaizda Former general counsel of the public policy group Greenlining Institute who called for scrutiny of unregulated lenders.

Greg Lippman Deutsche Bank mortgage trader. One of the few Wall Street traders to turn against subprime mortgages early on.

John Paulson Hedge fund manager who made $4 billion buying credit default swaps on subprime mortgage-backed securities.

Andrew Redleaf Head of the Minneapolis-based hedge fund Whitebox Advisors. Used credit default swaps to short the subprime mortgage market in 2006.

Josh Rosner Former Wall Street analyst who grew skeptical of the housing boom. Published a research paper entitled "A Home without Equity Is Just a Rental with Debt" in 2001.

KEY ACRONYMS

ABCP: Asset-backed commercial paper. Very short-term loans, allowing firms to conduct their daily business, backed by mortgages or other assets. Part of the "plumbing" of Wall Street.

ABS: Asset-backed securities. Bonds comprising thousands of loans—which could include credit card debt, student loans, auto loans, and mortgages—bundled together into a security.

AIG: American International Group.

ARM: Adjustable-rate mortgage.

CDOs: Collateralized debt obligations. Securities that comprise the debt of different companies or tranches of asset-backed securities.

CDOs Squared: Collateralized debt obligations squared. Securities backed by tranches of other CDOs.

CFTC: Commodities Futures Trading Commission. Government agency that regulates the futures industry.

CSE: Consolidated supervised entities. An effort by the Securities and Exchange Commission in 2004 to create a voluntary supervisory regime to regulate the big investment bank holding companies.

FCIC: Financial Crisis Inquiry Commission. Commission charged by Congress with investigating the causes of the financial crisis.

FDIC: Federal Deposit Insurance Corporation. Government agency that insures bank deposits and takes over failing banks. Also plays a supervisory role over the banking industry.

FHA: Federal Housing Administration.

GAO: General Accounting Office. Government agency that conducts investigations at the request of members of Congress.

GSEs: Government-sponsored enterprises. Washington-speak for Fannie Mae and Freddie Mac.

HOEPA: The Homeownership and Equity Protection Act. A 1994 law giving the Federal Reserve the authority to prohibit abusive lending practices.

HUD: Department of Housing and Urban Development. Sets "affordable housing goals" for Fannie Mae and Freddie Mac.

LTCM: Long-Term Capital Management. Large hedge fund that collapsed in 1998.

MBS: Mortgage-backed securities.

NRSROs: Nationally Recognized Statistical Ratings Organizations. The three major credit rating agencies, Moody's, Standard & Poor's, and Fitch, were granted this status by the government.

OCC: Office of the Comptroller of the Currency. The primary national bank regulator.

OFHEO: Office of Federal Housing Enterprise Oversight. Fannie Mae's and Freddie Mac's regulator from 1992 to 2008.

OTS: Office of Thrift Supervision. Regulated the S&L industry, as well as certain other financial institutions, including AIG.

PWG: President's Working Group on Financial Markets. Consists of the secretary of the Treasury and the chairmen of the Securities and Exchange Commission, the Federal Reserve, and the Commodities Futures Trading Commission.

REMIC: Real Estate Mortgage Investment Conduit. The second of two laws passed in the 1980s to aid the new mortgage-backed securities market by enabling such securities to be created without the risk of dire tax consequences.

RMBS: Residential mortgage-backed securities. Securities backed by residential mortgages, rather than commercial mortgages.

RTC: Resolution Trust Corporation. Government agency created to clean up the S&L crisis.

SEC: Securities and Exchange Commission. Regulates securities firms, mutual funds, and other entities that trade stocks on behalf of investors.

SMMEA: Secondary Mortgage Market Enhancement Act. The first of two laws passed in the 1980s to aid the new mortgage-backed securities market

SIV: Structured investment vehicle. Thinly capitalized entities set up by banks and others to invest in securities. By the height of the boom, many ended up owning billions in CDOs and other mortgage-backed securities.

VaR: Value at Risk. Key measure of risk developed by J.P. Morgan in the early 1990s.

ALL THE DEVILS
ARE HERE

Prologue

S tan O'Neal wanted to see him. How strange.

It was September 2007. The two men hadn't talked in years, certainly not since O'Neal had become CEO of Merrill Lynch in 2002. Back then, John Breit had been one of the company's most powerful risk managers. A former physicist, Breit had been the head of market risk. He reported directly to Merrill's chief financial officer and had access to the board of directors. He specialized in evaluating complex derivatives trades. Everybody knew that John Breit was one of the best risk managers on Wall Street.

But slowly, over the years, Breit had been stripped of his authority—and, more important, his ability to manage Merrill Lynch's risk. First O'Neal had tapped one of his closest allies to head up risk management, but the man didn't seem to know anything about risk. Then many of the risk managers were removed from the trading floor. Within the span of one year, Breit had lost his access to the directors and was told to report to a newly promoted risk chief, who, alone, would deal with O'Neal's ally. Breit quit in protest, but returned a few months later when Merrill's head of trading pleaded with him to come back to manage risk for some of the trading desks.

In July 2006, however, a core group of Merrill traders had been abruptly fired. Most of the replacements refused to speak to Breit, or provide him the information he needed to do his job. They got abusive when he asked about risky trades. Eventually, he was exiled to a small office on a different floor, far away from the trading desks.

Did Stan O'Neal know any of this history? Breit had no way of knowing. What he did know, however, was that Merrill Lynch was in an awful lot of trouble—and that the company was still in denial about it. He had begun to hear rumblings that something wasn't right on the mortgage desk, especially its trading of complex securities backed by subprime mortgages—that is, mortgages made to people wuth substandard credit. For years, Wall Street had been churning out these securities. Many of them had triple-A ratings, meaning they were considered almost as safe as Treasury bonds. No firm had done more of these deals than Merrill Lynch.

Calling in a favor from a friend in the finance department, Breit got ahold of a spreadsheet that listed the underlying collateral for one security on Merrill's books, something called a synthetic collateralized debt obligation squared, or sythentic CDO squared. As soon as he looked at it, Breit realized that the collateral—bits and pieces of mortgage loans that had been made by subprime companies—was awful. Many of the mortgages either had already defaulted or would soon default, which meant the security itself was going to tumble in value. The triple-A rating was in jeopardy. Merrill was likely to lose tens of millions of dollars on just this one synthetic CDO squared.

Breit started calling in more favors. How much of this stuff did Merrill Lynch have on its books? How bad was the rest of the collateral? And when in the world had all this happened? Pretty soon he had the answers. They were worse than he could possibly have imagined. Merrill Lynch had a staggering $55 billion worth of these securities on its books. They were all backed by subprime mortgages made to a population of Americans who, in all likelihood, would never be able to pay those loans back. More than $40 billion of that exposure had been added in the previous year, after he had been banished from the trading floor. The reckless behavior this implied was just incredible.

A few months earlier, two Bear Stearns hedge funds—funds that contained the exact same kind of subprime securities as the ones on Merrill's books— had collapsed. Inside Merrill, there was a growing nervousness, but the leaders of the mortgage desk kept insisting that its losses would be contained— they were going to be less than $100 million, they said. The top brass, including O'Neal, accepted their judgment. Breit knew better. The losses were going to be huge—there was no getting around it. He began to tell everybody he bumped into at Merrill Lynch that the company was going to have to write down billions upon billions of dollars in its subprime-backed securities. When the head of the fixed-income desk found out what Breit was saying, he called Breit and screamed at him.

Stan O'Neal had also heard that Breit had a higher estimate for Merrill Lynch's potential losses. That is why he summoned Breit to his office.

"I hear you have a model," O'Neal said.

"Not a model," Breit replied. "Just a back-of-the-envelope calculation." The third quarter would end in a few weeks, and Merrill would have to report the write-downs in its earnings release. How bad did he think it would be? O'Neal asked. "Six billion," said Breit. But he added, "It could be a lot worse." Breit had focused only on a small portion of Merrill's exposure, he explained; he hadn't been able to examine the entire portfolio.

Breit would never forget how O'Neal looked at that moment. He looked like he had just been kicked in the stomach and was about to throw up. Over and over again, he kept asking Breit how it could have happened. Hadn't Merrill Lynch bought credit default swaps to protect itself against defaults? Why hadn't the risk been reflected in the risk models? Why hadn't the risk managers caught the problem and stopped the trades? Why hadn't *Breit* done anything to stop it? Listening to him, Breit realized that O'Neal seemed to have no idea that Merrill's risk management function had been sidelined.

The meeting finally came to an end; Breit shook O'Neal's hand and wished him luck. "I hope we talk again," he said.

"I don't know," replied O'Neal. "I'm not sure how much longer I'll be around."

O'Neal went back to his desk to contemplate the disaster he now knew was unavoidable—not just for Merrill Lynch but for all of Wall Street. John Breit walked back to his office with the strange realization that he—a midlevel employee utterly out of the loop—had just informed one of the most powerful men on Wall Street that the party was over.

1

The Three Amigos

The seeds of financial disaster were sown more than thirty years ago when three smart, ambitious men, working sometimes in concert—allies in a cause they all believed in—and sometimes in opposition—competitors trying to gain advantage over each other—created a shiny new financial vehicle called the mortgage-backed security. In the simplest of terms, it allowed Wall Street to scoop up loans made to people who were buying homes, bundle them together by the thousands, and then resell the bundle, in bits and pieces, to investors. Lewis Ranieri, the messianic bond trader who ran the Salomon Brothers mortgage desk and whose role in the creation of this new product would be immortalized in the best-selling book *Liar's Poker*, was one. Larry Fink, his archrival at First Boston, who would later go on to found BlackRock, one of the world's largest asset management firms, and who served as a key adviser to the government during the financial crisis, was another. David Maxwell, the chief executive of the Federal National Mortgage Association, a quasi-governmental corporation known as Fannie Mae, was the third. With varying degrees of fervor they all thought they were doing something not just innovative but important. When they testified before Congress—as they did often in those days—they stressed not (heaven forbid!) the money their firms were going to reap from mortgage-backed securities, but rather all the ways these newfangled bonds were making the American Dream of owning one's own home possible. Ranieri, in particular, used to wax rhapsodically about the benefits of mortgage-backed securities for homeowners, claiming, correctly, that the investor demand for the mortgage bonds that he and the others were creating was increasing the level of home-ownership in the country.

4

These men were no saints, and they all knew there were fortunes at stake. But the idea that mortgage-backed securities would also lead inexorably to the rise of the subprime industry, that they would create hidden, systemic risks the likes of which the financial world had never before seen, that they would undo the connection between borrowers and lenders in ways that were truly dangerous—that wasn't even in their frame of reference. Or, as Ranieri told *Fortune* magazine after it was all over: "I wasn't out to invent the biggest floating craps game of all time, but that's what happened."

It was the late 1970s. The baby boom generation was growing up. Boomers were going to want their own homes, just like their parents. But given their vast numbers—there were 76 million births between 1949 and 1964—many economists worried that there wouldn't be enough capital to fund all their mortgages. This worry was exacerbated by the fact that the main provider of mortgages, the savings and loan, or thrift, industry, was in terrible straits. The thrifts financed their loans by offering depositors savings accounts, which paid an interest rate set by law at 5¾ percent. Yet because the late 1970s was also a time of high inflation and double-digit interest rates, customers were moving their money out of S&Ls and into new vehicles like money market funds, which paid much higher interest. "The thrifts were becoming destabilized," Ranieri would later recall. "The funding mechanism was broken."

Besides, the mortgage market was highly inefficient. In certain areas of the country, at certain times, there might be a shortage of funds. In other places and other times, there might be a surplus. There was no mechanism for tapping into a broader pool of funds. As Dick Pratt, the former chairman of the Federal Home Loan Bank Board, once told Congress, "It's the largest capital market in the world, virtually, and it is one which was sheltered from the normal processes of the capital markets." In theory at least, putting capital to its most efficient use was what Wall Street did.

The story as it would later be told is that Ranieri and Fink succeeded by inventing the process of securitization—a process that would become so commonplace on Wall Street that in time it would be used to bundle not just mortgages but auto loans, credit card loans, commercial loans, you name it. Ranieri named the process "securitization" because, as he described it at the time, it was a "technology that in essence enables us to convert a mortgage into a bond"—that is, a security. Fink developed a key technique called tranching, which allowed the securitizer to carve up a mortgage bond into pieces (tranches), according to the different risks it entailed, so that it could be sold to investors who had an appetite for those particular risks. The cash flows from the mortgages were meted out accordingly.

The truth is, though, that the creation of mortgage-backed securities was never something Wall Street did entirely on its own. As clever and driven as Fink and Ranieri were, they would never have succeeded if the government hadn't paved the way, changing laws, for instance, that stood in the way of this new market. More important, they couldn't have done it without the involvement of Fannie Mae and its sibling, Freddie Mac, the Federal Home Loan Mortgage Corporation. The complicated interplay that evolved between Wall Street and these two strange companies—a story of alliances and feuds, of dependency and resentments—gave rise to a mortgage-backed securities market that was far more dysfunctional than anyone realized at the time. And out of that dysfunction grew the beginnings of the crisis of 2008.

Almost since the phrase "The American Dream" was coined in the early 1930s, it has been synonymous with homeownership. In a way that isn't true in most other countries, homeownership is something that the vast majority of Americans aspire to. It suggests upward mobility, opportunity, a stake in something that matters. Historically, owning a home hasn't just been about taking possession of an appreciating asset, or even having a roof over one's head. It has also been a statement about values.

Not surprisingly, government policy has long encouraged homeownership. The home mortgage interest deduction is a classic example. So is the thirty-year fixed mortgage, which is standard in only one other country (Denmark) and is designed to allow middle-class families to afford monthly mortgage payments. For decades, federal law gave the S&L industry a small interest rate advantage over the banking industry—the housing differential, this advantage was called. All of these policies had unswerving bipartisan support. Criticizing them was political heresy.

Fannie Mae and Freddie Mac were also important agents of government homeownership policy. They, too, were insulated from criticism. Fannie Mae, the older of the two, was born during the Great Depression. Its original role was to buy up mortgages that the Veterans Administration and the Federal Housing Administration were guaranteeing, thus freeing up capital to allow for more government-insured loans to be made.

In 1968, Fannie was split into two companies. One, nicknamed Ginnie Mae, continued buying up government-insured loans and remained firmly a part of the government. Fannie, however, was allowed to do several new things: it was allowed to buy conventional mortgages (ones that had not been insured by the government), and it was allowed to issue securities backed by mortgages it had guaranteed. In the process, Fannie became a very odd creature. Half government enterprise, it had a vaguely defined social mandate from Congress to make housing more available to low- and middle-income Americans. Half private enterprise, it had shareholders, a board of directors, and the structure of a typical corporation.

At about the same time, Congress created Freddie Mac to buy up mortgages from the thrift industry. Again, the idea was that these purchases would free up capital, allowing the S&Ls to make more mortgages. Until 1989, when Freddie Mac joined Fannie Mae as a publicly traded company, Freddie was actually owned by the thrift industry and was overseen by the Federal Home Loan Bank Board, which regulated the S&Ls. People in Washington called Fannie and Freddie the GSEs, which stood for government-sponsored enterprises.

Here's a surprising fact: it was the government, not Wall Street, that first securitized modern mortgages. Ginnie Mae came first, selling securities beginning in 1970 that consisted of FHA and VA loans, and guaranteeing the payment of principal and interest. A year later, Freddie Mac issued the first mortgage-backed securities using conventional mortgages, also with principal and interest guaranteed. In doing so, it was taking on the risk that the borrower might default, while transferring the interest rate risk from the S&Ls to a third party: investors. Soon, Freddie was using Wall Street to market its securities. Volume grew slowly. It was not a huge success.

Though a thirty-year fixed mortgage may seem simple to a borrower, mortgages come full of complex risks for investors. Thirty years, after all, is a long time. In the space of three decades, not only is it likely that interest rates will change, but—who knows?—the borrowers might fall on hard times and default. In addition, mortgages come with something called prepayment risk. Because borrowers have the right to prepay their mortgages, investors can't be sure that the cash flow from the mortgage will stay at the level they were expecting. The prepayment risk diminishes the value of the bond. Ginnie and Freddie's securities removed the default risk, but did nothing about any of these other risks. They simply distributed the cash flows from the pool of mortgages on a pro rata basis. Whatever happened after that, well, that was the investors' problem.

When Wall Street got into the act, it focused on devising securities that would appeal to a much broader group of investors and create far more demand than a Ginnie or Freddie bond. Part of the answer came from tranching, carving up the bond according to different kinds of risks. Investors found this appealing because different tranches could be jiggered to meet the particular needs of different investors. For instance, you could create what came to be known as stripped securities. One strip paid only interest; another only principal. If interest rates declined and everyone refinanced, the interest-only strips could be worthless. But if rates rose, investors would make a nice profit.

Sure enough, parceling out risk in this fashion gave mortgage-backed securities enormous appeal to a wide variety of investors. From a standing start in the late 1970s, bonds created from mortgages on single-family homes grew to more than $350 billion by 1981, according to a report by the Securities and Exchange Commission. (By the end of 2001, that number had risen to $3.3 trillion.)

Tranching was also good for Wall Street, because the firms underwriting the mortgage-backed bonds could sell the various pieces for more money than the sum of the whole. And bankers could extract rich fees. Plus, of course, Wall Street could make money from trading the new securities. By 1983, according to *Business Week*, Ranieri's mortgage finance group at Salomon Brothers accounted for close to half of Salomon's $415 million in profits. Along with junk bonds, mortgage-backed bonds became a defining feature of the 1980s financial markets.

Tranching, however, was not the only necessary ingredient. A second important factor was the involvement of the credit rating agencies: Moody's, Standard & Poor's, and, later, Fitch Ratings. Ranieri pushed hard to get the rating agencies involved, because he realized that investors were never going to be comfortable with—or, to be blunt, willing to work hard enough to understand—the intricacies of the hundreds or thousands of mortgages inside each security. "People didn't even know what the average length of a mortgage was," Ranieri would later recall. "You needed to impose structures that were relatively simple for investors to understand, so that they didn't have to become mortgage experts." Investors understood what ratings meant, and Congress and the regulators placed such trust in the rating agencies that they had designated them as Nationally Recognized Statistical Ratings Organizations, or NRSROs. Among other things, the law allowed investors who weren't supposed to take much risk—like pension funds—to invest in certain securities if they had a high enough rating.

Up until then, the rating agencies had built their business entirely around corporate bonds, rating them on a scale from triple-A (the safest of the safe) to triple-B (the bottom rung of what was so-called investment grade) and all the way to D (default). At first, they resisted rating these new bonds, but they eventually came around, as they realized that rating mortgage-backed securities could be a good secondary business, especially as the volume grew. Very quickly, they became an integral part of the process, and so-called structured finance became a key source of profits for the rating agencies.

And the third thing Ranieri and Fink needed in order to make mortgage-backed securities appealing to investors? They needed Fannie Mae and Freddie Mac.

—∞—

At around the same time Ranieri and Fink were trying to figure out how to make mortgage-backed securities work, Fannie Mae was going broke. It was losing a million dollars a day and "rushing toward a collapse that could have been one of the most disastrous in modern history," as the *Washington Post* later put it. As interest rates skyrocketed, Fannie found itself in the same kind of dire trouble as many of the thrifts, and for the same reason. Unlike Freddie Mac, which had off-loaded its interest rate risk to investors, Fannie Mae had kept the thirty-year fixed-rate mortgages it bought on its books. Now it was choking on those mortgages. Things got so bad that it had a "months to go" chart measuring how long it could survive if interest rates didn't decline. It had even devised a plan to call on the Federal Reserve to save it if the banks stopped lending it money.

Two things saved Fannie Mae. First, the banks never did stop lending it money. Why? Because their working assumption was that Fannie Mae's status as a government-sponsored enterprise, with its central role in making thirty-year mortgages possible for middle-class Americans, meant that the federal government would always be there to bail it out if it ever got into serious trouble. Although there was nothing in the statute privatizing Fannie Mae that stated this explicitly—and Fannie executives would spend decades coyly denying that they had an unspoken government safety net—that's what everyone believed. Over time, Fannie Mae's implicit government guarantee, as it came to be called, became a critical source of its power and success.

The second thing that saved Fannie Mae was the arrival, in 1981, of David Maxwell as its new chief executive. Maxwell's predecessor, a former California Republican congressman named Allan Oakley Hunter, was not particularly astute about business, nor were the people around him. During the Carter administration, when he should have been focusing on the effects of rising interest rates on Fannie's portfolio, he had instead spent his time feuding with Patricia Harris, Carter's secretary of Housing and Urban Development.

Like Hunter, Maxwell had once been a Republican. A Philadelphia native, he graduated from Yale, where he was a champion tennis player, and then Harvard, where he studied law, before joining the Nixon administration as general counsel of HUD. When he was approached to run Fannie, he was living in California, running a mortgage insurance company called Ticor Mortgage, and he'd converted to the Democratic Party because he felt that in California that was the only way to have any influence. "I was a businessman," Maxwell says now. A businessman was exactly what Fannie Mae needed. Jim Johnson, the Democratic power broker who succeeded Maxwell as Fannie's CEO in the 1990s, would later say that he "stabilized the company as a long-term force in housing finance." Judy Kennedy, an affordable housing advocate who worked for Freddie Mac as a lobbyist in the late 1980s, puts it more grandly. She calls Maxwell a "transformative figure."

Maxwell was gracious and charming—the sort of man who sent handwritten notes, opened his office door to all his employees, and took boxes of books with him to read on vacation—but he was also incredibly tough, with blue eyes that could turn steely cold. He did not tolerate mediocrity. He couldn't afford to. "He was fighting for the survival of the company, and anyone, no matter what level, who was not up to the task left or was asked to leave," says William "Bill" Maloni, who spent two decades as Fannie's chief lobbyist. During Maxwell's ten-year reign, Fannie had four presidents and burned through lower-level executives. When Maxwell retired, the company's head of communications made a video that showed corporate cars moving in and out of Fannie's offices with body bags in the trunks.

Maxwell immediately began running Fannie in a more businesslike fashion. He tightened the standards for the loans that Fannie bought. He put in new management systems. Under Hunter, Fannie used to buy mortgages as much as a year in advance. That meant that lenders had time to see where interest rates were going, then shove off only unprofitable loans on Fannie. Maxwell changed that, too.

The Three Amigos   11

What he couldn't change was the combination of resentment and envy that Washington felt toward Fannie Mae. There was, Maxwell says, "tremendous disdain" for Fannie. "All over Washington, there were people doing stressful, important jobs for not a lot of money, and here was this place on Wisconsin Avenue where people did work that wasn't any more challenging—and yet, by Washington standards, they made huge amounts." He remembers taking his wife to a dinner party shortly after he arrived in town. "By the time we left, she was in tears, and I was close!" he later recalled.

Fannie's ostentatious headquarters didn't help. Under Hunter, the company had moved from modest digs on Fifteenth Street to a building in Georgetown that resembled a giant mansion. The front section had been occupied by an insurance company; to build the back to match perfectly, Fannie had a brickyard reopened specifically to supply the proper brick. "To many people, it was a living symbol of power and arrogance," says Maxwell.

Yet for all their resentment, people were envious of Fannie Mae's employees. They all wanted cushy jobs there—so they could get rich, too. "It happened over and over again," Maxwell says. "The same people who had power over you, whether they were congressional staffers or HUD employees or even members of Congress, wanted jobs and would unabashedly seek them. If you didn't hire them, then you had enemies."

Like Ranieri, Maxwell sang from the hymnal of homeownership. He'd later say that another reason for his conversion to the Democratic Party was his irritation at Republican attitudes toward affordable housing. Under Maxwell, Fannie created an office of low- and moderate-income housing, and the company helped pioneer the first deals that used the low-income housing tax credit program to create affordable rental housing. But he also understood that homeownership was Fannie's trump card: it's what made the company untouchable. Under Maxwell, Fannie also began to trumpet its contributions to affordable housing in advertisements. In addition, Fannie's press releases began to describe it, and Freddie, as "private taxpaying corporations that operate at no cost to taxpayers."

Also like Ranieri, Maxwell saw how critical mortgage-backed securities were to the future of the housing market—and to his company's bottom line. For Fannie, selling mortgage-backed securities was a way not only to get risk off its own books, but to earn big fees. Mortgage-backed securities represented an opportunity for Fannie to become even more central to the housing market than it already was, because the GSEs were the natural middleman between mortgage holders and Wall Street. If Fannie grabbed hold of that role—and kept it for itself—a profitable future was assured.

In public settings, Ranieri and Maxwell were generous in their praise for each other. "I think he's a genius, synonymous with Wall Street's entrance into mortgage finance," Maxwell told an audience of savings and loan executives in 1984. "David, as much as I, understood the implications of what I was trying to do," says Ranieri today. "He was my ally. We needed them and they needed us."

But under the surface, it was always an uneasy alliance. Ranieri was part of Wall Street. No one on the Street wanted to cede huge chunks of possible profit to the GSEs. "David and I jockeyed," Ranieri acknowledges. "The intellectual argument was, what should the government do? What should it be allowed to win at?" A person close to Ranieri put it more bluntly: "Despite his alliance with Fannie and Freddie, [Ranieri] was against them." He wanted Fannie and Freddie to have, at best, a junior role. Maxwell wanted to prevent Wall Street from shutting Fannie Mae out, and he wanted to establish the primacy of the GSEs in this new market. For all the noble talk about helping people buy homes, what ensued was really a fight about money and power.

What made Fannie and Freddie indispensable in the new mortgage market was one simple fact: the mortgages they guaranteed were the only mortgages investors wanted to buy. After all, the GSE guarantee meant that the investors no longer had to worry about the risk that homeowners would default, because Fannie and Freddie were assuming that risk. For some investors, GSE-backed paper was the only type of mortgage they were even *allowed* to buy. In many states, it was against the law for pension funds to purchase "private" mortgage-backed securities. But it was perfectly okay for them to buy mortgage securities backed by the GSEs, because those were treated like obligations from the government. States, meanwhile, had blue sky laws designed to prevent investment fraud, meaning that Wall Street firms had to register with each of the fifty states to sell mortgage-backed deals, a process they had to repeat on every single deal. Mortgage-backed securities issued by the GSEs were exempt from blue sky laws. In 1977, in one of the earliest efforts to put together a mortgage-backed securities deal, Salomon Brothers developed a bond made up of Bank of America mortgages. It was a bust. After that, almost all the early deals were ones in which Fannie and Freddie were the actual issuers of the mortgage-backed securities, while Wall Street was essentially the marketer.

Even before the advent of mortgage-backed securities, Fannie and Freddie had the reputation of being "difficult, prickly, and willing to throw their weight around at a senior level," according to one person who had regular dealings with them. It didn't matter. They couldn't be shut out of the market, because they *were* the market. By June 1983, the government agencies had issued almost $230 billion in mortgage-backed securities, while the purely private sector had issued only $10 billion. That same year, Larry Fink and First Boston pioneered the very first so-called collateralized mortgage obligation, or CMO, a mortgage-backed security with three radically different tranches: one with short-term five-year debt, a second with medium-term twelve-year debt, and a third with long-term thirty-year debt. (Fink still keeps on his desk a memento from the deal; it has a tricycle to memorialize the three tranches.) But as usual, the actual issuer of the mortgages wasn't First Boston. It was Freddie Mac. "They [the GSEs] were the enabler," Ranieri would later explain. "They wound up having to be the point of the spear."

The fees from these deals were plentiful, to be sure. The sheer excitement of building this new market was exhilarating. But there was something about being subservient to the GSEs—with all the built-in advantages that came with their quasi-government status—that stuck in Ranieri's craw. He wanted the role of the GSEs to be radically reduced. And if the only way he could get that done was to go to Washington and get some laws changed, then that's what he would do. Thus began the quiet war between Lew Ranieri and David Maxwell.

Ranieri had strong ties to the Reagan administration and knew he would find a receptive audience there. Like every president, Ronald Reagan professed to stand squarely on the side of the American homeowner. But David Stockman, his budget director; Larry Kudlow, one of Stockman's key deputies; and a handful of others, didn't believe that homeownership was necessarily synonymous with Fannie Mae. In particular, they didn't like the implied government guarantee. As market-oriented conservatives, they believed that the private sector was perfectly capable of issuing mortgage-backed securities without Fannie and Freddie. In 1982, President Reagan's Commission on Housing even recommended that the GSEs eventually lose their government status entirely.

With Ranieri's help, the administration drafted a bill to put Wall Street on a more equal footing with the GSEs. It was called the Secondary Mortgage Market Enhancement Act, although those in the know always used its slightly slippery-sounding acronym when they talked about it: SMMEA. Ranieri had another name for it: "the private sector existence bill." Failure to pass it, he warned Congress, would risk "turning the mortgage market of America into a totally government franchise." Ranieri was in Reagan's office when the act was signed into law in October 1984.

SMMEA exempted mortgage-backed securities, which constitute the secondary mortgage market (direct loans are the primary market), from state blue sky laws restricting the issue of new financial products. It removed the restrictions against institutions like state-chartered financial institutions, pension funds, and insurance companies from investing in mortgage-backed securities issued by Wall Street, even when they lacked a GSE guarantee. It also enshrined the role of the credit rating agencies, by insisting that mortgage bonds had to be highly rated to be eligible for purchase by pension funds and similar low-risk investors. Although there were worries that the rating agencies were being given too much responsibility, the bill's supporters reassured Congress that investors wouldn't rely solely on a rating to buy a mortgage bond. "GE Credit does not believe that investors in MBS will accept any substitute for disclosure," testified Claude Pope Jr., the chairman of GE's mortgage insurance business. The rating requirement "serves only as an additional independent validation of the issue's quality."

Helpful though it was, SMMEA didn't fully level the playing field. "No truly private company can compete effectively with Fannie Mae or Freddie Mac, operating under their special charter," Pope told lawmakers. What he meant, in part, was that because of the GSEs' implicit government guarantee, investors were willing to pay a higher price for Fannie- and Freddie-backed securities, since the federal government appeared to be standing behind them. For the same reason, Fannie and Freddie could borrow money at a lower cost than even mighty General Electric, with its triple-A rating. SMMEA or no SMMEA, the GSEs were still likely to dominate the market; in fact, they were even in a position to monopolize it, if they so chose. Investors still valued the GSE securities more than anything else Wall Street could produce.

There was a telling moment during one of the many congressional hearings on mortgage-backed securities. A congressman asked Maxwell whether he thought, as the congressman put it, "there is enough for everybody." "There is plenty," responded Maxwell. In response to a similar question, Ranieri countered, "I will have to completely differ." In truth, there was never going to be enough for both Wall Street and the GSEs.

The vehicle for shutting out Fannie Mae and Freddie Mac—or at least trying to—was a second piece of legislation Ranieri and Wall Street wanted.

Under the existing tax laws, it was quite possible that the cash flows from tranched securities could be subject to double taxation. (In 1983 the Internal Revenue Service actually challenged a Sears Mortgage Securities Corporation deal on these grounds, sending shudders of fear through investors.) So the inventors of mortgage-backed securities also wanted a bill that would lay out a specific road map for creating securities that wouldn't be taxed twice. Ranieri was emphatic—he thought this would be a "very powerful" tool. And while he never came out and said it shouldn't be given to the GSEs, his testimony makes it clear that that's what he thought. "If you do not give it to them, you have the potential to have the private sector outprice the agencies," he told Congress. "Do you wish to use [this structure] as a method to curtail the power of the agencies?" The Reagan Treasury agreed; the administration insisted that it would not support any legislation "that permits the government-related agencies to participate directly or indirectly in this new market," as a Treasury official testified. This bill, the official continued, should be "viewed as a first step toward privatization of the secondary mortgage market."

"It was directly symptomatic of another problem that existed later," Maxwell says now. "As we became bigger and had a bigger profile, everybody got scared." Says Lou Nevins, Ranieri's former lobbyist: "Fannie saw their ultimate trivialization if the bill passed and they couldn't be issuers." Fannie, in other words, felt it was fighting for its very survival. But Wall Street was fighting for something that, to it, was just as important: money. As with all new products, the profit margins were initially very high—up to 1 percent, says Nevins, meaning, for example, $10 million for assembling a $1 billion mortgage-backed security. The feeling on Wall Street, according to Nevins, was that "this is a gravy train, a gold mine, and we're not sure how long it is going to last, but if Fannie can be an issuer, the gold is going to dry up quickly."

And yet, ironically, to get a bill passed that took care of the double-taxation problem, Ranieri needed Maxwell's support. Maxwell wanted the legislation passed, too; the double-taxation problem was simply too threatening to the potentially lucrative new market. Realizing they needed each other, Ranieri and Maxwell put aside their differences and worked together to push the thing through Congress. To this day, though, there is disagreement over who did the heavy lifting. ("We had the brainpower and did most of the work on the Hill," Ranieri recalls; Maloni says that Fannie "did the lion's share of the work" pushing the bill through Congress.) In 1986, after a number of fits and starts, Congress finally passed the second bill as part of the Tax Reform Act of 1986. It was known as the REMIC law, referring to the real estate mortgage investment conduit, which became the shorthand phrase for deals in which mortgage-backed securities were carved into tranches. In essence, the law created a straightforward process for issuing multiclass securities and avoiding double taxation. Needless to say, it did not specifically prevent Fannie or Freddie from doing REMIC deals; had anyone insisted on that, Maxwell would surely have fought it instead of backing the bill.

Sure enough, the new market exploded. In December 1986, Fannie did its first REMIC offering. It sold $500 million of securities in a deal that was led by Ranieri's mortgage desk at Salomon Brothers. That year, according to the *New York Times*, the mortgage-backed securities market totaled more than $200 billion. Underwriting fees were estimated at more than $1 billion. And mortgage specialists were convinced REMICs would dominate the secondary market. "It became the way mortgages were funded in the United States," Nevins explains.

Almost as quickly, warfare broke out between Fannie Mae and Wall Street. "We worked hand and glove with the New York guys, and then they turned and tried to screw us," grumbles Maloni. Fannie Mae fought back with a display of bare-knuckled politics and public threats that if it didn't get its way, the cost of homeownership would certainly rise—an attitude that would characterize its approach to its critics for much of the next two decades.

The battle was joined in the spring of 1987, when five investment banks—Salomon Brothers, First Boston, Merrill Lynch, Goldman Sachs, and Shearson Lehman—banded together "in an effort to persuade the government to bar [Fannie] from the newest and one of the most lucrative mortgage underwriting markets," as the *New York Times* put it. The way Maxwell and Ranieri had dealt with the issue of whether Fannie should be allowed to issue REMIC securities prior to the passage of the law was by kicking the can: Fannie and Freddie were granted the ability to issue REMIC securities—but only temporarily. HUD was charged with the task of granting (or denying) Fannie Mae permanent approval, while the Federal Home Loan Bank Board had to make the same decision for Freddie Mac. The investment banks filed a hundred-page brief with HUD secretary Samuel Pierce, arguing that if HUD gave Fannie REMIC authority, they would "use their ability to borrow at lower costs to undercut the private sector," as Tom Vartanian, the lawyer hired by the investment banks to press their cause, told the *New York Times*.

It was a bitter fight. The big S&Ls, which also feared Fannie's market power, sided with Wall Street. The head of research at the United States

League of Savings Institutions, the lobbying organization for the S&Ls, told the *Times* that it cost Salomon two and a half times what it cost Fannie to issue a REMIC. Allowing Fannie to issue these securities, they complained, would force the private market out.

Fannie, in what would become its response whenever it was challenged, wrapped itself in the mantle of homeownership. It argued that its low costs also lowered mortgage rates for consumers, and that forcing it out of the market would make homes more expensive. In a March 1987 speech to the Mortgage Bankers Association, Maxwell said that the attack on Fannie Mae was part of a campaign by Wall Street and the big thrifts to "restore inefficiency to the housing finance system in order to increase their profits through higher home mortgage rates." He added, "They don't seem to care if this would close the door on homeownership for thousands upon thousands of American families."

In the end, Pierce ruled that Fannie could issue up to $15 billion in REMICs over the following fifteen months. Vartanian's clients trumpeted it as a victory, because the number wasn't unlimited, but as he says today, "it was a short-term victory. We lived to fight another day, and we lived to lose another day." Sure enough, by late 1988, Fannie had been granted "permanent and unlimited authority" to issue REMICs.

How did Fannie Mae persuade Pierce to rule in its favor? Not by sweet-talking, that's for sure; Maxwell had an iron fist inside that velvet glove of his. "We essentially gutted some of HUD's control over us in a bill that passed the House housing subcommittee," Maloni says today. In that bill HUD's ability to approve new programs was revoked. HUD went to Fannie, and essentially pleaded for mercy. "In return for us asking the Congress to drop the provision, HUD approved Fannie as issuers," says Maloni.

Maloni also called Lou Nevins and told him that if Salomon didn't back off, Fannie wouldn't do business with the bank anymore. (Maxwell denies knowing about the call.) For all their conflicts, Salomon Brothers had been Fannie Mae's banker, bringing its mortgage-backed deals to market and underwriting its debt offerings, making millions in fees as a result. This was a major threat. "It's like the post office saying we won't deliver your mail!" Nevins says. He remembers thinking to himself, "If they get away with this, there won't be a private company in the world that will stand up to them."

With the benefit of hindsight, it's hard to argue that REMIC authority was the cataclysmic event that either party feared it was at the time. While Fannie

issued its own securities, Wall Street made immense amounts of money marketing and selling them—Fannie never had the ability to find the Japanese
bank or the Midwest insurance company that might want a specific tranche.
And Fannie was always going to play an important role in the mortgage-
backed market because of its guarantees, which were prized by investors.
Essentially, it got to decide which mortgages were worthy of securitization
and which were not, and mortgage lenders had to offer mortgages that con-
formed to the GSEs' strict standards. Indeed, after all the hype over REMICs,
a series of big losses at several Wall Street firms—trader talk had it that Merrill Lynch lost over $300 million, which at the time was a big sum—caused
the market to cool on carving up cash flows in such extraordinarily complex
ways. At least for a time, the Street returned to old-fashioned pass-through
securities, the ones that didn't tranche the bonds, but simply sent the cash
flow along to investors. The hedge fund manager David Askin, who lost
hundreds of millions of investors' money buying mortgage-backed securities
that were supposed to have very low risk, told *Institutional Investor* that "not
all this stuff is for kids in the studio audience to try and do at home."

On the other hand, the future of the mortgage market might have been
very different if Fannie Mae had lost control of it at that critical juncture.
And the battle between Fannie and Wall Street did have consequences that
would linger for a very long time. The threats that Fannie had faced—not
just from a Wall Street that wanted to clip its wings, but from a White House
that wanted to take away its built-in advantages—deeply affected Fannie's
corporate mind-set. Its attitude became one of outsized aggression toward
even the most insignificant of threats. "You punch my brother, I'll burn your
house down" was the saying around the company. The idea that Fannie
should be stripped of its government advantages became, in Maloni's words,
"the vampire issue": it never completely went away. Fannie always felt that
its opponents, whether competitors or critics in the government, were out
to kill it. In this, it was absolutely right.

In addition, the REMIC fight established Fannie and Freddie as forces
not just in Washington but on Wall Street. The two companies completely
dominated the market for so-called conforming mortgages—that is, thirty-
year fixed mortgages under a certain size made to buyers with good credit
histories. "It was the end of the game," says Nevins. By the end of the 1980s,
there was more than $611 billion worth of outstanding GSE-guaranteed
mortgage-backed securities, according to a study by economic consulting

firm Empiris LLC. The outstanding volume of private mortgage-backed securities—the ones without GSE guarantees—was just $55 billion, less than one-tenth that amount. Fannie, meanwhile, went from losing a million dollars a day to making more than $1 billion a year. Its market value exploded from $550 million to $10.5 billion.

As for the larger dangers of mortgage-backed securities—the ones that would emerge in the years before the financial crisis—they were largely overlooked as Wall Street and the GSEs raced to establish a market for their new miracle product. Largely, but not entirely. At one congressional hearing, Leon Kendall, then chairman of the Mortgage Guaranty Insurance Corporation, a private insurer of mortgages, offered up a prophetic warning: "With all our concern in enhancing the secondary mortgage market, we should continue to have appropriate and equivalent concern relative to keeping people in houses." Historically, he noted, less than 2 percent of people lost their homes to foreclosure, because "what was good for the lending institution was also good for the borrower." But the new securitization market threatened to change that, because once a lender sold a mortgage, it no longer had a stake in whether the borrower could make his or her payments. He concluded, "The linkage, which I support fully, between the mortgage originator and the secondary market must be built carefully and appropriately. . . . Unless we have sound loans . . . we are going to find that the basic product we are trying to enhance and multiply will turn out soiled."

While securitization appeared to be alchemy, it wasn't, in the end, a magic trick. All the risks inherent in mortgages hadn't disappeared. They were still there somewhere, hidden, lurking in a dark corner. Dick Pratt, who had left the Federal Home Loan Bank Board to become the first president of Merrill Lynch Mortgage Capital, used to put it this way: "The mortgage is the neutron bomb of financial products."

There was one final consequence. After the REMIC battle, Wall Street realized it was never going to dislodge Fannie and Freddie from their dominant position as the securitizers of traditional mortgages. If it hoped to circumvent the GSEs and keep all the profits to itself, Wall Street would have to find some other mortgage product to securitize, products that Fannie and Freddie couldn't—or wouldn't—touch. As Maxwell later put it, "Their effort became one to find products they could profit from where they didn't have to compete with Fannie."

He added, "That's ultimately what happened."

2

"Ground Zero, Baby"

The birth of mortgage-backed securities didn't just change Wall Street and the GSEs. It changed the mortgage business on Main Street, too. Mortgage origination—that is, the act of making a loan to someone who wants to buy a home—had always been the province of the banks and the S&Ls, which relied on savings and checking accounts to fund the loans. Securitization mooted that business model.

Instead, securitization itself became the essential form of funding. Which meant, in turn, that all kinds of new mortgage companies could be formed—companies that competed with banks and S&Ls for mortgage customers, yet operated outside the banking system and were therefore largely unregulated. Not surprisingly, these new companies were run by men who were worlds apart from the local businessmen who ran the nation's S&Ls and banks. They were hard-charging, entrepreneurial, and intensely ambitious—natural salesmen who found in the changing mortgage market a way to make their mark in American business. Some of them may have genuinely cared about putting people in homes. All of them cared about getting rich. None of them remotely resembled George Bailey.

These new mortgage originators were of two distinct breeds—at least at first. One set of companies originated fairly standard loans to people with good credit, which they sold to Fannie and Freddie; Countrywide Financial was a good example of that kind of company. The second group had very different roots. They grew out of what was known as hard-money lending—lending made to poor people, primarily. ("Hard money" refers to the large down payments its customers had to make, even for a basic item such as a refrigerator.) These new companies moved hard-money lending into the mortgage market, making loans that would eventually become known as subprime. They couldn't sell to the GSEs, because, for a long time, the GSEs wouldn't buy such risky mortgages. On the other hand, this influx of new lenders created exactly what Wall Street had been searching for: mortgage products it could securitize without Fannie and Freddie.

———————

There is much irony in the fact that Countrywide Financial began life in that first group of companies, since it would later become the mortgage originator most closely associated with the excesses of the subprime business. But it's true. Its founder and CEO, a smart, aggressive bulldog of a man named Angelo Mozilo, believed strongly in the importance of underwriting standards— that is, in making loans to people who had the means to pay them back. In the early 1990s, a big competitor, Citicorp Mortgage, was forced to take huge losses, the result of making shoddy loans in a drive to increase market share. Mozilo's reaction was pitiless. "They tried to take a shortcut and went the way of every institution that has ever tried to defy the basics of sound underwriting principles," he told *National Mortgage News* in 1991.

There may have been another reason for Mozilo's withering dismissal of mighty Citigroup. Citi represented the establishment. Mozilo, Bronx born and Fordham educated, spent his life both wanting to beat the establishment and harboring a burning resentment toward it. "I run into these guys on Wall Street all the time who think they're something special because they went to Ivy League schools," he once told a *New York Times* reporter. "We're always underestimated. . . . I must say, it bothered me when I was younger— their snobbery and their looking down on us." When he was starting out, the business was "lily white," Mozilo's former partner Howard Levine recalls. Mozilo was an extremely dark-skinned Italian-American, and very sensitive about that heritage. He once told a colleague about returning from his honeymoon with his new wife, Phyllis, and stopping in Virginia Beach on the way home. They went into a restaurant to have dinner. "We don't serve colored," the waiter said. "I'm Italian," Mozilo replied. "That's what they all say," said the waiter.

Born in 1938, Mozilo was the son of a butcher who had emigrated from Italy as a young man. The Mozilos lived in a rental flat. "I saw my dad struggle all his life," Mozilo later explained. "He lived to be fifty-six and died of a heart attack." Mozilo's uncle, who worked for an insurance company, had the only white-collar job in the family. Young Angelo worked for his father until he was old enough to ask his uncle to help him find a job. At fourteen, he became a messenger for a small Manhattan mortgage company.

That's when Mozilo met Levine, who today is the president of ARCS Commercial Mortgage Company, a subsidiary of PNC Financial, the big Pittsburgh-based bank. "We were very anxious to be successful," says Levine. "Angelo in particular. This was our break."

By the time he graduated from high school, Mozilo had worked in every part of the company, and he continued to work there while attending Fordham. In 1960, the same year Mozilo graduated from college, the company merged with a larger company, United Mortgage Servicing Company, which was based in Virginia and run by a man named David Loeb. Though also from the Bronx, Loeb could not have been more different from Mozilo. "His parents were into ballet and opera," Mozilo later recalled. "He was fifteen years older, and I was frightened to death of him." But Loeb took a liking to Mozilo, to his scrappiness and ambition. Mozilo enrolled in night business school at New York University, but dropped out when Loeb decided to send him to Orlando, Florida. He was twenty-three years old.

Brevard County, on the coast not far from Orlando, was the perfect place to be in the housing business in the early 1960s. A few years earlier, the Soviet Union had launched the Sputnik satellite, and the space boom was on in the United States as America frantically tried to outdo its cold war rival. Brevard County included a small speck of land called Cape Canaveral. Space engineers flocked to the area, only to discover there was no place for them to live. As Mozilo would later tell the story to reporters, he remembered seeing people living in tents on the beach.

Mozilo met a group of developers who hoped to build one of the first subdivisions in the county. But they needed money. Mozilo wanted his company to lend them what they needed to build the subdivision, which was a common tactic back then. Loeb agreed, though the tactic was not without risk: the money they loaned to the developers was more than the company was worth.

Disaster struck. On the night before the grand opening, a huge storm swept through the area. When Mozilo arrived at the site, he'd later say, he saw furniture standing in water because the subdivision had been built in a basin. His heart sank. Yet it turned out not to matter: people were so desperate for homes that the subdivision sold out anyway.

In 1968, United Mortgage Servicing was bought out. Loeb and Mozilo left to start their own business. Mozilo was thirty years old, but he had already had sixteen years of experience in the industry. What was striking about this new venture was the sheer, naked ambition of it. Nonbank mortgage brokers had existed for a long time, but they were small and local, niche players at best. Mozilo and Loeb had no intention of being niche players. They were going to be big and they were going to be everywhere. The name of the company said it all: Countrywide.

They struggled at first. Since Countrywide wasn't a bank and couldn't gather deposits, the only way it could make loans was by getting a line of credit—called a warehouse line—from a bank or a Wall Street firm or a group of investors. Then, to replenish its capital, it had to sell the mortgages it originated. But since the securitization market didn't exist yet, that meant they were largely limited to loans that could be insured by the Federal Housing Administration or Veterans Affairs, since those were the only loans Fannie and Freddie were allowed to buy. It wasn't much of a business.

Loeb and Mozilo tried to raise money by selling stock on the New York Stock Exchange. They hoped to raise $3 million, but got only $450,000, according to Paul Muolo and Mathew Padilla in *Chain of Blame*. Things got so bad, Mozilo later told reporters, that he and Loeb had to lay everyone off and start again.

But even as they were holding on by their fingertips, the massive changes that would transform the mortgage business had begun. Rising interest rates were starting to kill the S&Ls. More important, not long after Countrywide was born, Fannie Mae was granted the right to buy conventional mortgages.

Almost overnight, mortgage originators like Countrywide began to dominate the home lending business. From a standing start, the market share of nonbank mortgage companies rose to 19 percent by 1989. Just four years later, it stood at an astonishing 52 percent, according to Countrywide's financial statements. By buying up the mortgages of companies like Countrywide, the GSEs made that growth possible, something Mozilo never forgot. As he once told the *New York Times*, "If it wasn't for them, Wells [Fargo] knows they'd have us."

Under the rules, Mozilo could sell only so-called conforming loans—those that met the GSEs' strict underwriting criteria. Loans were underwritten based on what was known in the business as the four Cs: credit, capability, collateral, and character. If you had late payments on a previous mortgage, and maybe any other debt, you didn't get a mortgage. The monthly payments for your home—the principal, interest, taxes, and insurance—couldn't exceed 33 percent of your monthly income. All of which was fine by Mozilo. It was the way he'd always done business.

On the other hand, Mozilo also pushed Countrywide to begin using independent brokers instead of relying on its own staff to make loans. This was decidedly not the industry norm. It was also one of the rare times Mozilo had an open disagreement with his mentor, Loeb, who protested that if Countrywide began relying on independent brokers, it would be hard to control the quality of the loans. In the days before the collapse of the S&Ls, says one industry veteran, "brokers' stock-in-trade was falsifying documentation." At least, that was the rap. And nonstaff brokers had no skin in the game; once they'd sold their loan to Countrywide and gotten their fee, they were out. "I think it's going to be a big mistake," Loeb said, according to *Chain of Blame*." But with S&Ls closing down by the hundreds, there was a cheap, ready-made workforce: out-of-work loan officers. Using them could help Countrywide grow faster. Loeb's resistance faded as brokers' reputation began to change, and as the company got aggressively behind this idea, all its competitors began using independent brokers as well. It soon became standard practice.

By 1992, just twenty-three years after its founding, Countrywide had become the largest originator of single-family mortgages in the country, issuing close to $40 billion in mortgages that year alone. Just as rising rates had crushed the S&Ls a decade before, so did falling interest rates now turbocharge Countrywide's growth. Lower interest rates helped more people afford homes, of course. But Countrywide began advertising a technique that allowed people who already owned their home to take advantage of lower rates. Refinancing, it was called. Often borrowers didn't just refinance their home, they pulled out additional cash against the equity in their homes. For the fiscal year ending in February 1992, refinancings accounted for 58 percent of Countrywide's business; two years later, they accounted for 75 percent of its business. Although refinancing allowed consumers to take advantage of lower interest rates, it really didn't have much to do with homeownership. Countrywide wasn't putting people into homes so much as it was making it possible for homeowners to use their homes as piggy banks.

During 1991 and 1992, Mozilo served as the chairman of the Mortgage Bankers Association. It was a sign that whatever lingering resentments Mozilo still felt, Countrywide was now part of the in-crowd.

What everyone remembers about Mozilo was how passionate he was about the business, about its success. He cared deeply about every aspect—he wanted to know everything, *had* to know everything. If he walked into a branch and saw that a fax machine was broken, he would stop everything and try to fix it himself. According to the *American Banker*, the thrift H. F. Ahmanson, desperate to compete with Countrywide, commissioned a report on the company in the early 1990s in an effort to understand its secret sauce. Mozilo, the report concluded, was a "hands-on manager, totally consumed by the business, a perfectionist." It also said he was a "dictatorial" boss who "is known to fire employees the first time they make a mistake." If this wasn't exactly true—longtime Countrywide executives often said that Mozilo's bark was worse than his bite—it was all part of his aura.

He did drive his employees incredibly hard, or those who succeeded drove themselves incredibly hard. He was both highly emotional and mercurial, and he operated from his gut. It wouldn't be uncommon for him to have "an allergic reaction to things," as a former executive puts it, before eventually coming around. He was perfectly capable of telling an employee that what he'd just said was the stupidest thing in the world. He expected those who worked for him to take whatever he dished out in the heat of the moment— and then do the right thing, even if it contradicted his command. If they did the wrong thing, following orders wasn't an excuse. Countrywide was not an easy place to work. "It was very, very competitive," recalls one person who knew the company well. "The politics were brutal. You had to eat, sleep, and drink Countrywide. It was a boys' club. There were a few women, but it was very autocratic." But employees took great pride in the company—and Mozilo. At getaways for top producers, people would clamor for a moment with him. He was the classic underdog who had achieved big things, after all.

He instilled something akin to fear in the investment community. Mike McMahon, a Wall Street analyst who followed Countrywide for more than twenty years, once took a group of investors to see Mozilo. During the meeting, one of them said that Countrywide's stock would be valued more highly if Mozilo disclosed more about its operations. Most CEOs would have dismissed the questioner with a platitude. Not Mozilo. He had a bad back that day, so he had to stiffly turn his whole body toward the man—"like Frankenstein," McMahon recalls. "No," Mozilo replied. "Fuck 'em." Then, ever so slowly, he turned his body back, almost menacingly, as if to say, "Who else wants to take me on?"

What everyone could see, though, was that Mozilo drove himself harder than anyone. For a long time he had a classic case of entrepreneurial paranoia—that gnawing fear that, someday, everything he had built would suddenly vanish. That's why he couldn't relax, even for a second. The company, after all, was in a boom-and-bust business, one that hit hard times when interest rates rose. It competed not just against other mortgage brokers but against giants like Wells Fargo and Bank of America. Margins were always tight. Securitization may have made the business possible, but it didn't make it easy. McMahon says that mortgage origination was a "negative cash flow business," meaning that the slim profits were eaten up by costs and commissions. There was profit in servicing mortgages, but that was realized over time. "The more they originated, the less cash they had," he says. In addition, because Countrywide had to appease the rating agencies in order to borrow money at a good rate, the company actually had to put aside more capital than banks did. "They were in a really, really, really competitive, low-margin commodity business with one hand tied behind their back on capital," says McMahon. Is it any wonder Mozilo's motto was "We don't execute, we don't eat"? According to *The New Yorker*, he once told a Countrywide executive, "If you ever stop trying to make your division the biggest and the best, that's the day you die."

Over time, Loeb faded into the background. Early on, Mozilo had moved Countrywide to California; the state represented a huge percentage of the mortgage market and accounted for as much as 50 percent of Countrywide's revenues in some years. Loeb, however, often worked from one of his homes in Manhattan or Squaw Valley, where he focused on managing Countrywide's risks. Mozilo became the public face of the company—and in some ways the public face of the industry as well.

With his trademark tailored suits and crisp blue shirts with white collars—which accentuated his perfectly white teeth and dark skin—Mozilo would testify before Congress, give interviews to reporters, make speeches at conferences, and meet investors. He took great pride in the business model he had helped create; he had, indeed, "showed them." By 2003, Countrywide was one of the best-performing companies in the country, with a stock price that had risen 23,000 percent in the twenty-one years since the start of the bull market that began in 1982. A glowing article in *Fortune* magazine noted that Countrywide had outperformed not just other mortgage companies and banks, but such storied stock market performers as Walmart and Warren Buffett's Berkshire Hathaway. Mozilo would later describe the publication of that article as one of the proudest moments of his life.

At precisely the same time Mozilo was building Countrywide, another entrepreneur was building a different kind of mortgage empire. His name was Roland Arnall. He was never in the limelight like Mozilo, and he never wanted to be. But he made far more money; by 2005, he was worth around $3 billion, according to *Forbes*. Arnall got rich by making loans to the borrowers that had long served as the customer base for the hard-money lenders: people who had bad credit, didn't make much money, or both. Though his companies never got the blame that would later be heaped on Countrywide, Arnall was the real subprime pioneer; in fact, his first company, Long Beach Mortgage, trained a slew of executives who would later go on to found their own subprime companies. "The Long Beach Gang," housing insiders used to call them. One of Arnall's subsequent companies was called Ameriquest. By 2004, it had become the largest subprime lender in the country.

A native of France, Arnall was born in Paris in 1939, on the eve of World War II. His mother was a nurse; his father, a tailor by trade, was in the army. Not long before Paris fell to the Germans, Arnall's father returned to Paris and warned his extended family they should leave as quickly as possible. Most of them refused. But Arnall's father took his wife and young son to the south of France, where they waited out the war using false papers that hid the fact that they were Jews. Arnall himself discovered that he was Jewish only after the war, a fact that stunned him. With the war ended, the family moved first to Montreal, where Arnall attended Sir George Williams College, and then, in 1950, to California, where Arnall sold flowers on street corners to make money for his family. "I know firsthand the precious gift of freedom," he once said.

Arnall exerted a powerful effect on those who came into his orbit. "He was scarily smart and charismatic," says Jon Daurio, who worked for Arnall from 1992, when Arnall recruited him to be the corporate counsel of Long Beach, until 1997. (Daurio would go on to found several other subprime lenders.) Daurio and his wife had dinner with Arnall when he was trying to convince Daurio to join Long Beach. "My wife is a lawyer, and smart," says Daurio. "She said, 'I don't understand 90 percent of what you talked about, but you're an idiot if you don't go work for him.'"

Even more than Mozilo, Arnall was known for running his companies with an iron fist. "He was very demanding, and not very tolerant," recalls a former executive. He had a penchant for enticing people to work for him, extracting what he wanted from them, and then losing all interest in them. "When he got what he wanted out of you, you were done," this person added.

Unlike Mozilo, Arnall was extremely secretive. He never gave press interviews. The documents his companies filed with the SEC divulged only the bare minimum required under the law. Arnall did not attend industry conferences, and his name was never on the door of his companies. He hated even having to talk to securities analysts. "I met with him once," recalls a former banking analyst. "We all had to sign forms agreeing not to disclose anything before we were allowed into the conference room. That never happened any other time in my twenty-plus-year career."

Yet he was never, ever rude to people the way Mozilo sometimes could be; that wasn't his style. On the contrary, he was gracious and polite to everyone, from janitors to community activists. He had old-world manners, was an avid reader and an intellectual. He was the sort who liked to remind people that if they had their health and their family, they had everything. And he gave away millions to charity. "He was quite concerned with society as a whole," says Robert Gnaizda, the former general counsel of the Greenlining Institute, a public policy and advocacy group, who spent a great deal of time dealing with Arnall's companies and came to know him well. "Except," Gnaizda added, "for this little niche, where he wasn't."

That little niche, of course, was subprime lending.

The way hard-money lenders had always made their money was simple: knowing that the default rate among their borrowers was likely to be high, they imposed onerous terms on their customers, who had no choice but to agree to them. They claimed collateral on anything they could haul away—cars, household goods, you name it. They extracted high fees just for making the loan. And they charged as much interest as they could get away with. They were also extremely tough-minded about collecting what was owed them, which meant they usually got paid back. And the high fees meant that those who paid up more than made up for those who defaulted.

The biggest hard-money lenders, finance companies like the Associates, Beneficial, and Household Finance, also made second-lien mortgages, which allowed strapped consumers to borrow against their homes to raise cash. But hard-money lenders had never offered first-lien mortgages, because the economics of a thirty-year fixed mortgage with a sizable down payment simply made no sense in that sector of the market.

What changed was the law. Specifically, a series of laws passed in the early 1980s, intended to help the S&Ls get back on their feet, wound up having profound unintended consequences. (They also backfired spectacularly and helped create a second S&L crisis within a decade.) The first law, passed in 1980, was the Depository Institutions Deregulation and Monetary Control Act; among other things, it abolished state usury caps, which had long limited how much financial firms could charge on first-lien mortgages. It also erased the distinction between loans made to buy a house and loans, like home equity loans, that were *secured* by a house, which would prove critical to the subprime industry.

Two years later came the Alternative Mortgage Transaction Parity Act, which made it legal for lenders to offer more creative mortgages, such as adjustable-rate mortgages or those with balloon payments, rather than plain vanilla thirty-year fixed-rate instruments. It also preempted state laws designed to prevent both these new kinds of mortgages and prepayment penalties. The rationale, needless to say, was promoting homeownership. "Alternative mortgage transactions are essential . . . to meet the demand expected during the 1980s," read the bill.

As the rules changed, the "Big Three" hard-money lenders—the Associates, Beneficial, and Household—began to expand into first-lien mortgages, which made economic sense for the first time. S&Ls, of course, had also gained new freedoms from the series of laws designed to get them back on their feet. The new breed of thrift operators started lending to consumers who would have never previously qualified for a mortgage. Thus was the subprime mortgage industry born.

One of the first to take advantage of the new opportunities was a thrift called Guardian Savings & Loan, run by a flashy, aggressive couple named Russell and Rebecca Jedinak. As federal thrift examiner Thomas Constantine would later write, "It started at Guardian. Ground zero, baby."

The Jedinaks moved into an aggressive form of hard-money lending. They offered loans—mostly refinancings—to people with bad credit, as long as those people had some equity in their house. "If they have a house, if the owner has a pulse, we'll give them a loan," Russell Jedinak told the *Orange County Register*. Kay Gustafson, a lawyer who briefly worked at Guardian, would later say that the Jedinaks didn't really care if the borrower couldn't pay the loan back because they always assumed they could take over the property and sell it. "They were banking on a model of an ever-rising housing market," she told the *Register*. In June 1988, Guardian sold the first subprime mortgage-backed securities. Over the next three years, the Jedinaks sold a total of $2.7 billion in securities backed by mortgages made to less-than-creditworthy borrowers, according to the *Register*. Fannie and Freddie were most decidedly not involved.

By early 1991, federal regulators had forced the Jedinaks out. The Resolution Trust Corporation, which had been established to clean up the second S&L mess, took over the thrift. Standard & Poor's noted that Guardian's securities were "plagued by staggering delinquencies." In 1995, the government fined the Jedinaks $8.5 million, accusing them of using Guardian's money to fund their lifestyles. They didn't admit to or deny the charges, and anyway, they'd already started another lender, Quality Mortgage. After the Jedinaks were barred from the business, they sold Quality Mortgage to a company called Amresco, which itself became a fixture of the 1990s subprime lending scene.

Roland Arnall was right behind the Jedinaks. Unlike them, he built businesses that would last—at least, for a while. Arnall got a thrift license in 1979, just as the rules were changing, and he named his thrift Long Beach Savings & Loan. Initially, he built multifamily housing and other real estate developments, but he soon spotted a much better opportunity. Taking note of the exorbitant fees charged by the hard-money guys, he realized he could cut those fees in half and still make plenty of money. In 1988, Long Beach began to use independent brokers, just like Mozilo, to make mortgages to people with impaired credit. By the early 1990s, Long Beach was also selling mortgage-backed securities—which Wall Street was eagerly buying. The company grew exponentially; between 1994 and 1998, Long Beach would almost quintuple the volume of mortgages it originated, to $2.6 billion.

In 1994, Long Beach chucked its thrift charter. The charter had outlived its usefulness. Now that a mortgage originator could sell the loans to Wall Street, there was no particular need to be a deposit-taking institution.

But how could it be that Wall Street was willing to buy and securitize mortgages that Fannie and Freddie wouldn't touch—mortgages made to people with a far higher chance of defaulting than traditional middle-class homeowners? This was something the founding fathers of mortgage-backed securities had never imagined was possible. Once, when Larry Fink was testifying before Congress in the 1980s, he was asked whether Wall Street might try to securitize risky mortgages. He dismissed the idea out of hand. "I can't even fathom what kind of quality of mortgage that is, by the way, but if there is such an animal, the marketplace . . . may just price that security out." By that, he meant that investors would require such a high yield to take on the risk as to make the deal untenable. And yet, less than a decade later, that is exactly what was happening.

Ironically, it was the government itself that had helped make Wall Street skilled at securitizing riskier mortgages—specifically the Resolution Trust Corporation. In cleaning up failed thrifts, the RTC wound up with hundreds of billions of dollars worth of assets—everything from high-rise office buildings to vacant plots of land—that it took from the S&Ls it was closing down. Eventually, the RTC decided that the best way to get rid of those assets was to securitize them and sell them to investors. Much of the RTC's raw material, though, qualified as risky and thus couldn't be backed by Fannie Mae or Freddie Mac.

Ah, but if the securities could get a double-A or triple-A credit rating, investors like pension funds would be able to buy them, even without the GSEs' seal of approval. It was the high rating, after all, that was required for them to hold the securities, not Fannie and Freddie's guarantee. Even before the RTC, Wall Street had been experimenting with ways to make risky securities less risky by issuing, for instance, a letter of credit promising investors payment in the event the cash flow from the assets wasn't enough. But the RTC allowed Wall Street to work on such techniques—"credit enhancement," they were called—on a far broader scale. Over time, people came up with all sorts of ways to do credit enhancements. You could get insurance from a third party—a bond insurer, say. You could "overcollateralize" the structure, meaning you put in more mortgages than were needed to pay the investors, so that there was extra in case something went wrong. Or (and this would come later) you could do a so-called senior/subordinated structure, where the cash flows from the underlying mortgages were redirected so that the "senior" bonds got the money first, thereby minimizing the risk for the investors who owned those bonds. Credit enhancements helped convince the rating agencies to rate some of the tranches triple-A, which in turn helped convince investors to buy them. "The innovative techniques that the RTC developed are now in the process of being used by private sector issuers," was the way Michael Jungman, the RTC's director of asset sales, put it in a 1994 lecture. Indeed.

Larry Fink, obviously, had never envisioned credit enhancements. But as a 1999 paper by economists at the conservative American Enterprise Institute noted, "The attraction of this segmentation of risk is that the senior (collateralized) debts appeal to investors with limited taste for risk or limited ability to understand the risks of the underlying loans." At last, Wall Street had a securitization business it could do on a large scale—and it didn't have to share a penny with the GSEs.

There was a final key to the rise of the subprime business. The federal government was behind it. Not in so many words, of course—and, to be fair, it is highly unlikely that many people in government truly understood what they were unleashing. But by the 1990s, government's long-running encouragement of homeownership had morphed into a push for *increased* homeownership. Thanks to the second S&L crisis, the percentage of Americans who owned their own home had actually dropped, from a historic high of 65.6 percent in 1980 to 64.1 percent in 1991. In a country where homeownership was so highly valued, this was untenable.

Thus it was that, early in his second term as president, Bill Clinton announced his National Homeownership Strategy. It had an explicit goal of raising the number of homeowners by 8 million families over the next six years. "We have a serious, serious unmet obligation to try to reverse these trends," said Clinton, referring to the drop in the homeownership rate. To get there, the administration advocated "financing strategies fueled by creativity to help home buyers who lacked the cash to buy a home or the income to make the down payments." Creatively putting people who lacked cash into homes was precisely what the new subprime companies purported to do.

Which also explains why the government had such a hard time cracking down on the subprime companies, even as it became apparent that there was widespread wrongdoing. Roland Arnall's company, Long Beach Mortgage, offered a case in point. In 1993, the Office of Thrift Supervision, a new agency created by Congress to regulate the S&Ls, alleged that Long Beach was discriminating against minorities by charging them more for their loans than they charged whites. Long Beach ducked this investigation when it gave up its thrift charter, leaving the OTS with no authority over the company.

A few years later—around the same time Clinton was announcing his housing initiative—the Justice Department began its own probe. Investigators found that Long Beach's brokers, most of them independent, were charging up to 12 percent of the loan amount over a base price. The amount they charged was "unrelated to the qualifications of the borrowers or the risk to the lender," according to the government. Younger white males got the lowest rates, while older, single African-American women fared the worst. In September 1996, then assistant attorney general Deval Patrick, an

African-American himself, announced a settlement with Long Beach. Although Long Beach denied the government's allegations, it agreed to pay $3 million into a fund that would go toward reimbursing borrowers who were allegedly overcharged. The Federal Trade Commission originally demanded half of Long Beach's net worth to settle the case, but Arnall had what Daurio calls a "brilliant" idea: the company offered to put $1 million toward partnerships with community groups for consumer education. Patrick and the FTC went along.

What the case mainly showed, though, was how difficult it was for the government to crack down on companies that were offering credit to people who would otherwise never be able to own a home. On the one hand, the Clinton administration's explicit policy was to get millions more American families into homes. Men like Arnall were making that possible. On the other hand, making it possible for poorer people to buy homes was inevitably going to mean charging higher fees and interest. Practices that banks viewed as disreputable were widely accepted in the subprime world. Cracking down too hard on the subprime companies might hurt their ability to make loans to their customer base—who were the exact same people the government was trying to help.

Ultimately, this was a heavily politicized gray area, difficult to police. It raised difficult questions about which practices were legitimate and which were not. The government's dilemma was obvious in the statement Patrick released when he announced the settlement. "We recognize that lenders understand the industry in ways we don't," he said. "That is why there is so much flexibility in the decree."

Clearing up the gray required a willingness to tackle the hard questions about what subprime lending was, and what was the proper way to conduct it. But that willingness was always in short supply, both then and later.

By the mid-1990s, the subprime market was exploding. Companies like Long Beach had shown how much money could be made, but the business got another kick from a different source: the Federal Reserve. In 1994, the Fed began to raise rates, and refinancings plummeted. That left "prime" lenders, whose loan volume dropped by as much as 50 percent, looking for a new source of loans. Guess what they found? Subprime.

The changes in interest rates also left Wall Street firms searching for a new product to sell. They had been making huge sums selling mortgage-backed securities that were tranched according to their interest rate and prepayment risk. When rates had fallen, so many people refinanced that the riskier tranches of the mortgage-backed securities lost much of their value.

Just in time came this new product: bonds backed by subprime mortgages, goosed by those "credit enhancements." For Wall Street, this new business presented a trifecta of opportunity. Street firms could make money selling and trading the mortgage-backed securities. But they could also make money by providing a warehouse line of credit so that the mortgage companies could make the loans in the first place. And they could make money by taking subprime specialists public.

It quickly became a frenzy. Traditional hard-money lenders like Associates, Household, and the Money Store saw their stocks soar. Subprime founders got very rich. For instance, the Money Store, which had been started by Alan Turtletaub in 1967 and became a household name after signing up Hall of Famer Phil Rizzuto to be its spokesman (1-800-LOAN-YES), went public in 1991 at $16 a share. By the spring of 1997, its stock had risen fivefold. In 1998, First Union bought the Money Store for $2.1 billion. Turtletaub's stake was estimated at $710 million.

There was also a proliferation of start-ups, making mortgage finance, for a brief moment, as hot as Internet companies. Dan Phillips, an ex-Marine who had been a loan officer at Beneficial, founded a company called FirstPlus Financial. The stock soared. Phillips, who once described old-school bankers as "accountants who make loans," made a fortune as well. He began building a 31,000-square-foot estate in North Dallas, complete with a pool house and lighted tennis court, according to the *Dallas Morning News*. Right around that time, Dan Quayle joined the board of FirstPlus.

There were plenty of others: First Alliance, Cityscape, Aames, and more. Steve Holder, who had been an executive at Long Beach, co-founded a company called New Century. Robert Dubrish, another Long Beach alum, founded Option One, which was bought by H&R Block in 1997. (Both Option One and New Century had former Guardian executives in key positions.) They were freewheeling entrepreneurs, grabbing for the brass ring; they didn't spend a lot of time worrying about crossing every *t* and dotting every *i*. As Paul Mondor, the director of regulatory compliance for the Mortgage Bankers Association, told the *American Banker* in 1997, "It's a high-risk, high-return market . . . it stands to reason you'll have flashier types who worry less about bending the rules."

From 1994 to 1999, the number of loans made by companies that identified themselves as subprime lenders increased roughly six times, from about

138,000 to roughly 856,000, according to the Federal Reserve. Over the same period, the dollar volume of subprime mortgage originations increased by a factor of nearly five, from $35 billion to $160 billion, or almost 13 percent of all mortgage originations, according to a joint study by HUD and the Treasury. Economists, including those at the Federal Reserve, credited subprime lending with the increased rate of homeownership, which by 1999 hit a record 66.8 percent. What tended to be forgotten, though, was that most subprime mortgages did not go toward the purchase of a new house, but rather were refinancings by existing homeowners. (According to a joint HUD–Treasury report, a staggering 82 percent of subprime mortgages were refinancings, and in nearly 60 percent of those cases the borrower pulled out cash, adding to his debt burden.)

It wasn't just the Democratic administration that saw a reason to applaud the rise of subprime lending, either. Conservatives were applauding, too. For instance, in that same 1999 American Enterprise Institute paper, the authors touted the virtues of something called high loan-to-value lending, or HLTV. That was industry jargon for loans with low or no down payments. (A loan with a 100 percent loan-to-value ratio has no down payment; a 90 percent LTV ratio has a 10 percent down payment; and so on.) "Consumer debt collateralized by the borrower's home is effectively a senior claim on his income, backed by an asset that would otherwise be protected from seizure by creditors if he were to file for bankruptcy," wrote the authors, Charles Calomiris and Joseph Mason. "Because HLTV lending can rely on securitization for the bulk of its financing, it provides a more diversified, and thus a more stable, source of consumer credit." They concluded, "HLTV lending is good for the American consumer and for the U.S. economy."

And all the while, Angelo Mozilo watched with amazement as subprime lending took off. It's not that he didn't believe in the virtue of increased homeownership. He did, passionately. The government's desire to get more people into their own homes aligned not just with Mozilo's business model but with his psyche. When he started in the business, after all, redlining—the practice of not making loans in poor neighborhoods—was standard practice in the banking industry. People with minority or immigrant background, like himself, had a harder time buying new homes than middle-class WASPs. Women had a harder time getting loans than men.

Mozilo felt that he and Countrywide were helping to democratize the housing market. "He always felt like he was compelled to help people get into homes," says Howard Levine. Once, during the administration of the first George Bush, Jack Kemp, Bush's HUD secretary, tried to scale back some government assistance for the mortgage market. Mozilo publicly denounced him as "the worst person who could possibly have been put in that position." It was a very impolitic thing to say, but Mozilo couldn't help himself.

When Clinton announced his housing initiative, Mozilo was an enthusiastic supporter. In 1994, he signed a pledge—part of an agreement between the Mortgage Bankers Association and HUD—to increase lending to minorities. He pushed hard to get Fannie and Freddie to guarantee mortgages with lower down payments, because the traditional 20 percent down payment, he believed, was the single biggest barrier preventing people from owning their own home.

And early on, Mozilo had made a commitment that his company would fund $1.25 billion of loans explicitly tailored to meet the needs of lower-income borrowers. But this program was a long way from subprime lending. The standards were fairly strict. The mortgages were all thirty-year fixed-rate loans. The losses were low. And it was a tiny percentage of Countrywide's business.

Mozilo, in truth, was horrified by the rise of subprime lending. It was a business, he groused, that made its money overcharging unsuspecting customers. Most subprime executives were "crooks," he railed to friends. But the growth was so dramatic that stock analysts started asking why Countrywide wasn't part of it. Meanwhile, the company's program aimed at lower-income customers, small to begin with, started to shrivel: loan volume dropped from $1.3 billion in 1996 to $600 million in 1997 to $400 million in 1998. Where were those customers going? There wasn't much doubt. They were going to companies like Long Beach.

In 1995, Countrywide hired Paul Abbamonto, himself a former executive at Long Beach, to help establish a subprime lending business at Countrywide. The new business was named Full Spectrum, and its goal, executives said, was to be less aggressive with margins than other subprime lenders were— meaning it would push its way into the business by charging less, even if it meant making smaller profits. "There was plenty of skepticism when Countrywide started Full Spectrum," recalls McMahon, the Wall Street analyst. "But I thought it was wise. Mozilo said that the mortgage business was morphing from one where there was prime and subprime into a home loan industry. There were borrowers at both ends of the spectrum, and Countrywide, being this company with a grandiose name, wanted to offer a product that filled all needs."

Countrywide didn't officially launch Full Spectrum until 1997, and the new division didn't make any loans until 1998. That year, it did $140 million in mortgage originations and home equity loans—which didn't even qualify as a drop in the bucket of subprime lending.

Much later, Countrywide's critics would claim that the company was responsible for starting the business of subprime lending. Some would even say that Mozilo did so out of a do-gooder's desire to get people who couldn't afford mortgages into homes. Neither of those things was true. Countrywide didn't start it, and Countrywide didn't get in because Mozilo wanted to do good. He got in because he felt he had no choice. If he stayed out of subprime, Countrywide would never be number one—and that was unacceptable.

As Howard Levine told *Business Week* in 1992: "Angelo will do whatever it takes to be number one."

3

The Big, Fat Gap

In 1991, David Maxwell retired as the chief executive of Fannie Mae. He was sixty-one years old and had held the post one day short of ten years. He walked away with a lump sum of $27.5 million, most of it accrued retirement benefits but still a shocking sum of money for Washington during that era. (He also turned down an additional $5.5 million that was owed him, fearing it would ignite criticism of Fannie Mae—and himself.) Fannie's shareholders, however, had no complaints. Maxwell had taken a troubled institution on the brink of insolvency and turned it into a well-oiled profit machine—professionally managed, financially strong, and politically powerful. Years later, Jim Collins, the well-known management guru, would name Maxwell the seventh greatest CEO of all time. (Charles Coffin, the first president of General Electric, was number one.) "If turnaround is an art," wrote Collins of Maxwell, then he "was its Michelangelo."

Maxwell had never been one to brag. His speeches always sought to cast Fannie Mae as merely one player among many making housing more affordable, rather than as the company with a dominant position in a critical market. But shortly after his retirement he gave an interview to the *Washington Post* in which he reflected on what he had accomplished. "It would take an event of such cataclysmic proportions as to result in a change of our form of government to put this company under," he concluded.

At the time, that statement didn't seem like much of an exaggeration. The year before, Fannie Mae's profits had exceeded $1 billion for the first time. Its market value had exploded. And perhaps most important, Fannie, along with Freddie Mac, had a virtual stranglehold over the market for conforming mortgages—a bit of industry jargon that directly reflected the power of the GSEs. Conforming mortgages, after all, were mortgages that conformed to the strict underwriting standards Fannie and Freddie demanded in return for their guarantee. Everyone in the mortgage business who could conform did so. They had little choice.

Long Beach Mortgage was just four years old when Maxwell retired; the subprime business was still a speck in the ocean. Countrywide was growing by leaps and bounds—not by making subprime loans, but by selling conforming mortgages to Fannie Mae. The vast majority of the nearly 60 million American homeowners were members in good standing of the middle class, with the financial wherewithal to make a down payment and monthly mortgage payments.

But Fannie Mae was never as invulnerable as it seemed to Maxwell in 1991. The company had enemies on all sides. From one direction, Wall Street was just starting to realize that subprime mortgages might allow them to effectively sidestep the GSEs, thus creating a competitive threat that seemed insignificant at the time but would ultimately prove life-threatening. From another direction, Fannie and Freddie's half-government/half-corporate structure meant that they were always going to face opposition in Washington—sometimes subterranean, sometimes overt, much of it ideological. Critics on the left felt that Fannie and Freddie weren't doing enough to help poor people buy homes. Critics on the right believed that the government-sponsored entities had no place in the private housing market, and that they should be forced to live or die competing on an equal basis with Wall Street's securitizers. Although this criticism ebbed and flowed over the years, it never entirely went away.

As Fannie Mae became ever more profitable and powerful, it also became more arrogant and high-handed. Yet at the same time, as the criticisms continued, it became increasingly paranoid. And as the sheer amount of money at stake grew exponentially over the ensuing decades, Fannie Mae became more determined than ever to protect both its own special privileges and its bottom line. It made for a lethal stew.

In 1992, the year after Maxwell retired, Congress passed a bill imposing on Fannie and Freddie two things they had never had to deal with before. The first was a regulator, called the Office of Federal Housing Enterprise Oversight, or OFHEO. The second was a clear definition of what had previously been the GSEs' vague mission to help lower-income Americans buy homes, including specific steps the GSEs were supposed to take to perform that mission. You might think that these two new facts of life would have had the effect of clipping Fannie and Freddie's wings—maybe even costing them some profits. They did nothing of the sort.

The main reason was Fannie Mae's new CEO, a smooth-as-silk longtime Democratic operative named Jim Johnson. A tall, forty-seven-year-old Minnesotan and a graduate of Princeton, Johnson was, as they say, a player. He had spent his twenties working on the campaigns of Eugene McCarthy and George McGovern, and then served as Vice President Walter Mondale's executive assistant during the Carter administration. In 1984, he had managed Mondale's failed presidential bid; a year later, he co-founded Public Strategies, a policy-oriented public relations firm, with Richard Holbrooke, the well-known diplomat. He counted among his friends senators, members of Congress, top administration officials, and even the president, Bill Clinton, whom he had first met at a reunion of former McCarthy campaign staffers. When he wasn't running Fannie Mae, he was serving as chairman of the Brookings Institution, Washington's leading liberal think tank, and heading up the capital's premier arts venue, the Kennedy Center for the Performing Arts. The *Washington Post* once called him "the chairman of the universe."

As Fannie Mae's CEO, though, Johnson also played a brand of take-no-prisoners political hardball that even Maxwell—no slouch himself in that department—would likely have shied away from. Maxwell had hand-picked Johnson for the job, and it was easy to see why. Like Maxwell, Johnson oozed charm. He was exceedingly smart; Maxwell recalls being dazzled by his brilliance the first time they met, at a dinner party in the 1980s. Also like Maxwell, he was a tough cookie who wasn't afraid to play rough to get his way.

The major difference between the two men was that Johnson's bare knuckles were much more visible than Maxwell's. Maxwell ran a smaller, less threatening company, and he had always had a sense of where the limits were, of what lines were best not crossed. Johnson didn't calibrate things that way. When it came to political fights, he believed in all-out warfare, no matter how important—or unimportant—the issue. "In daily life, he'd say things like, 'We're going to cut them off at the knees,'" recalls a former Fannie executive. Once, a government official in the middle of a negotiation with Johnson asked him jokingly what the possibility was that Fannie Mae might lose. There was no humor in Johnson's reply: "There is no probability that we lose."

Years later, Fannie's last real CEO, Daniel Mudd, would say about the Johnson years, "The old political reality was that we always won, we took no prisoners, and we faced little organized political opposition." One longtime critic, former Republican congressman Jim Leach, says that Johnson built "the greatest, most sophisticated lobbying operation in the modern history of finance."

Which was true. At first, the purpose of Fannie's lobbying machine was to bend the new legislation to its wishes as it wended its way through Congress. The bill had come about because there were people in the first Bush administration who worried that Fannie and Freddie were taking on risk that the taxpayers would likely have to absorb if the housing market ever tanked and they had to make good on their guarantees. At a minimum, these administration critics believed, Fannie and Freddie needed better, tougher regulation. As a general rule, banks had to put aside enough capital to cover around 8 percent of the assets in their portfolios. But Fannie Mae and Freddie Mac put aside only a sliver of capital, allowing them to employ more debt than their competitors could—and produce greater profits. The Treasury Department wanted Fannie and Freddie to be forced to put up more capital.

In 1990, even before Johnson took over as CEO, Fannie Mae engaged Paul Volcker, the legendary former Federal Reserve chairman, to defend Fannie Mae's low capital levels. This was a classic Fannie tactic—finding a highly respected expert to defend its position—that Johnson would also employ. In this case, Volcker argued that if Fannie reached the razor-thin capital levels it was arguing were sufficient, then it would be able to maintain its solvency under conditions "significantly worse than any experienced" in the postwar era. Volcker's endorsement gave Fannie's supporters "no small measure of comfort that the Treasury's considerably more Draconian proposals won't fly," wrote *Barron's*. As the bill neared passage, Fannie Mae rounded up other supporters to argue that increasing the firm's capital reserves would be bad for homeowners. Why? Because it would "limit credit availability and raise interest rates for home buyers," testified Stephen Ashley, then the president of the Mortgage Bankers Association. A few years later, Fannie named Ashley to its board. Another classic tactic.

As the legislation progressed, Johnson got his lobbyists—and several prominent housing activists—to convince Congress that the new regulator should be placed not within the Treasury or the Fed, which were both regarded as "antihousing," but at HUD, an agency with very little institutional understanding of banking regulation and risk. Sure enough, the new regulator was housed in HUD. And sure enough, the bill allowed the GSEs to hold far less capital than other financial institutions; by the mid-1990s, the GSEs' capital was about 2.75 percent of total assets.

There was another little twist that ensured that Fannie Mae would never have much to fear from the new law. Fannie maneuvered to have OFHEO—virtually alone among "safety and soundness" regulators—subject to the appropriations process. This meant that its annual budget was at the mercy of politicians, many of whom often took their cues from Fannie. As a result, one former Freddie Mac lobbyist says, OFHEO had two choices: "Appease Fannie and Freddie or get reamed in the budget."

Fannie's new "mission" requirements underwent a similar process. For instance, under the new law 30 percent of the mortgages the GSEs purchased were supposed to be loans made to low- and moderate-income families living in underserved areas. (The goals were increased slightly beginning in 1996.) But the goals were almost laughably meaningless. As the General Accounting Office later noted, they were actually *below* HUD's estimates of what the market naturally did already. And since "moderate income" meant those who made 100 percent of a certain area's median income, a mortgage made to your average American family counted toward the purported goals.

Johnson took great pride in the way Fannie had protected its profits and neutered the law. "It sounds a little muscular, but we wrote the housing goals in 1991 and 1992," he told friends. "We cooperated with their being written in such a way that they had no teeth."

When the bill was signed into law, Johnson declared victory. The legislation, he told the *Wall Street Journal*, "removes any cloud that remains about our government mandate." Fannie and Freddie, he seemed to be saying, were now officially untouchable. But like David Maxwell's earlier prediction, it only seemed that way at the time.

Not surprisingly, for the first roughly ten years of its existence, OFHEO was a notoriously weak regulator. There was a two-year stretch in the late 1990s when the agency didn't even have a director. Fannie executives didn't have much respect for OFHEO, and few bothered to hide it. When the regulator requested information, the GSEs would often respond that the information was confidential, explains Stephen Blumenthal, the former deputy director of OFHEO. "No one on Wall Street likes the SEC, but no one is crazy enough to fight with them. You try to develop a civil relationship. When I got to OFHEO, I was shocked. Fannie and Freddie were openly abusive to the agency and its staff." OFHEO itself would later contend that "the goal of [Fannie's] senior management was straightforward: to force OFHEO to rely on [Fannie itself] for information and expertise to such a degree that Fannie Mae would essentially be regulated only by itself." Which is pretty much what happened.

At the same time Fannie was stiff-arming its new regulator, it was embracing its mission requirements both to justify Fannie's government-bestowed advantages and to keep critics at bay. In this regard, the fact that its mission was now spelled out in a piece of legislation was a helpful thing.

The goals themselves, weak to begin with, were easy to game. For Fannie, they were almost beside the point. The real issue for Johnson was that the legislation gave him a huge new rhetorical advantage. His company—*by statute*—was helping low- and moderate-income Americans achieve the American Dream. The mission made it easy to explain to members of Congress why Fannie mattered. And when critics complained about Fannie, the company could hit back by labeling them "antihomeowner."

Fannie Mae had always employed people that insiders called housers, a mildly derisive term that referred to those idealists who believed homeownership was the cure to the world's ills. It wasn't long before Johnson became a houser, too. At least, he talked the talk. "The mission runs in our veins," he liked to say. Another of his favorite lines was a twist on the old saying about General Motors: "What's good for American housing is good for Fannie Mae." Fannie began advertising its connection to homeownership on shows like *Meet the Press*.

But Johnson went well beyond mere rhetoric. The GSEs' core problem, he liked to say, was that there was "nothing in the homeowner's life called Fannie Mae or Freddie Mac." Everything the GSEs did was behind the scenes. But for Congress, it was the homeowners who mattered, since they were the constituents. So Fannie had to find a way to demonstrate two key traits, which Johnson called "indispensability" and "tangibility." That, he'd say, would "allow us to survive."

Johnson solved this problem by establishing what Fannie Mae called partnership offices. Officially, these were operations dedicated to finding opportunities to purchase mortgages in a given state. Unofficially, they were the grassroots of a highly sophisticated political operation. Fannie's first partnership office was in San Antonio, which just happened to be home to Representative Henry Gonzalez, then the chairman of the House banking committee. (In 1994, he became the ranking minority member when the Republicans gained majority status in the House.) When Gonzalez retired in 1999, Representative John LaFalsce of Buffalo, New York, became the ranking Democrat. So Fannie opened a partnership office in Buffalo.

There was a certain formula to these offices. They were staffed by someone close to power—the son of a senator, a governor's assistant, a former congressional staffer. They held ribbon-cutting ceremonies, always with a politician present, to announce, for instance, that Fannie was going to put millions into a senior citizen center. There were as many as two thousand ceremonies a year in partnership offices all over the country. Members of Congress may not have understood how the secondary mortgage market contributed to homeownership, but they certainly understood the dispensation of pork.

Fannie Mae also funneled money to politicians. In addition to campaign contributions, Fannie set up a foundation that made contributions to politically useful causes. The foundation had existed in a small way since 1979, but in 1996 Johnson contributed $350 million of Fannie's stock and handed over responsibility for advertising to Fannie's foundation. Over the years, the foundation became one of the largest sources of charitable donations in the country. It made heavy donations to, among others, the nonprofit arms of the Congressional Black Caucus and the Congressional Hispanic Caucus.

Fannie hired key insiders to plum jobs. Tom Donilon, who had been the chief of staff to Secretary of State Warren Christopher, joined Fannie Mae when he left the government; so did Jamie Gorelick, who had been the deputy attorney general in the Clinton administration. Sometimes, when it suited his purposes, Johnson even hired Republicans, such as Arne Christensen, who had been the chief of staff to Newt Gingrich, the former House majority leader. "It was like the local Tammany Hall operation—a jobs program for ex-pols!" says one close observer.

Fannie and Freddie spent a staggering amount of money lobbying: $170 million in the decade ending in 2006, just a little less than the American Medical Association. But even the dollar tally understates Fannie's reach. Money alone couldn't have gotten a politician's barber to call him when Fannie Mae wanted something from Congress, as the *Washington Post* once reported. When one of Fannie Mae's few congressional critics, Jim Leach of Iowa, who succeeded Gonzalez as House banking committee chairman, proposed taxing Fannie and Freddie's debt issuances, rumors began circulating that he was going to be stripped of his chairmanship. That was Fannie's doing as well. "What do you think a Fannie pack is?" asks one critic. "Whenever there was a hearing, anyone involved would get a Fannie pack, which would consist of every single loan originated in their district that Fannie Mae had purchased in the last four or five years." Says former Louisiana congressman Richard Baker: "They ran a battle plan that would make Patton proud. It was twenty-four/seven and never anything left to chance."

And those who persisted in criticizing Fannie Mae? They learned to regret it. When some of Fannie's large competitors, worried about its growing dominance, launched an organization called FM Watch to keep tabs on the GSEs, Fannie openly threatened them. GE Capital CEO Denis Nayden told the *Wall Street Journal* that GE was on the "receiving end of multiple communications from Fannie Mae indicating that GE would suffer financial consequences if GE remained a member of FM Watch." Said Hank Greenberg, the chief executive of AIG: "They use their muscle to threaten competitors, and that's an outrage." Soon, FM Watch stopped disclosing the names of its members.

When the Congressional Budget Office published a report in May 1996 estimating that about 40 percent of Fannie and Freddie's profits were due to their implied government support, Fannie Mae denounced the report, calling it the work of "economic pencil brains who wouldn't recognize something that works for ordinary home buyers if it bit them in their erasers."

When the General Accounting Office wrote in a letter to house majority leader Richard Armey that the GSEs received a government subsidy amounting to $2.2 billion in 1995, the letter's author, James Bothwell, says that he received a call from Franklin Raines, who was then the vice chairman of Fannie Mae. According to Bothwell, Raines demanded that he take out the line about the subsidy—and if he didn't, Raines would make a call that might cost Bothwell his job. Bothwell refused. In the end, he didn't lose his job. (Raines denies the incident.)

And when, in 1996, the Treasury Department was preparing to issue a tough report on the GSEs, Fannie somehow managed to get it watered down—and turned into a largely positive report—before it ever saw the light of day. The early draft, for instance, said that if the GSEs were privatized, "Fannie Mae and Freddie Mac would be exposed to the full discipline of private capital market investors, rather than the weakened and distorted discipline resulting from GSE status." That sentence was gone from the final report. The draft also contained a paragraph that cited several reasons why ending government sponsorship "should also improve the safety and soundness of the housing finance market." That was gone from the final report, too. The fifth chapter of the draft disappeared entirely. It had been entitled

"Policy Options for Altering the Relationship Between the Federal Government and the GSEs."

No one who's talking can prove what happened, but those who know about the rewrite have long speculated that Johnson put in a call to his friend Bill Clinton or to Treasury Secretary Robert Rubin, another friend. Johnson has denied calling either man. The mystery was never solved.

The ferocity of Fannie Mae's response to criticism was strange, in a way. After all, Fannie Mae and Freddie Mac *did* play an important role in homeownership. Their guarantees allowed more people to buy homes. Over time, they made it possible for mortgage originators like Countrywide to overtake the dying S&L industry as the country's primary mortgage lender—thus keeping the mortgage spigot open even as the thrifts were shutting down.

And Fannie and Freddie had far more friends than critics, including some powerful Republicans. Republican senator Phil Gramm, an ardent champion of free markets, was in as good a position as any to cause Fannie and Freddie trouble; he became the chairman of the Senate banking committee in 1994. But Gramm always gave Fannie and Freddie a pass. Why? Because, like Johnson, Gramm saw the political fruit that homeownership could bear. According to a former banking committee staffer, the Republicans studied what it was that made people vote Republican. "The number one predictor of voting Republican was a job in the private sector," he said. "Number two, and it's a close second, is that you own your own home." He adds, "Gramm preached that gospel to all who would listen."

Then again, maybe Fannie's tendency, as Maloni later put it, "to throw one brick too many rather than one brick too few" wasn't so surprising after all. When you got right down to it, there was something about the GSEs' business model that made no sense. Nobody in his or her right mind would establish a company whose competitive advantage was built on a guarantee that was nowhere written down and that no one could say for sure even existed. Yet that was the premise upon which Fannie Mae and Freddie Mac had built their dominance. Their advantages were based in large part on the belief by investors that the government would never let the GSEs default.

When Fannie dealt with investors, it encouraged that perception. (It once claimed that its securities were even safer than triple-A-rated bonds because of the "implied government backing of Fannie Mae.") Yet whenever anyone in government brought it up, Fannie Mae went mildly berserk. To admit that it had government backing would mean admitting that taxpayer support was the key source of Fannie's huge profits—and that taxpayers would be on the hook if anything went wrong. And that was something Fannie could never concede. That's why even the most muted criticism was treated as life or death—because Fannie Mae always felt that it *was* life or death. Some former lobbyists used to compare Fannie to the old Oakland Raiders, whose motto in the seventies was "Just win, baby."

There was another reason why Fannie Mae was so quick to push back against its critics. Over time, the bulk of its profits were being generated from an activity that critics said—correctly—had nothing whatsoever to do with helping people buy affordable homes.

The business of stamping mortgages with its guarantee and turning them into mortgage-backed securities was a good, steady business. It gave Fannie Mae and Freddie Mac immense power in the marketplace. But while profitable, it wasn't off-the-charts profitable; it didn't generate the kind of profits that put companies in the upper echelon of American business. For that, Fannie and Freddie turned to another activity: they began to build up their own portfolios of mortgages and mortgage-backed securities, which they held on their own books, instead of selling them to investors.

Although owning a portfolio of mortgages had almost bankrupted Fannie in the early 1980s, the company never got rid of its portfolio entirely. "We always viewed it as a core part of the business," says Maxwell. Fannie's mantra was "Good times and bad," meaning it would be in the market when investors were eager to buy mortgages, as well as when they were uninterested—and the only alternative was for Fannie to hold the mortgages in a portfolio. Maxwell, typically, had kept the portfolio fairly small so it wouldn't attract too much attention.

Johnson, also typically, expanded it exponentially. The core idea behind the portfolio reflected, once again, the advantages of being a GSE. Fannie and Freddie would issue some of that low-cost debt their implied government backing made possible, use that money to buy higher-yielding mortgages, and pocket the difference. "The big, fat gap," Federal Reserve chairman Alan Greenspan used to call it disparagingly, a phrase that perfectly captures the almost moronic simplicity of the strategy. By the end of 1998, Fannie had a $415 billion portfolio of mortgages, up from just $156 billion in 1992. In its 1996 report to Congress, the Congressional Budget Office estimated that the profit margin on this business was four to five times higher than the guarantee business. By the end of the decade, it accounted for most of Fannie's profits.

This business also helped make Fannie even more of a force on Wall Street. Over the years, it paid Street firms hundreds of millions of dollars worth of fees to issue all the debt. "People dealt with them [Fannie and Freddie] as if they were sovereign credits," says one former Wall Streeter. "You just knew better than to get on the wrong side of them."

By the end of the decade, Fannie Mae had become America's third largest corporation, ranked by assets. Freddie was close behind. The companies were ranked one and two respectively on *Fortune*'s list of the most profitable companies per employee. Fannie's stock price had soared. Its market value under Johnson went from the $10.5 billion he'd inherited from Maxwell to over $70 billion. "There is no other financial institution in America with such a significant share of such a huge market," Johnson said in one speech, and he was exactly right.

<hr />

Here's the great irony of the mortgage market in the 1990s: to the extent that lower- and moderate-income Americans were being swept along in the rising tide of homeownership in the 1990s, it was happening not because of Fannie and Freddie, but despite them. The replacement of the S&L industry by the new mortgage origination companies; the toughening, in the 1990s, of the Community Reinvestment Act, which forced banks to make loans to people in poorer neighborhoods; even the rise of the subprime industry (though it was more focused on refinancings than new home loans)—these were all factors in helping poorer people own homes. Fannie and Freddie may have been given a federal mandate to help lower- and moderate-income Americans buy homes, but the GSEs were cautious about the credit risk they took. They preferred to game their housing goals rather than meet them, using methods that Fannie referred to internally as "stupid pet tricks." They wanted nothing to do with subprime. Subprime loans didn't conform. And anyway, there was so much money to be made elsewhere.

Many affordable housing activists found this infuriating. For all its sanctimony about its mission, they complained, the GSEs did very little for those who truly needed help. Both John Taylor, the CEO of the National Community Reinvestment Coalition, and Judy Kennedy, the former Freddie lobbyist in charge of the National Association of Affordable Housing Lenders, complained bitterly about Fannie and Freddie. Repeated studies by

HUD showed that the GSEs' purchases of loans made to lower-income borrowers lagged the market.

That's not to say Fannie and Freddie did nothing. When Countrywide ginned up its program to provide low-income mortgages, it sold them to Fannie through a special program Fannie had set up to handle such loans. But back then, programs like Countrywide's were small and highly controlled—experiments, really, and valid ones at that, because they sought an answer to an important question. As Dan Mudd would later ask, "Do you want to live in a country where someone who has a blemish on their credit, or someone who happens to be a minority, can't get a home? Where do you draw the line?"

Mostly, though, Fannie Mae made no apologies for its stance. "I used to say that the goal at Fannie was to have a seamless yes to anyone who wants to do anything for housing," Johnson later said. "But we didn't say yes to crap, to fraud. We were probing the boundaries, but it was carefully circumscribed."

Says a former Fannie executive: "About 98 percent of our mortgages were done at market rates. We were giving away a little at the edge of the big machine." This person adds: "Johnson's attitude was, 'I am not going to let the government define what affordable housing is to this company.'"

That would soon begin to change, however. In 1999, Andrew Cuomo, who had been appointed HUD secretary during Bill Clinton's second term and was a true believer in affordable housing, proposed increasing the affordable housing goals. To an unusual degree, Cuomo was immune to Fannie's charms and impervious to its threats. He'd already taken on Johnson on another issue, and did not back down when Fannie pushed back. In July 1999, the GSEs agreed that by 2001, 50 percent of the mortgages they guaranteed would be loans made to low- or middle-income Americans. One way the GSEs could meet those goals, of course, was by lowering their underwriting standards, just as the subprime industry had done. Indeed, the housers at Fannie had high hopes that their company could serve as the sheriff in the lawless world of subprime lending. An exhaustive study Fannie had done revealed that many subprime borrowers were so fearful of being rejected that they were willing to pay very high rates just to hear a yes. Some studies showed that plenty of subprime customers could have qualified for a prime loan— meaning they were paying far more for their mortgages than they had to. Fannie said it could use its clout to make sure that borrowers got a fair deal.

Later, many conservative critics of the GSEs would come to see this moment as the capitulation of Fannie and Freddie to the Clinton affordable housing drive. That wasn't really true. The real reason Fannie was willing to finally move into riskier territory was the same reason Countrywide did: profits. Subprime was taking off—and the GSEs were sitting on the sidelines. "Their motivation to enter this market is to continue a phenomenal record of amazing shareholder enrichment," Anne Canfield, a longtime critic of the GSEs, wrote at the time. There was another potential issue, too. At a congressional hearing in June of 2000, the Reverend Graylan Scott Hagler of the Plymouth Congregational United Church of Christ, in Washington, D.C., who also claimed that the GSEs were entering the subprime business to "maximize returns," said, "The real fear here is that when the economy goes south, or just through one of those cycles it periodically goes through, if Fannie and Freddie are engaged in these subprime markets, then they will get left holding the bag, and the American taxpayer with them."

Says a former Fannie executive: "It met our business goals. You have to start there. All the criticisms about Fannie being too shareholder driven and too profit driven—they are true! Shareholders were an important constituency at Fannie. For the smart people we brought in, they were the only constituency."

Still, Fannie moved cautiously. In 2000, it put out guidelines listing what sort of riskier loans it would buy; Cuomo used those guidelines in Fannie's affordable housing goals. Under the new rules, certain kinds of high-risk loans, ones that consumer advocates felt took undue advantage of borrowers, wouldn't count toward Fannie and Freddie's affordable housing goals. There is no data to prove that the GSEs avoided those loans, although neither company ever guaranteed large quantities of loans that they considered subprime.

In the end, though, it didn't really matter whether Fannie and Freddie moved into riskier mortgages quickly or slowly, reluctantly or gleefully. What mattered was that they entered this new market at all. In so doing, they gave their imprimatur to what had previously been an entirely separate universe. A line that had once been absolute was now blurring. "The whole definition of subprime was 'the stuff that Fannie and Freddie wouldn't touch,'" a former executive explains. No longer.

Much later, Maxwell would concede, with great sadness, that Fannie Mae had forgotten a simple question: Why are we here? If Fannie Mae had kept that question paramount, the company would have remembered that it didn't exist solely to generate ever-increasing profits or to keep pace with the private market, but to supply liquidity when the housing market needed it. If Fannie had remembered that, the company might have found its moral compass when it needed it most—and maybe left a different legacy.

4

Risky Business

The most cutting-edge firm on Wall Street in the early 1990s was not Drexel Burnham Lambert, which had dominated the 1980s with its junk bonds, or Goldman Sachs, whose sheer moneymaking prowess would first dazzle and then repulse the country during this last decade. No, the firm that everyone on Wall Street wanted to emulate was a one-hundred-year-old commercial bank: J.P. Morgan. During the same era that the subprime mortgage industry was rising from the primordial ooze and Fannie Mae was consolidating its power over the mortgage securitization market, J.P. Morgan was making an important series of innovations around the concept of risk.

Risk was the bank's obsession. It wanted to measure risk, model risk, and manage risk better than any institution had ever done before. It wanted to embrace certain risks that no bank had ever taken on, while shedding other risks that banks had always accepted as an unavoidable part of banking. To this end, J.P. Morgan (along with other firms, too) hired mathematicians and physicists—actual rocket scientists!—to create complex risk models and products. They were called "quants" because they tried to make money not by examining the fundamentals of stock and bonds, but by using more quantitative methods. They devised complex equations rooted in modern portfolio theory, which held as its core principle that diversification reduced risk. They searched for securities that seemed to move in tandem, and then used computers to take advantage of tiny discrepancies in their price movements. Their risk models were statistical marvels, based on probability theory. The new securities they invented, designed to shift risk from one firm's books to another's, were practically metaphysical. After the transaction was completed, the original security remained on the first firm's books, but the *risk* it represented had moved. These new products were called derivatives, because they were "derived" from another security. J.P. Morgan's chief contribution in this area was something called the credit default swap. Its breakthrough risk model was called Value at Risk, or VaR. Both products quickly became tools that everyone on Wall Street relied on.

What did these innovations have to do with subprime mortgages? Nothing, at first. J.P. Morgan and Ameriquest could have been operating on different planets, so little did they have to do with each other. But in time, Wall Street realized that the same principles that underlay J.P. Morgan's risk model could be adapted to bestow coveted triple-A ratings on large chunks of complex new products created out of subprime mortgages. Firms could use VaR to persuade regulators—and themselves—that they were taking on very little risk, even as they were loading up on subprime securities. And they could use credit default swaps to off-load their own subprime risks onto some other entity willing to accept it. By the early 2000s, these two worlds—subprime and quantitative finance—were completely intertwined.

Not that anyone at J.P. Morgan could see what was coming. Like Ranieri in the 1980s, the bank's eager young innovators were convinced they were making the financial world a better, safer world. But they weren't.

The chairman and CEO of J.P. Morgan in the early 1990s was a calm, unflappable British expatriate named Sir Dennis Weatherstone. Knighted in 1990, the year he took over the bank, Weatherstone had the bearing of a patrician despite working-class roots; his first job, at the age of sixteen, was as a bookkeeper in the London office of a firm J.P. Morgan would acquire. When he died in 2008 at the age of seventy-seven, an obituary writer described him as "dapper, precise, soft-spoken . . . unfailingly polite . . . a man no one disliked."

He was also a new kind of bank CEO. He had never been a commercial banker. His career had been spent as a trader in London. His last big assignment before moving to New York to join the J.P. Morgan executive suite was as the head of the firm's foreign currency exchange desk.

A reserved man who rarely granted interviews, Weatherstone was little known outside the banking industry. But his influence on J.P. Morgan—indeed, on banking itself—was profound. In the early 1980s, J.P. Morgan earned most of its money by making commercial loans. By 1993, nearly 75 percent of its revenues derived from investment banking fees and trading profits, the result of the bank moving to what one British journalist described as "new forms of finance." The most important of these new forms was derivatives. By 1994, the year Weatherstone retired, *Fortune* could quote a bank executive calling them "the basic business of banking."

The essential purpose of derivatives has always been to swap one kind of risk for another; that's why many common derivatives are called swaps. The earliest derivatives attempted to mitigate interest rate risk and currency risk. In the volatile economic environment of the 1980s, when interest rates and currency values could swing suddenly and unpredictably, big companies were desperate for ways to protect themselves; derivatives became the way. An interest rate swap allowed a company to lock in an interest rate and pay a fee to another entity—a counterparty, as they were called on Wall Street—willing to take the risk that rates would suddenly jump. (If rates dropped instead, the counterparty would make a nice profit.) The counterparty, in turn, would often want to hedge, or reduce, its own risks by entering into an offsetting trade with another entity. Which would then want to hedge *its* risks. And so on. Trading derivatives could often seem like standing between two mirrors and seeing the reflection of your reflection of your reflection, ad infinitum. Hedging derivative risk was a classic example of the old Wall Street saw that "trading begets trading."

Given his background, it is no surprise that Weatherstone was a big believer in derivatives; as a currency trader, he had undoubtedly structured his share of swaps. He was also very clear-eyed about the need for J.P. Morgan to move away from commercial lending and into more profitable areas like trading and derivatives.

Thus, one of Weatherstone's first acts when he became CEO in 1990 was to persuade the Federal Reserve to allow the bank to begin trading securities in the United States. This was a huge shift in U.S. policy; ever since the Great Depression, the government had kept commercial banking and investment banking apart. (Glass-Steagall, the 1933 law that mandated this change, forced J.P. Morgan to spin off its investment banking arm, which was rechristened Morgan Stanley.) In recent years, though, American banks had gotten back into the trading business, except that they did it from London instead of New York. Weatherstone argued that as banking changed, U.S. policy had to change, too, or it would risk losing its most profitable operations to the City of London. Though the Fed couldn't overturn the law, it could interpret Glass-Steagall in a different, looser way. Which it did. Little noticed at the time, this reinterpretation marked the transformation of banking from a sleepy business to a cutthroat one. Now that banks had trading desks, there was both more money to be made—and more pressure to make it.

Having run a trading desk, Weatherstone also had a deep understanding of risk—which meant, among other things, that he was more aware than other bank CEOs of how much he *didn't* know about the risks on J.P. Morgan's books. It made him uncomfortable.

All of J.P. Morgan's businesses had risks, whether it was buying or selling stocks and bonds, writing complex derivatives contracts, or making commercial loans to big companies. As head of the foreign currency exchange desk, Weatherstone had been attuned to all the risks in the portfolio he oversaw. But as CEO, he lacked the tools to get his arms around the various risks on the company's books, much less understand how they related to each other. Did the risks taken on one desk nullify the risks being taken on another desk—or did they exacerbate them? Even before he'd become the bank's CEO, Weatherstone decided that J.P. Morgan needed a new approach to risk.

The man he chose to lead this effort was a Swiss executive, Till Guldimann. Like Weatherstone, Guldimann had spent most of his career on trading desks. He, too, developed a keen interest in risk management, which he viewed as woefully unscientific. The traditional way of managing trading risks, for instance, was to impose a limit on how much capital a trader had at his disposal. But as a risk manager, Guldimann was often confronted with the problem of what to do when a trader wanted to increase his limit. "How should I know if he should get his increase?" Guldimann says. "All I could do is ask around. Is he a good guy? Does he know what he's doing? It was ridiculous."

There was never any question about how Guldimann and his team would approach this task. They would use statistics and probability theories that had long been popular on Wall Street. (The Black-Scholes formula, for example, developed in the early 1970s for pricing options, had become one of the linchpins of modern Wall Street.) The quants swarming Wall Street were all steeped in those theories—this was the essential building block of virtually everything they did. They knew no other way to approach the subject.

Sure enough, Value at Risk, or VaR, the model the J.P. Morgan quants came up with after years of trial and error, was built on a key tenet of the mathematics of probability, called Gaussian distribution. (It is named after Carl Friedrich Gauss, a German mathematician who introduced it in the early 1800s.) Its daunting name notwithstanding, the Gaussian distribution curve is something we're all familiar with: it is a simple bell curve, which looks like this:

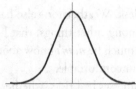

Why does a bell curve rise as it gets closer to the middle? Because the middle of the graph is where the smallest—and hence the most frequent—changes take place. Take a widely traded stock. It is going to rise or fall by twenty-five cents far more often than it will rise or fall by five dollars. So the twenty-five-cent movements will be clustered near the middle while the less frequent five-dollar movements will be farther along the sides of the curve, on either the plus or the minus side. And the truly enormous moves—the barely imaginable, once-in-a-lifetime events—will be so far outside the scale of the curve that they won't even show up. These rare events would eventually be called "fat tails" or "black swans."

Guldimann wasn't interested in black swans; that was a risk problem for someone else to solve. Instead, VaR was meant to measure market risk from one day to the next, with the working assumption that tomorrow would be more or less like yesterday. Guldimann's aim was to come up with a single number—a dollar figure—that would represent the amount of money the bank could lose over the next twenty-four hours with a 95 percent probability, assuming a normal market. Of course if it wasn't a normal market, then all bets were off.

VaR, as Guldimann and his team developed it, had a number of appealing features. First, it could be used to gauge the riskiness of any kind of portfolio, from the simplest loans to the most complex derivatives. Second, it could be used to aggregate risk across the entire firm. Third, it could be used to measure the risks being taken by individual traders. That meant that risk managers no longer had to ask around when a trader wanted to increase his limits. "Once we converted all the limits to VaR limits, we could compare," says Guldimann. "You could look at the profits the guy made and compare it to his VaR. If the guy who asked for a higher limit was making more money with less VaR, it was a good basis to give him more money."

Finally, VaR expressed risk as a single number. You didn't have to be a quant to understand it. For instance, if your firm's VaR was 45, then that meant that 95 percent of the time the most the firm could lose the next day was $45 million. For Wall Street CEOs not immersed in risk management practices, VaR gave them something they could readily understand.

By the early 1990s, Weatherstone had instituted something called the 4:15 Report. Every afternoon at 4:15—just fifteen minutes after the market had closed—all the top J.P. Morgan executives were sent a document that listed the firm's overall VaR for that day, as well as the VaR number for all the various trading desks around the world. No longer were executives in New York blind to the risks being taken in London, or Tokyo, or anywhere else in the world.

Later, many Wall Street CEOs would view their daily VaR number as an expression of their firm's worst-case scenario. But it was nothing of the sort. The most important information VaR conveyed was not the absolute number, but the trend over the course of weeks or months. Were the bank's risks increasing or diminishing? Were problems arising on this desk or that one? And so on.

And then there was the tail risk issue. The fact that VaR told you how much your firm might lose 95 percent of the time didn't say a thing about what might happen the other 5 percent of the time. Maybe you would lose a little more than the VaR number—no big deal. Or maybe you'd get caught in a black swan and lose billions. The fact that VaR had been created didn't mean you could stop worrying about risk.

Weatherstone understood this completely. "I remember meeting with him," says a former J.P. Morgan risk manager. "I would show him the VaR numbers and tell him that a certain currency trade had gotten 20 percent riskier. The currency guy would fight it. [Weatherstone] would listen to the arguments. He wouldn't say a lot. Then he would make a decision about whether the currency desk had taken on too much risk. And it was based not just on VaR but on the deeper discussion that it sparked." Which, for its creators at J.P. Morgan, was how VaR was supposed to work. Though it was an important data point, it was never meant to be the only data point.

Having created VaR, Guldimann then did something highly unusual: he gave it away. The theme of the bank's 1993 client conference was risk. By then, other firms were grappling with the same set of issues that had led J.P. Morgan to create VaR. When Guldimann explained the bank's new risk model at the conference, many of J.P. Morgan's clients began clamoring to learn more about it. Some of them asked if they could purchase the underlying system.

Most banks would have likely declined; after all, VaR was J.P. Morgan's intellectual property. But Weatherstone and Guldimann understood that if some banks took excessive risks they didn't understand, it would be bad for everybody, J.P. Morgan included. It would be better, they believed, if everyone had access to the same risk tools. But since they also didn't want to turn risk management into a side business, they decided to teach VaR to anyone who wanted to learn about it—free of charge. "Many wondered what the bank was trying to accomplish by giving away 'proprietary' methodologies and lots of data, but not selling any products or services," Guldimann wrote years later. "It popularized a methodology . . . and it enhanced the reputation of J.P. Morgan." By the late 1990s, VaR had become the de facto standard for risk models. Everybody used it. They had to.

∽

Even as Guldimann was popularizing VaR, another group of J.P. Morgan quants, in a different corner of the firm, was creating a new kind of derivative: credit default swaps. The project grew out of the same impulse as VaR—the bank's ongoing effort to better manage its own risks. In this case, though, the risk in question was perhaps the most basic in all of banking: the risk that a borrower might be unable to pay back his loan. Credit risk, in other words.

The best way to deal with the possibility of default of course, is to make good loans in the first place. That's why banks have underwriting standards. But even the soundest loan portfolio is going to have defaults; it's inevitable. Nobody can know what the future holds. Strong companies can become weak. Unforeseen events can take place. No loan is risk free.

Nor, of course, are bank portfolios always sound. The history of banking is filled with episodes of mania, going back at least to the South Sea Bubble in the 1720s, when bankers lost their heads and made foolish loans. In such instances, when a raft of bad loans couldn't be paid back, banks were suddenly shuttered and a financial crisis often ensued, requiring government intervention.

To protect against defaults, banks hold capital in reserve, which can be used to fill the hole in the balance sheet if loans go bad. In the late nineteenth century, the U.S. government forced banks to hold a staggering 30 percent of their capital in reserve. That onerous requirement eventually disappeared, but in the wake of the Latin American debt crisis of the 1970s—a crisis that nearly brought Citibank to its knees—federally mandated capital requirements made a comeback. U.S. banks were required by the Federal Reserve to set aside enough capital to cover 8 percent of their assets. In the view of the government, mandatory capital was a critical safety net. (As Alan Greenspan himself later wrote, "Adequate capital eliminates the need for an unachievable specificity in regulatory fine tuning.")

Around the same time, the idea of creating global capital requirements began to gain currency. The rationale was that in an increasingly globalized marketplace, it was important for all the big international banks to play by the same rules, so that one country's banks wouldn't have an advantage over another's. The group that was formed to put together these international rules was the Basel Committee on Banking Supervision, which began its work in 1974. By the time the Basel Committee proposed, finalized, and implemented its new capital rules, called Basel I, some eighteen years had passed.

Why did it take so long? Partly it was because international bureaucracies always take an absurd amount of time to get anything done. Partly it was because, during those eighteen years, banking was becoming increasingly complex and the proposed capital rules were constantly trying to catch up to that complexity. And partly—perhaps most important—it was because, throughout the process, the banks fought to both weaken the capital rules and turn them to their advantage.

Banks, you see, hate having to hold a lot of capital. Though they understand the importance of capital rules, they also know that every dollar of capital held in reserve is a dollar that can't be used to make a loan. So there has always been a struggle between regulators trying to impose capital requirements and banks trying to minimize them.

Prior to Basel I, every asset on a bank's books, no matter how risky, required the same amount of capital. Yet as banks broadened into derivatives and other areas that went well beyond commercial lending, it became increasingly clear that different assets had different risks. That's the complex reality the Basel Committee was trying to reflect.

Basel's solution was to adopt what it called risk-based capital requirements. That is, the amount a bank had to put aside in capital would depend on the riskiness of the asset. Commercial loans were in the riskiest bucket, requiring the full capital ratio. But mortgages were viewed as less risky, presumably because people would go to great lengths to avoid defaulting on their home, so they required less capital than a commercial loan. With some prodding from the banking industry, the Basel Committee agreed that private-label mortgage-backed securities—that is, mortgage bonds not backed by Fannie or Freddie—should have a risk weighting of 50 percent of the riskiest weightings, such as commercial loans. Mortgage-backed securities insured by Fannie Mae or Freddie Mac were viewed as the safest of all, since those loans were backed (implicitly) by the full faith and credit of the United States government. The capital they required was only 20 percent of that of a commercial loan.

The consequence of this new approach was obvious. Banks were going to stuff their balance sheets with mortgage products because they required less capital. Because highly rated securitized tranches required less capital, it made more sense for financial institutions to hold the securities rather than the original loans. The banks also kept pushing to change the rules in their favor. Starting in the mid-1990s, for instance, bank lobbyists repeatedly tried to get the regulators to lower the capital requirement on highly rated private-label securities to 20 percent, so their securities would be on equal footing with Fannie and Freddie's. (Fannie objected, of course.) In 2001 they finally succeeded, at which point banks had even more incentive to hold highly rated mortgage-backed securities.

Finally, banks searched for ways to game the Basel rules. For instance, under Basel I, banks could set up an off-balance-sheet investment vehicle, and so long as the duration of its credit line was less than one year, the bank didn't have to hold any capital against that vehicle. So, theoretically, a bank could sell a risky slice of a mortgage-backed security to such a vehicle, set the credit line to last one day short of a year, and hold no capital against it.

Once this risk-based methodology took hold, banks had an enormous incentive to move into assets that would require less capital—or to invent new products that would have the same effect.

Lo and behold, along came the product that would soon be the greatest capital reducer of them all: the credit default swap.

In simplest terms, a credit default swap is designed to accomplish the same task as an interest rate or currency swap—move risk from a party that doesn't want it to one that does. The risk in this case, however, is credit risk. A credit default swap is essentially an insurance policy against the possibility of default—credit protection, it came to be called. One party—a bank—would buy credit default swaps to protect against a default in its loan portfolio. A counterparty would sell the bank the credit default swap in return for a fee. So long as there was no default, the counterparty would keep collecting fees. But in the event of a default, the counterparty would have to pay the full amount of the loss to the bank. The loan itself remained on the books of the original lender.

There were a number of rationales behind J.P. Morgan's push to create credit default swaps. The first had to do with the bank's obsession with risk management. The one area where the bank's modern risk management approach had not taken hold was commercial lending. Over the years, big corporate loans had become increasingly less profitable as corporations turned to other funding mechanisms, like commercial paper. More and more, companies were using banks for inexpensive lines of credit that they needed only in emergencies—which is precisely when a bank doesn't want to extend credit. Yet banks were afraid to end these lines of credit because they didn't want to alienate their big corporate customers, who used many of their other, more profitable services.

What's more, although Basel may have viewed all commercial loans as equally risky, J.P. Morgan certainly did not. Was a loan to Walmart really as risky as a loan to Kmart? Yet the bank had no real way to distinguish the relative risk between the two. J.P. Morgan was reduced to making educated guesses. "We were extending credit," says one member of the credit derivative team, "and nobody was putting a price on it."

A tradable market for credit default swaps would change that. Traders buying and selling credit protection would allow the market to gauge the riskiness of a loan. If the cost of the credit default swap increased, that meant the chance of a default was rising; if it decreased, then the odds were decreasing. Even before a tradable market existed, J.P. Morgan's quants began using credit default swaps internally, to put a price on the risk of its own commercial loans. The old-line commercial lenders hated it, but this was exactly the kind of approach to risk that Weatherstone favored.

And the second reason the bank wanted to make credit default swaps a reality? If a tradable market developed, J.P. Morgan would certainly be a dominant player. It stood to make a lot of money. Commercial loans represented the stodgy past; credit derivatives represented the turbocharged future.

As for capital requirements, there is no doubt, when talking to people who were there at the creation, that the J.P. Morgan team always understood the potential for credit default swaps to reduce the need for banks to hold capital. After all, if a bank pays a counterparty to accept the default risk of its loan portfolio, doesn't that mean its credit risk has been reduced? And therefore, shouldn't it get capital relief? If the government went along, every big bank in the world would clamor to buy credit protection on its loan portfolio. The market wouldn't just be big; it would be *huge*. But for that to happen, the Federal Reserve would have to agree that credit default swaps did indeed transfer default risk. And who could say when, or even if, that would happen?

In 1994, J.P. Morgan put together its first credit default swap. It came about as a result of the *Exxon Valdez* oil spill. The oil giant, facing the possibility of a $5 billion fine, drew down a $4.8 billion line of credit from J.P. Morgan. This put the bank in exactly the kind of position it didn't want to be in. It couldn't say no, because that would alienate Exxon. Yet the loan wasn't going to make the bank much money, and it was going to tie up hundreds of millions of dollars in capital that would have to be placed in reserve.

The woman who came up with the idea of using a credit default swap to deal with this situation was Blythe Masters. Though she was not the head of the derivatives group, she was a key member of the team, a superb saleswoman who in later years would become the person most closely associated with J.P. Morgan's entrée into swaps. After Exxon drew down its $4.8 billion line of credit, she convinced the European Bank for Reconstruction and Development (EBRD) in London to participate in a swap deal where it assumed the default risk for the loan, with J.P. Morgan paying it steady fees for doing so. The loan stayed on J.P. Morgan's books.

Compared to what would come later, the deal was simplicity itself. J.P. Morgan was transferring the credit risk of a single loan to a single entity. Why was the EBRD willing to assume that credit risk? In truth, the reason was that the risk was minimal. Potential fine or no, Exxon was one of the strongest companies in the world, with 1994 revenues of close to $100 billion. It ranked third on the Fortune 500. Yet J.P. Morgan was going to pay the European bank substantial fees to assume the risk of an Exxon default. It seemed like free money.

And why was J.P. Morgan willing to pay those fees? Because even if it couldn't reduce its government capital, it was still removing a risk it did not want to bear, one that was weighing down its commercial lending risk profile. It had its own internal capital requirements, which would be reduced with this swap deal. And besides, the Exxon deal served as proof of a concept, and might help convince the government that swap deals merited capital relief. But that was still a ways off.

⌘

Just like mortgage-backed securities in the 1980s, the derivatives business needed government help in order to really take off. For instance, the industry needed Congress to tweak the bankruptcy laws, so that derivatives contracts could be "netted out" in case of a default. Without that change, if a bankrupt company owed its counterparties $500 million in swap deals, while the counterparties owed the company $300 million, the derivatives dealers would have to stand in line for its $500 million—while paying the company the $300 million. After Congress passed the "netting out" provision, the counterparties would then be owed $200 million instead.

But the derivatives dealers also wanted something even more important from the government: they wanted regulators to keep their paws off their shiny new product. For J.P. Morgan, which had been one of the leading derivatives dealers long before it came up with credit default swaps, this was its top Washington priority.

The person who led the lobbying effort for the bank, Mark Brickell, could not have been better suited to this task. A tall, thin, mildly disheveled man, Brickell wasn't like most Washington lobbyists. He wasn't a hired gun. Rather, he was a true believer, both in the virtues of derivatives and in the need for government to leave them alone. Handed this role in 1986, Brickell embraced it with a gusto that would never abate; even in the wake of the financial crisis, Brickell insisted—against all observable evidence—that derivatives had not been a leading cause.

Brickell graduated from the University of Chicago in the early 1970s, where he had studied economics and become a convert to the fierce free-market ideology that dominated its faculty—an experience he would later describe as one of the formative experiences of his life. After attending Harvard Business School, he toyed with a career in politics before joining J.P. Morgan in 1976, where he stayed for the next quarter century.

It was the growing popularity of interest rate and currency swaps in the mid-1980s that first caused regulators to begin asking questions about them. In response, the big banks, which dominated the business, formed a lobbying group in 1985, called the Independent Swaps and Derivatives Association, or ISDA. Brickell, representing J.P. Morgan, joined the following year. In 1988, he became its chairman.

Not long after Brickell joined ISDA, the Commodity Futures Trading Commission, a relatively new agency, published a notice saying that it planned to examine whether derivatives qualified as futures. If the answer was yes, then the CFTC would have regulatory authority over the swaps business. This was the first time anyone in government had raised such an idea—though it would hardly be the last. Over the course of the next decade, the question of whether derivatives should be regulated would arise regularly in Washington. Brickell's job essentially was to beat it back.

Brickell made at least four central arguments. The first was that because the major derivatives dealers were banks, they were already regulated by federal bank supervisors. His second argument was that the derivatives business was a hothouse of innovation, making the financial world less risky, and regulation would stifle further innovations. A third was that derivative transactions took place only among the most sophisticated investors, who didn't need the government looking over their shoulders. His final argument was that the market itself would impose the discipline needed to keep the growing business on the straight and narrow. Mistakes would lead to losses. Bad practices would cause other participants in the derivatives market to shun the offender. In making this argument, Brickell had a powerful ally in Alan Greenspan, who was also a believer in the power of market discipline—and a skeptic of regulation. It also didn't hurt that he had been on the J.P. Morgan board before becoming Fed chairman.

What Brickell did not talk about—or, rather, what he consistently pooh-poohed—was the fear that, in dispersing risk so widely, derivatives were transferring risk from a single institution to the entire financial system. All that hedging of derivatives—the reflecting mirror syndrome—was creating an interconnectedness among financial institutions that hadn't existed before. If one counterparty failed, what would happen to all the institutions holding its swap contracts? What would happen if the risks weren't properly hedged? Who kept track of the exposures major financial institutions held in their derivatives books?

In addition, derivatives also created an enormous amount of unseen—and unaccounted for—potential debt. A credit default swap is really a kind of IOU—a promise to pay a very large sum of money if something bad happens. Most of the time that promise would never have to be kept. But sometimes it would—potentially costing an institution billions of dollars it wasn't expecting to pay out.

To deflect Washington's concerns, in the early 1990s Weatherstone chaired an international committee on derivatives that came up with a four-volume tome of best practices for derivatives. Brickell was his aide-de-camp on the project. The report, entitled "Derivatives: Practices and Principles," impressed the bank regulators so much that some of them tried to codify the report into regulatory language. Brickell, of course, pushed back.

Brickell took care of the Commodity Futures Trading Commission, meanwhile, by simply claiming that derivatives were not futures and were therefore outside the agency's jurisdiction. If derivatives were ruled to be futures contracts, he said, the derivatives business would immediately be destroyed. Why? Because under the law, futures had to be traded on exchanges, and derivatives didn't trade on an exchange. What's more, the law said that any futures contracts that did not trade on an exchange were unenforceable. So if derivatives were declared futures, every derivative contract in the world would suddenly be worthless. Therefore they couldn't be futures.

It was a circular argument, but it worked. Shortly after the CFTC first expressed its interest in derivatives, President George H. W. Bush appointed Wendy Gramm as the agency's chairwoman. The wife of Senator Phil Gramm, the conservative Texas Republican, she had a PhD in economics and had been a high-level appointee at the Office of Management and Budget. After talking to Greenspan, the CFTC staff—and Brickell—Gramm ruled, in 1989, that derivatives were not futures. The *Wall Street Journal* ran an editorial with the headline "Swaps Saved."

Gramm's ruling did not put the issue to rest, however. On the contrary, prior to 1989 there were almost no congressional hearings about derivatives; over the next five years, there was a blizzard of them. Legislation to reauthorize the CFTC reopened the question of whether derivatives should be regulated like futures, leading to battles that went on for years. Court decisions that ruled that derivatives were, in fact, futures contracts had to be preempted by legislation. In 1992, the president of the New York Federal Reserve, Gerald Corrigan, made a widely noticed speech about the risks posed by derivatives. "High-tech banking and finance has its place, but it's not all that it is cracked up to be," he said in the speech. "I hope this sounds like a warning, because it is." The following year, a derivatives scandal broke out when two big companies, Procter & Gamble and Gibson Greetings, lost tens of millions of dollars on swap deals. Both later sued the issuing bank, Bankers Trust, claiming they had been misled about the risks those deals posed. In Orange County, a county treasurer had boosted the county's returns by using derivatives that Merrill Lynch had sold to him. When interest rates rose in 1994, the county lost so much money it had to file for bankruptcy.

Yet despite all the concern, the government never even came close to regulating derivatives. Brickell was relentless in his advocacy, but he had help. Shortly after making his speech in 1992, Corrigan left the New York Fed and joined Goldman Sachs; he was soon testifying in favor of derivatives. And Greenspan, who had a godlike status in Washington, was adamant that derivatives should be left alone. "Remedial legislation relating to derivatives is neither necessary nor desirable," he said at one congressional hearing. "We must not lose sight of the fact that risks in the financial markets are regulated by private parties." In other words, market discipline would take care of everything.

In the spring of 1994, James Bothwell of the General Accounting Office—the same man who had been threatened with the loss of his job after he wrote a tough report about Fannie and Freddie—released a report on the dangers derivatives posed. Though Bothwell was not a derivatives expert, he had a PhD in economics from Berkeley and had been working on his investigation for two years. Corrigan's 1992 speech had prompted five congressional committees to ask the GAO to look into derivatives. Bothwell and his team had surveyed fourteen major U.S. derivatives dealers—a fifteenth had refused to respond—and written a two-hundred-page report.

The GAO's report was far from a screed. "We were not against derivatives!" Bothwell says today. The report acknowledged how useful derivatives could be in managing risk. Still, Bothwell was stunned by what he had discovered. Brickell had consistently argued that since most derivatives dealers were banks, they were already regulated by the nation's bank supervisors. But Bothwell quickly realized that securities firms and insurance companies were also diving into the derivatives business, and that the securities firms had set up separate derivatives affiliates to avoid SEC oversight. The insurance companies also set up separate subsidiaries, and state officials, who were in charge of regulating insurers, told the GAO that these new subsidiaries were outside their authority.

The GAO team was also concerned by the see-no-evil attitude of the derivatives dealers. For instance, Bothwell's team asked the firms whether they were conducting stress tests on their portfolios, to gauge how they would do under "abnormal market conditions." Roughly one-third of the respondents said the question didn't even apply to them.

Most of all, the GAO was concerned about the elephant in the room: the possibility that derivatives posed systemic risk. Because the business was concentrated in a few hands, the failure of one dealer might "cause liquidity problems in the markets and could also pose risks to the others, including federally insured banks and the financial system as a whole," the report said.

Yet despite these concerns, the recommendations made by the GAO were hardly radical. "What we are pitching," Cecile Trop, the assistant director of the GAO, told Congress, "is an early warning system that will help in anticipating and responding to a financial system crisis, should there ever be one. That doesn't sound too onerous to us; it's a prudent and reasonable kind of approach."

No sooner had the report been issued than the industry fired back. Immediately following its release, not one but six leading financial trade associations put out a joint statement that was nothing short of apocalyptic: "We are convinced that any legislation having these effects will harm the American economy." ISDA issued a report about the GAO's work, arguing that adopting the GAO's suggestions would raise costs and reduce the availability of derivative products. It also said that the GAO had not proven that derivatives could create systemic risk. "The industry went after us and went after Congress to convince them that this was not a problem," says Charles Bowsher, who was then the head of the GAO, and had been Bothwell's only regulatory ally.

A month after issuing his report, Bothwell appeared as a witness before the House agriculture committee to defend it. (The agriculture committees in the House and Senate have jurisdiction over the CFTC.) As he walked into the hearing room, he was stunned at the line of people, most of them lobbyists, waiting to get in. There were cameras everywhere.

"What you see is that derivatives are growing up between the cracks in the regulatory system," he testified. "No one really has the authority over that type of activity."

Two years earlier, when Bothwell had testified about Fannie Mae and Freddie Mac, the response from Congress had been brutal. This was worse. The GAO produces "consistently overblown conclusions which are embarrassingly undersupported by the evidence and replete with undue editorializing," said Congressman Earl Pomeroy, a Democrat from North Dakota. "We have to be careful about excessive regulatory regulation," said Wayne Allard, a Republican from Colorado.

Then it was the regulators' turn to testify. Not a single one—not the FDIC, the SEC, the Treasury, the Fed, the CFTC, nor even the Comptroller—would support Bothwell. Their general view was summed up by Darcy Bradbury, a deputy assistant secretary at Treasury: "As a general principle, there should be a demonstration that there has been, or will be, a failure of market discipline before the need for such broad Federal regulation is advanced." When it was the industry's turn to testify, Gay Evans, who had succeeded Brickell as chairman of ISDA, said, "The GAO proposals for legislation have been rejected by all the key U.S. financial regulators, including the Federal Reserve. Therefore, Mr. Chairman, swaps and privately negotiated derivatives play a key role in reducing, not increasing, risks." *Therefore?*

In a follow-up report issued in 1996, the GAO explained, in one clear sentence, why it thought differently about this issue than everyone else: "Past experience has shown that firms can develop serious problems before the marketplace knows about them."

There is one final piece to this story. That fifteenth company, the one that refused to participate in the GAO's survey, was the insurance company American International Group, known on the Street simply by its acronym: AIG. "We got this call saying they couldn't help us, but at some point they'd explain that," Bowsher remembers. At that time, AIG was a relatively small player, with a derivatives desk one-third the size of Goldman Sachs's, which was the biggest derivatives dealer among the investment banks. But the GAO team knew that AIG's business was growing rapidly.

After the report was complete, Bowsher and Bothwell made it a point to go talk to all the CEOs in person, AIG included. They set up an appointment with AIG's chief executive, Hank Greenberg, and were summoned to his office on Wall Street, where they waited and waited in an anteroom. Bowsher wasn't bothered by the wait—he was used to imperial CEOs—and during their meeting he found Greenberg both candid and smart. At least, unlike the others, Greenberg never said the GAO report was stupid. What he did say was that he hadn't wanted to talk to them because he'd been having trouble with the person who ran his derivatives business. There had been big losses and a battle over control, but Greenberg had fixed all that. He'd "gotten rid of that person, and taken the losses," Bowsher recalls him saying. And now, Greenberg said, derivatives weren't something he had to worry about anymore.

5

A Nice Little BISTRO

In 1994, the year of that meeting with Bowsher and Bothwell, Maurice R. "Hank" Greenberg was sixty-nine years old and had been the chief executive of AIG for a remarkable twenty-six years. Perhaps even more remarkable, despite his age and the length of his tenure, he showed no signs of slowing down. He had no succession plan, and zero interest in creating one. Two of his sons had become high-ranking executives at AIG and were often mentioned as potential successors. Both eventually left to run other insurance companies once they realized that Greenberg was never going to give them the keys to the kingdom. He was dominant, brilliant, irascible, short tempered, controlling, obsessive—and by far the most successful insurance executive of his era, and perhaps any era. Since 1968, when AIG's founder, C. V. Starr, catapulted him over two higher-ranking executives to be the CEO, he had transformed Starr's company—which had been founded in Shanghai nearly fifty years earlier—from a quirky, privately held firm into the largest insurance company in the world. It had a stock price that outpaced its competitors, a reputation for treading where others wouldn't, and earnings growth so steady—topping $2 billion a year by the mid-1990s—that it was the envy of the industry. AIG wasn't just Greenberg's company; it was his creation, his baby, his sun and his moon and his stars. People sometimes joked that he planned to run it from the grave.

The son of a taxi driver from the Bronx, Greenberg was as up-by-his-bootstraps as a twentieth-century New Yorker could be. He ran away from home at seventeen to fight in World War II, took part in the Normandy invasion, attended the University of Miami and New York Law School, got drafted to fight again in Korea, and finally wound up in the insurance industry when he complained about the man interviewing him for a job—to the man's boss. In 1960, C. V. Starr lured Greenberg to AIG; two years later he put him in charge of AIG's struggling U.S. operations, which he turned into a roaring success. Six years later, with Starr just months from death, he anointed Greenberg as his successor.

Greenberg's passion for AIG went well beyond the norm—and woe to any company executive who didn't share that passion. He thought nothing of calling executives at three a.m. to discuss business—behavior for which he made no apologies. One Thanksgiving he called AIG executive Ed Matthews, his longtime consigliere. "We're just about to sit down for dinner," Matthews told him. "I just finished my dinner," replied Greenberg, who then proceeded to talk business for so long that Matthews's family had finished their own Thanksgiving dinner by the time the conversation ended. He would have weekly meetings with his key lieutenants, the main point of which sometimes seemed to be to give Greenberg the opportunity to berate them in front of their peers. "He could be unmerciful," recalls a longtime AIG hand. *Fortune* magazine, in one of the many AIG profiles it has published over the years, told of a time an executive being assailed by Greenberg couldn't take it anymore. "You know?" he finally conceded. "You're right." Greenberg shot back, "I don't need you to tell me I'm right."

Indeed, Greenberg felt sure he had a better understanding of the different divisions than the men running those divisions did. After all, it was Greenberg who had come up with the brainstorms, pushed into the new businesses, and engineered the mergers that had turned AIG into an insurance behemoth. AIG operated 300 insurance subsidiaries in 130 countries, and Greenberg had his finger on the pulse of every last one of them. Or so, at least, it seemed. "A lot of the strategy was run out of Hank's head," says a former AIG executive. "He had most of the ideas about how to run the businesses." And he fully expected his executives to carry out those ideas, no questions asked.

One famous story involved Iranian-American executive K. C. Shabani, who Greenberg sent to Iran in the early 1970s. Because Shabani knew some family members of the shah of Iran, Greenberg assigned him the task of convincing the shah to allow AIG to operate inside the country, something no foreign insurance company was then allowed to do. Once in Tehran, Shabani discovered that the only way AIG could get into Iran was if the parliament passed a law inviting it in. He returned to the United States and told Greenberg that the chances of this happening were remote. "If I were you, I'd give up," he said, according to *Fortune*.

"I didn't ask you what was necessary to do this," replied Greenberg. "I just asked you to get it done." He did. Among other things, Shabani married the shah's social secretary, having at some point gotten divorced from his American wife. Sure enough, the law was passed in 1975, and AIG ran a profitable business in Iran until the Iranian revolution four years later.*

To put it another way, Greenberg didn't so much manage his executive team as control them, running AIG as a not-so-benevolent dictatorship. One way he did this was by establishing for the top AIG brass one of the most generous—yet most onerous—bonus plans ever devised. Each year, the three hundred top executives were granted "units of participation" in a company called Starr International Company, or SICO. SICO, which was based in Panama, was AIG's largest shareholder, and its value rose as AIG's shares rose. Greenberg, in turn, was SICO's biggest shareholder, with 25 percent of the company, and SICO's board was made up almost entirely of AIG executives. Here, however, was the catch: you couldn't get your hands on your accumulated SICO bonuses until you turned sixty-five. If you were still with AIG when you turned sixty-five, you could walk away with tens of millions of dollars. But if you left the day before your sixty-fifth birthday, you got nothing. Greenberg, of course, was the one who decided how many units of participation you got.

There was, however, one piece of AIG that Greenberg didn't control. It was known as AIG Financial Products—FP, everyone called it. It was the part of the company in the derivatives business. Headquartered in Wilton, Connecticut, and London, it was run by Howard Sosin, who was every bit the control freak that Greenberg was, and who made it plain that he expected Greenberg to stay out of his playpen. Even though the division was making plenty of profits, this was hardly a situation that could continue indefinitely. And it didn't: eventually Sosin faltered, at which point Greenberg pounced. That is what Greenberg was referring to when he spoke to Bowsher and Bothwell. He had finally managed to put FP under his thumb.

Starting a derivatives business at AIG was one of the very few moneymaking ideas that had not sprung, fully formed, from Hank Greenberg's fertile mind.

---

* The rest of the story shows the other side of Greenberg. After the shah fell, Shabani spent a year in an Iranian prison, and on several occasions his Iranian guards pretended they were about to execute him. According to *Fallen Giant* by Ronald Shelp with Al Ehrbar, Greenberg personally took charge of the effort to free him. Although he was finally released from jail, he was still not permitted to leave the country. Greenberg did not give up, however; eventually, AIG managed to smuggle Shabani out of the country, at a cost to the company of about a million dollars.

This also explains why he didn't control it at the start. Although, as an insurance company, AIG was in the risk business, it did not necessarily follow that insurance companies were diving into derivatives. Insurance companies were generally conservative institutions; if they used derivatives at all, it was as a customer of a big bank like J.P. Morgan, trying to hedge an interest rate or a currency risk. Under Greenberg, AIG had built a reputation for its willingness to take on unusual, one-of-a-kind risks: AIG wrote kidnapping insurance, it insured satellites, it even wrote insurance on the first ostrich farm in Texas. Greenberg used to boast that AIG's balance sheet was so big that it could take on risks other companies couldn't. But derivatives? Greenberg hadn't really thought of it as a potential new line of business.

It was Sosin who brought the idea to Greenberg. Sosin was the prototypical modern Wall Streeter. A native of Salt Lake City, he had gotten a PhD from Stanford, taught finance at Columbia Business School, and put in a stint at Bell Laboratories before joining Drexel Burnham Lambert in the early 1980s. He was, in other words, a quant. Drexel in those days was best known for its most infamous executive, Michael Milken, the man who popularized junk bonds and built a huge business around them. Sosin wasn't interested in junk bonds; instead, like any good quant, he gravitated toward complex derivatives, becoming one of the pioneers in developing ever more complicated forms of swaps.

The problem for Sosin was that, at Drexel, derivatives were never going to replace junk bonds as the firm's bread and butter. Drexel also didn't have a particularly good credit rating, which meant its borrowing costs were higher than its competitors'. This made it difficult to run a profitable derivatives desk. Sosin had big ideas about doing swap deals that no one had ever done before, with durations of fifteen or twenty or even thirty years, instead of the much shorter durations that were then the norm. He needed to find a different corporate parent to make that happen.

By the fall of 1986, Sosin and several Drexel colleagues were searching for a company that could back them. They were particularly interested in companies with lots of heft and capital, and a triple-A credit rating. Then, as now, there were fewer than a dozen companies with triple-A ratings. Warren Buffett's conglomerate, Berkshire Hathaway, and General Electric both had triple-A ratings; so did AIG, a fact in which Greenberg took immense pride—and which he jealously guarded.

Sosin was introduced to Greenberg through former Connecticut senator Abraham Ribicoff. (Ribicoff and Greenberg were old friends.) Greenberg was clearly enamored with Sosin, but because this was a realm outside his area of expertise, he took a backseat in the negotiations that ensued. Ed Matthews was his point man in dealing with Sosin.

What Sosin wanted was complete autonomy—and, of course, coming from Wall Street, a piece of whatever profits he generated for AIG. And that's what he got: the contract he signed with AIG in January 1987 called for the formation of a joint venture, with AIG owning 80 percent and Sosin 20 percent. Sosin and his team got to command 38 percent of FP's profits, which were designated "incentive compensation." Sosin, in turn, would have "sole discretion" in distributing his share of the pie to his staff. In truth, part of the reason Greenberg was willing to cut such a sweet deal was that he didn't really comprehend just how profitable FP was going to be. Besides, as someone who was there would later recall, "Hank liked getting married and never thought about getting divorced."

Almost immediately, the new joint venture was taking on larger risks than most other swap dealers. Without question, the key to the business was the triple-A rating and the enormous balance sheet of the parent company, which not only gave FP cost advantages, but made it a very desirable counterparty. Nobody worried that AIG would have problems if it lost money in a derivatives trade. It was also extremely well run. Sosin kept close tabs on FP's risk profile, which, in turn, allowed him to take larger risks—and generate larger profits. (FP built special computer systems that could track the ever-changing value of its swap deals far more closely than anybody else in the business, for instance.) Under Sosin, FP did indeed specialize in swaps that went out as far as thirty years, controlling the risks by using a technique called dynamic hedging, which involved constantly recalibrating—and rehedging—its positions. ("The hedging challenges are extraordinary at thirty years," one competitor told the *Wall Street Journal* in 1993. "We haven't done [them]. . . .they're too risky.") But FP's willingness to do long-dated deals also allowed it to charge higher fees than its competitors. In its first six months, FP generated $60 million. Greenberg was amazed.

There are other things people remember about the early years at FP. One was that as controlling as Sosin was, the environment he created was far more collaborative than other AIG businesses. Greenberg liked people to say, "How high?" when he said, "Jump." Sosin wanted people who were willing to question deals, and he created a culture where people could express skepticism without fear of being reprimanded. Sosin also instilled in his troops a sense that they were an elite vanguard, battling bigger and more powerful forces. To some degree, they were. Despite AIG's strong balance sheet and triple-A rating, FP was much smaller than other players with big derivatives desks, lacking the built-in client base of a Goldman or a J.P. Morgan. So it had to be more creative. Marketers at FP would come up with some exotic new product, sell it to clients, and then ride it as hard as they could for two or three years. Eventually, though, the big boys at Goldman Sachs and J.P. Morgan would come out with their own version of the FP product, at which point the profit margins would be squeezed and FP would move on to something even more exotic. Sosin's propensity for pushing the edge of the derivative envelope caused the *Wall Street Journal* to label him the "Dr. Strangelove of derivatives."

The other thing that traders noticed was that Hank Greenberg was simply not part of their lives. Elsewhere in the company, Greenberg had no compunction about calling a midlevel manager in some division somewhere to find an answer to a question he had. That never happened at FP. The special computer system Sosin had built for FP was not shared with the rest of AIG; on the contrary, he had a clause in his contract stipulating that if he ever left the company, he could take the whole system with him. Any time Greenberg did anything that Sosin considered meddling, he would erupt. In 1990, for instance, Drexel imploded and Greenberg quickly snatched up a handful of Drexel traders, with the idea of having them create a new currency trading operation for AIG. When he told Sosin what he had done, Sosin replied that under the terms of their joint venture, only FP could engage in currency trading for AIG. He refused to allow it.

Greenberg responded by sending Sosin a letter informing him that AIG planned to terminate its joint venture agreement. Sosin reacted by undertaking a search for another triple-A company to back him, knowing that he had the contractual right to take his computer system with him. When Greenberg heard through the grapevine what Sosin was doing, he blinked. Within two months, he had patched things up with Sosin and brought him back into the fold—though he did get Sosin to lower the incentive compensation pool from 38 to 32 percent. "AIG Chairman Greenberg announced renewed agreement with Howard Sosin on AIG financial products," read the headline of the press release announcing the deal, making it sound as if Sosin had simply re-upped. No one had any idea Sosin had almost walked out the door.

Why was Greenberg so worried about Sosin leaving AIG? Money, of course. In 1991—just four years after it had opened for business—FP generated $105 million in profits, according to *Business Week*, and was the fastest-growing part of AIG. (The article also claimed that Sosin was taking home between $3 million and $5 million, an amount that was almost certainly too low.) In a legal brief filed in 1995 by Randall Rackson, who served for many years as Sosin's right-hand man before falling out with him, Rackson reported that FP's cumulative profits between 1988 and 1992 were "in excess of" $1 billion.

To journalists and stock analysts, AIG had always been something of a black box. Quarter after quarter its earnings went in only one direction—up—no matter what calamities had taken place around the globe. Hurricanes, floods, earthquakes, big lawsuits—all the bad things that insurers wrote insurance against crushed their profits when the disasters finally struck. Except at AIG. People who followed AIG often chalked this up to the business genius of Hank Greenberg, who seemed to be able to will the company into the kind of double-digit earnings that investors craved. "I thought of him as a great CEO," says one former analyst, "but I didn't quite get how he did it."

The author of that *Business Week* article, though, put forth another explanation. AIG's diversified units protected it from having to take the big earnings hits that other insurers regularly suffered. The magazine singled out AIG's various financial services divisions, which it said were generating some 25 percent of AIG's profits. "Although AIG, too, has been hit," the magazine wrote, "suffering $150 million in property-damage claims from Typhoon Omar and Hurricanes Andrew and Iniki, it has been shielded by the cash its life insurance and finance arms continue to churn out." As it turns out, this wasn't the whole truth, either, though it would take another dozen or so years for people to figure that out.

It is nearly impossible for derivatives dealers to never lose money, no matter how careful they are or how well hedged. Under Sosin, FP had had a remarkable run, writing some $80 billion worth of long-dated contracts and then hedging them brilliantly as circumstances changed. But in 1993, Sosin made his one big mistake: he lost a lot of money on a swap contract.

By then, Sosin had become extraordinarily wealthy. Unlike Greenberg, who lived well but not extravagantly, Sosin used his new wealth to fund a lavish lifestyle. Among his residences was one in Fairfield, Connecticut, a five-story mansion that locals called "the castle." According to a *Wall Street Journal* account at the time, "It boasts an elevator, indoor and outdoor swimming pools, a squash court and an elaborate security system, including metal gates and a guard at the end of the driveway." The FP offices in Connecticut and London were every bit as lavish—true to his control-freak self, Sosin had overseen every detail—which stood in marked contrast to AIG's shabby headquarters near Wall Street.

Given how events transpired, it seems pretty clear that Greenberg had been waiting for Sosin to slip up. The fact that Greenberg had had to back down in 1990 was an intolerable situation. There was only one indispensable person at AIG, after all, and it wasn't Howard Sosin.

Two years after Sosin had signed his new deal, FP lost $100 million in a complicated deal with Edper, the holding company of the Canadian billionaires Edward and Peter Bronfman. According to the *Washington Post*, FP had a second deal with Edper, which was not losing money but nonetheless "spooked" Greenberg. Greenberg had a document drawn up that gave AIG more control over the joint venture and "placed restrictions on transactions into which AIG-FP could enter," according to the Rackson lawsuit. In February 1993, Sosin sent AIG his "notice of termination," which he set for the end of the year. If he stayed through 1993, he would retain control of FP's incentive compensation, which he estimated at $250 million.

This time, however, Greenberg was ready. He set in motion a secret plan, one that "verged on a covert operation," the *Washington Post* would later write. Enlisting the company's auditors at PricewaterhouseCoopers, Greenberg set up a secret office near FP's Connecticut office. There, they built a computer system from scratch that was able to, in effect, reverse engineer FP's trades. Sosin's secret sauce was now Greenberg's as well.

Then, when Sosin began an arbitration proceeding against AIG, as part of his effort to stay on until the end of the year, Greenberg hit back hard. He accused Sosin of fraud and breach of duty—exactly the kind of allegations that, if proven, would strip Sosin of his right to any of the $250 million. The two sides fought over FP's executives, with Greenberg offering them promotions and Sosin dangling the prospect of a big chunk of whatever incentive compensation he won. Most of the executives stayed loyal to Sosin.

In November, the two sides settled, with Sosin agreeing to take $200 million, a portion of which he paid to the executives who had left with him.* A month before the settlement, the *Wall Street Journal* published a lengthy article about the dispute, reporting that Sosin "was holed up with his team in a secluded office in Westport, Conn., plotting a comeback." But to make

---

* Rackson sued because he claimed that he alone was never paid by Sosin.

a comeback, Sosin needed another triple-A-rated company to back him, and that he never found. He was never again a factor in the derivatives business.

At FP, life went on. By the spring of 1994, Greenberg had chosen a new executive to run AIG-FP, which was no longer a joint venture but a full-fledged division of AIG. That man was Tom Savage, a well-liked FP veteran with a PhD from Claremont Graduate University who'd gotten his start working on Larry Fink's mortgage desk at First Boston. "He was from Minnesota," recalls one of his former traders. "He had a quiet, unemotional, analytical approach." Another former trader described him as "mild mannered, intelligent, and extremely risk averse."

There was no question that FP was going to stay in the derivatives business. There was also no question that things were going to be different. Greenberg wanted a larger share of the profits for AIG. He wanted FP traders to defer some of their compensation in case a deal went sour. He wanted to be informed—on a daily basis at first—about every deal FP was working on. And he wanted to be sure that FP never did anything that would put the parent company in danger. "Tom spent most of his time managing Hank Greenberg," recalls an ex-trader. "It was not an easy task." Early on, Greenberg warned Savage, "If you ever do anything to my triple-A rating, I'm coming after you with a pitchfork."

<hr />

It was probably inevitable that FP would one day get into credit derivatives. Part of its self-image, after all, came from its willingness to find the bleeding edge of the derivatives business, and get there before everyone else. By the late 1990s, nothing was more bleeding edge than credit derivatives.

In another sense, though, there was nothing inevitable about it at all. Savage, like Sosin, was a firm believer in having a deep, ongoing understanding of the risks FP took. It was a point of pride among FP's executives that although they were derivatives traders, they were unusually careful ones. The problem for AIG when it began building deals around credit default swaps was that the risk models they used seemed to suggest that they came with virtually no risk at all. Which ultimately caused FP to let down its guard. The traders and executives didn't do the constant calibrating, didn't bring the skepticism, didn't do the worst-case-scenario modeling or put on the hedges that they might have if they'd sensed danger lurking. Their internal models told them that there was a 99.85 percent chance that they would never have to pay out a penny. "The different nature of those trades from any other trades FP had done opened the door to all the problems that came about," Savage told the *Washington Post*.

It was J.P. Morgan that lured AIG into the credit default swap business. The bank's initial 1994 swap deal—the one that insured against an Exxon default—had gone off without a hitch. Since then, J.P. Morgan had done a handful of similar deals, while at the same time using credit default swaps internally to better evaluate its loan portfolio. In 1997, after the bank lost millions in bad loans during the Asian financial crisis, the credit derivatives team was put in charge of the bank's commercial lending department, much to the horror of the old-time commercial lenders. They began using swaps to perform risk analysis on the loan portfolio. Credit default swaps were truly becoming central to the way the bank did business.

As for the regulators, once they began to understand what credit default swaps did, they warmed up to them. Bank regulators, it turned out, *liked* the idea of banks off-loading some of their default risk to other entities; in theory, it meant that banks were less likely to fail if they made bad loans. In fact, by 1996, the Federal Reserve agreed with J.P. Morgan that a bank should get some capital relief if it used credit derivatives. It put out a statement saying that if a bank used credit default swaps to move a borrower's default risk off its balance sheet, it would be allowed it hold less capital.

What J.P. Morgan had not been able to create was a tradable market for credit default swaps. Such a market was important to the bank for several reasons. First, it would give the bank a new line of securities to create, market, and trade. Second, if a tradable market existed for credit derivatives, the market itself could be used to establish a company's default risk. This would give J.P. Morgan a better way of measuring the risks in its own commercial loan portfolio, while also giving speculators the means to bet on the possibility of a company's default, even if they had no economic interest in the company.

In the late 1990s, the bank—again, with Blythe Masters leading the way— found a way to create a credit product that investors loved. It did so by ingeniously combining credit derivatives with securitization. Instead of having a credit default swap reference a single company like Exxon, J.P. Morgan bundled together a large, diversified basket of credit derivatives that referenced hundreds of corporate credits. It was different from other kinds of securitizations in one critical way. Investors in mortgage-backed securities owned pieces of actual mortgages. But those who invested in J.P. Morgan's invention didn't own a piece of the actual corporate loans. Instead, they owned credit default swaps—the performance of which was determined by the performance of the underlying corporate credits. The credit default swaps referenced the actual loans, which were owned by others. Because securities like these were built out of credit derivatives rather than real assets, they came to be called synthetics.

Just as with mortgage-backed securities, synthetic securities were tranched, usually into three slices. The first, and smallest, was called the equity portion; it produced the heftiest return because it came with the most risk. In the event of a default, the equity holders would be the first to be wiped out. The second slice was called the mezzanine tranche; its holders would begin to lose money only after the equity holders had been completely wiped out. The third and largest tranche generated the smallest return, because it was supposed to carry only the tiniest of risks. Modern financial theory suggested that it would take a monstrous financial catastrophe for the defaults to eat through both the equity and the mezzanine tranches and hit the holders of the third tranche. After all, the credits were diversified, which was supposed to ensure a high degree of safety. J.P. Morgan's models suggested that the possibility that defaults would hit the third tranche was so remote that no capital needed to be held against this final tranche. The bank called this tranche super-senior—so named because it was supposed to be safer than even the senior, triple-A tranche in a typical securitization.

The first such synthetic deal, which J.P. Morgan put together in 1997, was called the Broad Index Secured Trust Offering, or BISTRO. If the name made eyes glaze over, the intricacies of putting it together were even more mind-numbing. The swaps covered $9.7 billion worth of corporate credits spread out among some 307 companies, according to *Fool's Gold*, Gillian Tett's authoritative account of the creation of credit derivatives. Thanks to the diversification of the credits, J.P. Morgan calculated that only $700 million worth of notes would be required to ensure the entire $9.7 billion. So the bank set up a shell company—a so-called special purpose entity, or SPE— to which it would make insurance-like payments. The SPE, in turn, sold $700 million worth of notes to investors, beginning in December 1997. The payments from J.P. Morgan flowed through the shell company to the investors. After much wrangling, the big credit rating agencies agreed that there was very little risk in these securities and rated most of them triple-A. The BISTRO notes were quickly snapped up.

So where did AIG come in? As would so often be the case with credit derivatives, the issue had to do with capital requirements. Despite their enthusiasm for credit derivatives, bank regulators were leery about BISTRO, particularly that "riskless" super-senior tranche. Yes, it would take a genuine financial calamity to get to the point where the entire $700 million would be eaten up by defaults. But what it if happened? Who would be on the hook if there were so many defaults that they reached into the super-seniors, as mathematically improbable as that was? The answer was J.P. Morgan.

For the regulators, that's all that mattered. The fact that J.P. Morgan was still theoretically on the hook in a worst-case scenario—as unlikely as it might be—meant that the bank had not completely eliminated the default risk on its portfolio. Therefore, the regulators concluded, banks that held the super-seniors got no capital relief—not unless they could truly find a way to off-load every last penny of the default risk.

Thus did J.P. Morgan begin looking for a way to buy credit protection for the super-seniors, so it could show regulators that it had indeed gotten rid of that risk. And thus did it find FP, which was almost uniquely positioned to provide such protection. Because it was a derivatives dealer operating inside an insurance company, FP had no capital requirements. It was already doing a lot of derivatives business with J.P. Morgan. And the parent company's triple-A rating meant that there could be no doubt—could there be?—that FP had the financial wherewithal to back up its promise to insure the super-seniors. In the BISTRO deal, J.P. Morgan bought credit protection from AIG, which took on the risk of a super-senior default. Not that anybody at AIG thought there was any risk; they were every bit as convinced as J.P. Morgan that this was a riskless transaction. "The models suggested that the risk was so remote that the fees were almost free money," Tom Savage would later tell the *Washington Post*. "Just put it on your books and enjoy the money."

Inside FP, the biggest proponent for getting involved in BISTRO-type deals was not Savage, but one of his deputies, Joe Cassano, who had risen from the back office to become the chief operating officer of FP. Although he had come with Sosin from Drexel, he did not have a quant background; the son of a Brooklyn cop and a graduate of Brooklyn College, Cassano had learned the business by starting at the bottom and working his way up. It was Cassano who Blythe Masters first approached about getting involved in BISTRO, and it was Cassano who became the deal's champion internally. The fees would likely be small—because the perceived risk was so low—but it was a business that FP could dominate, Cassano argued. (The fees would grow considerably over time.) If this structure proved popular, FP was likely to become the insurer of choice for everybody's super-seniors, not just J.P. Morgan's.

And the regulators? Once again, they eventually saw things exactly as J.P. Morgan had hoped they would. They ruled that when banks bought credit protection for their super-senior holdings, they could cut their capital requirements for the underlying credits by 80 percent. This became the rule that the Basel Committee embraced, and it was adopted by regulators around the world. Not surprisingly, every big bank in the world began clamoring for a chance to bundle their credit risk into BISTRO-like structures. The business took off, just as J.P. Morgan—and now AIG—had hoped it would.

Years later, by which time he was running FP—and not long before the first glimmers of the financial crisis could be seen on the horizon—Cassano spoke at an investment conference in which he boasted about being involved in that original BISTRO deal. "It was a watershed event in 1998 when J.P. Morgan came to us, who were somebody we worked with a great deal, and asked us to participate," he said. "These trades were the precursors to what's become the CDO market today."

CDO stood for collateralized debt obligation, which is what that BISTRO-type structure was eventually called. By 2007, when Cassano made those remarks, Wall Street churned them out as if they were coming off an assembly line. There was, however, one giant difference between the early BISTRO deals and the CDOs of 2007. At the heart of the early BISTRO deals was corporate debt. But at the heart of the CDO market of 2007 was something far more dangerous: mortgages.

6

The Wizard of Fed

Inevitably, the nation's first subprime boom ended badly.

In its first iteration in the mid- to late-1990s, the subprime business had all the earmarks of a classic bubble. Subprime companies would go public and their stocks would skyrocket. Company founders got rich making loans to people who had never before been able to qualify for a mortgage. Shoddy business practices became the norm. Nobody seemed to care. Greed replaced fear, as it always does in a bubble. And then—*poof!*—it was over.

The first crack in the facade came when a crop of companies specializing in subprime auto lending went belly-up amid rising delinquency rates. That made investors nervous about securitizations based on any kind of subprime loans. Then, in the fall of 1998, came a financial crisis that ripped through Asia and so unsettled Wall Street that all the big banks and securities firms became momentarily cautious.

To compound matters, the subprime mortgage companies began taking unexpected write-downs. It had long been common industry practice for the subprime companies selling loans to Wall Street to keep what were called the residuals. These were the riskiest pieces of the securities, the ones that nobody else wanted; most of the time, they were the ones that came with the highest prepayment risk. Accounting rules required the companies to estimate the future value of the cash flows and book them as upfront profits, which they did very aggressively. But as more companies entered the business, they began to poach from each other by refinancing borrowers' mortgages. More refinancings meant more people prepaying their mortgages—crushing the already overvalued residuals. As one subprime originator after another took big write-downs on their residuals, years of supposed profits were erased. Josh Rosner, who was then an analyst at Oppenheimer Securities, had played a hand in taking many of these companies public. "They were all liars," he says now.

Spooked by the write-downs, Wall Street began to pull the plug on the subprime machine, withdrawing the warehouse loans that had been its lifeblood. One after another, the companies went bankrupt. Much of their supposed profit turned out to be illusory. One company, FirstPlus, had reported $86 million in earnings in the first nine months of 1997, but had eaten through $994 million in cash and had had to raise a stunning $1 billion in Wall Street financings, according to a presentation given by hedge fund manager Jim Chanos. Those were the kinds of "results" that can exist only in a bubble. In 2000, First Union shut down the Money Store, the subprime lender it had bought just two years earlier for $2.1 billion. "At the end of the day, we're saying we made a bad acquisition," First Union CEO G. Kennedy Thompson told the *New York Times*.

Along with the bankruptcies came a wave of lawsuits and complaints from consumer advocates, who accused the subprime industry of engaging in predatory lending. Customers, they said, had been gulled into taking on expensive mortgages—and paying exorbitant fees—by unscrupulous lenders. Many subprime refinancings replaced simple, affordable thirty-year fixed mortgages. "We and others were saying to the Fed, state legislators, anyone who would listen in D.C., that lending was getting out of control," says Kevin Stein, the associate director of the California Reinvestment Coalition.

Even back then, there was a legitimate debate over who ultimately was more culpable: the lender or the borrower. After all, borrowers often wanted to get their hands on the money every bit as much as lenders wanted to give it to them. Not everyone was being gulled; many borrowers were using the rising values of their homes to live beyond their means. And there were plenty of speculators, betting that they could outrun their mortgage payments by flipping the house quickly. The line between predatory lending and get-rich-quick speculating—or a desperate desire for cash—was often difficult to discern.

But in the larger scheme of things, did it really matter who was at fault? The key point was this: *A lot of people were getting loans they couldn't pay back.* Wasn't *that* the real problem?

Prior to securitization, lenders had to care about the creditworthiness of borrowers. They held the loans on their books, and if a borrower defaulted, they took the hit. That's why borrowers who didn't have much money couldn't get mortgages: lenders were afraid they would default. Securitization severed that critical link between borrower and lender. Once a lender sold a mortgage to Wall Street, repayment became someone else's problem. The potential consequences of this shift were profound: sound loans are at the heart of a sound banking system. Unsound loans are the surest route to disaster. But at the time, almost no one seemed to realize that the wave of poorly under-written loans that securitization seemed to encourage was a monstrous red flag.

The subprime business back then was still relatively small. The collapse of dozens of subprime companies didn't remotely threaten the banking system. It didn't have much of an effect on the housing market, either. But it was still significant. For the bank regulators charged with ensuring that the banking system remain sound, this was the canary-in-the-coal-mine moment, the signal that something was seriously wrong.

Or rather, it should have been.

In Alan Greenspan's memoir, *The Age of Turbulence*, a five-hundred-plus-page tome published the year before the financial crisis, the phrases "subprime mortgage" and "predatory lending" don't merit so much as a mention. Greenspan's book is a triumphant account of his eighteen and a half years as Fed chairman—years during which, by his account, he put out economic crises, kept inflation under control, and deftly manipulated interest rates to ensure that the economy hummed and the markets rose. Before the financial crisis tarnished his reputation, Greenspan's self-image—Fed chairman as economic Superman—was widely shared. Congressmen fell all over them-selves to praise him when he made his semiannual appearances on Capitol Hill. His interest rate decisions were invariably lauded. Many economists viewed him as the greatest Fed chairman ever, even greater than Paul Volcker, who had tamed the raging inflation of the 1970s. The small handful of favored journalists who had off-the-record access to Greenspan regurgitated his pro-nouncements as if they had been handed down by the Oracle of Delphi. To many people, Greenspan *was* the Oracle of Delphi.

Although the country was understandably fixated on Greenspan's handling of monetary policy, the Fed had always had other roles, too. It had supervi-sory authority over the big bank holding companies. It was supposed to be the guardian of the "safety and soundness" of the banking system. It even had a Division of Consumer and Community Affairs, to look after the interests of bank customers. The Fed, in other words, was a regulator. Greenspan, however, was not.

As a young economist, Greenspan had come under the spell of Ayn Rand, the author of *The Fountainhead* and *Atlas Shrugged*, two of the most influential odes to capitalism ever written. The capitalism Rand believed in was "full, pure, unregulated, laissez-faire capitalism," as she once put it, the kind that didn't put regulatory roadblocks in the way of red-blooded entrepreneurs. Greenspan met Rand in the early 1950s, became part of her inner circle, and remained close to her until she died in 1982.

A conservative economist like Greenspan is always going to tilt against regulation. But Rand gave his leaning a philosophical underpinning and helped turn him into a true free-market absolutist. He came to believe that regulation always had unforeseen negative consequences, and that the market itself was far better at embracing the good and driving out the bad than any well-meaning government mandate. That's what he meant by market discipline.

Greenspan's antiregulatory philosophy did not prevent him from working for the government, however. As an adviser to Richard Nixon's presidential campaign in 1968, he reasoned that it was better "to advance free-market capitalism from the inside, rather than as a critical pamphleteer," he says in *The Age of Turbulence*. In 1974, President Ford asked Greenspan to become the chairman of the president's Council of Economic Advisers. "I knew I would have to pledge to uphold not only the Constitution but also the laws of the land, many of which I thought were wrong," he writes. (He concludes, "Compromise on public issues is the price of civilization, not an abrogation of principle.")

When he was nominated to be Fed chairman, Greenspan took the job knowing that he was "an outlier in [his] libertarian opposition to most regulation." Therefore, he says, his plan was to focus on monetary policy and let other Fed governors take the lead on regulatory matters. That's not really how it played out, however. Greenspan was too dominating a presence, and his views were too well known. Fed economists who believed in the superiority of market discipline tended to do well in Greenspan's Fed; those who didn't languished.

There is no question, looking back, that Greenspan's Federal Reserve could have taken steps to cure the growing problems with subprime lending before they got worse. It had the authority. There was a law on the books called the Home Ownership and Equity Protection Act, or HOEPA, that gave the

Federal Reserve the power to flatly prohibit mortgage lending practices that it concluded were unfair or deceptive—or designed to evade HOEPA. "The Federal Reserve [has] ample authority to encompass all types of mortgage loans within the scope of any regulation it promulgates," wrote Raymond Natter, a lawyer who had worked on the bill when he was on the staff of the Senate banking committee.

There is also no question that the problems with subprime lending weren't a secret. After the crisis of 2008, a common refrain arose that no one saw it coming. But that was never true. State attorneys general had filed lawsuits. Housing advocates had continually beaten the tom-toms. Repeatedly and in graphic detail, Congress and the regulators—including Greenspan—had been told what was happening on the ground.

Robert Gnaizda, then the general counsel of the Greenlining Institute, which, among other things, advocates for consumer protections for people of diverse backgrounds, started meeting with the Fed chairman in the early 1990s. He raised the problem of the many mortgage originators that existed outside the banking system and were unsupervised by any federal agency. "We won't argue about whether federal regulators are doing a good job," Gnaizda says he told Greenspan. "Let's look at the unregulated lenders."

"He had no objections other than saying he wouldn't do anything," Gnaizda says now. "He was very gracious and polite, but there was also an imperious quality to him."

A few years later, Gnaizda and John Gamboa, Greenlining's executive director, met with Greenspan again. In advance of the meeting, Gnaizda had sent the Fed a pile of loan documents, which Greenspan had read. "Even if you had a doctorate in math, you wouldn't understand these instruments and their implications," Greenspan acknowledged during the meeting. The Fed chairman had just given a speech in which he had famously recommended adjustable-rate mortgages. Gamboa asked Greenspan if he had an adjustable-rate mortgage. "No," replied Greenspan. "I like certainty."

John Taylor, of the National Community Reinvestment Coalition, was another housing activist who used to meet with the Fed. "Their response was that the market would correct any problems," Taylor says. "Greenspan in particular believed that the market would not produce, and investment banks would not buy, loans that did not make sense. He genuinely believed that."

But anyone who knew anything about the subprime business could see that wasn't true. A prototypical example was First Alliance Mortgage Company, or Famco. A star of the early subprime scene, Famco went public in 1996, allowing its founder and his wife to take $135 million out of the company. Within two years, however, its abuses had become so widespread, and so well known, that several state attorneys sued to force the company to stop.

Famco's abuses were not the result of a few bad apples; they were baked into the company's business model. As former loan officer Greg Walling explained in an affidavit, Famco recruited top auto salesmen who knew nothing about mortgages and had them memorize something called the "Track," which was a how-to for the hard sell. They were taught never to tell customers that a teaser rate meant their interest rate would increase. They were never to divulge the actual principal amount of the loan; if they did, the customers would be able to see the enormous fees that Famco had tacked on. The sales force, meanwhile, was highly motivated to charge the highest fees it could get away with: big commissions kicked in when the fees exceeded fifteen points. According to the Massachusetts lawsuit, an incredible 35 percent of Famco mortgages in Massachusetts had fees over 20 percent.

Did Wall Street know what was going on? You bet it did. Famco *told* its investors that most of its subprime loans went to people with relatively good credit—which meant borrowers were essentially being ripped off, since they didn't need to pay a big fee to get a good rate. In 1995, Eric Hibbert, a Lehman Brothers executive, wrote a memo, later obtained by both the *Wall Street Journal* and the *New York Times*, describing Famco as a "sweat shop" specializing in "high-pressure sales for people who are in a weak state." He added, "It is a requirement to leave your ethics at the door."

Did Lehman Brothers then decide it couldn't do business with a company as sleazy as Famco? Of course not. Starting in 1998—the same year the states filed suit—Lehman gave Famco a warehouse line of $150 million and helped it sell $400 million in mortgage-backed securities, according to one lawsuit. The shoddy quality of the loans seems to have been as much of a nonissue for Lehman as it was for Famco; since Wall Street was just passing the loans along to investors, it didn't have to care whether the money would be paid back, either.

In 2000, Famco declared bankruptcy. A jury later found that the company had systematically defrauded borrowers. Lehman was found guilty of "aiding and abetting the fraudulent scheme." But the firm's punishment—a $5 million fine—was negligible. This was market discipline? Good practices driving bad ones out? It was just the opposite: bad practices were driving out the good ones. In the mortgage industry at least, Greenspan's beloved theory was being blown to smithereens on a daily basis. And still he refused to do anything.

Actually, that wasn't quite true. In the spring of 2000, Greenspan announced the formation of a nine-agency task force, including all the bank supervisors, to look into predatory lending. By then, the complaints and lawsuits had become so numerous that Washington officials could scarcely keep ignoring them. The Senate had held hearings. Three prominent senators, including Paul Sarbanes, the ranking Democrat on the Senate banking committee, introduced bills to ban predatory lending. The Treasury Department and HUD put together a National Predatory Lending Task Force. Its conclusion in a 2000 report: "Treasury and HUD believe that new legislation and new regulation are both essential." The Federal Trade Commission started bringing cases.

Sarbanes, for one, knew the terrible damage predatory loans could do; Baltimore, in his home state of Maryland, had been hit hard by rising foreclosures, many of them the result of subprime lending abuses. But the chairman of the Senate banking committee, Phil Gramm, opposed any move to regulate subprime lending. His staff at the Senate banking committee issued a report saying that it made no sense to regulate predatory lending practices because it was impossible even to say what predatory lending was. To do otherwise, the report said, "threatens to subject those regulated to the abuses of arbitrary and capricious governmental action at worst."

For that matter, Greenspan's task force was more a sop to Congress than a serious effort to grapple with the problem. Actions mattered more than words, and Greenspan didn't act. The Fed's preferable solution seemed to be more disclosure, so that borrowers could better understand the terms of their loans and make informed decisions. More disclosure appealed to his libertarian instincts. But as everyone in the mortgage business knew, increased disclosure had done virtually nothing to stamp out lender abuses. Over the years, there had been numerous disclosure requirements added to the law. Yet to the average home buyer, mortgage documents remained largely incomprehensible. "I don't think there is such a thing as a real sophisticated borrower," Bill Dallas, who founded a subprime company called First Franklin in the 1970s, told the *American Banker* in 1998. "Basically they put their lives in the hands of originators, and we guide them." Phil Lehman, an assistant attorney general in North Carolina, described disclosure statutes to Fed officials in 2000 as "the last refuge of scoundrels."

One thing the Federal Reserve was required to do under the 1994 HOEPA law was hold hearings from time to time, to gain an understanding of the latest problems in the lending industry. In 2000, it held a series of HOEPA hearings in San Francisco, Charlotte, Boston, and Chicago. For anyone trying to understand why regulators were having so much trouble dealing with predatory lending, these hearings were an illumination.

The man who chaired them was Edward Gramlich, a Federal Reserve governor. Ned Gramlich was an unusual Fed governor. Despite a stint as a Fed research economist decades earlier, he had not spent his career steeped in the intricacies of monetary policy. Public policy was his passion. He was the author of a highly respected textbook on cost-benefit analysis. Before being named to the Fed board of governors, Gramlich had been a professor at the University of Michigan, where he taught economics and public policy. He was a bighearted, self-effacing man, much beloved inside the Federal Reserve building.

Not long after his arrival at the Fed in 1997, Gramlich was asked by Greenspan to head up the Fed's committee on consumer and community affairs. This was not a prestigious post for a Fed governor, and Gramlich knew very little about the subject. But he dove in eagerly, becoming one of the country's leading experts on the subprime business—and one of its leading critics. In 2007, Gramlich wrote a short book entitled *Subprime Mortgages: America's Latest Boom and Bust.* "In the subprime market," he wrote, "where we badly need supervision, a majority of loans are made with very little supervision. It is like a city with a murder law, but no cops on the beat."

Gramlich, however, was not temperamentally suited to be the cop on the beat. As the hearings opened, he explained that the purpose was to see whether the HOEPA regulations should be tightened to force lenders to "consider the consumer's ability to pay." Given what would happen—indeed, given what was *already* happening—it would be hard to think of a more important line of inquiry. Yet Gramlich's questions weren't so much answered as they were parried. And he was too gentle a soul to push back.

One of the people testifying that day, for instance, was Sandor Samuels, the chief legal counsel for Countrywide. He objected to the idea that borrowers should be required to disclose their income—something you would think lenders would want to know before making a six-figure loan. "Let me just say, very briefly, that we think this is a very dangerous area to get into," Samuels replied when asked about income disclosure. "Because the reality is that, in many communities, including many minority communities and immigrant communities, sometimes it's difficult to document income."

Gramlich: "The obvious question is: If you can't document the income, how . . . do you know they can pay the loan back?"

Samuels: "Right. And I would say that there are certain reality checks, let's just say . . . if a waiter in a restaurant puts down that he or she is making three hundred thousand dollars a year, we're going to ask what kind of restaurant they're working at."

Around and around they went. Every objection the Fed panel brought up to a subprime practice got the same response: cracking down would mean denying worthy borrowers the opportunity to own a home. Finally, Gramlich asked Samuels for his advice on the best way to keep predatory lending practices in check. "We believe increased competition is the key," Samuels replied, echoing Greenspan. Wall Street simply wouldn't buy bad loans in bulk. Wall Street, of course, was already doing precisely that.

Gramlich ended the hearings by more or less throwing up his hands. "There are many practices that might be good most of the time, but end in abuse some of the time, so it's difficult to simply ban practices," he said. Should the government try to discourage house flipping? If it did that, it might also prevent people from taking advantage of falling interest rates. Should it forbid balloon payments? For certain borrowers, a balloon payment might make sense. And on and on. The hearings didn't so much end as they sputtered, ignominiously, to a close.

There came a moment—it's not clear exactly when—when Ned Gramlich went to see Alan Greenspan. He wanted the Fed to take a more active role in policing the subprime business. And he had a specific policy idea. According to the *Wall Street Journal*, Gramlich thought the Fed should "use its discretionary authority to send examiners into the offices of consumer finance lenders that were units of Fed-regulated bank holding companies." (The GAO recommended the same thing, but the Fed had formally adopted a policy of not conducting such exams in early 1998.) Such companies were major subprime lenders. Gramlich had toyed with idea of placing his proposal in front of the entire seven-member Fed board. But he decided to see Greenspan privately so as not to put the Fed chairman in an awkward spot in front of the other Fed governors.

The details of that meeting have never emerged. Gramlich died of cancer in 2007, at the age of sixty-eight. Greenspan told the *Wall Street Journal* that he didn't remember much about the conversation, but it was certainly not a heated discussion. Gramlich presented his idea; Greenspan turned it aside. "He was opposed to it, so I didn't pursue it," Gramlich told the *Journal* three months before his death. He, too, proffered few details.

Yet that meeting would later become a touchstone for Greenspan's critics. It was proof, they would say, that the Fed chairman wouldn't take on the subprime lenders—or the larger problem of too many people getting loans they could never repay—even when asked to do so by a fellow Fed governor. And they were right. But Gramlich's unwillingness to push Greenspan any further than the Fed chairman was willing to be pushed made it easy for Greenspan to ignore him. Shamefully, Greenspan would later publicly blame *Gramlich* for failing to bring the issue to the board, which, as he surely knew, Gramlich had done to save Greenspan from embarrassment.

Not long before he died, Gramlich, upset at the criticism Greenspan was starting to receive, penned a note to his old boss. "What happened was a small incident," he wrote, "and as I think you know, if I had felt that strongly at the time, I would have made a bigger stink." But he hadn't made a stink. That was the point. Making a stink was simply not how Gramlich led his life, even with something that mattered to him as much as subprime lending.

―――∞―――

Josh Rosner had also begun complaining to the Fed about subprime mortgages. By 2000, he had left his job at a mainstream Wall Street investment bank and joined a small independent research firm. Once a huge believer in the new subprime companies, he had become deeply critical of them. Companies he had invested his clients' money in had gone out of business. He had watched the lawsuits pile up over their seamy business practices. "I unintentionally helped kill my clients," he says today. "I was so dispirited."

Rosner had a foreboding that went well beyond that of most subprime critics. Gramlich worried about subprime lending because it took advantage of unsophisticated buyers and often cost people their homes. But Rosner saw that the delinking of borrower and lender could have more far-reaching consequences. Well connected in Washington, he began showing up at the Fed to express his concern. Fed officials would respond by saying that it wasn't their job to determine who should or shouldn't get a mortgage. "I'd say, but it *is* the Fed's job to ensure that the system is stable," Rosner recalls.

There were two essential reasons for Rosner's fears. The first was that his close reading of the data showed that most of this frenetic mortgage lending really had nothing to do with getting people into homes, since the vast majority of subprime loans were refinancings. That was true of the prime market as well. He calculated that the dollar volume of refinancings during the 1990s was $3.4 trillion, more than the entire volume of mortgage origination in the 1980s! A little-noticed Freddie Mac study noted that more than 75 percent of homeowners who refinanced in the last three months of 2000 had taken out mortgages at least 5 percent higher than the ones they retired. They were using their homes as piggy banks. "Refinancing offers the potential to increase the absolute debt burden of the average U.S. household without materially reducing other consumer debts," Rosner wrote at the time. Surely, he thought, all this additional consumer debt was likely to end badly.

The second reason for Rosner's fears was that he could also see from the data that fewer and fewer home buyers were putting down 20 percent, which had long been the standard to get a mortgage. By 1999, in fact, more than 50 percent of mortgages had down payments of less than 10 percent. Angelo Mozilo, who was becoming an increasingly prominent figure in the mortgage industry, believed passionately that big down payments prevented otherwise capable borrowers from being able to own a home. For much of his career, he had fought to be able to originate mortgages with little or no down payments. And mostly, he had won. Wall Street now regularly securitized loans with down payments of 10 percent or less, and even Fannie and Freddie were allowed to buy low-down-payment mortgages (although they required a private insurer to absorb some of the risk). But Rosner picked up on yet another little-noticed study, this one by Fannie Mae, showing that low-down-payment loans triggered greater losses. "Put simply, a homeowner with little or no equity has little or no reason to maintain his/her obligations," Rosner wrote. Having equity in one's home was much more than a barrier keeping people from buying a home, he came to believe. It was the key to homeownership. Down payments, more than any single thing, meant that you were a homeowner.

On June 29, 2001, Rosner published a research piece that summed up his thinking, entitled, "A Home without Equity Is Just a Rental with Debt." No one seemed to take much notice. He was working from home one day when the phone rang. On the other end was an elderly man. "I just read your paper and want to discuss it with you, but I can't hear very well on the phone," he said. "Would you be able to sit down with me in person?"

"Sure," Rosner responded politely. "Are you in the city?"

"I'm in Lexington, Massachusetts," the caller explained. Rosner, again being polite, said he'd call when he was next headed to Boston for meetings, and asked for the man's name.

"My name is Charles Kindleberger," the caller replied. Kindleberger was the author of *Manias, Panics, and Crashes*, which documented market crises through the ages and was widely viewed as a classic. Rosner had long admired it. The next morning, Rosner flew to Boston and spent the day with Kindleberger, who was ninety-one. Kindleberger told Rosner that if he published another edition of *Manias, Panics, and Crashes*, he would use "A Home without Equity" as the final chapter.

⌀⌀⌀⌀

There was at least one bank regulator in Washington during this era who tried to do something to curb subprime lending abuses. Her name was Donna Tanoue, and from 1998 to 2001 she was the chair of the Federal Deposit Insurance Corporation. Her concern stemmed from the simple fact that subprime lenders were shutting down. When those lenders were banks, it was the FDIC, which insures deposits for the federal government, that had to pick up the pieces. Tanoue's solution—an obvious one, really—was for the subprime companies to hold more capital against those loans. "Subprime lenders," she said during one congressional hearing, "are twenty times more likely than other banks to be on the agency's problem list and accounted for six of the last eleven failures." By late 2000, she went even further, arguing that banking regulators needed to "sever the money chain that replenishes the capital of predatory lenders and allows them to stay in business." She was talking about Wall Street's purchase and securitization of subprime loans. The FDIC even issued draft guidelines instructing banks on how to avoid purchasing predatory loans for their securitizations.

The industry was apoplectic about the draft guidelines. Patricia Alberto, an executive at J.P. Morgan, wrote a letter in protest. "The regulatory agencies and the public, in their quest to eradicate predatory lending, have issued 'guidelines' that have the effect of imposing a large portion of the responsibility for ferreting out and eliminating predatory lending by others to the large banks in the industry, because they are in a position to provide liquidity to the marketplace," she said. Well, yes: that was exactly what Tanoue was trying to do.

When Tanoue testified before the House banking committee, defending her plan to increase the capital that had to be held for subprime loans, Representative Carolyn Maloney, a Democrat from New York, replied bluntly, "I am concerned that adopting any arbitrarily high capital standard for subprime lending will unnecessarily reduce the number of subprime lenders."

In early 2001, the banking regulators did issue "guidance" requiring institutions with heavy concentrations of subprime loans to hold more capital against those loans. But the definition of what constituted subprime lending was vague. And "guidance" was only guidance, which lenders could adopt or ignore as they saw fit, depending on how zealously the regulators enforced it. No antipredatory lending bill was ever passed; no strictures against most of the practices were ever enforced; no serious effort was ever made to make financial institutions pay more attention to the loans they were buying and securitizing.

Yet even the guidance, as weak as it was, met with a firestorm of criticism. John Reich, a new member of the FDIC board, told the *American Banker* that the regulators were in the wrong, and that "we should have done it right the first time." He clarified that "doing it right" meant consulting with the banking industry. James Gilleran, who became the head of the Office of Thrift Supervision in late 2001, would later say of his agency, "Our goal is to allow thrifts to operate with a wide breadth of freedom from regulatory intrusion." A few years later, a picture was taken of Gilleran and Reich with the representatives of three bank lobbying groups. They were taking a chain saw to the red tape of excessive regulation. In 2005, Reich replaced Gilleran as the director of the OTS.

And yet, and yet. Even though the bank supervisors refused to take steps to curb subprime lending, the smarter ones—the Office of the Comptroller of the Currency, in particular—also didn't want its institutions to make these loans. Via the examination process, which isn't public, the OCC quietly started making life difficult for any national bank that had a big subprime business. Early on, in August 2001, Bank of America announced it was selling its ninety-six subprime lending branches and its $26 billion loan portfolio. Four years later, in a decision that every bank noticed, the OCC forced Laredo National Bank, in Texas, to make restitution to every borrower who had gotten a loan without the bank taking care to "adequately consider creditworthiness." "OCC ran every national bank out of the business," says a former Treasury official.

Admirable though this effort may have seemed, it was both problematic and a little perverse. Because the OCC's effort was not matched by the Office of Thrift Supervision, thrifts began grabbing the subprime market share the big banks were abandoning. Subprime lending also began to migrate into state-regulated institutions, where, as Gramlich once put it, federal regulators have "no obvious way to monitor the lending behavior of independent mortgage companies."

And one other thing. What the OCC forgot was that even if the big banks were no longer making the majority of subprime loans, those loans were still finding their way into the banking system. All the big banks were also in the securities business, and they were all making fortunes securitizing subprime loans originated by others. And big and small banks alike continued to hold mortgage-backed securities on their balance sheets. But no one, not the banking supervisors, nor the Securities and Exchange Commission, nor the Federal Reserve, was bothering to track this. That risk was supposed to be gone.

7

The Committee to Save the World

In February 1999, *Time* magazine put a photograph of Alan Greenspan, Robert Rubin, and Larry Summers on its cover. Greenspan by then was the most famous economic policy maker in the country, and probably the world, but Rubin, the Treasury secretary, and Summers, his deputy—who would become Treasury secretary himself five months later—weren't far behind. On the cover, Greenspan stood front and center, flanked by a smiling Rubin and a stern-faced Summers, the three of them looking both smug and heroic. Then again, they had a lot to be smug about. Ever since Rubin had become Treasury secretary in January 1995, the three men had successfully fended off one major financial crisis after another.

First came the 1994 Mexican crisis, which had Mexico's creditors bracing for a default of its sovereign debt, an event that would have sent tremors through the global economy. The crisis was averted when the Treasury Department and the Fed, after weeks of around-the-clock effort, maneuvered to have the Exchange Stabilization Fund loan Mexico $20 billion, guaranteed by the United States. That was followed, in short order, by full-blown crises in Russia (which did default), Asia, and Latin America, as well as near crises in Egypt, South Africa, the Ukraine, and elsewhere. Each time, the three men helped contain the crisis while keeping it walled off from the U.S. economy. They did the same in the fall of 1998, when a giant hedge fund, Long-Term Capital Management, collapsed. An LTCM bankruptcy could have been devastating for Wall Street, since the big firms were all on the hook for tens of billions of dollars of LTCM's losses, both as lenders and as counterparties.

"In late-night phone calls, in marathon meetings and over bagels, orange juice, and quiche, these three men . . . are working to stop what has become a plague of economic panic," *Time* wrote breathlessly. "By fighting off one collapse after another—and defending their economic policy from political meddling—the three men have so far protected American growth, making investors deliriously, perhaps delusionally, happy in the process." Who wouldn't be smug after being described in such terms? *Time* called them "The Committee to Save the World."

One thing the article glided over, though, was *why* these crises kept taking place. To the extent the Committee to Save the World had answers, they were as smug as that cover photo. The developing world, they said, was new to this business of trusting in markets. They didn't act enough like, well, us, with our supremely efficient market-driven economy. "A Thai banker who breaks the rules by passing $100,000 to his brother-in-law puts the whole system at risk," is how the author of the article, Joshua Cooper Ramo, characterized their thinking.

Even the Long-Term Capital Management disaster didn't dent their enthusiasm for the way our own markets had evolved. LTCM was a firm that relied entirely on the tools of modern finance, chief among them derivatives, risk models, and debt. Its leverage ratio was a staggering 250 to 1, meaning that it had borrowed $250 for every $1 of equity on its balance sheet. The notional value of its derivatives book was more than $1.25 trillion, and the fact that LTCM traded almost exclusively in derivatives was the central reason it had been able to accumulate so much debt. Derivatives didn't come with capital requirements. Derivatives transactions could be done entirely with borrowed money. And derivatives positions housed in secretive hedge funds—even massive, bring-down-the-system positions—didn't have to be disclosed to anyone.

Yet when Greenspan was asked about the Long-Term Capital Management crisis, he shrugged it off as the price of modernity. Faster markets, he told Ramo, gave rise to "the increased productivity of mistakes"—whatever that meant. Added Ramo, paraphrasing Greenspan: "Computers make it possible to push a button and destroy a billion dollars of wealth." Clearly, the staggering increase in the number of derivatives contracts, with notional value topping $50 trillion by early 1999, didn't cost Greenspan any sleep. He liked derivatives. He especially liked the fact that they were unregulated. As one former Capitol Hill aide later put it, Greenspan viewed the derivatives market as akin to "the way the Europeans once viewed the New World. It was a virgin market. A beautiful, unregulated, free market." Summers felt likewise.

But Rubin was different. Derivatives made Rubin nervous. During his years as a trader and manager at Goldman Sachs, he had seen derivatives trades spiral out of control. He knew that if something went seriously awry they had the potential to create immense damage. "I thought both derivatives and leverage could pose problems," he wrote in his 2003 memoir, *In an Uncertain World*. And yet at the same time LTCM was collapsing, Rubin was standing arm in arm with his fellow Committee members, blocking the last serious attempt anyone in government would make to oversee derivatives prior to the financial crisis of 2008.

In this misguided stance, Greenspan was blinded, as ever, by ideology. Summers was blinded by his deep-seated need to be viewed as a brilliant man, which in this case meant embracing, uncritically, the complexities of modern finance. As for Rubin, he was blinded by pride.

The Goldman Sachs that Bob Rubin joined in 1966, a young man just a few years removed from Yale Law School, was not the Wall Street juggernaut we know today. Not even close. Though nearly a century old, with a noble history, Goldman had nonetheless spent most of that century struggling to become an elite firm. During the Depression, Goldman was nearly brought to ruin by an excitable senior partner named Waddill Catchings, who had made a series of disastrous investments during the roaring twenties that dragged the firm down for the next decade plus. According to *The Partnership*, a history of Goldman Sachs written by Charles Ellis, it was saved in part by the forbearance of the ruling Sachs family, which covered its losses for the next twenty years, and in part by the savvy senior partner Sidney Weinberg, who had joined the firm as a janitor in 1907, took it over after Catchings was ousted, and ruled it until his death in 1969.

Weinberg was a Wall Street giant—Mr. Wall Street, the press called him. He rebuilt Goldman as a place where the relationship between a corporate client and its Goldman Sachs investment banker was paramount. More often than not, that investment banker was Weinberg himself. As late as 1956, when he was sixty-five, Weinberg served as Ford's investment banker when the automaker went public. At the time, it was the biggest IPO in history, and it finally catapulted Goldman Sachs into Wall Street's top tier.

The senior partner who succeeded Weinberg was Gus Levy, a gruff, no-nonsense trader who had built the firm's trading department more or less from scratch. In the early 1950s, Levy had been one of the innovators in risk arbitrage, and the firm had one of the leading "arb" desks on Wall Street.

For most of its modern life, Goldman Sachs has been a firm with two cultures—a genteel investment banking culture, represented by Weinberg, and a rough-and-tumble trading culture, exemplified by Levy. In many ways, the two men could not have been more different. Yet Levy, a college dropout who joined Goldman at the age of twenty-three, completely shared Weinberg's beliefs in how Goldman Sachs should act as a firm. A Goldman man, whether banker or trader, worked impossibly hard, eschewed flashy cars and clothes, and was utterly devoted to the firm. He was maybe just a little smarter than his Wall Street peers, but he didn't make a big show of it. His Goldman colleagues were his closest friends. He didn't tell tales out of school. He took great pride in his work, but it was a quiet, understated pride. Senior executives at Goldman did not have palatial offices with private bathrooms. The rugs and furniture were a little shabby. The firm's offices in lower Manhattan lacked so much as a single sign identifying it as Goldman's headquarters.

Most of all, Levy subscribed to Weinberg's lifelong belief that acting ethically on behalf of its clients was the single most important thing Goldman Sachs did. Anything that created even the appearance of a conflict with its clients was not just discouraged, but forbidden. That's why, for instance, when corporate raiders like Carl Icahn and T. Boone Pickens began their takeover attempts in the late 1970s, Goldman refused to advise them, despite the substantial fees they were paying. The hostile takeover movement, the firm believed, was not in the best interest of its corporate clients. A few years after Levy died, in 1976, one of his successors, John Whitehead, set down a list of Goldman's fourteen business principles. The first one began, "Our clients' interests always come first."

Levy was also Bob Rubin's mentor. Rubin started his Goldman career on the risk arbitrage desk, which he quickly found he had an affinity for. Levy soon realized it as well, and began both encouraging Rubin—in his gruff, no-nonsense way—and talking him up with the other Goldman partners. Within five years, Rubin himself was named a partner.

Rubin had the rarest of skills: he could rise through the ranks of Goldman Sachs faster than just about anyone ever had before without arousing either jealousy or animosity. He was admired equally by superiors, peers, and underlings. On the surface, he appeared to be the opposite of prideful. In meetings—even meetings filled with important partners—he made a point of soliciting the opinion of the most junior associate, and then seeming to hang on his every word. He had a way of making his bosses want to see him do well. His colleagues were drawn to his almost preternatural calm. When a problem arose and he was asked his opinion, he invariably responded, "What do you think?"

"There is no one better at the humility shtick than Bob," says one former colleague who remains a Rubin admirer. "The line 'just one man's opinion' was something he would utter a dozen times a day." He inspired intense loyalty.

He also delivered the goods. In 1981, when Goldman Sachs bought J. Aron, a commodities firm whose executives then included Goldman's current CEO, Lloyd Blankfein, Rubin was put in charge of overseeing the new acquisition. With his help, the firm began to move its business in a direction that made it vastly more profitable. He pushed Goldman to begin trading options, which it had long shied away from, even hiring Fischer Black, the MIT professor and coinventor of the famous Black-Scholes options pricing model. Goldman's options trading desk soon became immensely profitable as well. As co-head of the fixed-income research department in the mid-1980s, Rubin helped transform the fixed-income division from a second-tier player into a worthy competitor to such bond strongholds as Salomon Brothers and First Boston. By 1990, he was the co-head of the entire firm. (He shared the title with Steve Friedman, who had also run the fixed-income department with him.) By the time Rubin left for the Clinton administration in 1993—where he spent two years as the head of the National Economic Council before becoming Treasury secretary—Goldman had become the envy of Wall Street. Rubin departed for Washington as the most admired man at the most admired firm.

In August 1996, a year and a half after Rubin became Treasury secretary, Bill Clinton appointed a lawyer named Brooksley Born to be the new chairman of the Commodity Futures Trading Commission. She was a formidable figure in Washington legal circles, a longtime partner at Arnold & Porter, with a practice that dealt with regulatory and financial services issues. She was also a player on the national legal scene, a co-founder of the National Women's Law Center, a member of the board of governors of the American Bar Association, and an adjunct professor at the law schools of Georgetown and

Catholic University. After Clinton won the presidency, she was rumored to be on the short list for attorney general.

As a female law student in the early sixties, Born had faced her share of slings and arrows. When she became the president of the Stanford Law Review—the first woman to do so—a dean told her that "the faculty stood ready to take over the law review if [she] ever faltered," as she later recounted in the *Washington Post*. Although she graduated first in her class—another first for a woman at Stanford Law—the school declined to recommend her for a Supreme Court clerkship. She wangled tea with Justice Potter Stewart, who told her point-blank that he wasn't ready for a female law clerk.

Perhaps as a result, she had a steely side. Though always polite and cordial and collegial, she was tough when it came to things she cared about. She took her new post with the same resolve that had long characterized her.

It wasn't long before she was focusing her attention on derivatives. In the years since Wendy Gramm had ruled that they didn't constitute futures, the business had exploded. Sumitomo, a large Japanese commodities dealer, had been caught using over-the-counter derivatives as part of an effort to corner the copper market. The Procter & Gamble and Orange County debacles were still fresh on people's minds. After she had been in office for a while, Born also began to hear rumors that firms were using swaps to doctor their quarterly financial statements.

As she looked more closely, she realized there was some question as to whether the grounds for the Gramm exemption still applied. After all, it was only supposed to pertain to one-of-a-kind derivatives between sophisticated counterparties. Yet swaps had become so commonplace that many of them were practically standardized and used off-the-shelf contract language. If derivatives were becoming standardized, Born wondered, shouldn't they also be traded on exchanges? Shouldn't they be classified as futures? And shouldn't they be regulated?

Although the Sumitomo market manipulation case had been exposed before she took office, the agency conducted its investigation—and imposed a hefty fine—on Born's watch. The experience made her realize that "we were trying to police a very rapidly growing part of the market for manipulation and fraud, but we knew nothing about the market," she later said. "There were no record-keeping requirements. No reporting requirements. It was totally opaque."

Born was in many ways a political naïf. She ran an agency with fewer than six hundred employees. She lacked both the power base and the political skills to sway members of Congress or her fellow regulators. All she knew was that derivatives were a gigantic market and that some bad things had happened in the past, and that meant, in all likelihood, that bad things might very well happen in the future. And no one in the government had a clue. Born and others at the CFTC started calling derivatives "the hippopotamus under the rug."

About a year into her tenure, Born hired a top Washington litigator, Michael Greenberger, to be the director of the CFTC's division of trading and markets, which made him one of her top deputies. The hiring itself suggested what a tin ear she had for politics: Greenberger had never been involved in commodities, and so had no natural allies on the agriculture committees that oversaw the CFTC. He and Born had gotten to know each other serving on the board of an agency that helped the homeless. But he was no rube—he had spent his career involved in complex litigation and had argued several cases before the Supreme Court. Like his new boss, he also knew how to be tough when he needed to be. Not coming out of the commodities industry, he later said, gave him an advantage over just about anyone else who might have taken that job. "Because I was not dependent on the futures business, I really did not care what the futures industry thought of me." Not long after he came on board, Greenberger had a meeting with Born. "I remember her telling me that we have a lot of things to do, but that I had to start focusing on over-the-counter derivatives," he says.

Thus it began.

That Bob Rubin worried about derivatives was not the result of some conversion experience that took place after he joined the government. He had felt the same way during his years on the fixed-income desk at Goldman Sachs. It's not that he hadn't traded in derivatives—what was an option, after all, but a kind of derivative?—or that he didn't understand their value as a hedging device. But he had always had a healthy fear of them, because he understood better than most that in a crisis, their combination of excessive leverage and counterparty exposure could make them an immensely destructive force.

"I remember Bob at Goldman in the 1980s," says a former colleague. "He was always the guy saying, 'I'm not sure how much principal risk we should be taking with the derivatives book.' When it got to be a $1 billion book, the traders wanted $2 billion. Bob would agree reluctantly. By the time Bob left, it was probably a $10 billion or $12 billion book. But Bob was always worried."

His fear stemmed from something almost no one else in government could claim: actual experience with a derivatives meltdown. It happened in the late 1980s when a sudden, unexpected shift in interest rates—unforeseen by Goldman's risk models, needless to say—wreaked havoc on the bond and derivatives markets. "Bonds and derivative products began to move in unexpected ways relative to each other because traders hadn't focused on how these securities might behave under the extremely unlikely market conditions that were now occurring," Rubin writes in his memoir. "Neither Steve nor I was an expert in this area, so our confusion was not surprising. But the people who traded these instruments did not fully understand these developments, either, and that was unsettling. You'd come to work thinking, *We've lost a lot of money but the worst is finally behind us. Now what do we do?* And then a new problem would develop. We didn't know how to stop the process." He concludes: "What happened to us represents a seeming tendency in human nature not to give appropriate weight to what might occur under remote, but potentially very damaging, circumstances."

Once he got to Washington, Rubin found himself surrounded by people who viewed his lack of enthusiasm for derivatives as an amusing eccentricity. Most of the young turks he brought with him to Treasury were gung-ho about derivatives. His core group of young assistant secretaries—including a thirty-seven-year-old Treasury wunderkind named Timothy Geithner—approved of derivatives. Larry Summers used to tell Rubin that his attitude about derivatives was a little like a tennis player who wanted to keep using wooden rackets when everyone else had moved to graphite. And of course there was Greenspan, whose enthusiasm for derivatives knew no bounds. During the derivatives battles in the mid-1990s, dozens of officials from the Fed and Treasury—including Greenspan—testified in favor of unregulated derivatives and argued that the best thing the government could do was stay out of the way. Despite his qualms about derivatives, Rubin never once said anything publicly to contradict the Clinton administration party line.

Oddly enough, it was the SEC that sent the first shot across the bow: in December 1997, it proposed that the investment banks it supervised put their derivatives businesses in a separate unit, and register them—voluntarily!—with the agency. Under this plan, derivatives dealers would have capital requirements (but they would be lower than the parent firm's!) and they would have to use risk models to calculate the riskiness of their derivatives book (but they could use their own internal VaR!). In fact, the derivatives transactions themselves wouldn't even be regulated by the SEC. The plan was called "Broker-Dealer Lite."

When the SEC put its plan out for public comment, Greenberger quickly drafted the CFTC's response. Writing that the SEC proposal raised serious "jurisdiction" issues, the CFTC argued that if any agency should by rights be overseeing derivatives it should be the CFTC. Born would later say that she didn't care who wound up regulating derivatives, so long as it was done right. The SEC's "lite" approach hardly qualified. She then instructed Greenberger to draft a policy paper. The draft he came up with, thirty-three pages long, was called a concept release; it asked market participants and others a series of open-ended questions aimed at "reexamining" the agency's approach to derivatives. Should players in the swap markets be required to report their positions to the government? Should swaps be sold through a central clearing facility? Should the CFTC impose capital requirements on derivatives transactions? Should derivatives dealers be made to conform to certain internal control standards? And so on.

The draft of the concept release was completed in March 1998. As an independent regulator, Born had the right to simply publish it and let the world react. But she didn't do that. Viewing herself as someone who wanted to collaborate with other regulators, she sent it around to all the other important actors—not just the other regulators, but lobbyists, key legislators, and the Treasury Department—to solicit their feedback.

Feedback? Blowback was more like it. "One day I walked into Brooksley's office," says Greenberger. "She put down the phone and all the blood was drained from her face. She said, 'That was Larry Summers.' He had been screaming at her." Summers had told her that he had just been visited by a group of bankers who said that if the CFTC insisted on pursuing their concept release, they would move their derivatives business to London. "Summers wanted us to stop," says Greenberger. Adds Born: "There was so much pressure. The derivative dealers did not want this market looked at—at all. For some of them, derivative trading made up 40 percent of their profits."

A month later, the President's Working Group met to discuss Born's concept release. The PWG, as it's called, consists of four regulators: the chairs of the Fed, the SEC, and the CFTC, plus the Treasury secretary. But this had become such a hot-button issue in Washington that virtually all the bank regulators were there: Larry Summers. John Hawke, the comptroller of the currency. Ellen Seidman, the director of the Office of Thrift Supervision. William McDonough, the president of the New York Fed. "It was a very tense meeting," recalls one person who was there. The date was April 21, 1998.

The purpose of the meeting, it quickly became clear, was to persuade Born to back off. The other regulators made all the old arguments about the dangers of classifying derivatives as futures. Born, for her part, said that CFTC was a long way from trying to regulate derivatives; all it was trying to do was ask some useful questions and glean some useful answers. "Greenspan thought even asking the questions was dangerous," recalls Born.

And where was Rubin? Given his history of concerns about derivatives, you might have expected him to be Born's one ally in the room. During the Asian financial crisis, Rubin had asked one of his aides to find out how much derivatives exposure U.S. financial institutions had to South Korea. "We couldn't find out," this aide recalled. Rubin was stunned. But in this meeting, Rubin sided, without hesitation, with his fellow regulators. His reaction to Born's arguments was almost visceral—a far cry from the man who was so admired for his ability to listen and ask questions. He bullied Born in a way that seemed out of character to anyone used to watching him manage a meeting. "It was controlled anger," Greenberger later recalled for the *New York Times*. "I've never seen him like that before or after."

Late in the meeting, Rubin turned to Born and said brusquely, "My general counsel says you have no jurisdiction."

"Our view is that we have exclusive jurisdiction," she replied.

Rubin: "Would you agree to discuss this with our general counsel before you issue the concept release?"

Born: "Of course."

One suspects that Rubin thought this exchange would cause the issue to go away. Instead, it gave Born hope. She was a big-time lawyer after all; a frank and fruitful exchange of views with the general counsel of the U.S. Treasury was a fine outcome. It played to her strengths. Except that for the next two weeks she couldn't get Treasury's lawyer on the phone. That's when her steely side emerged. In Born's view, if the general counsel couldn't be bothered to explain Treasury's legal reasoning, then she saw no reason to delay the publication of the concept release. On May 7, the CFTC published it.

The other three members of the PWG were incensed. Rubin, Greenspan, and Arthur Levitt, the chairman of the SEC, immediately sent a letter to Congress requesting that it block the CFTC's effort to solicit comments.

Rumors were spread that Born was just an impossible woman—too shrill and strident to work with the august members of the Committee to Save the World.

Over the next few months, Born testified more than fifteen times in a series of highly charged congressional hearings about the concept release. It was an extraordinary spectacle: in one hearing after another, an array of Clinton regulators lined up to publicly denounce the action of another Clinton regulator. Congressional Republicans were only too happy to pile on.

In a hearing before the Senate banking committee in July, for instance, Greenspan made the specious claim that derivatives were already adequately supervised: "I would say that the comptroller and ourselves for the banks and the SEC for other organizations create a degree of supervision and regulation which, in my judgment, is properly balanced and appropriate."

Jim Leach, the committee chairman, then addressed John Hawke, repeating Born's complaint in her testimony that the proposed legislation "would delegate review of federal law governing derivatives markets from the jurisdiction of the CFTC and SEC to a body dominated by banking regulators with no expertise in derivatives and market regulation." Leach continued, "I would like to ask Mr. Hawke—The name of the Treasury secretary of the United States at this time is Robert Rubin. Does he have a background in financial supervision and financial market participation?"

"If he were here, he would say he spent twenty-seven years in that," replied Hawke.

Leach: "I would continue to ask Mr. Hawke—The name of the chairman of the Federal Reserve Board of the United States is Alan Greenspan. Does he have a background in financial market participation?"

Hawke: "I believe he does."

More than a decade later, you can still hear them chuckling at that exchange.

The concept release got nowhere. Persuaded by Greenspan et al., Congress slipped a provision into an agriculture bill that prevented the CFTC from acting on derivatives for six months—which just happened to be the amount of time left in Born's term as chairman.

Three months later, Long-Term Capital Management blew up.

It would be hard to overstate the feeling of terror the LTCM collapse inflicted on Wall Street. The Russian crisis was taking place at virtually the same time; indeed, it was the precipitating event that had led to LTCM's problems. The markets were incredibly volatile. The Dow Jones Industrial Average dropped 512 points one day in late August—the fourth largest drop in history—only to gain nearly 400 points one day in early September. The fear that the financial crisis, having swept through Asia and Russia, was about to hit the United States was palpable.

The main reason it didn't was that the New York Fed ordered all the big Wall Street firms into a room and insisted that they hammer out a rescue plan. In the end, fourteen firms injected equity into LTCM, effectively taking it over. (Only Bear Stearns refused to participate.) In other words, it was government action—not market discipline—that prevented disaster.

Washington was every bit as terrified as Wall Street—as it should have been. The potentially destructive power of derivatives had been exposed. For that matter, all the tools of modern finance—excessive leverage, probabilistic risk models, unseen counterparty exposure—had been shown to be flawed. When Wall Street finally got a look at Long-Term Capital's books, for example, it was astounded by the size of the firm's total counterparty exposure: $129 billion. Up until that moment, LTCM's lenders had only known about their own small piece of it.

During a hearing on October 1, 1998, even the Republicans on the Senate banking committee fretted about whether the LTCM disaster signaled the beginning of another S&L-style crisis. If ever there was a moment when Bob Rubin could have used his immense stature to do something about the derivatives problem he had supposedly spent years worrying about, this was it. Even hard-line deregulators might have followed his lead. But he did nothing of the sort. During that October hearing, Chairman Leach said to Born, "We owe you an apology." One last time, Born pleaded with Congress to grapple with "the unknown risks that the over-the-counter derivatives market may pose to the U.S. economy." Even after LTCM, she remained the only administration official willing to talk about the need for government oversight over the derivatives business.

Six months later, the President's Working Group issued a report on LTCM, which focused much more on the firm's excessive leverage than its derivatives book, and which made exactly one regulatory recommendation: unregistered derivatives dealers should be required to report their financial risk profiles on some kind of regular basis. In a footnote, Greenspan dissented even from that recommendation.

Although Brooksley Born signed her name to that report, she was unhappy with it, feeling that it only reinforced the government's laissez-faire attitude toward derivatives. When the White House called and asked if she wanted a second term, she declined. By June 1999, she had returned to Arnold & Porter, where she resumed her practice until she retired in 2003.

A few weeks after Born left the government, so did Rubin. Rubin never spoke to Born again after that April 1998 meeting. Immediately after the Long-Term Capital Management fiasco, she had reached out to Gary Gensler, then a high-ranking official at Treasury—later, ironically, the chairman of the CFTC—asking him to convey a message to Rubin. "We all seem to be on the same side now," she told Gensler, hoping he would convey to Rubin that she wanted to work with him on the derivatives issue. Rubin never responded. Not long afterward, she attended a meeting at the Treasury Department in which she tried to congratulate Rubin for his role in containing the crisis. He brushed past her without saying a word.

Years later, Rubin's defenders would claim that it was Born's hard-nosed approach that had turned him against her. She was too strident, they said, too legalistic, not deferential enough to the Treasury secretary. "If she had just been more collaborative," said one such defender, "Rubin might have been her ally."

Arthur Levitt, the SEC chairman, was one of those who had been told by Treasury that Born's supposed stridency made her impossible to work with. Years later, though, he worked with her on a project and found her completely collegial. He later told the PBS documentary show *Frontline* that he felt Treasury had misled him. For his part, Greenberger believes that Rubin didn't take her seriously because he didn't view her as a bona fide member of the establishment like himself.

Even so, why should Brooksley Born's personality or her background have been the deciding factor? Derivatives either were a problem or they weren't. Rubin either understood the trouble they might someday cause or he didn't. If, as he says, he did understand the problem, then allowing his position to pivot on whether or not Born showed him the proper deference would seem, in retrospect, a pretty serious dereliction of duty. Robert Rubin had spent most of his career affecting a kind of egoless management style. His treatment of Born—his willingness to put his personal irritation ahead of the important public policy issues that derivatives posed—suggests that he wasn't quite as egoless as he let on.

It fell, finally, to Larry Summers to make sure that derivatives could never again be threatened by a regulator like Brooksley Born.

After Rubin left the Treasury Department, he took a position with Citigroup as "senior counselor," where he had no operational responsibilities but was nonetheless paid around $15 million a year. Clinton named Summers as his replacement. A few months later, the President's Working Group issued a long-awaited report on derivatives—a report that had been prompted by the furor over Born's concept release. "A cloud of legal uncertainty has hung over the OTC derivatives markets in the United States in recent years," read the cover letter accompanying the report. The report recommended that that uncertainty be remedied by Congress. It was: Phil Gramm pushed through the Commodities Futures Modernization Act in 2000, which Clinton—with Summers's enthusiastic support—signed into law. The new law explicitly stated that derivatives were not futures and could not be regulated by the CFTC—or any other government regulator. It was the last bill Clinton signed before leaving office.

A year earlier, the president had signed a law that repealed Glass-Steagall, which had split commercial from investment banking so many years before. Gramm-Leach-Bliley, as the new law was called, also had Summers's strong support. One of its nods to modern finance was a provision that "expressly recognized and preserved this authority for national banks to engage directly in asset-backed securitization activities," as Comptroller of the Currency John Dugan would note many years later.

In most respects, though, the repeal of Glass-Steagall was largely symbolic, a recognition of changes that had already taken place. By 1999 all the big banks had investment banks and trading desks. And in any case, the real problem was not that the wall that had long separated commercial and investment banks had been torn down. Nor was it that the CFTC was not allowed to regulate derivatives. No, the core problem was that even as the old regulatory firmament was disappearing, nothing was being created to replace it. If Rubin and Summers deemed the CFTC as not the right agency to regulate derivatives, they should have given the task to some other agency they felt could handle it. Their defenders point out that the Republicans had firm control of both houses of Congress, and that is certainly true. But that wasn't the only reason nothing was done to shore up the nation's financial system. The other reason was that Bill Clinton's Treasury was every bit as complacent as Alan Greenspan's Fed.

After the financial crisis, one man who had worked closely with Rubin at Treasury would exclaim: "My God, I wish I had done more."

8

Why Everyone Loved Moody's

In September 2000, Dun & Bradstreet, a sleepy, 160-year-old business information company, spun off a sleepy subsidiary. The subsidiary was Moody's, the credit rating agency, which Dun & Bradstreet had owned since 1962 and which had just hit the century mark itself.

Along with its two competitors, Standard & Poor's and Fitch Ratings, Moody's was in the business of gauging the possibility that a bond would be repaid on time and in full. It did so by using a series of letter grades known as ratings. Its highest "investment-grade" rating, triple-A, meant that the bond had the same risk of default as a Treasury bond: almost none. Bonds rated double-A to triple-B minus were also investment grade—riskier than triple-As, but still safe enough for widows and orphans. Anything below a triple-B minus was a "junk" bond, considered too risky to be bought by pension funds and other institutional investors that were legally bound to hold only safe investments.

The business of rating bonds was as steady as a thing could be. Everybody used the three rating agencies, and everybody understood what those letter grades represented on the risk spectrum. In the prospectus it issued prior to becoming a public company, Moody's boasted that it rated $30 trillion of the world's debt across one hundred countries.

"Steady," however, is not the same as "fast growing." Though it was immensely profitable, Moody's 1999 revenues of $564 million would have barely dented the Fortune 2000, much less the Fortune 500. When its stock began trading, most investors yawned. Warren Buffett, who always liked to buy stocks others overlooked, took a 15 percent stake in Moody's, but that was mainly because he liked the company's impregnable market position and its steady cash flow.

As events would prove, though, Moody's *was* poised to start growing faster—a lot faster. In addition to corporate and government bonds, Moody's had begun rating "structured financial products," Wall Street's catchall euphemism for mortgage-backed securities, off-balance-sheet vehicles, derivatives, and the like. (S&P and Fitch were doing the same.) Although Moody's had been reluctant to rate mortgage-backed securities when first approached by Lew Ranieri in the 1980s, that reluctance was long gone. By the time Moody's became a stand-alone company, its structured finance business was growing much faster than its traditional bond rating business.

Structured financial products needed more than just a rating, though. They needed a *high* rating. The whole purpose of an asset-backed security was to take assets that could never merit a triple-A rating on their own and transform them into products safe enough to be rated that highly. Triple-A securities could be bought by investors like money market funds and pension funds. They could be used by banks to reduce capital requirements. The combination of tranching—with its cascading levels of risk that used the riskier tranches in the capital structure to protect the higher-rated tranches—and the other credit enhancement techniques that fortified the triple-As made that possible.

The rating agencies had always been stingy about bestowing triple-A status on corporate debt. In 2007, for instance, only six companies had a triple-A rating. Yet when it came to tranches of mortgage-backed securities, the rating agencies handed out triple-As like candy. Literally tens of thousands of mortgage-backed tranches were rated triple-A.

In the early years, the securities performed well. That was true even of the relatively small batch of asset-backed securities that used subprime mortgages. They had plenty of credit enhancements, and besides, housing prices were going up, the way they were "supposed" to, which kept defaults to a minimum. But the rating agencies continued to slap their triple-As on subprime securities even as the underwriting deteriorated—and as the housing boom turned into an outright bubble, waiting to burst. When it did burst, the rating agencies, and the investors who had depended on them, were caught flat-footed.

There were many reasons why the rating agencies continued to grant triple-As long after they should have stopped: an erosion of standards, a willful suspension of skepticism, a hunger for big fees and market share, and an inability to stand up to Wall Street. Not least, Moody's and the other rating agencies turned their backs on their own integrity. "The story of the crisis," says a former Moody's executive, "is how Moody's put its profits ahead of what was right."

After an internal meeting held in the fall of 2007, as the financial crisis was gaining steam, a Moody's employee complained that he would like more "candor" about the company's "errors," as he called them. "[They] make us look either incompetent at credit analysis or like we sold our soul to the devil for revenue, or a little bit of both."

A little bit of both, indeed.

John Moody, the founder of Moody's, was a muckraking journalist who in 1900 published something called *Moody's Manual of Industrial and Miscellaneous Securities*. This publication, which investors took to immediately, formed the origins of Moody's. At first, it offered statistical information about stocks. Then Moody began adding analysis, ranking stocks with letter grades. Finally, he shifted his focus from stocks to bonds. This was his eureka moment.

There has always been far less information available about bonds than stocks. Bonds don't trade on public exchanges, and most of the information about them is held by the investment bankers and traders who are trying to sell them. Moody saw his manual as a means of leveling the playing field. As the circulation of his publication grew, others copied him. Henry Varnum Poor, who edited the *American Railroad Journal*, engaged his son to begin rating bonds in 1922; after a merger with Standard Statistics in 1941, the company became known as Standard & Poor's.

The credit rating business didn't change much until the 1970s, when two things happened. First, the rating agencies, which by then included a smaller upstart, Fitch Ratings, upended the way they generated revenue, abandoning the subscriber model in favor of charging issuers directly. The switch made undeniable business sense. Bond ratings had become important enough that many investors wouldn't buy an unrated bond. Subscriptions were always going to be optional for the subscriber, but a rating had become mandatory for issuers.

The rating agencies' new business model came with an obvious conflict: now that they were being paid by bond issuers, the rating agencies were potentially beholden to the same people whose bonds they were rating. For a long time, the potential conflict had kept Moody's and S&P from taking that step. In 1957, for instance, a Moody's executive told the *Christian Science Monitor*, "We obviously cannot ask payment for rating a bond. To do so would attach a price to the process, and we could not escape the charge, which would undoubtedly come, that our ratings are for sale. . . ." Now Moody's was insisting it could manage this conflict.

The second change came in 1975, when the Securities and Exchange Commission began to use ratings to determine how much capital broker-dealers had to hold. The higher a bond's rating, the less capital the broker-dealer had to hold against it. This made ratings even more important, but it also begged the question of whose ratings would count toward reducing capital. To prevent a proliferation of fly-by-night bond raters, the SEC decreed that Moody's, S&P, and Fitch were nationally recognized statistical rating organizations, or NRSROs.

By the time mortgage-backed securities arrived on the scene, ratings were ingrained in the very fiber of the capital markets. Lenders put ratings triggers in bond agreements—stipulations that a ratings downgrade could cause a debt payment to accelerate or collateral to come due. The government had literally hundreds of rules based on ratings. One said that 95 percent of the bonds held by low-risk money market funds had to have an investment-grade rating. Another said that schools participating in government financial aid programs needed to maintain a certain rating. State regulators used ratings to determine the capital that insurers had to hold. "The resulting web of regulation is so thick that a thorough review would occupy hundreds, perhaps thousands of pages," wrote Frank Partnoy, a professor at the University of San Diego School of Law and a longtime critic of the rating agencies.

As well intentioned as many of these rules were, they overlooked two problems. The first is that the bond market was essentially outsourcing its risk management to the rating agencies. The universal acceptance of the ratings resulted in almost no independent research by the fund managers who actually bought the bonds. They simply assumed that if the rating agency had given a bond a double-A or a triple-A, it must be safe. Nor was this some dark secret. As the Office of the Comptroller of the Currency put it in 1997, "Ratings are important because investors generally accept ratings . . . in lieu of conducting a due diligence investigation of the underlying assets. . . ."

Second, the rules imbued the rating agencies with an "almost Biblical authority," to borrow a phrase first used in 1968 by New York City's finance administrator, Roy Goodman. But that authority wasn't remotely deserved. The agencies had charts and studies showing that their ratings were accurate a very high percentage of the time. But anyone who dug more deeply could find many instances when they got it wrong, usually when something unexpected happened. The rating agencies had missed the near default of New York City, the bankruptcy of Orange County, and the Asian and Russian meltdowns. They failed to catch Penn Central in the 1970s and Long-Term Capital Management in the 1990s. They often downgraded companies just days before bankruptcy—too late to help investors. Nor was this anything new: one study showed that 78 percent of the municipal bonds rated double-A or triple-A in 1929 defaulted during the Great Depression. To critics like Partnoy, the fact that ratings carried the force of law explained a troubling paradox: even as proof piled up that the agencies made mistake after mistake, their power continued to grow.

In retrospect, the surprise is not that the rating agencies would eventually be corrupted by their business model, but that it took so long to happen. For many years, whatever mistakes they made were the result of misguided analysis, not out-and-out cravenness. This was especially true of Moody's, which had a reputation among bond issuers as a "hard-ass," according to a former employee. The Moody's culture, introverted and nerdy, was more akin to academia than Wall Street. Analysts would answer their phones after many rings, if at all. Moody's analysts were standoffish toward the issuers who paid their salaries—a little like journalists during the heyday of newspapers, when they could thumb their noses at advertisers. Credit analysts at Moody's didn't worry about the revenue that might be lost if they refused to give an issuer the rating it sought. That was someone else's problem. In the early 1990s, Moody's actually refused to rate a then popular structured product, on the grounds that a rating might lead investors to expect more than they were likely to get.

This last anecdote was recounted in a 1994 article in *Treasury and Risk Management* magazine entitled "Why Everyone Hates Moody's." After polling ninety-nine corporate treasurers, the magazine concluded that "ingrained in Moody's corporate culture is a conviction that too close a relationship with issuers is damaging to the integrity of the rating process." Moody's was actually proud of that characterization. A company executive responded by saying that the survey left out "our most important constituency . . . investors."

What caused Moody's to change were three things. The first was the inexorable rise of structured finance, and the concomitant rise of Moody's structured products business. The second was the 2000 spin-off, which resulted in many Moody's executives getting stock options and gave them a new appreciation for generating revenues and profits. And the final factor was the promotion of a former lawyer named Brian Clarkson within structured finance.

A Detroit native who had graduated from Ferris State University in Michigan and then practiced law at a tony New York firm, Clarkson joined Moody's as an executive in 1991, without ever having worked as a credit analyst. One of his early tasks was to rate mortgage-backed securities issued by Guardian, the subprime mortgage originator founded by the Jedinaks in California. The bonds, needless to say, eventually blew up, but if there was a lesson in that, it was lost on Clarkson and his bosses. By 1995, he had become the co-head of the asset-backed finance group.

Clarkson went off like a bomb inside Moody's. He developed a reputation for being nasty to those who couldn't fight back and for never forgetting a slight. "At my level, any watercooler discussion of his management style included the words 'fear and intimidation,'" a former Moody's lawyer, Rich Michalek, later told the Senate Permanent Subcommittee on Investigations. Mark Froeba, another ex-Moody's lawyer, told investigators that the company's top executives "recognized in Brian the character of someone who could do uncomfortable things with ease, and they exploited his character to advance their agenda." That agenda was using structured finance to boost revenues, market share, and—above all—Moody's stock price.

Clarkson had no problem with this agenda. "We're in a service business," he once told the *Wall Street Journal*. "I don't apologize for that." But what exactly did that mean for a company that rated bonds? It wasn't just a case of answering the phones on the first ring. Under Clarkson, former analysts say, it also meant caring about whether the issuers—meaning the small group of investment banks who mattered—were happy with the ratings they got.

Clarkson's co-head of the asset-backed group was longtime Moody's analyst Mark Adelson. Adelson was, in some ways, the opposite of Clarkson—a careful, cautious, somewhat skeptical analyst. He had been involved in structured finance seemingly forever; as a young lawyer in the 1980s, Adelson had worked on several of the early deals put together by Lew Ranieri and Larry Fink. Perhaps because of his long experience, he was always less willing to accept uncritically many of the arguments made for mortgage-backed securities. When underwriters began reducing their credit enhancements, claiming that the securities had proven themselves with their good performance, Adelson didn't buy it. The fact that an asset class like housing had performed well in the past said nothing about how the same asset class was going to perform in the future, he believed. For a very long time, Moody's backed Adelson, for which he would always be grateful. But his skepticism was out of sync with both the market and the new Moody's. "My view wasn't the most widely held one at Moody's," he says now. "You spend a lot of time doing soul-searching when you're looking one way and everyone else is looking the other way." As Clarkson was rapidly promoted, Adelson was eventually moved out of asset-backed securities. In 2001, he quit.

There had long been tension between the corporate bond side of Moody's and the structured finance side; Clarkson's ascension signaled that structured finance had won. More than that, the *culture* of the structured finance side had won. Bond analysts, even in the good old days, regularly faced pressure to issue favorable ratings, but Moody's had always backed them when they resisted. Not anymore. Soon after Clarkson took charge, Moody's began making a point of informing its analysts of the company's market share in various structured products, according to a lawsuit filed in 2010 against Moody's by the state of Connecticut. If Moody's missed out on a deal, the credit analyst involved would be asked to explain why. ("Please . . . advise the reason for any rating discrepancy vis-à-vis our competitors," read one e-mail.) Michalek, who had a reputation as a stickler, said that Goldman Sachs once requested that he not be assigned to its deals. Gary Witt, the Moody's executive who took the call from Goldman, later testified that he was told that not complying with its request "would result in a phone call to one of my superiors."

"When I started there, I don't think Moody's managers knew what their market share was," says one former employee. "By the peak of subprime, there were regular e-mails every time Moody's didn't get a deal." Another former managing director says that Clarkson used to tell people, "We're in business and we have to pay attention to market share. If you ignore market share, I'll fire you."

"When I joined Moody's in late 1997," Mark Froeba told investigators, "an analyst's worst fear was that he would contribute to the assignment of a rating that was wrong, damage Moody's reputation for getting the answer right and lose his job as a result. When I left Moody's, an analyst's worst fear was that he would do something that would allow him to be singled out for jeopardizing Moody's market share, for impairing Moody's revenue or for damaging Moody's relationships with its clients, and lose his job as a result." (In prepared testimony for the Financial Crisis Inquiry Commission, Clarkson denied that "Moody's sacrificed ratings quality in an effort to grow market share.")

Examples:

- In August 1996, after Commercial Mortgage Alert noted that Moody's share of commercial mortgage-backed securities was just 14 percent—largely because it was being tougher in certain areas than S&P or Fitch—Clarkson responded by saying, "It's the right time to take a second look." Moody's market share soon rose to 32 percent.

- In 2000, Moody's had 35 percent of the mortgage-backed securities market, according to Asset Backed Alert. By the first half of 2001, it had jumped to 59 percent. Rivals claimed Moody's had lowered its standards, but Clarkson attributed Moody's rise to a "reshuffling" of its analysts. Several former Moody's executives say that analysts weren't "reshuffled." They were fired. (Clarkson said that complaints by rivals that Moody's had lowered its standards were "sour grapes.")

- Another example: Moody's was initially more conservative on securitizations in cases where, in addition to the first lien, there was a second-lien mortgage. But that was a problem because S&P had a different, looser standard: it concluded in 2001 that as long as second-lien loans were attached to no more than 20 percent of the mortgages in the pool, it would treat the entire pool as if it didn't have additional risk. "The other agencies took the same position shortly thereafter," Richard Bitner, a former subprime lender, later told the Financial Crisis Inquiry Commission. He added, "The rating agencies effectively gave birth to the subprime piggyback mortgage." Those were subprime mortgages in which the homeowner avoided putting up any cash and got two loans—one for the mortgage itself and another for the down payment.

The great advantage issuers had in seeking triple-A ratings is that they rarely needed all three agencies to be involved in any one deal. Investors liked having two agencies rate a deal, but nobody cared about having all three involved. So issuers could play the agencies off each other. They didn't really care which rating agencies bestowed the rating. All that mattered was the rating itself. "The triple-A was the brand, not Moody's," says a former Moody's structured finance managing director.

Like everyone else utilizing risk models, the rating agencies used the mathematics of probability theory to arrive at their ratings. A given mortgage-backed deal might contain as many as ten thousand mortgages. As every investor is taught, diversification spreads risk, so one question was, how diversified were the mortgages? If they all came from California, they were less diversified than if some were from California, some from Idaho, and some from Connecticut. The working assumption was if home prices dropped in California, they would remain stable, and even keep rising, in other parts of the country. The Wall Street term for spreading risk this way—and there are more complex variants—is correlation. Correlation is essentially a way of describing, in numerical terms, the likelihood that if one security defaults, others would default in tandem. Zero correlation means that one default would have no effect on anything else in the security; 100 percent correlation means that if one defaults, everything else would, too. The closer the mortgage-backed security came to zero correlation, the greater the percentage of tranches that could be labeled triple-A. Underwriters often added credit enhancements to boost the percentage of triple-A tranches.

One obvious flaw of this approach is that nowhere in the process was anyone required to conduct real-world due diligence about the underlying mortgages. As the SEC later noted, "There is no requirement that a rating agency verify the information contained in RMBS loan portfolios presented to it for rating." (RMBS stands for residential mortgage-backed security.) A second problem is that the rating agency models were built on a series of assumptions. One assumption was that if housing prices declined, the declines would not be severe. Another was that the housing market in California was indeed uncorrelated with the housing market in Connecticut. And then there was the fact that assumptions could be changed. If the bankers didn't like the outcome of the analysis, maybe a little rejiggering might be in order.

For instance, UBS banker Robert Morelli, upon hearing that S&P might be revising its RMBS ratings, sent an e-mail to an S&P analyst. "Heard your ratings could be 5 notches back of moddys [sic] equivalent," he wrote. "Gonna kill your resi biz. May force us to do moodyfitch only . . ." Internally, the rating agencies had a term for this: ratings shopping. Even Clarkson acknowledged that it took place. "There is a lot of rating shopping that goes on," he told the *Wall Street Journal*. Of course, he saw nothing wrong with it. "People shop deals all the time," he shrugged.

Ratings shopping was a classic example of why Alan Greenspan's theory of market discipline didn't work in the real world. The market competition between the rating agencies, which Greenspan assumed would make companies better, actually made them worse. "The only way to get market share was to be easier," says Jerome Fons, a longtime Moody's managing director. "It was a race to the bottom." A former structured finance executive at Moody's says, "No rating agency could say, 'We're going to change and be more conservative.' You wouldn't be in business for long if you did that. We all understood that."

"It turns out ratings quality has surprisingly few friends," Moody's chief executive, Raymond McDaniel, told his board in 2007. "Ideally, competition would be primarily on the basis of ratings quality, with a second component of price and a third component of service. Unfortunately, of the three competitive factors, ratings quality is proving the least powerful." He added, "In some sectors, it actually penalizes quality by awarding ratings mandates based on the lowest credit enhancement needed for the highest rating."

Just as LTCM exposed the dangers of derivatives in 1998, there also came an early moment when the failings of the rating agencies were exposed for all to see. The moment was December 2, 2001, the day Enron filed for bankruptcy. Although Enron had been faking a portion of its profits for years—and though it had been in precipitous decline since October, when the outlines of its fraudulent practices were first revealed—the rating agencies didn't downgrade the company's debt until four days before its collapse. Investors in both Enron's stock and its bonds lost millions. The Enron bankruptcy—quickly followed by similar debacles at WorldCom, Tyco, and a handful of other companies—became a huge, ongoing news story. And the fact that the rating agencies had failed to sniff out any of them was a big part of the scandal narrative.

Government investigators put together thick reports about the failings of the agencies. The rating agencies were excoriated in congressional hearings. Senator Joseph Lieberman said they were "dismally lax" in their coverage of Enron. At one hearing, the S&P analyst who had covered Enron confessed that he hadn't even read some of the company's financial filings. There was a strong sense that something was going to be done to reform the rating agencies.

Perhaps to appease Washington—and fend off regulation—Moody's agreed to adopt a code of conduct. Among other things, the code stated that "the determination of a credit rating will be influenced only by factors relevant to the credit assessment." It also stated that "The credit rating Moody's assigns . . . will not be affected by the existence of, or potential for, a business relationship between Moody's and the issuer."

In its lawsuit, the state of Connecticut alleged that shortly after Moody's unveiled its code of conduct, two experienced compliance officers were fired and replaced by employees from the structured finance department. The head of the department later complained, "My guidance was routinely ignored if that guidance meant making less money." Investigators also allege that during a dinner party after a board meeting, the president of Moody's walked by the head of compliance and said, quite loudly, "Hey . . . how much revenue did Compliance bring in this year?"

In other words, nothing changed. Not a single analyst at either Moody's or S&P lost his job as a result of missing the Enron fraud. Management stayed the same. Moody's stock price, after a brief tumble, began rising again. The ratings remained embedded in all the rules and regulations. The conflict-ridden business model didn't change. "Enron taught them how small the consequences of a bad reputation were," says one former analyst.

The dirty little secret was that nobody really wanted to reform the rating agencies. Investment bankers needed to be able to continue gulling, cajoling, and browbeating the agencies into handing out triple-A ratings. Investors wanted to be able to rely on ratings instead of having to do their own research. Regulators found that in devising rules about risk taking, using ratings was the easiest path.

"Most of the big investors—they like ratings to be scapegoats," says Jerome Fons. "They say, 'Oh, we do our own analysis,' but then when things go bad—well, it's the fault of the credit rating agencies." Or as Clarkson later ranted to other Moody's executives during an internal meeting in the fall of 2007, "It's perfect to be able to blame us for everything. . . . By blaming us, you don't have to blame anybody else."

———— ∞ ————

Of all the securities whose existence depended on their ability to get a triple-A rating, none would become more pervasive—or do more damage—than collateralized debt obligations, or CDOs. CDOs, which had first been invented in the late 1980s but didn't become wildly popular until the 2000s, were a kind of asset-backed securities on steroids. A CDO is a collection of just about anything that generates yield—bank loans, junk bonds, emerging market debt, you name it. The higher the yield, the better. Just as with a typical mortgage-backed security, the rating agencies would run the CDO's tranches through their models and declare a large percentage of them triple-A.

There would also be a triple-B or triple-B-minus slice, which was called the mezzanine portion, as well as an unrated equity tranche, which got paid only after everyone else had collected their returns. One astonishing fact is that the CDO managers didn't always have to disclose what the securities contained because those contents could change. Even more astonishing, investors didn't seem to care. They would buy CDOs knowing only the broad outline of the loans they contained. So why were they willing to do so? Because the way they viewed it, they weren't so much buying a security. *They were buying a triple-A rating.* That's why the triple-A was so key.

Like so many of the other financial products bursting onto the scene, CDOs weren't necessarily a bad idea. Done correctly, they could give investors broad exposure to different kinds of fixed-income assets at whatever level of risk they desired. But CDOs were fraught with risks and conflicts. Debt was being used to buy debt. CDO managers were paid a percentage of the money in the CDO, meaning they had an incentive to find stuff to buy—good, bad, or indifferent. Wall Street firms, who usually worked hand in glove with the managers, could earn hefty fees. According to one hedge fund manager who became a big investor in CDOs, as much as 40 to 50 percent of the cash flow generated by the assets in a CDO went to pay the bankers, the CDO manager, the rating agencies, and others who took out fees.

What's more, CDOs could also give banks and Wall Street securities firms both the means and the motive to move their worst assets off their balance sheets and into a CDO instead. And since the rating agencies could be counted on to rate a big chunk of the CDO triple-A, nobody would be the wiser.

Is it a surprise to learn that just as the rating agencies had failed to sniff out Enron and WorldCom, they also drastically misjudged the first batch of CDOs? Perhaps not. Sure enough, in 2002 and 2003 the rating agencies were forced to downgrade hundreds of CDOs—in no small part because they contained the bonds of certain companies the agencies had also woefully misjudged. A handful of investors sued the CDO managers and the firms that had underwritten them. But because the CDO issuance was still small, neither the lawsuits nor the losses made headlines. For a short while, CDO volume declined.

And how did Wall Street respond? By devising a new type of CDO, one that would be backed not by corporate loans, but by mortgage-backed securities. The idea, says one person who was prominent in the CDO business, was that the original rationale for CDOs—loan diversification—had proven to be flawed. But if you bought real estate, he said, "you were golden. You were safe."

There were a few critical differences between CDOs composed of securitized mortgages and CDOs composed of corporate loans. The former contained not two but three levels of debt. Instead of "merely" using debt to buy the debt of a company, CDOs were using debt to buy the debt from a pool of mortgages, which was itself homeowner's debt. A second critical difference was that bonds backed by mortgages generally had higher yields than similarly rated corporate bonds. Defenders of mortgage-backed securities tended to explain away this anomaly, once again, by claiming that investors didn't understand mortgage-backed bonds as well as corporate bonds, and thus demanded a higher yield for what was really a very safe asset. And to be sure, that was one possibility. Another possibility, though, was that the market understood quite well that mortgage-backed securities were riskier than corporate bonds and was compensating by insisting on a higher yield.

Wall Street didn't really care which explanation was correct. All it cared about was that it had discovered an anomaly it could take advantage of. And, oh, did it ever. Firms bought mortgage-backed bonds with the very highest yields they could find and reassembled them into new CDOs. The original bonds didn't even have to be triple-A! They could be lower-rated securities that once reassembled into a new CDO would wind up with as much as 70 percent of the tranches rated triple-A. Ratings arbitrage, Wall Street called this practice. A more accurate term would have been ratings laundering.

Soon, CDO managers were buying the lowest investment-grade tranches of mortgage-backed securities they could find and then putting them in new CDOs. Once this started to happen, CDOs became a self-perpetuating machine, like cells that won't stop dividing. From the very beginnings of the mortgage-backed securities business, marketers had always had to work hard to find enough investors to buy the lower-rated tranches. The triple-As were easy to sell because investors around the globe that were legally confined to conservative investments, or didn't want to hold the capital against a higher-risk investment, embraced their higher yield relative to their super-safe rating. The triple-B and -B-minus tranches were a harder sell, with a much smaller universe of potential investors. But once the CDO machinery *itself* became the buyer of the triple-Bs, there were suddenly no limits to how big the business could get. CDOs could absorb an infinite supply of triple-B-rated bonds and then repackage them into triple-A securities. Which everybody could then buy—banks and pension funds included. It really *was* alchemy, though of a deeply perverse sort.

In time, CDOs became by far the biggest buyers of triple-B tranches of mortgage-backed securities, purchasing and reassembling an astonishing 85 to 95 percent of them at the peak, according to a presentation by Karan P. S. Chabba, Bear Stearns's structured credit strategist. Among other consequences, this practice helped perpetuate the worst, most dangerous securities, because they were the ones that had the highest yield relative to their rating. One Wall Street executive would later liken CDOs to "purifying uranium until you get to the stuff that's the most toxic."

Lang Gibson, a former Merrill Lynch CDO research analyst, wrote a novel after the crisis in which a character describes the CDO market as a Ponzi scheme. You can see his point. As the triple-Bs were endlessly recycled, CDOs begat CDO squareds (in which triple-B portions of CDOs were reassembled into a new CDO) and even CDO cubeds (reassembed triple-B tranches of CDO squareds). The rise of ratings arbitrage helped push sales of CDOs from $69 billion in 2000 to around $500 billion in 2006. It was an endless cycle of madness.

The rating agencies were at the very heart of the madness. The entire edifice would have collapsed without their participation. "Get the rating out the door—that was it," says a former S&P executive. Once a tranche of a mortgage-backed security was stamped triple-A, nobody ever went back and reanalyzed it as it was rebundled into a CDO. "We simply assumed triple-A was a triple-A," says a former Moody's managing director who worked on CDOs.

The analysts in structured finance were working twelve to fifteen hours a day. They made a fraction of the pay of even a junior investment banker. There were far more deals in the pipeline than they could possibly handle. They were overwhelmed. "We were growing so fast, we couldn't keep staff, and we were grossly underresourced," recalls a former Moody's structured finance executive. Moody's top brass, he says, thought the mania would end with home prices flattening out, and as a result they wouldn't add staff because they didn't want to be stuck with the cost of employees if the revenues slowed down. "They were so stingy," he says. At both Moody's and S&P, former employees say there was a move away from hiring people with backgrounds in credit and toward hiring recent business school graduates or foreigners with green cards to keep costs down.

And of course nobody had the time or the inclination to examine the actual mortgages upon which this entire edifice had been built. If they had done so—if they had taken a hard look at the subprime mortgages that were at the heart of the securities they were rating triple-A—it would have meant putting an end to an immensely profitable business. "It seems to me that we had blinders on and never questioned the information we were given," a former Moody's executive later wrote. "It is our job to think of the worst-case scenarios and model them. Why didn't we envision that credit would tighten after being loose and housing prices would fall after rising? After all, most economic events are cyclical and bubbles inevitably burst."

After leaving Moody's, Mark Adelson joined Nomura Securities, where he was the head of structured finance research. At securitization conferences, he would look around at the audience and think to himself, "No one in that room had ever loaned or collected back one red cent. Any schmuck can lend it out. The trick is getting it back!"

In the fall of 2007, after it all started melting down, a Moody's managing director wrote in a memo, "My recommendation is that we do not rate ABS [asset-backed securities] CDOs. The reasoning behind this recommendation is that due to the complexity of the product and multiple layers of risk, it is NEVER possible to have the requisite amount of information to rate." But that had been true long before 2007.

By the fall of 2005, Moody's market capitalization had grown to more than $15 billion. That was roughly the same as Bear Stearns. Yet Bear Stearns had 11,000 employees and $7 billion of revenue, while Moody's had 2,500 employees and $1.6 billion of revenue. Moody's operating margins were consistently over 50 percent, making it one of the most profitable companies in existence— more profitable, on a margin basis, than Exxon Mobil or Microsoft. Between the time it was spun off into a public company and February 2007, its stock had risen 340 percent. Structured finance was approaching 50 percent of Moody's revenue—up from 28 percent in 1998. It accounted for pretty much all of Moody's growth.

And in August 2007, Brian Clarkson was named president of Moody's. His compensation that year was $3.2 million.

9

"I Like Big Bucks and I Cannot Lie"

It was the 2004 holiday season, and a college student—let's call him Bob—was home in Sacramento. One night, out on the town, he met another young man—Slickdaddy G, Bob nicknamed him. Slickdaddy G, who was twenty-six, was a "larger-than-life personality type," Bob recalls. "He had perfectly highlighted blond hair, short and gelled, perfect white teeth, perfect bronzed skin." He also had his own limo driver and a seemingly endless supply of money. Bob joined Slickdaddy G for a night of club hopping, picking up pretty girls and drinking Dom Pérignon. The crew ended up at a penthouse apartment—it was just called "the P"—where an "insane party" was taking place. "A DJ, and more girls, booze, and drugs than you can imagine," says Bob. "It was one of the crazier experiences of my life to this point." The next morning, Bob asked Slickdaddy G, "What the hell do you do?"

"Ameriquest" came the reply. "I'm in the mortgage business."

Incredibly, the subprime mortgage business, which had been left for dead, had come roaring back, bigger than ever. Never mind that most of the mortgage originators during the first subprime bubble—subprime one, let's call it—had gone bust, or that giving mortgages to shaky borrowers had led to a rather unsurprising rise in foreclosures. And never mind that the subprime financial model had been very nearly discredited. "Subprime one," says Josh Rosner, "was the petri dish."

The second subprime bubble was as wild as anything ever seen in American business. During subprime two, kids just out of school—sometimes high school—became loan officers, some of them pulling down $30,000 or $40,000 a month. (Slickdaddy G told Bob that in one especially good month he took home $125,000.) In some places, like Ameriquest's Sacramento offices, where Bob had taken a job in 2005, drug usage was an open secret, former loan officers say, especially coke and meth, so that the loan officers could sell fourteen hours a day. And the money poured in.

It wasn't just Ameriquest, either. In 2006, at a Washington Mutual retreat for top performers in Maui, employees performed a rap skit called "I Like Big Bucks." To the tune of "Baby's Got Back," the crew rapped:

> *I like big bucks and I cannot lie*
> *You mortgage brothers can't deny*
> *That when the dough rolls in like you're printin' your own cash*
> *And you gotta make a splash*
> *You just spends*
> *Like it never ends*
> *'Cuz you gotta have that big new Benz.*

What triggered subprime two—besides some very short memories—was Alan Greenspan's decision to push interest rates down to near historic lows during the first few years of the new century to keep the economy from faltering. (He was reacting to the bursting of the Internet bubble.) Low interest rates drove down mortgage rates, making home purchases more attractive while driving up investor demand for yield. And despite the rampant lending abuses that characterized subprime one, the government continued to smile on the subprime phenomenon because of its supposed benefit in helping more Americans buy homes. Naturally, Greenspan held this view. "Where once more marginal applicants would simply have been denied credit, lenders are now able to quite efficiently judge the risk posed by individual applicants and to price that risk accordingly," he said in April 2005.

But there was another factor as well. Piece by piece, over the course of nearly two decades, a giant money machine had been assembled that depended on subprime mortgages as its raw material. Wall Street needed subprime mortgages that it could package into securitized bonds. And investors around the world wanted Wall Street's mortgage products because they offered high yields in a low-yield environment. Merrill Lynch, Morgan Stanley, UBS, Deutsche Bank, even Goldman Sachs, which had stayed away from subprime one (too small-fry), moved heavily into the business. By 2005, the securities industry derived $5.16 billion in revenue from underwriting bonds backed by mortgages and related assets, Fox-Pitt Kelton analyst David Trone told Bloomberg. That accounted for a staggering 25 percent of all bond underwriting revenue.

Mortgage originators sought to supply the riskier mortgages Wall Street craved—no matter what. The fraud that took place during subprime one paled in comparison to what happened during subprime two. Even borrowers who qualified for a traditional mortgage might be pushed toward a high-fee, high-interest-rate subprime product. And "nontraditional" mortgages—meaning those that were more lucrative for lenders than the old thirty-year fixed-rate mortgage—held by prime borrowers became a whole new category: Alt-A mortgages, they were called.

Nor did every prime borrower need to be pushed. As subprime two moved into bubble territory, more and more people wanted so-called affordability products—loans with low "teaser" rates that would quickly reset at a new, higher rate, for instance, or even "negative amortization" loans, in which the borrower paid less than the interest due, so that the principal got bigger, instead of smaller. Often, borrowers used the low teaser rate in the hopes of flipping their new home at a higher price before the new rate kicked in. Speculation was widespread.

The actual purchase of new homes was only part of what drove this new bubble. As Rosner had begun to suspect, millions of Americans were using subprime mortgages to profit from the rise in the value of homes they already owned. A big chunk of Ameriquest's business, for instance, was something called cash-out refinancings, meaning that borrowers refinanced their mortgages based on the increased value of their homes and pulled out the excess cash for spending. By February 2004, fully two-thirds of the loans made by New Century, another huge subprime lender, were cash-out refis. From 2001 to 2006, more than half the subprime originations and more than one-third of all Alt-A loans were used for refinancings, according to Jason Thomas, a former economist at the National Economic Council who is now at the George Washington University finance department. According to the *Wall Street Journal*, total household debt in America doubled, from $7 trillion to $14 trillion, between 2000 and 2007. Debt related to housing was responsible for 80 percent of that increase.

And of course housing prices themselves were going through the roof, which both enabled and exacerbated everything else. Since 1940, according to data compiled by the S&P/Case-Shiller home price index, the average home increased in value by 0.7 percent a year. But between 2001 and 2006, fourteen of the twenty largest metropolitan areas in the country saw home values rise by more than 10 percent a year. Median home prices in hot areas like Phoenix and Las Vegas increased by an inflation-adjusted 80 percent.

The ratio of home prices to income, which had hovered between 2 and 4 since the Great Depression, shot up in some places to as high as 12, according to data collected by the financial blogger Paul Kedrosky.

During subprime one, the new subprime companies had been marginal players in an enormous housing industry. In subprime two, the subprime companies dominated the industry. Washington Mutual turned itself into the biggest thrift in the country by moving aggressively into the riskiest forms of subprime lending. New Century and Option One, bit players during subprime one, became multibillion-dollar companies.

And then there was Ameriquest. . . .

——⊶∞⊷——

In April 1996, Roland Arnall moved out of the house he shared with his wife of thirty-seven years, Miriam Sally Arnall. During their divorce proceedings, he told her that because "things were not going that well with his business," her "financial future would be uncertain" unless she settled quickly, she later alleged in a court filing. ("Please do not consider this any kind of threat," Arnall's lawyer told her in a letter.) In the divorce, which was finalized in April 1998, she got $11 million, tax free, and their homes in Los Angeles and Palm Springs. Arnall also paid her legal fees. He, in turn, got full control of his brand-new company, Ameriquest Capital Corporation, or ACC.

As it turns out, Arnall's financial future was spectacular. In the spring of 1997, before the divorce was concluded, Arnall had spun off a division of Long Beach in an initial public offering. Arnall's name was mentioned only once in the offering documents, as the owner of 69.9 percent of the parent company. His company sold all of its shares to outside investors, reaping a little over $120 million in the process. A few years later, the new publicly held Long Beach was sold to Washington Mutual, marking the thrift's entrée into subprime lending. By then, however, Arnall was already in the process of creating a new subprime empire, under the umbrella of ACC. His most promising new venture was Ameriquest.

ACC became a holding company for more than a dozen entities, including Ameriquest and Town and Country, two retail subprime lenders with their own sales force, and Argent, which sold loans through independent brokers. According to the *American Banker*, from 2001 to 2004 ACC's loan volume grew more than twelvefold, to $82.7 billion, putting ACC atop the list of subprime lenders that year. According to figures published by the *Los*

Angeles Times, between 2002 and 2004 ACC generated $7.6 billion in revenue and earned $2.7 billion in profits. Ameriquest itself made more than $80 billion in loans in 2004, its peak year.

In some ways, Arnall followed his old playbook: he made high-priced loans to people who would eventually have trouble paying them back, and he sold the loans to Wall Street. But he did it on a much bigger scale than Long Beach, boosted by a massive advertising campaign. Ameriquest paid $2.5 million a year for the naming rights to the Texas Rangers stadium, and another roughly $3 million to sponsor the Rolling Stones' A Bigger Bang tour in 2005. It spent untold sums on commercials, blimps, and sponsorship of everything from NASCAR to the popular PBS program *Antiques Roadshow*. The company's slogan was—what else?—"The Proud Sponsor of the American Dream."

Executives were extremely well paid. Wayne Lee, who had worked for Arnall since 1990, spent one year as Ameriquest's CEO before quitting in the spring of 2005. He later said in a deposition that in 2004 and 2005 he had received yearly bonuses of around $5 million on top of his roughly $330,000 in salary. His severance agreement was truly astounding. In return for working a maximum of twenty-five hours every three months and agreeing to neither compete with nor disparage ACC, the company agreed to pay him $50 million.

As for loan officers, they got a small base salary, but made most of their money on commissions—typically 15 percent of all the revenue they generated. And the perks were fabulous. Every year Ameriquest hosted an event called the Big Spin in Las Vegas for hundreds of top producers. In 2004, Jim Belushi was the emcee and the rock band Third Eye Blind played. In 2005, the head of national sales, Mary Jo Shelton, was shot out of a cannon to start the festivities, and the Black Eyed Peas played. One loan officer, Joe McGregor, just out of college, won a Hummer that year. When someone asked him if he was excited, he replied, "Well, yeah. I've already got one." The company also gave its top three hundred loan officers an all-expenses-paid trip to Hawaii in 2005.

"The amount of money the company had to throw around was staggering," says a former corporate employee. "These guys in sales who were twenty-five years old and maybe had a couple years of college were making incredible money and driving Porsches. It felt like something was wrong."

When they weren't partying, the young loan officers at Ameriquest were under enormous pressure to move loans. "It was a chop shop, and the whip was always being cracked for more," says Mark Bomchill, describing the Ameriquest office in Minnesota where he worked from 2002 to 2003. Two other former loan officers, interviewed separately, used the same description: "Think *Glengarry Glen Ross*." Loan officers were often required to make a certain number of outbound calls each day—a hundred fifty, says Bob—and there were "power hours" for cold-calling. Managers were "brutal to those who weren't closing loans," recalls another former employee. Firms took anyone—"car wash guys, let alone car salesmen," laughs Bob. Executives said they hired young, inexperienced people to keep costs down, though former loan officers say the real reason was that inexperienced loan officers were less likely to realize that "they were screwing people over," as one of them put it. The branches were run a little like frat houses. Once, says Bob, a handful of loan officers were blindfolded while a manager yelled out lines from the movie *Boiler Room*.

Fraud was an everyday occurrence. "You'd look over and there would be a guy altering W-2s," says Bomchill. One loan officer, Lisa Taylor, who worked in Ameriquest's Sacramento office from 2001 to 2003, filed a sexual harassment and wrongful dismissal case alleging that Ameriquest management "condoned, encouraged and participated in extensive document alteration, manipulation and forging in order to sell more loans." Taylor later told the *Los Angeles Times* that she'd walked in on coworkers using a brightly lit Coca-Cola vending machine as a tracing board so loan agents could copy borrowers' signatures onto blank documents. (She also said in her complaint that Ameriquest had hired a "self-avowed porno king who made no secret of the fact that he sold sex toys online in his spare time.")

In 2003, Ameriquest tried to tighten up its lending standards. Among other things, it changed its compensation guidelines so that loan officers were no longer rewarded for tacking on additional fees, and it implemented new software designed to prevent fraud. But the relentless pressure for loan volume never changed, and in the branches there always seemed to be ways of getting around the new policies. "It is absurd to suggest that their 2003 changes 'solved' the problems," says one longtime critic.

Ameriquest's core product was something called a 2/28 loan, meaning it had a low fixed rate for two years, and then converted to a higher adjustable rate for the remaining twenty-eight years. What made a 2/28 loan particularly pernicious is it often came with a three-year prepayment penalty. That meant that the borrower either had to refinance at year two—and pay a hefty fee—

or pay the higher rate for a year before refinancing without having to pay a penalty.

Then there were the points and fees Ameriquest charged. In theory, borrowers pay up-front points to reduce the interest rate on their loan. And in theory, risk-based pricing—or charging consumers based on the risk they represent—means that riskier borrowers should pay more. Indeed, that's the essential justification for subprime lending.

It would be hard to call what went on at Ameriquest risk-based pricing. Ameriquest had a rule capping the points and fees on any one loan at 5.5 percent. (This was to avoid running afoul of several state laws with similar caps.) But, according to a former loan officer, the goal in the branches was to charge as close to that limit as possible. The creditworthiness of the borrowers mattered a lot less than whatever the loan officer thought he could get away with.

A spreadsheet of all the loans Ameriquest made in the month of February 2005 offers a vivid illustration. One customer with a midgrade credit score got a loan of $750,000—and paid the maximum in points and fees. The revenue to Ameriquest was $41,226. Another customer with a $750,000 loan paid so little in fees and points that the loan generated only $1,830 for Ameriquest. Yet that second customer was far less creditworthy than the first. Another example from that same spreadsheet: Two borrowers, both with the same credit score, took out 2/28 loans of roughly the same amount. One of them paid over 3 percent in points to get a 6.5 percent interest rate (revenue to Ameriquest: $31,320). The other paid almost no points for the same rate (revenue to Ameriquest: $2,559). Ameriquest's total revenue for just that one month was $87.5 million on $2.5 billion in loans.

Ameriquest also had special "portfolio retention" branches, whose job it was to prevent Ameriquest borrowers from refinancing with competitors. They would pay fees to the big credit bureaus and get alerts whenever an Ameriquest customer requested a credit check. That was standard practice in the industry, according to former loan officers. But they also sometimes did something far sleazier. Bob says that certain Ameriquest employees would hack into the system and print out a sheet with everything about a borrower: the size of their loan, their social security number, birth date, and contact information. The loan officer would then call borrowers who hadn't even voiced an interest in a refinancing, offering a new loan with a reduced interest rate—and hefty new fees for Ameriquest. "The reality was you were screwing people again and again and again," Bob says. (ACC says that it was "against company policy to misuse company assets, including customer information," and points out that every employee received and signed a document acknowledging this.)

And what happened when complaints about these practices leached into public view? Once again, Arnall fell back on his old playbook: he spent whatever it took to make them go away. In late 1999, the grassroots organization ACORN picketed twenty Ameriquest offices, accusing it of deceptive lending tactics. Ameriquest responded by committing to fund $360 million in ACORN-originated thirty-year fixed-rate loans. ACORN stopped picketing. (Very few of the loans were ever made.) In 2001, a group of Ameriquest borrowers filed a class action lawsuit against the company—the first of many. In settling, Ameriquest agreed to pay up to $50 million in reimbursement. Three years later, the state of Connecticut charged Ameriquest with violating a state law regarding refinancings. The company paid $670,552 to settle the charges. In 2005, Connecticut announced a second settlement over the same issue. Ameriquest blamed the problem on new employees who didn't know the rules. It paid $7.25 million to move on. "Roland was not a cheapskate," says Greenlining's Robert Gnaizda. "He spent money if he thought it would be helpful."

As Ameriquest became the country's dominant subprime lender, Arnall himself became extraordinarily wealthy. In 2004, he made the Forbes 400 list of richest people in America, with a net worth of $2 billion. The following year, the magazine estimated his net worth at $3 billion, ranking him seventy-third on the list. (He tied with Yahoo co-founder David Filo.) By then, he and his second wife, Dawn Arnall, owned a $30 million, ten-acre compound in Los Angeles, and a 650-acre ranch in Aspen, snuggled between two ski resorts. The former property had been owned by Sonny and Cher in the 1970s; the latter was the second most expensive home in the country, according to a list compiled in 2004 by *Forbes* magazine. It cost Arnall $46 million.

Through it all, he never changed. Although Ameriquest had a far higher profile than Long Beach ever had, Arnall himself remained in the shadows. His companies never went public. Others served as their chief executives. He remained ever demanding, yet ever gracious, respectful even of the company janitors. The wealthier he got, the more he spent on quiet philanthropy—and on political contributions, mainly to Republicans.

And from his office in ACC's bland twelve-story headquarters in Orange

County—the epicenter of the subprime industry—he never, ever spoke about the practices that permeated the branch offices. Headquarters, in fact, acted as if the company were a paragon of subprime virtue, rather than a place that oozed with sleaze and fraud. In July 2000, for instance, Ameriquest publicly committed to a set of best practices, which included promises to let two years pass before refinancing any loans and to refrain from offering loans with balloon payments and negative amortization. The following year, Ameriquest's chairman, Stephen Prough, testified before the Senate banking committee; Ameriquest had been invited to testify because many in Washington considered Ameriquest a model subprime lender.

Yet the evidence suggests that the best practices were mainly honored in the breach. One example: after an exhaustive analysis of public records, the *Los Angeles Times* determined that nearly one in nine 2004 Ameriquest mortgages was a refinancing of an existing Ameriquest loan less than twenty-four months old—precisely what the company had promised it wouldn't do. (ACC says that many of Ameriquest's borrowers were not pushed into these refinancings but came to the company of their own volition. The *Times* also noted, however, that Ameriquest's refinancing rate was higher than that of six competitors included in its analysis.)

The question of how much Arnall knew about his company's sordid lending practices is something we'll never know; Arnall died in 2008, after being diagnosed with esophageal cancer, and without ever being pinned down about what, exactly, his involvement was. Even to some at ACC, he was a mysterious figure. He tended to float above the problems and never got involved in the nitty-gritty of the business. "Never, ever did I ever see him pick up a loan file," says a former executive.

On the other hand, how could he not have known? The company was constantly being hit with accusations, investigations, and lawsuits charging fraud and deceptive practices. "We were inundated with stories about the conduct of the sales personnel—everything from drug use and fraud to theft and gang affiliation," says another former executive. At best, Arnall seemed to have practiced a kind of willful ignorance.

In January 2003, as questions about Ameriquest's practices were heating up, the company hired a mortgage veteran named Ed Parker to investigate fraud in the branches. At first, Parker says, he was hopeful he would be given the authority to do the job right. In his first investigation, he helped shut down a branch in Michigan after looking at twenty-five hundred loan files and discovering that the loan officers were all using the same few appraisers to inflate the value of properties. The fraud wasn't subtle—there would even be notes in the files spelling out the value the appraisers had been told to hit. Ameriquest repurchased the loans from lenders who had bought them.

But Parker says that other executives made comments that caused him to think they didn't really want him to be such a zealot. He soon decided that, as he later put it, "I was not brought in to do a job. I was brought in to provide cover." In Fresno, he discovered that branch employees were manipulating bank statements to make it appear that the prospective borrowers had more cash reserves than they did. They would cut and paste information from one borrower's statement to another's. Several of the implicated employees had been promoted to branch managers. At other California branches, Parker discovered that stated-income letters were being manufactured that misrepresented the age of elderly borrowers. One loan application stated that the borrower was a forty-four-year-old consultant who earned $8,000 a month. In fact, the borrower was seventy-four. In the Florida branches, says Parker, "there were just so many problems with the loans." He would record what he found, send it to management—and nothing would happen. He says he was turned down for promotions, cut out of decision making, and eventually fired in July 2006. In a lawsuit Parker filed alleging employment discrimination, he claimed that Ameriquest was "engaged in massive fraud for years." He says now, "My problem was, they did not want to know."*

What Arnall's defenders say—indeed, what all the defenders of the subprime originators would say after the fact—is that the true villains were not the lenders on Main Street but the investment firms on Wall Street. Wall Street, after all, was both making the warehouse loans on which the subprime companies depended and then buying up their mortgages and securitizing them. The Wall Street firms, in fact, were dictating what kind of mortgages they would buy and at what price. They wanted the riskiest subprime mortgages they could get their hands on, because those were the mortgages that generated the most yield. In a presentation to the board of directors, Washington Mutual executives noted that subprime loans were roughly seven times more profitable than prime mortgages, because the company could sell them for

---

* ACC calls Parker a "disgruntled former employee" and notes that an arbitrator decided against his claim for wrongful dismissal. The arbitrator did not opine on Parker's allegations of fraud. But he wrote that "there is no evidence that anything that happened to Parker in terms of his employment was connected" to his reporting of problems.

so much more. WaMu used to award its sales staff a bonus if they could tack on a prepayment penalty to the loan—which was something else Wall Street wanted.

"Wall Street set the product guidelines," says a former Ameriquest executive. "I can't say to the consumer, 'Here's your rate.' Wall Street figures out what investors are willing to pay. They design it and they present it to you. If they say, 'Don't put it on my warehouse line,' that means you can't make the loan." This executive claims that he wanted to offer loans without prepayment penalties, but he couldn't, because Wall Street wouldn't buy them. "Ultimately, the market is driven not by what is best for borrowers, but by what products investors can invest in," Ameriquest's vice president for capital markets, Ketan Parekh, told a trade publication in November 2004.

Jon Daurio, the executive who had worked for Arnall at Long Beach and then went on to form several other subprime companies, recalls a meeting in 2003 with some representatives of Bear Stearns. "How can you increase your volume?" the Bear Stearns bankers asked him. "We said, tongue in cheek, 'Well, we can do a 100 percent loan-to-value stated-income loan for 580 FICO scores!' Translated, that meant making loans with no down payment and no income verification to borrowers with very low credit scores. Daurio continued: "They said, 'Okay!' We said, 'No problem! Let's do this all day!' And we did it, in massive quantities."

Perhaps the most dangerous manifestation of Wall Street's demands was something called a payment option adjustable-rate mortgage, or a pay option ARM. Pay option ARMs gave consumers the right to choose whatever rate they wanted at the start, from a very low teaser rate to a higher rate that more resembled a thirty-year fixed mortgage. The teaser rate, which most people chose, was so low that it often didn't include all the interest, much less principal, meaning that additional interest was accumulating even as the borrower was paying the mortgage. Most pay option ARMs had reset triggers, so that if the borrower's loan balance reached, say, 115 percent of the original amount, he or she would automatically have to begin paying the full rate. Because the amount due each month could escalate so suddenly and dramatically, the phrase "payment shock" became an unwelcome, but very common, feature of pay option ARMs.

Wall Street loved pay option ARMs. So Ameriquest, New Century, WaMu, all the big subprime lenders began trafficking in them. They were extremely lucrative. WaMu, according to its internal presentations, could make more than five times the profit selling an option ARM to Wall Street than a prime fixed-rate loan.

The only party that was leery of them, in fact, were the *customers*—and rightfully so. Their terms were so pernicious that they wound up crushing hundreds of thousands of borrowers even before the bubble had ended. In the fall of 2003, WaMu held a series of focus groups to figure out how to sell more pay option ARMs. According to a summary of the focus groups, "Very few people simply walk through the door and ask" for an option ARM. In fact, the summary continued, most borrowers said that pay option ARMS were a "moderately or very bad concept." They also said things like, "It's really scary to me what's going to happen in five years" and "I have this feeling of impending doom." Most customers said that they "felt good being able to pay a portion of the principal each month because it seemed to be the right thing to do."

But customers could be persuaded to take a pay option ARM with the right sales pitch. WaMu, for instance, noted that if the salesperson told the borrower that "price appreciation would likely overcome any negative amortization," they often came around. Pay option ARMs, in other words, were sold, not bought. "Participants generally chose an option ARM because it was recommended to them," the WaMu summary said. (A Federal Reserve Bank of Atlanta study later correlated financial literacy to mortgage delinquencies, implying that unsophisticated consumers were the ones most likely to fall for this kind of pitch.)

Later, after everything had come to an end, an Ameriquest loan officer named Christopher Warren—who, like Bob, worked in the Sacramento office—posted a rambling confession online about his years in the mortgage business. Of his three years at Ameriquest, where he said he started as a teenager, he wrote: "[M]y managers and handlers taught me the ins and outs of mortgage fraud, drugs, sex, and money, money and more money. My friend and manager handed out crystal methamphetamine to loan officers in a bid to keep them up and at work longer hours. At any given moment inside the restrooms, cocaine and meth was being snorted by my estimates [by] more than a third of the staff, and more than half the staff [was] manipulating documents to get loans to fund, and more than 75 percent just made completely false statements . . . A typical welcome aboard gift was a pair of scissors, tape and white out. . . ." He left, he said, with the personal information of 680,000 Ameriquest customers to start a company called WTL Financial. His new company, he admitted, faked credit scores, pay stubs, and bank statements in order to sell $810 million in securities backed by his loans. He could get away with it because Wall Street didn't care.

After posting his confession, Warren tried to flee the country but was arrested at the Canadian border with $1 million in Swiss bank certificates and $70,000 stuffed in his cowboy boots. The case was pending as of fall 2010. (ACC says that Warren was terminated for "egregious acts" and that it has found no research to support his hacking claims. The company also says it is "patently unfair" to use Warren as an example of a typical employee.)

Had Ameriquest been an outlier, that would have been bad enough. But it wasn't. Its aggressive practices were copied by subprime competitors across the country—because they felt if they didn't copy Ameriquest, they'd lose the business to someone who had. "I think Ameriquest was the trendsetter," says Bomchill. "They spewed their slime everywhere."

"Ameriquest was a problem for us because they were a large company and everyone was trying to compete with them," says an executive at another large lender. "If we denied a loan, we'd track who ultimately did the loan and a lot of times it was Ameriquest. Every time we rejected a loan, the sales force would call up and say, 'Well, Ameriquest is doing this.' I would say, 'Just because Johnny jumped off a bridge doesn't mean you have to follow.'"

But they all did jump off the bridge. Including—eventually—the biggest lender of them all: Countrywide.

10

The Carnival Barker

Angelo Mozilo had long had a conflicted attitude toward subprime lending. On the one hand, he looked down his nose at the likes of Ameriquest and Roland Arnall, and didn't want Countrywide, or himself, to be viewed in the same light. "There is a very, very good, solid subprime business and there is this frothy business," he once told investors. "[It] is very important that you understand the disciplines . . . that Countrywide has." On the other hand, Mozilo couldn't bear to see Countrywide's market share eclipsed by the subprime companies. And market share remained his obsession. By the middle of 2003, he was promising investors that Countrywide "would get our overall market share to the ultimate 30 percent by 2006, 2007." At the time, its share of the mortgage market was a little over 10 percent.

Mozilo would later frame the choices Countrywide faced in stark terms. "Ameriquest changed the game," he said to a friend. "If you had said, 'Nope, I'm not going to do this because it's not prudent,' you would have had to tell shareholders, 'I'm shutting down the company.'" The reality, however, was never that simple. Mozilo had created a company that had the desire to be not just big and good but biggest and best embedded in its DNA. Taking a pass of a large segment of the business wasn't Countrywide's style. And then, as subprime two gained steam, Countrywide was increasingly riven by internal divisions. The way those conflicts played out may have helped influence Countrywide's future course every bit as much as Ameriquest's unquenchable thirst for subprime lending.

By the early 2000s, Angelo Mozilo wasn't remotely the hands-on manager his frequent CNBC appearances would suggest. This wasn't by choice; he was struggling with a variety of health issues. He had spinal cord problems so serious he had trouble walking at times, according to one person who knows him well. He had neck surgery, back surgery, and another elective surgery, which went badly, this same person says. An old acquaintance who hadn't seen him for several years was shocked when he next saw Mozilo. "He looked like an old man," he says.

David Loeb, Countrywide's other founder, wasn't around, either, having retired as president and chairman in early 2000. (He died of neuropathy in 2003.) Loeb was in some ways the invisible founder, yet he had played a critical role in Countrywide's success. Access to capital, the sale of loans in the secondary market, the management of interest and credit risk—these were the important but low-profile aspects of the business Loeb focused on.

Loeb's departure hadn't been entirely graceful. As he got older, his behavior became more erratic. In July 1999, for instance, the news broke that Loeb had sold a million shares of his Countrywide stock. High-ranking executives at publicly owned companies are never supposed to sell stock without first clearing the sale with the legal department and informing the rest of the management team and the board. Loeb had done neither. When one executive called to ask him why he had sold the stock without telling anybody, Loeb just chuckled.

After Loeb left, Mozilo seriously entertained the idea of selling Countrywide. There were lots of potential suitors knocking on his door, and he hired Goldman Sachs to find the best fit. Although Countrywide came close to selling to a big British bank—and to Washington Mutual—both deals fell apart.

Even without a sale, there were plenty of executives internally with the ambition and skill to run the company. Countrywide's core group of executives had joined when the company was young and small. Like Mozilo, most of them lacked an Ivy League pedigree but made up for it with a combination of business savvy and fanatical work habits. Most of them had that same chip on their shoulder toward the financial establishment that Mozilo had. That attitude was ingrained in the culture of the company and was a big part of the reason why Countrywide was always striving to outdo the big boys—even after it had become one of the big boys. For Countrywide's top executives, that deep-seated need to prove themselves never completely went away.

Chief among these executives was Stanford Kurland, a graduate of California State University Northridge, who was hired by Countrywide in 1979 after spending the early part of his career as Countrywide's auditor. Kurland had an intense, bookish demeanor and a slow, almost hesitant way of speaking that served to mask his deep emotion and strong will. In 1995, he became the chief operating officer of Countrywide Home Loans, the prime mortgage division that had always accounted for the bulk of Countrywide's business; four years later, Kurland became the division's CEO and joined Countrywide's board. In 2004, he became president and chief operating officer of the parent company. To the employees, he was as much the boss as Mozilo. "It was always 'Angelo and Stan want to do this,'" recalls a former executive.

Kurland was the one who took on the tasks that Loeb had always handled, making sure that Countrywide's increasingly intricate plumbing worked perfectly. This was no small task at a company that was funding tens of billions of dollars' worth of loans every month. "He was the inside guy, the numbers guy, the operations guy," says a former analyst. In 2000, Paine Webber analyst Gary Gordon wrote a report celebrating Countrywide's "wonderful discipline." That discipline was very much Kurland's doing, and he took great pride in it. He'd later tell people that while he was there, "there was never a single issue." He was right. Other mortgage originators occasionally had trouble with funding or the sale of their loans. Countrywide never did.

Kurland also pushed Countrywide to diversify. He wanted Countrywide to be one of the most admired financial services providers in the country, not just a big mortgage maker. To that end, Countrywide bought a bank in 2000. Because the bank was regulated by the Office of the Comptroller of the Currency, Countrywide itself became a bank holding company, which was supervised by the Federal Reserve. Kurland used to tell people that being under the supervision of the country's two most important bank regulators gave Countrywide extra credibility.

The purchase of the bank also forced Mozilo to leave the board of another bank, a subprime lender called IndyMac, based in Pasadena. IndyMac, which would be taken over by the FDIC during the financial crisis, had begun life as Countrywide Mortgage Investments. Founded by Mozilo and Loeb, it was a real estate investment trust, or REIT, that served as an outlet for Countrywide's so-called jumbo loans, the ones that were too big for the GSEs to buy. (REITs pay out most of their profits as dividends to their shareholders.) Starting in the early 1990s, it began to aggregate loans from other lenders and turn them into mortgage-backed securities. It also began to originate its own Alt-A mortgages. In other words, the company was starting to compete with Countrywide. Despite the growing conflict, Mozilo stayed on the board (as did Loeb), exercised stock options, and collected some of the company's rich dividends. His son Mark began working there in 1996. And when Mozilo finally left the board after Countrywide bought a bank, it was because he had no choice. IndyMac also owned a bank, and bank regulations don't allow anyone to serve as a director on two bank holding company boards. When Mozilo stepped down from the board, IndyMac forgave an outstanding $3.3 million loan and paid him another $3.6 million to cover any taxes he might owe on his stock options.

Taking the money was an outrageous move—and to some at Countrywide, a sign that money was starting to matter too much to Mozilo. In 2000, he owned 2.8 million shares of Countrywide stock (including options) and would take home $6.6 million in compensation—a number that would rise to $10.1 million by 2001 and $23.6 million by 2003. Yet he wanted more. "There are CEOs of companies to whom the most important thing is if they made more than the next guy," says someone who knew him well. "Mozilo was getting caught up in all of that."

If Stan Kurland was in charge of Countrywide's plumbing, a very different kind of executive was in charge of producing all of its loans. His name was David Sambol; he had joined Countrywide in 1985 and become its head of loan production in 2000. (He was named chief operating officer for the home loan division in 2004.) Like Kurland, Sambol had gone to California State University Northridge and had worked briefly as an accountant. For many years, the two men appeared to be friendly. They were both highly intelligent, proud men who cared deeply about Countrywide's standing and its market share goals. About Sambol, a former executive says, "he bled Countrywide." But there the similarities ended.

Sambol was a super-aggressive salesman, very much in the Mozilo mode, though he lacked Mozilo's charm and warmth. He did not always make a good first impression. "His style was one of attack," says a former executive. "He would attack everything around him that didn't report to him. He would be relentless, and very convincing until you challenged him with facts. But when you called him out, it never bothered him. It rolled right off his back and he was on to the next thing." This aspect of Sambol's character gave rise to an internal nickname: Teflon Dave. Another former executive who was a fan of Sambol's says, "He loved the details, he loved knowing the details, and he loved putting people through the wringer to see if they knew the details." People also made fun of his dictatorial nature. Other executives would pretend they were Sambol and say to each other, "You don't understand. You're not capable of understanding. I see all of the colors of the rainbow."

Inside Countrywide, it was very apparent that Sambol was "all about building his own kingdom," as a former executive puts it. He was dismissive of everything that he hadn't personally created. And while one former executive says that Sambol did care about risk, above all, Sambol wanted to win. "There was a clear mentality from his organization that these [subprime] guys are outcompeting us, we've got to do this, we just lost another loan," recalls a former executive. Soon after taking charge of the sales force, Sambol made several changes aimed at putting Countrywide on a more even footing with its subprime competitors. The most important of these was to the compensation system: instead of taking home a flat salary, loan officers would earn commissions based on volume, according to the *American Banker*.

There was always friction at Countrywide between those who worried about risk and controls and those who wanted to sell more loans. But for a long time, the friction was manageable, maybe even healthy. "Really great organizations have friction," says another former executive. "But friction can become cancerous."

For Countrywide, the friction started to become a sickness in 2004, when the Federal Reserve began to raise interest rates. Normally, rate increases signal that it's time for mortgage originators to pull back on loan production. But in this new world, loan production did not decline. Those, like Kurland, who worried that higher rates brought increased risks of default felt as though they were trying to hold back a flood. In lighter moments, they began to joke that they were becoming the CNOs—the chief nuisance officers. Kurland complained to confidants that on some days he felt his role was increasingly being relegated to that of the "no" guy. "The people who are propelled upward in many cases in corporate America are the guys who said yes to an idea that worked," he later told a friend. "The guys who said no to a big failure—there's no list for that. That's why we end up with bubbles."

When Countrywide had first moved into subprime lending back in the late 1990s, Kurland and Mozilo had both believed that the market was moving toward risk-based pricing, and the lines between prime and subprime were going to go away. And they convinced themselves that Countrywide would establish standards that would keep the truly troubled borrowers away, while capturing the more creditworthy subprime borrowers, those who were just a step below prime. Initially, the company was very careful.

Kurland issued three rules for subprime lending at Countrywide, according to several former executives. First, all of its subprime loans had to be sold, by which he meant the entire thing, including the residuals that most subprime companies held on their books. Second, the borrowers had to either make a 20 percent down payment or get mortgage insurance to cover the first 20 percent of the loan. Finally, Countrywide couldn't offer any subprime loan products that had a higher probability of default than an FHA or VA loan.

These rules, however, seemed to constrain the company less and less as time went on—and whatever reservations Mozilo had about subprime lending seemed to fade the bigger the market got. Within a few years of making subprime loans, Countrywide could offer an astonishing 180 different products. In 2004, the *American Banker* accused Mozilo of sounding like a "carnival barker" as he listed some of them: "We have ARMs, one-year ARMs, three-year, five-year, seven- and ten-year. We have interest-only loans, pay option loans, zero-down programs, low or no-doc programs, fast and easy programs, and subprime loans." Sambol told investors that "it's our intent to carry every product or program for which there is reasonable demand. . . . [I]f your customer can legitimately qualify for a loan anywhere else in the U.S., they'll qualify at Countrywide." In a complaint the SEC later filed against Mozilo, Sambol, and former CFO Eric Sieracki, the agency alleged that Countrywide referred to this as its "matching" strategy: if a competitor offered a loan product, Countrywide would match it.*

Besides, with Wall Street willing to buy anything, mortgage issuers willing to guarantee anything, and estimates about the probability of default open to assumptions, Kurland's rules could be rendered basically meaningless. Indeed, one former executive says that if he could go back and do one thing differently, he would look at the models about how loans were supposed to perform and say, "I'm not going to believe them."

"We had meetings where I would say, 'Are you sure you're comfortable with that?'" says this person. "And they would bring in the quants!" And so, the matching strategy came to mean that Countrywide repeatedly loosened its guidelines for both the loans its own sales force originated and the loans it purchased from others, according to the SEC. Other subprime companies, for instance, adopted a loan strategy called risk layering, in which two or three different risks—no-doc, adjustable-rate, credit-impaired

---

* The case was scheduled to go to trial in October 2010, shortly before the publication of this book.

borrower—were wrapped together in one loan. These were risks that were never meant to coexist, and blending them greatly increased the chances of default. Yet since Countrywide's competitors were making risk-layered loans, Countrywide made them, too. It was madness. "Subprime one was just really high rates for borrowers with bad credit," says Josh Rosner. "That's different than the loan itself being a bad product."

"When you are the biggest, you have a responsibility to not give credibility to bad products—whether you're Countrywide, Fannie, Freddie, or any of the big mortgage lenders out there that were doing this," says a former Countrywide executive. Countrywide did just the opposite: by mimicking the products of competitors, no matter how dangerous, it gave them an imprimatur they didn't deserve.

There was a final problem with the company's subprime guidelines. If a borrower couldn't meet the guidelines, Countrywide would try to make the loan work anyway. This was not some rogue effort by aggressive branch managers to sidestep the rules. It *was* the rule: Countrywide called it the exception pricing system. Every lender had some version of this, but, according to the SEC, Countrywide "liberally" used its exception policy for loans that didn't fit into even the loosened guidelines. One former Countrywide executive says that Mozilo told the sales force to listen to Sambol, not Kurland; in its complaint, the SEC corroborates that in part, saying the company's rules about a kind of subprime loan known as an 80/20—the customer took out two loans in order to borrow 100 percent of the money needed to purchase a home—"were ignored by the production division."

In 2005, John McMurray, Countrywide's chief risk officer, wrote in an e-mail to Sambol, "As a consequence of [Countrywide's] strategy to have the widest product line in the industry, we are clearly out on the 'frontier' in many areas." The "frontier," McMurray added, had "high expected default rates and losses."

Those in the industry could see the change, even if Mozilo still refused to acknowledge it. Says a former industry executive: "Roland [Arnall] thought he [Angelo] was a hypocrite. It was an odd thing, Countrywide acting holier than thou. Countrywide was in the same game."

But to the outside world, the picture couldn't have seemed more glorious. By the end of 2004, Countrywide had leaped in front of Wells Fargo to be the nation's largest mortgage company. It originated a stunning $363 billion in mortgages that year. A year later, Countrywide originated almost $500 billion in mortgages. Sambol and other executives had taken to telling investors that Countrywide expected to originate $1 trillion worth of mortgages by 2010. They were halfway there.

———— ✤ ————

It was pointless to expect Washington to do anything to stop the abuses that characterized subprime two. In addition to Ned Gramlich, the only people in Washington who seemed to care about the issue were Senator Paul Sarbanes and Sheila Bair, the assistant secretary of the Treasury for financial institutions during the first few years of the Bush administration. But as a Democratic senator, Sarbanes had no leverage in the Republican-dominated Senate. And Bair, a moderate Republican from Kansas, didn't have much leverage, either. Realizing that pushing for new regulation was futile, she tried to get the industry to write a voluntary code of conduct for subprime lending. She chaired a big meeting that included Ameriquest, Citibank, J.P. Morgan, Countrywide, and others. But that idea soon petered out. "The problem," says one former regulator, "is that they were all making too much money."

So it was left to local officials to try and stop the abuses. And try they did. But at every level, those who took on the lending machine found themselves stymied by lender lobbying and federal bank regulators who actively—and successfully—sought to thwart local officials. It would be hard to imagine a more telling example of how the nation's bank regulators had become captive to the institutions they were charged with regulating.

Take Cleveland, which had been hit hard by the first subprime bubble and feared the consequences of a second bubble. In 2001, the city council passed a law banning balloon payments and mandating counseling for borrowers who were seeking certain loans. The law also required lenders to submit key information, including the total points and fees paid on each loan. In response, the Ohio state legislature, which was controlled by Republicans, passed its own, much meeker law, saying that only the state had the right to regulate lending. Mortgage lobbyists proudly acknowledged that they had largely written the state's bill. Then a group of lenders called the American Financial Services Association sued Cleveland, arguing that the city's law was now illegal. A court ruled in favor of the AFSA in 2003; Cleveland's law was overturned.

That same story played out in Oakland, Los Angeles, and elsewhere. Communities tried to strengthen state laws that had been watered down by lender lobbying, only to face lawsuits from the AFSA. The AFSA dubbed this its "municipal litigation" program; in most of these battles, the AFSA's most public spokesman was its Ameriquest representative. From 2002 to 2006 Ameriquest, its executives, and their spouses and business associates donated at least $20.5 million to state and federal political groups, according to the *Wall Street Journal*.

States that wanted to do something about subprime lending didn't fare much better. In the fall of 2002, Georgia governor Roy Barnes, a Democrat, signed into law the Georgia Fair Lending Act, which prohibited loans from being made without regard for the borrower's ability to repay. It also provided "assignee liability," meaning that the investment bank that securitized the loans—and the investors who wound up owning the mortgage—could both be sued if the loan violated the law. The outcry was instantaneous. Mozilo called the new law "egregious." Ameriquest said that it could no longer do business in Georgia. A group of Atlanta lenders filed a class action lawsuit. The rating agencies jumped in on the side of the bankers, with S&P and Moody's both saying they would no longer rate bonds backed by loans that were originated in Georgia.

But the most crushing blow came from the national regulators—especially the Office of Thrift Supervision and the OCC, which oversaw roughly two-thirds of the assets in national banks. Siding with the banks against the states and cities that were trying to stop abusive lending, the two federal regulators asserted something called preemption. What that meant, in effect, was that institutions that were regulated by the OTS or the OCC were immune from state or local laws. In theory, preemption makes sense—companies always want to be able to play by one set of rules, instead of having to adapt to fifty different laws in fifty different states. Federal preemption basically says that federal rules always take precedence over state rules.

But in this case, there was no meaningful federal rule. "[N]either of these federal agencies replaced the preempted state laws with comparable, binding consumer protection regulations of their own," wrote Patricia McCoy, the director of the University of Connecticut's Insurance Law Center, in 2008. And the preemption doctrine was never intended to give banks free rein to make abusive loans to people who had no chance of being able to pay them back. But perhaps the most important thing was the message it sent. "It gave lenders a sense that they had a protector in the government," says Prentiss Cox, who ran the consumer enforcement division in the Minnesota attorney general's office until 2005.

Preemption also became a recruiting tool for the regulators trying to expand their own empires. Incredibly, American financial institutions had the ability, under certain circumstances, to switch regulators—an idea that had long been promoted by Alan Greenspan. His essential belief was that having multiple, overlapping regulators was good for the system because, as he once put it in testimony before the Senate banking committee, it served as a "valuable restraint on any one regulator conducting inflexible, excessively rigid policies." ("The present structure," he added, "provides banks with a method . . . of shifting their regulator, an effective test that provides a limit on the arbitrary position or excessive rigid posture of any one regulator.") Jerry Hawke, the comptroller of the currency, took that idea a step further— rather than sit back and wait for institutions to come to the OCC, he actively talked up the "advantages" of being regulated by the agency he headed. In early 2002, for instance, the OCC issued a press release with this startling headline: "Comptroller Calls Preemption a Major Advantage of National Bank Charter." A former regulator says that he viewed his job as "a salesman for the national charter. He would make sales calls. The OCC used preemption as its advertising."

Just about a year after the OCC first began trumpeting the virtues of preemption, the OTS joined in, announcing that the thrifts it oversaw were exempt from the key provisions of Georgia's new law. The OTS's move helped make the state's law moot. "Either we will have an unlevel playing field and a rush of people to go get OTS charters or we will see a leveling out of the playing field by having the state legislature" change the law, said a spokesman for the mortgage lobby. Sure enough, by the spring of 2003, the law had been replaced by a much weaker one.

The OTS had long asserted preemption when states passed laws that it didn't think its thrifts should have to follow. But in early 2004, the OCC went all in, decreeing that *all* institutions under its watch would be exempt from *all* state and local laws aimed at predatory lending.

After Wachovia moved its mortgage company into its federally chartered bank in order to take advantage of the OCC's preemption policy, the state of Michigan argued that it should still be able to regulate Wachovia's local lending unit. Wachovia sued. The OCC filed a supporting brief. The fight went all the way to the Supreme Court, which in 2007 sided with Wachovia.

And so it went. New Jersey, which passed a predatory lending law in the fall of 2003, repealed it a year later after the lending community, along with the rating agencies, followed the Georgia playbook. In New York, the OCC asserted preemption when then attorney general Eliot Spitzer simply tried to get data from national banks in order to see if they were complying with fair-lending laws. "I think the reality is that the refusal to permit our inquiry, and the assistance of the OCC in helping the banks stop it, was symptomatic of a world where nobody wanted to look at anything," Spitzer later said.

John Dugan, who replaced Hawke in 2004 as comptroller of the currency, would later argue that national banks were only a small part of the problem. He wasn't completely wrong; by the OCC's calculation, national banks originated 12.1 percent of nonprime loans between 2005 and 2007. But his argument missed the larger point. Preemption created competition between the OCC and the OTS—and the OTS, which regulated institutions like Indy-Mac and WaMu, was indisputably a weaker regulator. Secondly, preemption meant that even the state-chartered lenders didn't have to curb their abuses, because states were reluctant to pass or enforce strict rules for their institutions that federally regulated institutions were allowed to duck. Says Kevin Stein, the associate director of the California Reinvestment Coalition: "Banks said, 'We don't have to comply.' The OCC said, 'They don't have to comply.' The state legislatures said, 'If we can't pass a law that regulates federally chartered banks operating in our state, then we're not going to regulate state-chartered lenders, because then they can't compete.' It was a legislative and regulatory race to the bottom."

Finally, subprime loans continued to make their way, unchecked, into the national banking system, thanks to securitization. It really didn't matter who originated them. States had no way of cutting off that all-important funding source. And the national regulators, with their energy focused on making sure that "their" institutions were free from pesky state laws, idly stood by.

What none of the regulators could see was the most obvious fact of all: if cities and states all over the country felt the need to enact their own laws— as twenty-five states, eleven localities, and the District of Columbia had by 2004, according to a GAO report—didn't that suggest there was a problem that needed fixing? Even the FBI seemed to think so. In October 2004, Chris Swecker, the assistant director of the criminal investigative unit of the FBI, told Congress that "mortgage fraud is pervasive and growing." He explained, "The potential impact of mortgage fraud on financial institutions and the stock market is clear. If fraudulent practices become systemic within the mortgage industry and mortgage fraud is allowed to become unrestrained, it will ultimately place financial institutions at risk and have adverse effects on the stock market. Investors may lose faith and require higher returns from mortgage-backed securities." And *still* the regulators remained unconcerned.

There was one halfhearted effort to enact a national law to curb some of the subprime lending abuses. But while some lenders, including Ameriquest and New Century, did want national legislation to avoid the constant need to beat back state and local laws, the powerful Mortgage Bankers Association didn't put its weight behind a law. One former lobbyist says that the deciding factor was Angelo Mozilo, who told him, "No regulator is going to tell me what kind of products I can offer." According to the *Wall Street Journal*, Countrywide spent $8.7 million between 2002 and 2006 on political donations, campaign contributions, and lobbying to defeat antipredatory lending legislation. Old-school Republicans always felt, here's the channel of commerce and here are the curbs, says Chris Hoyer, who runs the plaintiffs' firm James Hoyer in Tampa, Florida. "Go over them, and we'll kill you. As soon as someone starts to cheat to get market share, and their market share gets bigger, well, guys are gonna cheat to keep and get market share. That's why you have old-school rules. Bad shit happens if you let the curbs down."

—❧—

For the few who remember the old world of mortgages, and the concept of risk, those were surreal days. Dave Zitting, an old-fashioned mortgage banker with a homespun style, runs the Arizona-based Primary Residential, which makes mortgages across the country. Zitting started in mortgage banking in 1988, when he was eighteen, and aside from one year spent bagging groceries, he's never done anything else. He grew up in a world where making a loan was all about the four Cs—credit, collateral, capacity, and character. "We thought of a loan like an airplane," he says. "It couldn't fly unless it had all four parts." As he watched the growing insanity, he says he went from feeling scared to leave a C out to thinking, "What good am I? Have I just been fooling myself that I'm doing a job? Holy shit, maybe these guys are on to something—maybe paying for a home has nothing to do with the four Cs." When he started in business, there were three loan products. By 2005, there were six hundred. The rule, Zitting says, was "Breathe on a mirror, and if there's fog, you got the loan."

In 2005, Zitting began to dip his toe into the subprime market, although he insisted on tight controls. Every subprime loan that was offered at a branch was underwritten again at headquarters. He still remembers the day in June 2005 he got a call from a wholesaler who bought his company's loans. This wholesaler was "one of the largest organizations on the planet." (Zitting, who is still in the business, won't name the company, other than to say, "They're not around anymore.") They flew him to their headquarters because they wanted to talk to him. Around a conference table sat a dozen men in suits. "They said, 'Dave, what's going on? Your company sells us the lowest amount of approved loans of anyone we do business with,'" Zitting recalls. Because Zitting used this company's software, they could see that their system was approving loans that Zitting was then rejecting at headquarters.

"Oh, it's simple," Zitting told them. "We check the credit at corporate, and not a lot make it through."

"That's why we flew you out," one of the suits responded. "We don't like that. You need to trust our system, and if you do, your volume will go up by leaps and bounds."

"How do I know the borrower will pay?" Zitting asked.

"You don't need to worry about that," they responded.

The next day, Zitting says, he got the "trade tapes" for the subprime loans he was selling, which showed the prices various buyers were willing to pay. June had been a big month for him: Primary Residential had underwritten $9 million of subprime loans. Usually, the offer was close to what the buyer had been promising verbally, but this day, the offer was surprisingly low. So Zitting called up the guy he dealt with. "I said, 'Something is screwed up in the secondary market,'" he recalls. "He said, 'I've been fielding those calls all day.'" It was a moment when the subprime market was tightening up, almost as if the bubble was coming to an end. Although the moment didn't last very long, it was enough for Zitting.

"Dave," the man said. "I like you. Get out."

"Excuse me?" Zitting replied. He thought to himself, "I just came from a meeting where people were telling me not to turn down loans."

The man said, "If you ever say I said this, I'll deny it, but if you want your company to be around, you will not fund another subprime loan. There is going to be a bloodbath."

And so, Zitting says, he called an emergency board meeting and he shut down his tiny subprime business, even though his firm had just spent $400,000 buying some necessary software. "All my friends in the business were laughing all the way to the bank," he says. Over the next two years, he watched his business pals make millions and buy private jets and mansions. He remembers thinking to himself, "What the crap?"

11

Goldman Envy

Goldman Sachs went public on May 4, 1999, ending a 130-year partnership and ushering in a new era, with shareholders to answer to, a board of directors to provide oversight, and a chief executive officer instead of a senior partner. Even at a time when Internet IPOs were all the rage, Goldman's public offering stood out. The stock was priced at $53 a share, but it opened at $76—the opening was delayed an hour because the demand was so strong. By day's end, it stood at $70 a share, giving it a market valuation of $33 billion. The $3.6 billion the company raised in the offering made it the second largest IPO ever. The *average* take for the 350 former and current partners who owned most of Goldman's stock was $63.6 million. Senior partner–turned-CEO Jon Corzine held shares that were suddenly worth $305 million. Hank Paulson, who would become CEO within days of the IPO, had a stake worth $289 million. One Wall Street competitor told *BusinessWeek*, "To have priced this much paper—as a nontechnology stock—is incredible."

To an outsider, the Goldman IPO must have seemed like a no-brainer. But people connected to the firm knew that the act of going public had been the culmination of a long struggle that had left many scars. As early as 1986 Bob Rubin and Steve Friedman, who were still co-heads of the fixed-income department—but were already pushing hard to reshape the Goldman culture—floated the idea of an IPO. It got nowhere. Over the next five or six years, the subject would occasionally bubble up, sometimes in small discussions, sometimes at firm-wide meetings, but the resistance to an IPO from the majority of the partners (and former partners, who retained an ownership stake in the firm even after they retired) remained strong. Some feared it would destroy what made Goldman special; some worried that they would be disadvantaged compared to other partners who had larger stakes; some didn't want to see Goldman's financials—and their compensation—printed in the newspapers.

In truth, however, Goldman badly needed to go public. Merrill Lynch, Lehman, and Morgan Stanley were already public companies, as were most other big Wall Street firms. Big, publicly held banks like Citibank and J.P. Morgan were Goldman competitors. Transformational deals were taking place that were reshaping Wall Street, and those deals used stock as currency. Wall Street firms that went public suddenly had what Charles Ellis, the Goldman historian, calls "substantial permanent capital." They could take more risk. They could grow more rapidly. They were no longer reliant on the partners' capital. Firms that didn't go public would, in all likelihood, be left behind.

When Corzine became senior partner in 1994, he made it his mission to persuade his partners about the necessity of an IPO. In this he succeeded. The deal was originally supposed to happen in the fall of 1998, but had to be postponed, embarrassingly, when Goldman got caught up in the Russian crisis and the collapse of Long-Term Capital Management. Even when the IPO finally took place the following spring, it was not without internal turmoil. Shortly before it finally went off, Corzine was ousted in a palace coup, replaced by Paulson. (Although the change in leadership was announced prior to the offering, Corzine stayed on until the IPO was completed.) And John Whitehead, he of the famous fourteen business principles, wrote an anguished letter to all the Goldman partners: "I don't find anyone who denies that the decision of many of the partners, particularly the younger men, was based more on the dazzling amounts to be deposited in their capital accounts than on what they felt would be good for the future of Goldman Sachs."

The IPO was a critical turning point for Goldman Sachs. Over time, its culture *did* change, as the company—you couldn't really call it a firm anymore—became focused on such measures as return on capital, stock performance, and growth. A firm where senior partners used to say "Trees don't grow to the sky" began instead to talk about aggressive goals for return on equity. The trading side of the firm—for which "substantial permanent capital" was its lifeblood—eventually overwhelmed the investment banking side, in terms of profits, stature, and ethos.

And starting in the early 2000s, Goldman, having adjusted to life as a public company and having transformed itself into a money machine, went on a run the likes of which has rarely been seen in the annals of corporate America. Its 2003 revenues were $16 billion. They rose to $21 billion in 2004,

$25 billion in 2005, and nearly $38 billion in 2006—more than double what it had been just three years before. Its market cap that year topped $88 billion. Somehow, Goldman always seemed to be in the sweet spot of every market. Somehow, Goldman always seemed to react to big market shifts faster than anyone else. Somehow, Goldman never seemed to make a wrong move.

But nobody could quite say how. As Goldman began generating most of its revenue from trading, it became impossible for outsiders to see how Goldman was making its money. Trading can mean a lot of things. It can mean acting as a market maker or trading for one's own account—or both. It can mean treating clients fairly or "ripping their faces off," as traders sometimes put it. It can mean trading plain vanilla bonds or peddling complex derivatives deals. Competitors began to whisper that Goldman had become increasingly ruthless, increasingly cutthroat, and increasingly concerned only about its own bottom line—and its bonuses. "They'd cut your ear off for a nickel, rip your throat out for a quarter, sell their grandmother for a penny, and sell two grandmothers for two pennies!" groused one private equity executive.

The rest of Wall Street watched Goldman's metamorphosis with a mixture of envy, frustration, and resentment. But even as Goldman's peers questioned and criticized its transformation, they also tried to copy it. The money—both the profits the firm produced and the paychecks its partners got—made Goldman the firm that everyone else had to keep up with. And to the outside world, it looked like they had become like Goldman. They all embraced risk taking and they all began to produce outsized profits. And yet the crisis would show that they weren't like Goldman at all.

∞

In his memoir, *On the Brink*, Paulson recalls the moment when he went to talk to Corzine after the coup had been completed. Corzine had just learned his fate; he'd been informed by John Thain, Goldman's CFO and Corzine's close friend. (In 2007, Thain was named chief executive of Merrill Lynch; during the worst weekend of the financial crisis, he negotiated its merger with Bank of America.) "Hank, I underestimated you," said Corzine, according to Paulson. "I didn't know you were such a tough guy."

In fact, there was a lot about Hank Paulson that was surprising. He was a devout Christian Scientist, whose worst vice was too many Diet Cokes. Despite a nine-figure net worth, he inveighed against conspicuous consumption. He was almost absurdly frugal, a trait he inherited from his father, an

Illinois jeweler. He and his wife, Wendy, whom he married during his second year at Harvard Business School, were avid conservationists and fanatical bird-watchers. Though they obviously lived in New York, the Paulsons' homestead was in the Midwestern prairie, on a farm in Barrington, Illinois. It was where Paulson had grown up.

As a leader, Paulson was cut from a very different cloth than, say, Bob Rubin. He once told his alumni magazine that "I'm not an inspirational leader. I'm just not." He didn't lead by charm, or by leading people to his way of thinking by asking, "What do you think?" Rather, he was a force of nature, and his management style was marked by a kind of brutal pragmatism. His preferred mode was revving into action rather than sitting back, waiting, and patiently strategizing. He was direct to a fault, utterly lacking the verbal slickness that dissembling requires. At about six foot two with a build that still mildly resembled the Dartmouth football player he'd once been, and a gravelly voice to boot, Paulson had an aggressiveness about him that made people think he was much bigger than he was, and which could intimidate people into silence. These qualities also led some people to underestimate Paulson, as Corzine had. But doing so was a mistake: he had a mind that was surprisingly detail-oriented, nuanced—and clever.

He also had an astonishing work ethic. "Hank is a heat-seeking missile," says a former Goldman partner. "If you say Motorola might do a financing, he calls Motorola seven thousand times. He doesn't stop." (Paulson would always tell the firm's bankers that they had to have something new to offer with each and every call.) He hated—*hated*—losing, whether he was on the ski slopes or trying to land a deal.

Unlike his predecessor, Corzine, or his eventual successor, Lloyd Blankfein, Paulson was an investment banker, not a fixed-income trader; he had spent the early part of his career doing banking deals out of Goldman's Chicago office. (Prior to joining Goldman, Paulson had served as an assistant to John Ehrlichman in the Nixon administration.) He became a partner in 1982, eight years after joining the firm, rising to be co-head of the firm's investment banking department and then its chief operating officer before taking over as CEO in 1999.

Investment banker though he was, Paulson did not try to turn back the clock. He saw clearly that trading and fixed income weren't just the future of the firm—they were the present. The last hurrah for the investment bankers at Goldman had been the Internet bubble, which burst in early 2000, not long after Paulson took control of the firm. When it collapsed, the business changed in ways that hurt Goldman. Clients demanded low-priced loans in exchange for banking business, and Goldman found itself at a deep disadvantage, up against full-service banks like Citi and J.P. Morgan. Paulson had to lay off nearly three thousand employees and reduced his old investment banking division by 10 percent. A sentimentalist he was not. Never again would investment banking—the raising of capital for companies—be a sizable component of Goldman's results.

In fact, in the years after Paulson took over, the investment bankers who had risen to the top of the firm—and were jockeying to be Paulson's heir apparent—were pushed aside. Thain, for instance, left to run the New York Stock Exchange. By 2003, it was clear that Paulson's heir apparent was a trader: Lloyd Blankfein, who ran the fixed-income, currency, and commodities division. In June of that year, Blankfein, then forty-nine, became a Goldman board member; in December, he was named president and chief operating officer. (Paulson, however, always made a point of saying he wasn't going anywhere. "There is no fear, and for those who want me to go, no hope," he told *Fortune* in 2004.)

Blankfein had joined Goldman via its acquisition of J. Aron, the commodities trading firm. An up-by-his-bootstraps kid from the Bronx who put himself through Harvard and Harvard Law, Blankfein had joined J. Aron as a gold salesman in 1981, the same year Goldman bought the firm. The two organizations couldn't have been more different. While Goldman was becoming a white-shoe firm, J. Aron was a tough, street-savvy, highly entrepreneurial trading shop—"street fighters," in the words of Dennis Suskind, the former J. Aron executive who hired Blankfein. It had the classic traders' rough-and-tumble culture. Blankfein himself later joked that at J. Aron "we didn't have the word 'client' or 'customer,' we had counterparties—and that's because we didn't know how to spell the word 'adversary.'" For years, J. Aron had its own separate elevator bank at Goldman's headquarters at 85 Broad Street, preventing the staffs from intermingling. "It created a feeling inside J. Aron of 'us against the world,'" says a former Goldman managing director.

As soon as Goldman acquired J. Aron, profits plummeted. Despite being new to the firm, Blankfein played a key role in rebuilding it. He proved that he had a sixth sense about making money and a rare ability to manage traders. His power began to grow. In 1997, he became co-head of Goldman's entire fixed-income department. As he rose, he lost weight (about fifty pounds), quit smoking, and shaved his beard. He also repurposed his rapier-sharp wit into an engaging, self-deprecating sense of humor. Says a former

Goldman trader: "Lloyd got really refined, but he used to be just a killer." Blankfein had all the verbal dexterity Paulson lacked, and although he wasn't physically prepossessing, tough-talking trader types were drawn to him. One partner described it as a bit of a "sun god phenomenon."

As Blankfein rose, he pushed hard to complete the transformation that had begun under Rubin and had accelerated under Paulson. What this meant, broadly speaking, was that Goldman no longer sat on the sidelines dispensing advice. The new Goldman was at the center of the action. It had a proprietary trading operation and a large private equity business. It used its money to invest alongside clients, to get trades done—and, sometimes, to compete with clients or trade against them. In the trading business, Goldman wasn't just hedging its risk, but actively seeking to profit for its own account. In other words, instead of trying to avoid conflicts of interest with clients, Goldman embraced them—and made money from them. It was an attitude that one competitor in 2004 described as "somewhere between mercenary and pragmatic." Hedge fund managers and private equity executives alike complained that while they no longer trusted the firm, they did business with Goldman because they had to—the firm was so dominant and so much better at everything than everyone else that you pretty much had no choice. By 2004, trading accounted for 75 percent of Goldman's profits, while investment banking had shrunk to about 6 percent. Soon there was a widespread cliché: Goldman was just a giant hedge fund that was engaged in proprietary trading and investing for its own account.

Goldman always insisted that it had something no hedge fund had: customers. And that was true. As Goldman's chief financial officer, David Viniar, explained it on a 2003 call, "There is a small percentage of our trading that is purely proprietary and there is a small percentage that is purely customer driven. But the great majority of what we do will be driven by trading with customers where customers ask us to do a transaction, or we'll hedge something for them and then we may hold a position for a while or we may lay it off in pieces to the market. It's very hard to break out what is proprietary and what is customer."

And when Blankfein insisted that nothing had changed and that Goldman recognized that its success was due to its client franchise, well, that was true in a way, too. It was customers that instigated the transactions that put Goldman at the center of the action. Goldman might earn a fee from a deal or make its money by putting its own capital to work as part of the deal, or both. It might be on the other side of a trade in order to satisfy a client, to offset another risk elsewhere in its book, or because Goldman thought the other side was where money could be made. The many facets of Goldman's involvement might help clients, because it might get a trade done that would otherwise be difficult, or it might hurt them in ways that were hard to see from the outside. Or maybe both. At one point, Goldman's bankers—whom Blankfein began to refer to as the "front of the house," meaning they were the salespeople for the firm's products—were told that they should sell more derivatives. But if a banker asked Goldman's foreign exchange desk for a price on a currency swap, neither the banker nor the client had any way of knowing how much profit margin the trading desk was building in. Was the client still a client to whom Goldman owed some sort of responsibility, or was the client now merely a counterparty? In this new era, Goldman's first duty was to its own bottom line, which accrued to its shareholders. Clients were a means to that end, not an end in and of themselves.

Goldman's client franchise gave it another big advantage: customer trades gave the firm extraordinary insight into what was happening in the market. Blankfein would speak of being "so close to clients that you can see the pattern better than anyone else." What he meant, although he didn't put it this way, was that Goldman had become the house in the casino: it could see all the cards, whereas the other players could see only their own hands.

Goldman always defended its transformation as not only smart, but necessary. At a meeting of managing directors in London in the fall of 2007, Blankfein told the assembled crowd that, without the change, "we would have been irrelevant." And if that was an overstatement, it was certainly true that Goldman would have been a far smaller firm. But it was also true that Goldman's single-minded focus on maximizing profits made its partners extraordinarily wealthy. In 2003, Paulson made $21.4 million while Blankfein made $20.1 million; in 2004, the men made $29.8 million and $29.5 million respectively, according to company filings. Not very long ago, a million-dollar payday was considered a sterling year. Now bonuses of $5 million, $10 million, $15 million were not uncommon.

And the more Goldman grew, and the more the men at the top of Goldman earned, the more jealous the rest of the Street became.

There was one key way in which Goldman Sachs *didn't* change—and this had as much to do with its success as the many ways in which it did change. Goldman Sachs practiced risk management with an unblinking rigor that no other firm on Wall Street came close to matching—not even J.P. Morgan, which had practically invented modern risk management. The firm most certainly did not take VaR—or any other modern risk model—as gospel; a former risk manager says the phrase "The model says so" was potentially a firing offense. When it came to managing risk, Goldman had what can only be called a kind of humility, a belief that the model was only as good as its inputs and that faith in the model had to be balanced with the informed judgment of human beings. Goldman understood that risk could bring rewards, yes, but it could also bring disaster.

There were several specific things that the firm did differently than its peers. Goldman was a stickler for using what's known as mark-to-market accounting, meaning that it marked its books, every day, at the price at which securities traded in the market. CFO David Viniar traced this discipline to the old Goldman Sachs partnership. "People came into the partnership at a certain value, and they left the partnership at a value," he'd say. If a trader said there wasn't a price for a particular position, Goldman might force him to sell a little bit, just to see what the price was. There was no pretending.

Goldman also carefully monitored its access to cash, which is critical for an investment bank. Unlike commercial banks, which have government-insured deposits, investment banks are wholesale funded, which basically means they have to constantly raise capital in the markets. If the markets shut down for an extended period of time, they're dead. That's why Goldman kept what was basically a piggy bank full of short-term securities—$40 billion in 2004—set aside in case of emergency. "We asked how much money, under the most adverse conditions, could disappear on any given day," Paulson writes in his memoir. That was very different from the VaR standard for calculating potential daily losses. VaR assumed normal markets rather than adverse ones.

There were also several squishier aspects to Goldman's approach to risk management. At most Wall Street firms, the back office—made up of the controllers and risk managers and accountants—is a kind of no-man's-land. Back office employees don't produce revenue, are paid less, and are generally treated like inferiors. But at Goldman, this organization was called "the Federation," and it was powerful. It included a separate group of controllers who independently checked traders' marks. At its helm sat Viniar, who himself sat on Goldman's privileged thirtieth-floor executive suite, right next to Paulson and Blankfein.

But the single most important thing was this: at Goldman, people talked to each other, all the time, about what was going on in the firm and on the trading desks—both the good and the bad. Viniar once joked that his teen-age son said to him about Gary Cohn—Blankfein's longtime consigliere, who became chief operating officer and president in 2006—"You two are like camp counselors. You talk to Gary more than me or Mom." Says a former trader who once had to confess big losses to Cohn: "I told him bad stuff and he handled it. If the guy who ran a desk told the president of most other firms the news I gave Gary, he wouldn't handle it." Information didn't get stuck in silos, and because Blankfein came from the trading business, he could have a conversation with traders and understand it. Those simple acts—a trader telling his manager that something was wrong, the executive understanding what the trader was saying—would turn out to be disconcertingly rare among Wall Street's highly paid and supposedly accomplished elite.

A mile or so north of Goldman's Wall Street offices, in a high-rise complex a stone's throw from Ground Zero, stood the headquarters of another venerable Wall Street institution, one with a name that, to most Americans, was far better known than Goldman Sachs. This firm was Merrill Lynch. It had been founded in 1914 by an intense, ambitious stockbroker named Charlie Merrill, whose notion of how to succeed on Wall Street was completely different from anyone else's at the time. Merrill's idea—nay, his lifelong crusade—was to sell stocks and bonds to the American middle class. For most of its history, Merrill made its money by "bringing Wall Street to Main Street," a phrase its founder coined. Merrill Lynch was the "Thundering Herd" that was "Bullish on America." It had brokerage offices all over the country and employed, at its peak, some sixteen thousand brokers. Merrill's core brokerage division was a good, solid, profitable business. This was especially true after 1982, when the combination of a long bull market and legal changes that caused people to begin investing for their own retirement turned tens of millions of middle-class Americans into investors.

Merrill had a fixed-income division and an investment banking division. It had equity analysts who were highly rated by *Institutional Investor*, the arbiter of such things. It had businesses that ranked high on the "League Tables." And it had been an absolute trailblazer in going public, which it did in 1971, only the second firm to do so. (The first was the much smaller Donaldson, Lufkin & Jenrette.) Yet it was never held in the same esteem as Morgan Stanley and Goldman Sachs. Goldman, especially, made so much more money—and with so many fewer people! It dealt with sexy hedge funds and counterparties rather than middle-class Americans. By the early 2000s, there was no firm suffering from a worse case of Goldman envy than Merrill Lynch.

The primary reason for this was that, in 2002, Merrill Lynch elevated its president, E. Stanley O'Neal, to be the new CEO. O'Neal had joined Merrill as a trader on the junk bond desk in 1987, when he was thirty-five. Proud, prickly, intolerant of dissent, and quick to take offense at perceived slights, O'Neal had never worked as a stockbroker, and had no particular affection for the business that had long been Merrill's heart and soul. His burning ambition was to change Merrill. He wanted to transform its "Mother Merrill" culture, which he viewed as bloated and soft—"not adequate to the times," he once told a colleague—and he wanted to put new emphasis on trading, especially fixed-income trading, where the fat profits lie. Under O'Neal, Merrill got into the business of lending money to private equity firms. It boosted its proprietary trading desk. It greatly expanded its commodities trading business. And it bulked up its mortgage desk. Most of all, O'Neal pushed Merrill to take more risks and bigger risks—Goldman Sachs–like risks. After all, isn't that how one made Goldman Sachs–like profits?

Stan O'Neal was the kind of man who could bristle even at comments that were meant as praise, so it is no surprise that he never found the label "African-American CEO" to his liking. Yet his was one of the great African-American success stories in modern business. O'Neal was born in the tiny town of Wedowee, in eastern Alabama, an hour due north of Auburn. It was, says a friend, "a tough town where it was dangerous for black people to look directly at white people"; well into the 1990s one of its prominent citizens publicly crusaded against interracial marriage. O'Neal's grandfather was a slave. His father was a poor farmer who moved his family to Atlanta when Stan was twelve. They lived in a housing project until his father established himself as an assembly line worker at a nearby General Motors plant. After high school, O'Neal was accepted into a work-study program by the General Motors Institute (now known as Kettering University). GM then hired him as a shift foreman upon his graduation, and gave him a merit scholarship when he was accepted at Harvard Business School. Once O'Neal had his MBA, General Motors put him in its treasury department and gave him a series of promotions.

Although he was clearly a comer at GM, O'Neal took a job at Merrill because he felt that it offered him more opportunity. By 1990, he had been put in charge of the junk bond desk, where he quickly impressed the top brass with both his effectiveness and his ruthlessness, something he would continue to do as he made his way up the ladder. As the head of the brokerage division when the Internet bubble burst, he laid off thousands of brokers—without asking his then boss, CEO David Komansky, for permission. As chief financial officer in the late 1990s, he sent Komansky an analysis of the company that was far tougher and more clear-eyed than the Merrill culture was accustomed to—criticizing the firm's low profit margins and concluding that "the root causes of our uncompetitive margins are both structural and cultural." Far from being put off by O'Neal, Komansky was impressed. "The one thing about Stan," Komansky later told *The New Yorker*, "was that he gets things done."

By July 2001, O'Neal had been named president of Merrill Lynch. Komansky had planned to stay on as CEO for a few more years, until he turned sixty-five, but two events forced him out earlier. The first was 9/11. Several Merrill employees died in the attack, and the firm's headquarters were badly damaged. During and after the attacks, O'Neal took charge while Komansky seemed paralyzed. "O'Neal filled the vacuum," recalls one former executive. Concluding that Wall Street was unlikely to recover quickly after 9/11, O'Neal instituted big layoffs. Komansky cautioned him against such a move, fearing a public backlash so soon after the terrorist attacks, but O'Neal had no patience for such thinking.

Secondly, though, O'Neal simply wasn't willing to wait a few more years to become CEO. He was ready now. Before being named president, he'd had rivals for the top job. He outmaneuvered them, and then, as president, pushed them aside. Once he became president, he cultivated key allies in the firm who had ties to board members; they began agitating for O'Neal to take over, arguing that the firm couldn't wait to make the changes O'Neal had in mind. By the end of 2002, Komansky had turned over the reins to O'Neal. Though he had hoped to stay on as board chairman, Komansky soon acceded to O'Neal's demand that he give up that role as well.

Thanks to all the jockeying around O'Neal's ascension, the Merrill Lynch executive suite had become a very political place. His appointment as CEO didn't end the palace intrigue. Strangely, though, the next round of intrigue came not from his many enemies in the firm, but from two of his closest allies. One was Arshad Zakaria, the head of global markets and investment banking. The other, Tom Patrick, who had been Merrill's chief financial officer under Komansky, was effectively O'Neal's number two, though he lacked the title of president. O'Neal had told the board he didn't feel any need to fill the position.

Within a matter of months, Patrick began going behind O'Neal's back to the board, pushing board members to insist that O'Neal name a president and promoting Zakaria for the job. (The reason behind Patrick's ploy has always been a mystery, even to people at Merrill.) Although Zakaria did not openly join Patrick's effort, he knew about the lobbying, and was lurking in the shadows. At least one board member was ready to do Patrick's bidding.

But then, in July 2003, somebody whispered in O'Neal's ear and told him what was going on. O'Neal responded fiercely. He went to the board, laid out what Patrick and Zakaria were doing, and demanded that the board back him—which it did. He then had Patrick escorted from the building. By early August, Zakaria was gone as well.

Almost every executive associated with Merrill Lynch at the time would later point to these firings as a critical event in the O'Neal era—and not for the better. O'Neal had always been insular; he was the kind of man who liked to play golf by himself. Now he became isolated. He had been wary; now he became suspicious of everyone around him. Patrick and Zakaria were extremely competent executives; he replaced them with more pliable lieutenants. He trusted no one but himself.

Although O'Neal didn't realize it, this was not the way to compete with Goldman. Goldman's executive committee members all participated in discussions about all the various businesses. O'Neal, by contrast, insisted that the company's executives speak only to him about their businesses and not discuss the businesses with one another. The Goldman brass insisted on knowing bad news; Merrill executives trembled at the thought of giving O'Neal bad news. Whenever Goldman's CEO had to make an important decision, he consulted with a handful of advisers to solicit their advice. O'Neal rarely asked for input when he was preparing to make a decision, and under no circumstances did he want to be challenged once he had made up his mind.

A few years after the ouster of Patrick and Zakaria, Greg Fleming, one of the few O'Neal lieutenants who had the temerity to disagree with him, was having dinner with him, pressing him on a handful of issues. As the dinner was concluding, O'Neal said, "This is getting too painful."

"Stan, I don't understand what you mean by 'too painful.' I'm just disagreeing with you," replied Fleming.

"I don't think we can have dinner anymore," said O'Neal. They never did.

The Merrill culture, pre-O'Neal, had always been fearful of risk. There was a good reason for this: when the firm got too aggressive, it often got burned. Merrill, after all, was the firm that persuaded Orange County to trade derivatives in the early 1990s, resulting in the county's 1994 bankruptcy—and a huge black eye (and a $30 million fine) for Merrill. In 1987, during the early days of mortgage-backed securities, a Merrill Lynch mortgage trader named Howard Rubin lost $250 million on one trade. That loss was big enough that Merrill stayed away from taking significant risks in the mortgage business for years. A decade later, during the Long-Term Capital Management crisis, Merrill struggled to maintain its liquidity, fearing at one point that its biggest retail money market fund might "break the buck," a potential disaster. (O'Neal had been Merrill's chief financial officer during the LTCM crisis.)

"Anytime a trader lost $50 million," recalls a former Merrill trader, "it was like the Spanish Inquisition." You couldn't take big risks without accepting the possibility of big losses, and that was something that Merrill just couldn't stomach. Taking a lot of risk just wasn't part of its culture.

O'Neal pushed hard to change that, according to former Merrill executives. He was constantly asking the various desks why they weren't taking on more risks. Sometimes when he saw the firm's VaR number, he would actually get angry—it wasn't *high* enough, which to him meant that Merrill wasn't taking the kinds of risks it should be taking. He backed his department heads when they wanted to hire aggressive young turks while getting rid of those who didn't have the risk appetite he was looking for. And he constantly compared Merrill's performance to Goldman's. "You didn't want to be in Stan's office on the day Goldman reported earnings," recalls one of his former lieutenants.

Everybody on Wall Street had a big mortgage desk, Merrill Lynch included. By the time O'Neal became CEO, they were all beginning to focus on underwriting collateralized debt obligations that included at least some percentage of subprime mortgages. With this new CDO market up for grabs, Merrill decided to go all in. Within just a few years, Merrill was the dominant underwriter of CDOs, taking the business from nine CDO deals worth $2.2 billion in 2002 to thirty-eight deals worth nearly $19 billion in 2004. It went from fifteenth in the ranking to first. Between 2002 and 2007, Merrill Lynch underwrote one hundred CDOs, twenty-seven more than runner-up Citigroup. Merrill's management viewed its number one ranking as proof positive it could play with the big boys, and that ranking became something to be preserved at all costs.

The man who had the ultimate authority over the mortgage desk for Merrill Lynch in those days was a veteran trader named Jeff Kronthal. He had spent his career around mortgage-backed securities; while still in his twenties, he had run the mortgage desk for Lew Ranieri at Salomon Brothers. Kronthal had joined Merrill in the late 1980s, just a few years after O'Neal, overseeing its trading desks until the mid-1990s, when he took over its derivatives business. Although he spent much of the 1990s pushing a reluctant Merrill to take more trading risk—he thought its tepid risk limits constrained its ability to make sizable profits—he also had a healthy fear of mortgage-backed securities. He had watched them get increasingly risky over the years. His essential view was that Merrill's role should be to create structures that allowed investors to gain the exposure to risk they wanted to take. But Merrill itself should never assume those risks. "They are things you want to sell, not hold," he used to tell the traders who worked for him.

In O'Neal's push to have the firm take on more risk, Kronthal found himself in a tricky position. He had had a few run-ins with O'Neal over the years, but Patrick and Zakaria, both good friends of his, had persuaded him to stay. Once they were gone, Kronthal didn't have any protectors in the executive suite.

More important, everyone around him was creating CDOs as fast as they could. Kronthal's boss, Dow Kim, headed all of fixed income. "Stan was constantly pounding on him about why we weren't making as much in fixed income as Lehman or Goldman," says a former Merrill executive. As O'Neal pushed Kim, Kim pushed Kronthal.

From below, meanwhile, Kronthal was trying to keep the CDO team under control. That was no small task, either. The team was headed by Chris Ricciardi, an aggressive thirty-four-year-old trader. A decade before, while at Prudential Securities, Ricciardi had been part of a group that had first come up with the idea of bundling mortgages into a CDO. After successful stints at Prudential and then at Credit Suisse, Ricciardi and most of his team joined Merrill Lynch in July 2003, where he quickly ramped up the firm's CDO business. Kronthal and his crew of veteran traders viewed Ricciardi warily. "He was dangerous," says one former Merrill trader. "He didn't care about rules. If one of his managers didn't give him the answer he wanted, he sought out another manager. All he cared about was himself and his team. He was always threatening to leave and take his team with him." Kronthal's belief was: let him go. But Dow Kim thought Merrill needed ten more salesmen just like him. He was exactly the kind of aggressive risk taker that O'Neal wanted at Merrill.

According to someone who did business with him, Ricciardi was surprisingly mild mannered for someone with such an outsized reputation. "He didn't have a lot of flash," this person says. But he was a natural leader, the kind of person who, as a college student, had put together groups that made money painting houses. And, this same person says, "he was very smart and he could articulate a case." One investor recalls looking at an early Ricciardi deal that included credit card receivables as well as mortgage-backed securities. It had a very limited default history. The investor asked what would happen to the security if the credit card defaults started to rise. Ricciardi had no good answer, and the investor walked away from the deal. But Ricciardi still managed to maneuver the rating agencies into giving most of the deal a triple-A rating.

Ricciardi knew exactly what he'd been hired to do. "The strategy has been to be a high-volume underwriter, with a focus on areas that are very popular," he told a trade publication in early 2005. What was popular, of course, was subprime mortgages. To ensure that it had a steady source of subprime mortgages to securitize and then bundle into CDOs, Merrill took a 20 percent stake in Ownit, a mortgage originator founded by Bill Dallas. A Merrill executive joined the Ownit board. By 2006, says Dallas, Merrill was pushing him to make loans that would generate more yield for Merrill's CDOs.

"They never told us to make bad loans," Dallas says now. "They would say, 'You need to increase your coupon'"—meaning make loans with higher yields. "The only way to do that was to make crappier loans." Between the fourth quarter of 2005 and the first quarter of 2006, Ownit went from being a company whose loans were virtually all fully documented to becoming a company that was, in his words, "no-doc-centric. We became more of a subprime lender."

In short order, Merrill would then create mortgage-backed securities out of the mortgages it bought, warehouse the new securities until they could be bundled into a CDO, and negotiate hard with the rating agencies—and tinker with the CDO's structure—to get most of the security labeled triple-A. (E-mails would later reveal at least one instance in which Merrill specifically linked its fee to a high rating.)

Ricciardi and his team picked the firms that would manage the assets in the CDOs once they'd been created, and the investors who bought the tranches. They had big, sophisticated investors all over the globe lined up to buy Merrill's CDO tranches. But Ricciardi was also not above pitching smaller-fry. According to the *Wall Street Journal*, "Merrill distributed some of its riskiest CDO slices through its global network of wealthy private clients." In 2004, at New York's Harvard Club, the *Journal* added, "salesmen described the merits of CDO investing to doctors, hedge-fund managers and businessmen." Merrill's risk managers, meanwhile, would hold regular meetings to try to figure out who Ricciardi was selling his CDOs to and whether the buyer was truly an appropriate investor.

Finally, Ricciardi was in the vanguard of the practice of rebundling the triple-B mezzanine portion of the CDO into new CDOs. Thus would triple-Bs be turned into triple-A tranches, which were much easier to sell. "Ricciardi could find someone to buy any piece of shit," says a former Merrill executive.

Kronthal didn't have any moral objection to the CDO business. Nobody on Wall Street did. But as an old hand at the business, he was keen to make sure that Merrill itself wasn't warehousing too many CDO tranches. For instance, he imposed a $1 billion limit on triple-A tranches that could be held as an investment on Merrill's own books. Largely because of Kronthal's caution, by the spring of 2006, Merrill had around $5 billion or $6 billion in its total exposure to CDOs with mortgage-backed tranches. Most of the exposure consisted of securities Merrill was warehousing until they could be bundled into new CDOs. It was hardly a small number, but it was a manageable one. It didn't put the firm at risk.

In early 2006, Ricciardi suddenly left Merrill. He jumped to Cohen & Co., a firm that managed many of the CDOs that Ricciardi had sold at Merrill. He became the firm's president. For Dow Kim, his departure was a blow. Kim quickly assured the rest of the CDO staff that the firm would do "whatever it takes" to stay number one. He said the same to Stan O'Neal.

A few months later, in April, Merrill's directors and top executives went to Pebble Beach for an off-site. During one of the working sessions, the discussion centered on Merrill's fixed-income department. "The world has changed," O'Neal told the assembled executives, according to several people who were there. Fixed income and credit, he added, were no longer cyclical in nature. There was going to be an ongoing demand for fixed-income products. "We need to continue our ability to take risk and manufacture products," he said.

By then, Kronthal was beginning to fear the mortgage market was becoming overheated. His bosses, starting with O'Neal, felt otherwise. They wanted more people like Ricciardi, not fewer. They wanted to buy a mortgage orig-inator, just like Lehman and some of the other firms had. They wanted to raid other firms to bring in aggressive young talent. Kronthal thought the hour was getting late, and Merrill would be better served pulling back.

At the off-site, Kronthal and his team gave a series of presentations outlin-ing the risks—and the possibilities—in Merrill's various fixed-income desks. In 2005, Kronthal had been Merrill's highest-paid nonexecutive employee, with a bonus of more than $20 million. That sum was a testament to the profits his desks were making at Merrill. To the board that day, Kronthal and his team were portrayed as the graybeards, the seasoned hands who knew how to take smart risks.

Six weeks later, they were all fired.

12

The Fannie Follies

George W. Bush believed in homeownership, too.

In June 2002, nine months after 9/11, the president traveled to Atlanta, where, in an African-American church on the city's south side, he unveiled his homeownership agenda. Entitled "Blueprint for the American Dream," it promoted homeownership among minorities. The administration's goal, Bush said, was to raise the number of minority homeowners by 5.5 million by 2010. "Part of being a secure America is to encourage homeownership," he said, thus making homeownership seem somehow a part of the battle against terrorism.

Sitting in the audience that day was a man named Franklin Delano Raines, the chief executive of Fannie Mae. It was a triumphant moment for Raines, and not only because he was a minority himself—the first African-American CEO of a Fortune 500 company. Along with Leland Brendsel, the chief executive of Freddie Mac, Raines had gone to Atlanta that day at the behest of the White House, which wanted him to be part of the administration's orchestration of the events of that day. (The two men flew back on Air Force One.) For all the controversies that had dogged the GSEs, the new administration seemed to be signaling that it could live with Fannie and Freddie just the way they were. A few months later, at a White House conference on minority homeownership, the president went out of his way to praise Raines's stewardship of Fannie Mae.

And yet, if Raines thought he could rest easily, he was dead wrong. Within a year, the Bush White House would be engaged in a bitter war with Fannie and Freddie. By the end of 2004, the war would cost Raines his job, while Fannie Mae would be forced to restate billions of dollars in earnings in one of the largest accounting scandals in American history.

These events created an envious amount of *Sturm und Drang* in Washington. But ultimately, very little changed. The administration had started the war because it feared that Fannie and Freddie had become so big they posed a systemic risk to the financial system. The White House wanted to force the GSEs to pare back the risks on its books. Yet the "intifada," as Raines would later call it, arguably wound up making matters worse, because it helped push the GSEs into buying riskier mortgages at exactly the wrong time. Just as important, this intense focus on the dangers Fannie and Freddie posed to the system allowed Congress and regulators to turn a blind eye to the systemic risks that were building up, inexorably, in the private market. After all, if clipping the wings of the GSEs was your primary objective, then you wouldn't be inclined to look skeptically at their private competitors, would you?

Frank Raines, as everyone called him, was the quintessential postmodern Horatio Alger; born poor, he attached himself to the meritocracy and rode it for all it was worth. He grew up in Seattle, his father a custodian for the city parks department, his mother a cleaning woman for Boeing, a company whose board Raines would later serve on. After he became Fannie Mae's CEO, Raines liked to recall that his father didn't make enough money to get a thirty-year fixed-rate mortgage. The only way he could buy a home was to pay an exorbitant rate of interest to a hard-money lender.

Raines earned a scholarship to Harvard, where he joined both the Young Democrats *and* the Young Republicans and was named a Rhodes Scholar. After graduating from Harvard Law School, he interned in the Nixon White House and then served in the Carter administration before leaving to become a partner at Lazard Frères, where he spent the next eleven years. Deciding that he had had enough of the nonstop travel that was the life of an investment banker, he quit without knowing what he was going to do next. In 1991, Jim Johnson offered him the vice chairmanship of Fannie Mae, the same job Johnson had held when he was Maxwell's protégé. Raines said yes; Fannie's offices were just a mile and a half from Raines's home in Washington.

Five years later, he jumped back into government, becoming the head of the Office of Management and Budget at the beginning of Bill Clinton's second term. When Raines asked the president how long the job would last, Clinton replied, "Until you balance the budget." Within two years, the Clinton administration had indeed produced a balanced budget, the first in a generation, for which Raines reaped enormous credit. When he returned to Fannie Mae in 1998—with a promise from Johnson that he could soon take it over—his political stock could not have been higher. Charismatic, smart, and tough, he had "extraordinary presence," recalls Andrew Lowenthal, a lobbyist whose clients once included Freddie Mac. "You see him, you meet him, you want to believe him." There were people in Democratic circles who speculated that he might someday become the first black president of the United States.

By all appearances, the Fannie Mae that Raines inherited was a well-oiled machine. It utterly dominated the traditional mortgage market, guaranteeing almost three-quarters of a trillion dollars worth of securitized mortgages, many of them thirty-year fixed-rate loans. It was so powerful that it essentially dictated the terms under which prime borrowers could get such loans. Its other, far more profitable business—buying up mortgages and mortgage-backed securities to keep on its own books—was growing by leaps and bounds. It held, by then, more than half a trillion dollars worth of mortgage assets on its books. Fannie was just beginning to tiptoe into riskier mortgages, but it was doing so cautiously; it didn't care for credit risk. To the extent that subprime mortgages could help the company meet its affordable housing goals, Fannie had better ways to reach those goals—ways that wouldn't dent its profits.

By the end of the 1990s, Fannie and Freddie's combined assets exceeded the GDP of any nation except the United States, Japan, and Germany, according to a research report by Sanford Bernstein. There was even talk—encouraged by the GSEs—that Fannie and Freddie's thirty-year note was going to replace thirty-year U.S. Treasury debt as the United States' benchmark bond.

Then there was the GSEs' regulator, the Office of Federal Housing Enterprise Oversight. It was a nonfactor—woefully understaffed, dependent on Fannie and Freddie for information, and regularly trounced by Fannie's congressional allies on the rare occasions it tried to assert itself. Fannie's capital requirements were minimal. Its leverage was sky high—over 60 to 1. Its earnings were growing steadily, while its stock rose tenfold during the decade. Fannie's executives, their compensation tied to the company's earnings goals, got very rich. It still had critics, of course, but it had proven time and again that it could swat them away like an irritating fly.

Which perhaps explains why, not long after becoming CEO in 1998, Raines met with some of the company's investors and laid out an extraordinary target. He felt confident, he said, that the company could double its earnings per share over the next five years, from $3.23 to $6.46. That number became a kind of mantra within Fannie Mae; even its chief internal auditor—who is supposed to be immune to earnings concerns—once told his troops, "By now, every one of you must have 6.46 branded in your brains. You must be able to say it in your sleep, you must be able to recite it forwards and backwards, you must have a raging fire in your belly that burns away all doubts, you must live, breathe, and dream 6.46. . . . After all, thanks to Frank, we all have a lot of money riding on it."

In retrospect, it is hard to see this target as anything but hubris. For all their power, the GSEs' business model was seriously constrained. Being a government-sponsored enterprise had a few minuses as well as pluses. One of the major drawbacks was that Fannie and Freddie's charters prevented them from diversifying into other businesses. The only business they could be in was the one they already dominated: the secondary market for home mortgages. And with the rate of homeownership approaching 68 percent by 2002 (an all-time high), how much could that market really grow? A former Fannie executive recalls that after Raines announced his new target, "All the vice presidents in the company looked at each other and said, 'How is this going to work?'"

In truth, the only way Fannie Mae could continue its rapid growth was to keep expanding its controversial mortgage portfolio. As you'll recall, there was no particularly good "housing" reason for Fannie Mae to have such a gargantuan portfolio, especially in good times, when there were plenty of buyers of mortgages and mortgage-backed securities. (In bad times, an argument could be made that it was important for Fannie and Freddie to buy up mortgages to keep the mortgage market going. Since the financial crisis, in fact, that is precisely what the GSEs have been doing.) Fannie's critics were mainly worried about the interest rate risk in the portfolio—and the more the portfolio grew, the more the fears grew as well. To hedge that risk, Fannie and Freddie were huge buyers of derivatives, quite likely the biggest in the country. But hedges don't always work, and critics feared that if there was an abrupt shift in interest rates and Fannie began taking big losses, the taxpayers would be the ones picking up the tab. After all, Fannie had come close to the brink many years earlier, before David Maxwell saved the company.

If there was one thing Raines had inherited from Jim Johnson, it was a pugnacious attitude toward anyone who dared criticize Fannie Mae; indeed, it sometimes seemed as if he were trying to outdo his predecessor. "I think

Frank's fear was that he couldn't be tough enough, and he overcompensated," says a former Fannie executive. For his part, Raines would later say, "We never had any illusion at Fannie that we were all-powerful. If we were all-powerful, we wouldn't have had to fight so many battles. All day every day, we felt besieged." As Fannie Mae really did become besieged, so did the ferocity of Fannie's response—to the company's, and the country's, ultimate detriment.

The first real shot across Fannie's bow during the Raines era came even before the Bush administration took office. Toward the tail end of Clinton's second term, Richard Baker, a Republican congressman from Louisiana and a longtime critic of the GSEs, introduced a GSE reform bill.*

Larry Summers, who was by then the Treasury secretary, decided to come out in favor of the reforms. There was no way Baker's bill was going to pass; the combination of a lame-duck Democratic administration, a Republican-controlled Congress, and Fannie and Freddie's political power made that obvious. But Summers wanted to sound the alarm about the portfolio risks. He got the White House to agree, telling Clinton's chief of staff, John Podesta, that although Treasury would testify for the bill, it wouldn't invest any political capital. Maybe, Summers thought, the next administration would pick up the cudgel.

It was strange, in a way. Within the administration, Summers invariably took the Greenspan position that the market was better equipped to recognize and handle risk than Washington regulators. And, like Greenspan, Summers's belief that the market cured all problems blinded him to the systemic risks that were building up.

But he could see all too clearly the risks posed by Fannie and Freddie. For officials like Greenspan and Summers, there was something offensive about the GSEs. The moral hazard that existed in the banking system—and that would be all too obvious during the financial crisis—was something policy makers couldn't see. But the moral hazard posed by Fannie and Freddie? *That* they could see plain as day.

In late 1999, Summers made a speech at a Women in Housing & Finance conference, which included one sentence about Fannie and Freddie: "Debates about systemic risk should also now include government-sponsored enter-

---

* In response, Fannie hired a telemarketing company, which blanketed the Hill with tens of thousands of letters protesting the bill. Some of them turned out to be from dead people. When asked how much the campaign cost, Fannie said that information was "proprietary."

prises, which are large and growing rapidly." That one line got Fannie's attention; Summers got his first taste of Fannie's legendary pushback. Fannie's vice chairwoman, Jamie Gorelick, called Treasury to complain about the "attack." Raines called Summers personally. Both expressed outrage.

A few months later, it was Take Your Daughters to Work Day. Summers brought his two daughters, as one former Treasury executive recalls. Another employee said to them, in an obvious reference to the GSEs, "What would you tell your daddy to do if there are people who are doing a lot of harm, and Daddy could take them on, but they might do Daddy some harm, and nothing he does may do any good?"

"Oh, is Daddy like Rosa Parks?" asked one of Summers's daughters.

Finally, on March 22, 2000, assistant Treasury secretary Gary Gensler testified in favor of Baker's bill on behalf of the administration. Among other things, he said that the U.S. Treasury should consider cutting off the GSEs' $2.5 billion lines of credit with the federal government.

All hell broke loose. At the hearing, Gensler was berated by Fannie's many defenders. Yields on GSE debt rose dramatically, meaning that investors suddenly viewed Fannie and Freddie as riskier bets. This, in turn, reduced the spread Fannie could earn on its portfolio, which threatened Fannie's earnings. Fannie reacted even more intemperately than usual, calling Gensler "irresponsible," "unprofessional," and (of course) antihousing.

Congress quickly rose to Fannie's defense. Within a week, Rick Lazio, the Republican chairman of a key housing subcommittee, announced that he would oppose any legislation that would, as he put it, increase costs to home buyers. Senate Minority Leader Tom Daschle, a Democrat from South Dakota, went on C-SPAN to say that Fannie had done a "phenomenal job" over the years, and "if it ain't broke, don't fix it."

That wasn't quite the end of the story. Behind the scenes, for a period of about a year, the Treasury Department also held a series of unpublicized meetings with Fannie's top executives. The meetings were conducted at Fannie Mae's instigation. In an effort to appease its critics, Fannie Mae had put together a series of "voluntary" initiatives that it hoped to get Treasury to sign off on, which included such measures as disclosing more information about its interest rate risk. It was classic Fannie Mae: keep your friends close and your enemies closer. But the chemistry between Summers and Raines was "horrible," in the words of one former executive. "The two of them were so alike," this person explains. "They were both arrogant, stubborn sons of bitches, and they both viewed themselves as the smartest guy in the room."

Summers simply didn't believe the Fannie team when they explained why it was necessary for Fannie to own that huge portfolio of mortgages. And he absolutely scoffed when Fannie insisted that it received no subsidy and posed no risk to taxpayers. "They made the mistake of insulting his intelligence," says a former Treasury official.

The initiatives turned into a small comedy of errors. Freddie Mac, having gotten wind of Fannie's plans, did an end-around, working out a deal to announce the initiatives with Richard Baker. The weekend before the announcement, however, Fannie Mae discovered that Freddie was going to one-up it. So it joined in and took part in the announcement. But the point of the exercise had always been to get Treasury to sign off on the initiatives, which would have signaled to the marketplace that Treasury was finally aligned with Fannie's business model. That never happened. And without the Treasury on board, the initiatives did little to quell the criticism.

It was pure political calculus that initially caused the Bush administration to decide to leave Fannie and Freddie alone. It's not that the White House didn't understand the issue, or that there weren't a smattering of critics inside the administration. But Fannie also had its internal defenders: the head of the National Economic Council was Steve Friedman, the former Goldman Sachs senior partner who had run the firm with Bob Rubin. He had been on Fannie's board of directors. Besides, Fannie and Freddie could be useful props to help support Bush's homeownership bona fides.

Yet one of the leading Fannie haters in the Bush administration wasn't some anonymous White House economist; he was the head of OFHEO. His name was Armando Falcon Jr. and he was Fannie and Freddie's regulator.

Like Raines, Falcon was a product of the meritocracy. The son of an aircraft technician from San Antonio, Texas, Falcon had gone to the University of Texas law school, and then Harvard's Kennedy School of Government, before landing a job in 1990 as general counsel of the House banking committee. After losing a race for Congress, Falcon was nominated to head OFHEO. He was in his early forties when he ran the agency, a seemingly shy, hesitant man who liked poker and cigars. He lacked the charisma and brilliance of someone like Frank Raines. He was easy to underestimate. As he came to understand just how difficult the GSEs were to deal with—and how powerless OFHEO was to do anything about them—he first became frustrated and then deeply angry.

Every year, it seemed, OFHEO's proposed budget was cut, either by Congress or the White House. When Falcon first took office, he later recalled, he discovered that some risk examinations were being put off because the agency didn't have the manpower to conduct them. The agency estimated that it needed sixty examiners to do its job properly; it had seventeen. OFHEO's entire budget, which ranged between $19 million and $30 million, was less than the total compensation of the four top executives at Fannie and Freddie.

In 2000, the year after he took the job, "Representative Maurice Hinchey bravely offered an amendment on the floor of the House to increase OFHEO's budget," Falcon would later testify. "The amendment was angrily opposed by the chairman of the VA, HUD appropriations subcommittee, who lashed out at me personally for encouraging the amendment." It didn't pass.

Given its live-and-let-live attitude toward the GSEs, the Bush White House was not an early supporter of OFHEO. Nevertheless, in 2002, Falcon decided to initiate a study on the systemic risks posed by the GSEs. It would be hard to imagine a more important topic for OFHEO to tackle. It would also be hard to imagine a topic more likely to inflame Fannie Mae.

By early 2003, OFHEO was set to release its report. In truth, it wasn't all that tough. "The possibility of either Enterprise failing or contributing to a financial crisis [is] remote," it concluded. But it also raised the possibility— small though it was—that Fannie or Freddie could get into trouble and "cause disruptions to the housing market and the financial system."

Most companies would have accepted such mild criticism with, at most, a press release rebuttal. But, according to Falcon, Raines and Fannie Mae immediately went into overkill mode. A few days before the report was set to be issued, Raines called Falcon and asked him not to issue it. "When I reaffirmed my plans," Falcon later said, "he threatened to bring down me and the agency." Fannie lobbyists then called Treasury and other regulatory agencies, asking them to press OFHEO not to release the report. (Raines calls Falcon's allegations "totally made up." Although he called Falcon to tell him that "it was highly unusual for a regulator to issue a report saying its regulated companies might bring down the financial system," he insists there was no threat.)

Fannie was just getting started. February 4, 2003, was the day Falcon had set for releasing the report. He had flown to New York to give a speech outlining its findings. As he waited to give the speech, he got a call from the White House personnel office informing him that the administration was about to announce his replacement. It was none other than Mark Brickell, the former J.P. Morgan derivatives lobbyist. Although Falcon's term still had a year and a half to go, he dutifully wrote a resignation letter. Not surprisingly, the news coverage of Brickell totally drowned out any coverage of OFHEO's report. Falcon was humiliated.

And yet, Falcon wound up keeping his job. In part, Brickell said a few too many impolitic things during his confirmation hearings later that year. But more than that, the political winds were shifting. Whereas it had once been in the administration's interest to play nice with Fannie and Freddie, it was suddenly in the administration's political interest to show it could get tough on the GSEs. Although there was no love lost between Falcon and the Bush administration, the White House realized that his doggedness—and, for that matter, his anger—could be useful. When Brickell withdrew his nomination, the White House decided to stick with Falcon. The war between the GSEs and the White House was on.

∞

It was the Enron scandal that caused the political winds to change. The Enron scandal spooked the White House; Bush had been friends with Enron CEO Ken Lay and had even bestowed on Lay one of his famous nicknames—"Kenny Boy." When the administration looked around in the wake of the Enron debacle to see what other potential business scandal might hurt it, it was hard to miss Fannie and Freddie.

The Enron scandal had another, more practical consequence: it caused Freddie Mac to hire a new accounting firm. Freddie's longtime firm, Arthur Andersen, had been forced out of business after being indicted for its role in the Enron debacle. In the fear-ridden business environment of 2002, Freddie's new accountants at PricewaterhouseCoopers scrubbed Freddie's books and found them seriously wanting. It forced Freddie Mac to restate its earnings going back years. In January 2003, around the same time OFHEO was sending around its report on systemic risk, Freddie Mac announced that it would be restating its earnings "materially" for at least the past two years. The restatement, when it was unveiled six months later, was a stunner: since 2000, Freddie had *understated* its earnings by some $5 billion. (The purpose of the understatement had been to produce smooth earnings growth.) Freddie's entire senior management team had to step down.

Fannie responded to Freddie's problems with astonishing—yet unsurprising—self-righteousness. Raines publicly accused Freddie of causing "collateral damage." The frequently asked questions section on Fannie's Web site included the following statement: "Fannie Mae's reported financial results follow Generally Accepted Accounting Principles to the letter. . . . There should be no question about our accounting."

The Freddie restatement was yet another humiliation for Falcon. Not long before Freddie revealed that it would have to restate its earnings, Falcon had publicly pronounced the company's internal controls "accurate and reliable." Furious at having been so wrong about Freddie Mac, Falcon decided to launch an investigation to see if Fannie had the same problems. OFHEO hired Deloitte & Touche, the big accounting firm, to dig into Fannie's books.

The White House piled on, yanking Bush's presidential appointees from the GSEs' boards. Then, in the fall of 2003, it put its weight behind a bill to toughen regulation of the GSEs—a bill that Fannie's lobbyists managed to water down, causing the White House to pull its support. (The bill failed.) Around the same time, John Snow, the new Treasury secretary, even called for a receivership provision should Fannie or Freddie become insolvent. Amazingly, there was no real procedure in place for reorganizing the GSEs in the event of a bankruptcy. The larger implications were clear: the government was signaling that it would not stand behind Fannie and Freddie's debt.

Some White House aides began to jokingly call the campaign against the GSEs "Operation Noriega," after the strategy the United States used to roust former Panamanian strongman Manuel Noriega. (It bombarded him with loud rock music.) The administration helped spur anti-Fannie and anti-Freddie op-ed columns and editorials. It also got HUD in the act, which announced that it would begin steadily increasing the GSEs' affordable housing goals from 50 percent of their purchases to 56 percent. "It was consciously punitive," says a former Fannie executive. The real significance wasn't so much the percentage increase as it was the fact that the GSEs, for the first time, had specific single-family goals in metropolitan areas. It could no longer use apartment buildings or refinancings to get around the rules. Dow Jones got a copy of an e-mail a Fannie staffer had written: "You just cannot appreciate how truly bad this is—from a purely Republican standpoint," it read, in reference to the new, tougher goals.

Even Greenspan got involved. He and Raines were social friends, but he simply didn't buy Fannie's rationale for its enormous mortgage portfolio. "The explanation they gave was utter nonsense," Greenspan later said.

The White House assault seemed to embolden the Fed chairman, who began speaking out regularly against Fannie and Freddie. His most pointed comments came in 2004, when he told Congress, "To fend off possible future systemic difficulties, which we assess as likely if GSE expansion continues unabated, preventive actions are required sooner rather than later." (Fannie, of course, responded in kind; even Greenspan wasn't immune.)

In the fall of 2004, OFHEO announced the preliminary results of its investigation. Fannie, the agency said, had willfully broken the complex accounting rules surrounding derivatives to facilitate smooth earnings growth. Whereas Freddie had understated its earnings, OFHEO charged Fannie with overstating them and willfully breaking accounting rules.

The clear implication was that Fannie Mae was cooking its books so that the executives could line their pockets. During the previous five years, the company had, indeed, doubled its earnings just as Raines had promised when he first became CEO, generating tens of millions of dollars in management bonuses. OFHEO was now saying that much of that profit was basically the result of accounting fraud. OFHEO also said that Fannie, under Raines, had fostered an environment of "weak or nonexistent internal controls." Raines responded in a highly unusual way. Throwing down the gauntlet, he demanded that the SEC reinvestigate the company's accounting.

Fannie had one more trick up its sleeve. An aide to Kit Bond, a Republican senator from Missouri, played poker with Bill Maloni, Fannie's top lobbyist. Bond sat on the appropriations committee that oversaw OFHEO. Before the results of the OFHEO investigation were made public, Bond sent a letter to HUD's inspector general, requesting that it investigate not Fannie or Freddie, but *OFHEO*. (A draft of Bond's letter, which was nearly identical to the letter that was actually sent, was later found on Fannie Mae's computer system.) Separately, the committee also called for $10 million of OFHEO's budget to be withheld until Falcon was removed.

There is no question that OFHEO actions were well beyond the bounds of normal regulatory behavior. Like the White House, it had gone to war with Fannie Mae, leaking damaging information to the press and actively seeking to embarrass the GSEs. To put it bluntly, it was out to get Fannie. Which is precisely what the HUD inspector general wrote in his report.

The inspector general's report was supposed to be confidential. But Fannie had a long history of strategic leaks itself. Sure enough, just before a key hearing, it managed to get the HUD report into the hands of members of Congress. Not surprisingly, when the hearing began, the committee members went after OFHEO and Falcon instead of Raines.

"This hearing is about the political lynching of Franklin Raines," said

Congressman William Lacy Clay, an African-American Democrat from Missouri.

"Is it possible that by casting all of these aspersions . . . you potentially are weakening this institution in the market, that you are potentially weakening the housing market in this country?" chimed in Congressman Artur Davis, Democrat of Alabama.

In responding to the OFHEO charges, Raines was unapologetic. "These accounting standards are highly complex and require determinations on which experts often disagree." A congressional aide would later say, "I have never seen anyone treated as disrespectfully as Armando Falcon was by the Democrats and Franklin Raines."

Raines, however, had overplayed his hand. In demanding that the SEC look at Fannie's account, he assumed it would side with the company rather than its regulator. But he had calculated wrong. On December 15, 2004, at a meeting that included Raines, Falcon, and Justice Department officials, the SEC's chief accountant, Donald Nicolaisen, announced that Fannie Mae's accounting did not comply "in material respects" to the accounting rules.

Raines was flabbergasted. "What did we get wrong?" he asked, his voice wavering. Nicolaisen held up a sheet of paper. If the four corners represented what was possible under GAAP accounting rules and the center was perfect compliance, he told Raines, "you weren't even on the page." Fannie's representatives tried to argue that if they couldn't get it right, no one could. Nicolaisen wasn't having it. "Many companies out there get it right," he said.

The restatement was astounding. OFHEO alleged that Fannie Mae had overstated its earnings by $9 billion since 2001, representing a staggering 40 percent of its profits. (Ultimately, Fannie restated its earnings by a "mere" $6.3 billion.) OFHEO also reported that Raines had been paid $90 million between 1998 and 2003—$52 million of which was directly tied to Fannie's meeting its earnings targets. Raines and his number two, CFO Tim Howard, were forced to step down. Fannie agreed to pay a $350 million civil penalty to the SEC and $50 million to the Treasury. As part of a consent decree with OFHEO, Fannie agreed to hold 30 percent additional capital and stop growing the portfolio. Freddie agreed to the same measures.

There are many former Fannie executives, including Raines and Howard, who will go to their graves believing that the entire scandal was drummed up by OFHEO and the White House solely to bring Fannie down. In August 2006, the Justice Department took the rare step of publicly announcing that it was dropping its investigation into Fannie Mae's accounting; no criminal charges were ever filed. For that matter, the SEC never filed civil charges against any individual, either. And an investigation by the law firm Paul, Weiss exonerated Raines of any wrongdoing. While OFHEO settled with Raines and Howard, it did so on terms that can only be described as incredibly generous. The bulk of Raines's settlement—some $25 million—came from stock options he had received that were so out of the money they'd likely never be worth anything anyway. Raines today describes the accounting scandal as "a dispute among accountants," because Fannie's outside accountants had agreed with its original interpretation of GAAP. Derivatives accounting *is* incredibly complex, and the line between sloppiness, aggressiveness, and fraud is often difficult to discern. The fact that the SEC—which had no dog in the fight—agreed with OFHEO suggests that the scandal was real. The fact that the Justice Department declined to prosecute suggests that maybe it wasn't.

Whichever the case, Raines had no one to blame but himself. CEOs of regulated companies may grouse privately about their regulator, but few are so foolish as to let the relationship become so openly hostile. Whether because of sloppy accounting or something less excusable, Fannie gave its regulator enough rope to hang it with. Having abused its regulator for years, how could Fannie expect OFHEO not to use that rope?

Here's the stunning thing, though: despite scandals at both Fannie and Freddie, despite a Republican White House, despite some powerful enemies in Congress—like Richard Baker and Senator Richard Shelby, the chairman of the Senate banking committee, even despite the importunings of Alan Greenspan—Congress and the administration took no steps to impose new regulation on the GSEs. That wouldn't happen until much later.

"Can you imagine if they all had said, 'Enough is enough. We're sending legislation to the Hill to privatize Fannie and Freddie and end their beneficial status with the federal government?" asks a former Fannie lobbyist. "At the time, the Republicans never believed they could get that done. And on the other side of the political spectrum, Democrats like Barney Frank and Senator Chris Dodd would never have supported such an effort, because the companies would no longer be bound to support affordable housing. You were never going to get to the middle."

In truth, the Treasury Department could have done something about the GSEs even without new legislation. During the early stages of Operation Noriega, Treasury had researched an obscure provision in a 1954 law that appeared to give the Treasury the right to limit the GSEs' issuance of debt.

Treasury and the Justice Department concluded that Treasury did, indeed, have that right. By exercising it, they could have shut down the GSEs entirely. But they never tried. Even the Bush administration was afraid to see what would happen to the mortgage market without Fannie and Freddie.

Fannie's new CEO was Daniel Mudd, a self-deprecating ex-Marine who had run General Electric's Japanese operation before joining Fannie Mae in 2000. The son of the well-known television journalist Roger Mudd, the new chief executive could not have been more different from his three predecessors. He wasn't a Democrat, a Washington power player, or a houser. He and Raines had never been close, and Mudd had thought about leaving the company because he didn't like its "arrogant, defiant, my-way Fannie Mae," as he later put it. When he became CEO, he embarked on a strategy of conciliation. "I thought for a very long time that it was our fault, because we were heavy-handed, because we had a propaganda machine," he said. Though he tried to patch things up with the administration, no one in the White House would take his calls.

On the other hand, the White House was the least of Mudd's problems. While Washington had been transfixed by the war between Fannie and the White House, something every bit as dramatic was taking place in the marketplace: Fannie's stranglehold on the secondary mortgage market was weakening. And not just by a little. In 2003, Fannie Mae's estimated market share for bonds backed by single-family housing was 45 percent. Just one year later, it dropped to 23.5 percent. As a 2005 internal presentation at Fannie Mae noted, with some alarm, "[P]rivate label volume surpassed Fannie Mae volume for the first time."

There was no question about why this was happening: the subprime mortgage originators were starting to dominate the market. They didn't need Fannie and Freddie to guarantee their loans—and for the most part didn't want the GSEs mucking around in their business. The subprime originators sold their loans straight to Wall Street, which, unlike the GSEs, didn't really care whether they could be paid back. "The subprime market needed the companies who created all the rules to go away," says subprime entrepreneur Bill Dallas. "Fannie and Freddie were in the penalty box. They were gone."

As Fannie's market share dropped, the company's investors grew restless— so restless that Fannie hired Citigroup to look at what Citi called "strategic alternatives to maximize long-term Phineas [the code name the Citi team gave Fannie] shareholder value." In a July 2005 presentation, Citi concluded that Fannie shouldn't privatize, because its charter was its "core asset," accounting for up to 50 percent of its current market capitalization. Among Citi's key recommendations for increasing that market capitalization: Fannie should begin guaranteeing "non-conforming residential mortgages"—i.e., subprime.

Fannie's relationship with its biggest customer, Countrywide, was also increasingly difficult. In some years, Countrywide generated a quarter of the loans purchased by Fannie; and the company had long supported certain key Mozilo causes, like low down payments. "The single defining quality of that relationship was the mutual dependence," says one lobbyist. But now the balance was shifting, because Countrywide had other options. Unlike the pure subprime companies, Countrywide wanted Fannie in the subprime market. Countrywide originated so many loans that Mozilo wanted as many buyers as he could get, even Fannie. Besides, Countrywide liked the idea of having Fannie impose some order on the Wild West of subprime, with its insistence on sound underwriting standards. That would probably help Countrywide, with its long history of working hand in hand with the GSEs, and hurt the pure subprime companies like Ameriquest and New Century.

Instead, because Fannie wouldn't buy riskier loans, its share of Countrywide's business shrank. According to an internal Fannie Mae presentation, in mid-2002 Fannie bought more than 80 percent of Countrywide's mortgages. By early 2005, that had shrunk to about 20 percent. "This trend is increasingly costing us business with our largest customer," noted the presentation.

The new, tougher housing goals of the Bush administration also ratcheted up the pressure. How was Fannie going to achieve those goals without adding subprime mortgages to its books? The products it had carefully tailored for low-income borrowers were no longer appealing in a world where those borrowers could get much bigger mortgages from a subprime originator by making up their income. But Fannie couldn't just dive headlong into the subprime market. Its systems weren't able to gauge the risk of subprime mortgages. "[W]e are not even close to having proper control processes for credit, market, and operation risks," wrote the company's chief credit officer, Enrico Dallavecchia, in an e-mail. The irony was painful: HUD had increased and toughened Fannie's housing goals at the precise moment when the market was willing to make loans—often terrible loans that quickly soured, to be sure—to any low-income person who wanted one. "The difference between what the market produced and what we had to produce grew bigger and bigger," says a former Fannie executive.

"All these voices on the outside were saying, 'You are not relevant,'" Mudd later recalled. "And you have an obligation to be relevant."

Fannie's traditional arrogance soon gave way to angst; Mudd would later say that going to work felt like "a choice between poking my eye out and cutting off a finger." Fannie's internal struggles were on vivid display at a getaway for executives in the summer of 2005. In a slideshow entitled "Facing Strategic Crossroads," the first question Fannie asked itself was "Is the housing market overheated?" The next question: "Does Fannie Mae have an obligation to protect consumers?" Executives debated whether the new dominance of subprime products was a permanent change or a temporary phenomenon. The presentation went on to lay out the two "stark choices" Fannie faced. One was to "stay the course," which meant staying away from subprime lending and seeing continued market share declines. The other: "Meet the market where the market is." Which meant subprime. The presentation concluded on a plaintive note. "Is there an opportunity to drive the market back to the thirty-year FRM [fixed-rate mortgage]?"

Although the company vowed at the meeting to stay the course, in truth it had already begun to stray. First the GSEs bought for their portfolios the safest subprime securities in the marketplace: the triple-A-rated tranches of residential mortgage-backed securities. (Neither GSE ever bought CDOs.) They'd begun buying these securities in the earlier part of the decade because they offered decent yields. But when the housing goals became harder to fulfill, the triple-A tranches provided an easy way to meet their mission numbers. Eventually, the Street began designing a special GSE tranche that was packed with loans that satisfied the affordable housing requirements. And HUD allowed the GSEs to count these purchases toward their goals.

Over time, Fannie and Freddie became two of the world's largest purchasers of triple-A tranches. In the peak year of 2004, the GSEs bought about $175 billion in triple-As, or 44 percent of the market. While there were plenty of buyers for triple-A-rated securities, the very size of the GSEs' purchase undoubtedly helped inflate the housing bubble.

Putting triple-A subprime securities on its books was, like some of Fannie's other methods of meeting its housing goals, a stupid pet trick. It didn't help low-income Americans buy homes. Because the GSEs weren't determining which loans they would buy, they lost the opportunity to enforce any standards on the lenders. And, as housing advocate Judy Kennedy points out, putting subprime securities on its books was a perversion of its affordable housing mission. From the government's perspective, GSEs existed to buy up loans to poor and middle-income borrowers—even if that came at the expense of its profits. By buying Wall Street's securities, the GSEs were able to earn more of a return on their affordable housing investments, rather than less.

Fannie and Freddie turned out to be almost as clueless as your average investor. They, too, relied on the rating agencies, although Fannie did so with a tiny bit of caution. ("Although we invest almost exclusively in triple-A-rated securities, there is a concern that rating agencies may not be properly assessing the risk in these securities," noted a Fannie internal document in the spring of 2005.) Not enough caution, however. After the crisis, HUD would report that the value of the Wall Street–created securities owned by Fannie and Freddie fell as much as 90 percent from the time of purchase.

The GSEs also began buying, guaranteeing, and selling those not-quite-subprime Alt-A mortgages. Fannie executives insist that they never bought or guaranteed more than a few billion dollars worth of loans they considered subprime. They never guaranteed loans with layered risks, for instance. But many of the borderline loans they guaranteed would certainly be categorized as subprime by others in the marketplace. To this day, former Fannie Mae executives will insist that they chose the securities they guaranteed more carefully than others. And maybe they did; after the crisis, Fannie and Freddie defenders would point out that in every mortgage category, from prime to Alt-A to subprime, the GSEs' loans defaulted at rates below the national average.

But just as with the purchase of triple-A securities, guaranteeing Alt-A loans had little to do with housing goals and everything to do with profits and market share. They were simply more profitable than guaranteeing thirty-year fixed loans. "We were lured into it by the big margins," says a former executive. Both companies got warnings about the true state of market—Fannie from the outside and Freddie from the inside. Michelle Leigh, a vice president at IndyMac, later claimed in a lawsuit that she tried to warn Fannie about the Alt-A loans it was buying from IndyMac, which were riddled with problems. Fannie didn't respond, and increased its purchases of loans from the company, according to the lawsuit.

Over at Freddie, chief credit officer David Andrukonis warned the company's new CEO, Dick Syron, the former chairman of the Boston Federal

Reserve, about the riskiness of no-income, no-asset loans. (They were called NINA loans.) "Freddie Mac should withdraw from the NINA market as soon as practical," Andrukonis wrote in the fall of 2004. "Today's NINA appears to target borrowers who would have trouble qualifying for a mortgage if their financial position were adequately disclosed." He added, "What better way to highlight our sense of mission than to walk away from profitable business because it hurts the borrowers we are trying to serve?"

Between 2005 and 2007, about one in five mortgages Fannie and Freddie purchased or insured was Alt-A or subprime, according to a study by Jason Thomas. By the end of 2007, Fannie Mae had $350 billion in Alt-A exposure and another $166 billion in exposure to mortgages that it defined as subprime or whose recipients had FICO scores of less than 620. Freddie had $205 billion in Alt-A exposure and $173 billion in exposure to subprime or sub-620 FICO scores. Thomas calculates that that meant the GSEs owned about 23 percent of the subprime mortgage-backed securities outstanding at that time and a whopping 58 percent of the total Alt-A mortgages outstanding.

There was no worse time to accumulate exposure to Alt-A and subprime loans than the 2005 to 2007 time period. Some critics would later point to these massive purchases in an effort to blame the entire crisis on Fannie and Freddie. But as Thomas points out, it's precisely because they were so late to the party that their losses would be so immense.

Another irony is that, in the end, OFHEO, despite its brief stance as an aggressive regulator, failed as miserably as the GSEs. As Raines would later point out, "Fannie and Freddie succumbed to the pressure, and they did so right in front of OFHEO." After the accounting scandal, OFHEO had examiners in Fannie's offices on a full-time basis. There was very little that Fannie Mae did that OFHEO didn't know about. OFHEO's 2006 report to Congress had a cover letter that read in part, "OFHEO is working with the Enterprises to provide guidance on subprime . . . mortgages." OFHEO had the right to suspend the affordable housing goals if the agency felt they threatened the GSEs' capital position. At any moment along the way, OFHEO could have stopped the GSEs from buying risky loans by citing "safety and soundness" concerns. But it didn't. Like the other regulators who were charged with looking after the health of the financial system, OFHEO simply didn't appreciate the credit risk until it was too late.

The last, and most painful, irony is that the two longtime rival armies in the securitization market—the investment banks and the GSEs—would end up magnifying each other's sins rather than keeping each other in check.

Without the GSEs' buying power, the private market would never have been as big as it got. And without Wall Street, there never would have been all those bad mortgages for the GSEs to binge on.

Which is why some Fannie defenders argue that the GSEs, rather than being the villains of the crisis, were really the victims. That may be, but they were far from innocent victims.

13

The Wrap

His temper. That's what AIG-FP traders always mentioned whenever they talked about their old boss, Joe Cassano. Yes, they would also take note of his wide-ranging intelligence, and the way he knew every FP employee's name, and the pleasure he took in handing out multimillion-dollar bonuses each December—"like Santa Claus," recalls a former executive. But his temper tended to dominate conversations about him, because that's what everyone at FP had to cope with every day.

It was brutal and indiscriminate—"terrifying when unleashed," says an ex-trader. "Sometimes he could seem uncontrollable." Cassano would rage at traders who were making the company a fortune and traders who were on a losing streak. He would go out of his way to embarrass executives in front of their peers, and blow up over the most inconsequential things. "Talking to him was like walking on eggshells," says another former FP executive. "You were always worried about what would set him off."

Once, he got mad because a trader wore a V-neck sweater over a T-shirt. From two desks over, he loudly berated the man and then sent him home to change into a collared shirt. A new hire, speaking to Cassano for the first time, told him that the firm was making 50 basis points on a certain $1 billion transaction. "I said that was $5 million a year," recalls the trader. Cassano erupted: "How dare you do the math on me!" He was a bully. It was his fatal flaw.

Cassano had taken over AIG-FP when Tom Savage retired in 2001. Though he had been Savage's top deputy, it was no sure thing that Cassano would get the top job. But Hank Greenberg had taken a shine to Cassano; a tough, up-from-the-streets manager who cared about AIG to the exclusion of all else, Cassano surely reminded Greenberg of himself. It also helped that

Cassano never forgot who was boss. "Joe managed Hank beautifully," says a former colleague.

Cassano had learned the derivatives trade from the ground up, having begun his FP career in the back office. In the late 1990s, when the London office was floundering, Savage moved him there to fix the situation. He did, making London his home and traveling to the Connecticut office one week a month. When AIG-FP first began selling credit default swaps, Cassano ran the business. He may have lacked a degree in high finance, but nobody could say he didn't know derivatives.

He also cared deeply about the business. His former employees all stress that as well. Whenever an executive said a deal couldn't be done because of some deficiency with FP, Cassano would respond with fury. "He took that kind of thing personally," says a former trader. "In his eyes, you were blaming his company for why you were ineffective." In his mind, FP had no deficiencies. Cassano's devotion to FP was also why his former colleagues all say that he would never, ever do anything that he thought might damage it. Which, in retrospect, was the most surprising thing about him. Joe Cassano was positively risk averse.

Ever since Howard Sosin's departure in 1993, Greenberg had insisted that FP executives defer half their compensation to protect against deals later going sour. Cassano himself went much further. In 2007, for instance, he was paid $38 million, but pulled out only $1.25 million, keeping the rest in his deferred compensation pool. He had no incentive to take foolish risks. Whenever FP devised a new product, he took it to Greenberg to get the CEO's blessing. He made traders pull back from positions he thought were becoming too risky. "The company took minimal risk," says one former trader. When deals were brought to him, Cassano would pick them apart, looking for hidden risks. "He would say, 'Be careful out there. Don't take big positions,'" recalls the former trader. "He wasn't a cowboy."

"It was an extremely well-run business," this trader continues. "But there was one blind spot."

The blind spot was AIG-FP's credit default swap business. Ever since that original BISTRO deal with J.P. Morgan, FP had created a profitable niche by taking on the risk of insuring the super-senior tranches of CDOs. These were the top-tier, triple-A tranches, the ones that got hit only if all the lower tranches got wiped out. Although it had been a sexy little business in the beginning, with innovative deals and healthy margins, it had become fairly humdrum. For the first four or five years, the credit default swap business was focused primarily on corporate credits—first writing protection against the possibility that a particular company's debt might default, and then insuring the super-senior tranches of CDOs that were primarily made up of corporate loans. But as competitors entered the business, the spreads narrowed and the profits dwindled. Soon, FP's traders were looking for new ways to use credit derivatives to make money.

FP found several things. It created a business aimed at helping banks—primarily European banks—evade their capital rules. AIG-FP sold credit default swaps to banks that held a variety of highly rated paper; the FP wrap, as it was called, allowed them to decrease their capital. There was nothing illegal about this; seeking "capital relief" had become widespread ever since the adoption of risk-based capital standards. Nor did FP hide what it was doing. It called the business—appropriately enough—"regulatory capital." By the time of the financial crisis, AIG-FP had insured around $200 billion of highly rated bank assets.

And in 2004, AIG-FP began selling credit protection on triple-A tranches of a new kind of CDO, called a multisector CDO. In this, AIG-FP was following the evolution of the CDO business itself, which had gone from BISTRO—a CDO made up of one bank's corporate loan portfolio—to CDOs that consisted of disparate corporate credits, to this new multisector CDO. Multisector CDOs were "highly diversified kitchen sinks," as one FP trader put it, that included everything from student loans to credit card debt to prime commercial real estate mortgage-backed securities to a smattering of subprime residential mortgage-backed securities. The theory, as always, was that diversification would protect against losses; the different asset classes in a multisector CDO were supposed to be uncorrelated. A Yale economist named Gary Gorton was hired to work up the risk models, which showed—naturally!—that the possibility of losses reaching the super-senior tranches was so tiny as to be nearly nonexistent. To FP's executives, wrapping the super-seniors felt like free money.

The executive who marketed credit default swaps for AIG-FP was Al Frost. Many FP executives were wary of him, viewing him as someone who had a way of shoehorning his way into businesses started by others. But he was a Cassano favorite and a member of the boss's inner circle. Like everyone else, he feared Cassano's temper. "He was more worried about Joe's temper than about bringing him straight information," says someone who worked with him.

Frost was a glad-hander, with friends up and down Wall Street. As these new multisector CDOs were being developed, Frost was among the people at FP who soon realized there was a need for someone to wrap the triple-A tranches—a need that AIG-FP was uniquely capable of filling. AIG-FP by then was an experienced, trusted credit default swap counterparty that knew the ins and outs of swap contracts. And FP's swaps were especially appealing to underwriters because they were backed by the parent company's own stellar triple-A rating.

Or were they? Here was a question that no one at FP—or its counterparties—ever thought much about: What did it really mean to be backed by AIG's triple-A rating? It most certainly did not mean that the parent company's capital reserves were at FP's disposal. AIG was an insurance company; there were severe limits as to how it could deploy its capital reserves. Says a former AIG executive: "We had capital, but it wasn't mobile." Much of AIG's capital was walled off in the company's insurance units, where it could only be used to shore up that particular division. Surprisingly little of it could be moved to FP, even in a crisis. In truth, despite being owned by the world's largest insurance company, AIG-FP was really a stand-alone derivatives dealer. The parent company did not have its back.

"If you run a derivatives company," says a former AIG-FP executive, "all you have to do is be wrong once, given the amount of leverage and the size of the book." Hank Greenberg viewed AIG's triple-A rating as critical to his business model, yet he never realized that the very existence of AIG-FP put that triple-A rating at risk.

That same uncritical belief in the strength of AIG's triple-A was the reason FP never bothered to hedge its exposure to the super-senior tranches it was insuring. This was a sharp departure from the company's usual practice. But AIG executives felt that because the deals were deemed to be riskless, "why would you hedge a riskless transaction? And if you did hedge," says a former FP trader, "you would be getting protection from someone who was unlikely to be around, because it was a lesser entity." In other words, any financial event powerful enough to cause losses to the super-seniors was also likely to bring down the counterparties.

Written into FP's contracts were so-called collateral triggers, which allowed counterparties to demand that AIG put up collateral—that is, cold, hard cash—if certain events took place. One trigger was a drop in AIG's credit rating to single-A. A second trigger was a downgrade of the super-seniors.

And the third trigger was a decline in the market value of the securities AIG had wrapped—even if those securities retained their triple-A rating.

It is hard to know for sure if these triggers were there from the start. Frost ran his department like a little fiefdom; he tended to impart information on a need-to-know basis. (Through his attorney, Frost denies that he didn't talk freely about what was going on in his business.) AIG-FP's chief competitors in wrapping triple-A CDO tranches were the so-called monoline insurers, like MBIA and Ambac. Their business model did not allow for collateral triggers. AIG-FP's willingness to agree to the triggers gave it a big marketing advantage.

It is also unclear who else in the company knew about the triggers. Cassano knew, of course. Greenberg says he knew as well, but they didn't trouble him: "At the time, the business was so small, and besides, we had the triple-A." But almost nobody else at AIG appears to have known about them—not AIG's risk managers, not the executives who oversaw Cassano and FP, and not other FP executives. Every quarter, AIG-FP sent a memorandum to AIG management, updating its positions and exposure. The collateral calls were never a part of those memos, according to former AIG executives. "I don't think Joe ever really focused on them. It was just another facet of the deal," says one executive. Cassano and Frost appear to have assumed it was simply not possible that they would ever have to put up collateral. In the days when Sosin and then Savage had run AIG-FP, it is likely that the collateral triggers would have been discussed openly with FP and the AIG executive suite. But Cassano's FP was a much more secretive place; former AIG executives say they had to practically conduct interrogations to pry even the most mundane information out of FP. It wasn't until 2007, when Cassano acknowledged the collateral triggers on a conference call with investors, that most AIG executives first found out about them.

"It was startling news," says a former trader. "It was the stupidest thing we ever did."

By the time FP was getting into the multisector CDO business, Hank Greenberg was in his late seventies. He still didn't have a succession plan. He still ruled AIG with an iron fist. And he was still heralded as the Great Man of modern insurance. Even though by 2004 AIG ranked tenth on the Fortune 500, with almost $100 billion in revenue and more than $11 billion in profits,

Greenberg still managed to churn out 15 percent earnings gains each year. It seemed a miracle.

As ever, the intricacies of AIG remained largely in Hank Greenberg's head. And those intricacies had become truly bewildering, beyond the ken of most mere mortals. When AIG set up a new subsidiary, it often launched a dozen or more surrounding subsidiaries to take advantage of tax laws, reinsurance possibilities, a whole gamut of small advantages. It had, literally, hundreds of such subsidiaries. "There was a kind of scheming mentality," says someone familiar with the AIG culture. "They always seemed to be thinking, 'How do we beat the system?'"

Most CEOs have maybe a half dozen top executives reporting directly to them; Greenberg had nearly thirty direct reports. That meant that only Greenberg and maybe his longtime sidekick Ed Matthews had a complete grasp of AIG's convoluted businesses. It also meant that nobody besides Greenberg and Matthews understood all the risks the company was taking. "In other firms, there are checks and balances," says a former AIG consultant. "So far as I could tell, AIG had no formal risk function." In effect, Hank Greenberg was AIG's one-man risk department.

"Hank ran the company unlike any other twentieth-century company," says another AIG consultant. "Even though it had gotten huge, there was no big company infrastructure. The systems were completely antiquated. It still gathered its earnings data every quarter by hand. And all decisions were made by him to a remarkable degree."

To put it another way, while outsiders may have thought they were seeing an earnings machine, insiders saw something that more resembled a Rube Goldberg contraption. Why did AIG have such an antiquated infrastructure? Because Greenberg didn't like to pay for anything that didn't generate revenue. So he scrimped on computers and software that other companies bought as a matter of course, and refused to pay the salaries necessary to hire a first-rate operations staff.

Why did he have thirty direct reports? Because that way he could keep all his division managers segregated from each other. "Hank wanted people to operate with the idea that they had their own little private P&L and they were only responsible for what happened in their cell," says a former AIG executive.

Many of AIG's subsidiaries were also interlocking. So for instance, National Union Fire Insurance Company, a big insurance subsidiary, had a significant ownership stake in ILFC, AIG's airplane leasing company. An operation called AIG Foreign Life—an overseas life insurance company that was one of the company's crown jewels—had a large portion of its capital in AIG stock. And of course SICO, the company that Greenberg used to accumulate his top executives' retirement money and which he himself ran, was AIG's largest stockholder.

Although Greenberg obviously was in command of everything that went on at AIG, its formal internal controls and processes—the kind that every public company has in place—were decidedly subpar. AIG's longtime banker was Goldman Sachs; the firm was constantly involved in AIG deals, and Greenberg had close ties with the firm's top investment bankers. Yet one former Goldman banker recalls that whenever a new deal was in the works, the junior bankers working on it would find, as he put it, "deficiencies" in AIG's internal controls. "In the due diligence calls, the company always did end runs around our questions and said they were aware of internal control problems and were working on fixing them. If we weren't satisfied with the answers, we would have to go to senior relationship people at Goldman and get the go-ahead for the deal. Half the time," he adds, "the senior people didn't want to hear any shit about AIG's problems." The deals always got done.

And then there was AIG's risk taking. Though he had built a very large company, Greenberg still wanted his executives to be risk-taking entrepreneurs in the way they approached their businesses. "He repeatedly made the point that AIG's balance sheet was so big and so highly rated that AIG could take risks that no other company had the strength to take," says a former executive. That was the whole point of having a triple-A, after all: AIG could take more risk, and be rewarded for it. "Being that big, and that prone to risk taking—it's just not a good combination," says a former AIG executive. "Those two things together do not equal prudence."

And it wasn't just one or two subsidiaries, either. The airline leasing subsidiary, the investment arm, the insurance companies—they were *all* seeking out risks they could take from leveraging the triple-A rating. Among other consequences, this led a surprising number of AIG divisions to invest in subprime mortgages. FP, of course, was insuring super-senior CDO tranches. But AIG also had a mortgage originator making subprime loans. It had a mortgage insurance unit that was guaranteeing subprime loans. And it had a securities lending program that was investing in subprime mortgages.

It's worth pausing for a moment on that last one, to get a sense of just how willing AIG was to push into risky areas. The purpose of any securities lending program is to loan stock from a company's investment portfolio to short sellers. (A short seller has to borrow stock in order to short it.) The borrower puts up cash as collateral, which the lender is supposed to invest in short-term liquid securities that can be quickly cashed in when the borrower returns the stock. For that reason, most companies with securities lending programs invest the cash in low-yielding, short-term commercial paper. But AIG decided to invest a portion of the money in largely illiquid CDO tranches. Its executives reasoned that since the short sellers would never all ask for their money back at the same time—*would they?*—they could keep some of the cash in CDOs and turn the wider spreads into bigger profits. The possibility that something might happen someday that would cause all the borrowers to demand their money at the same time was, once again, viewed as implausible. By 2007, the company had $78 billion from the securities lending program tied up in mortgage-backed securities. "It was incredibly irresponsible," says someone who was there.

When you got right down to it, there was something almost Wizard of Oz–like about the way AIG was run. It was simply not the company it was purported to be. Behind its impressive facade was a tough, stubborn old man who refused to groom a successor, refused to run his company the way modern companies were supposed to be run, and refused to play by anybody's rules but his own. Those attributes were about to hurt both him and his beloved AIG.

AIG's stock peaked toward the end of 2000, at around $103 a share. It was, by then, a very rich stock, with a much higher valuation than its competitors; keeping it that way was deeply important to Greenberg. But over the next year or so, as the Internet bubble burst, the Enron and WorldCom scandals broke out into the open, and the 9/11 attacks took place, all insurance company stocks suffered, including AIG's. By 2002, the stock was struggling to stay above $65 a share.

In retrospect, it appears that these were not the only factors causing the stock to drop. The market was beginning to realize that AIG was going to have increasing difficulty meeting Greenberg's 15 percent earnings target. Partly, that was simply a function of AIG's mammoth size: the bigger AIG got, the harder it became to tack on 15 percent in additional profits each year. Analysts call this the law of large numbers.

There had long been suspicion that Greenberg got to his 15 percent target not just by pushing his executives to take more risk, but by taking advantage of complex accounting rules to help smooth out earnings, disguise under-writing losses, and tuck away surpluses that he could use for a rainy day. AIG had set up a series of reinsurance companies in places like Bermuda and Barbados—away from the prying eyes of U.S. regulators—which, although ostensibly independent, did almost all their business with AIG. Reinsurance companies exist to take on risk that insurers like AIG want to lay off, but state regulators had long suspected that AIG did at least some of its reinsur-ance deals to pretty up its books. AIG was by no means an Enron—its busi-nesses were very real and so, for the most part, were its profits. But wasn't it at least a little implausible that, year after year, its earnings never did anything but go up by 15 percent?

Once, a Wall Street analyst took some clients to see Greenberg and asked him point-blank how he managed to produce that steady stream of earnings growth "in this highly volatile industry," as he put it. "Aren't you concerned that the SEC or someone is going to look at AIG and ask if you are manag-ing earnings?"

Greenberg was not happy with the question, but he gave a surprisingly straightforward answer. "Look," he replied. "We are in the long-tail liability business"—meaning that, though the risks AIG insured didn't occur very often, the payout was very large when they did. "If there is one thing we have learned, it is that there are risks we can't anticipate, so when we have extra capital we are justified in setting it aside." He added, "What do you want? Do you want steady growth? Or do you want up 60 percent one quarter and down 15 percent the next?" The analyst recalls thinking that Greenberg had just admitted he was managing earnings.

It was around this same time—with the stock sliding and the market wondering if AIG was finally bumping up against the law of big numbers—that the company found itself in a series of small scandals. The first came in 2001. The SEC accused AIG's National Union unit of constructing what amounted to a sham insurance transaction to help a company called Bright-point hide nearly $12 million in losses a few years earlier. "It was some dinky-assed insurance deal that they did that fudged around with the accounting at the end of the day," says a former executive. And yet it took two years to settle the case—years in which AIG, and Greenberg, infuriated the SEC by dragging its feet on producing documents. "He was arrogant to those people," recalls this same former executive. "Uncooperative." When the case was finally settled—with AIG paying a $10 million fine—the SEC went out of its way to criticize the company's behavior. "The penalty," the agency said in its press release, "reflects AIG's participation in the Brightpoint fraud, as well as misconduct by AIG during the Commission's investigation of this matter."

Even as the SEC was prosecuting the Brightpoint deal, the agency opened up a second AIG investigation. This was a much bigger deal, and the guilty party this time was AIG-FP. The SEC eventually charged FP with conducting a series of fraudulent transactions that helped PNC, the big Pittsburgh bank, hide more than $750 million in dubious loans. The allegations were serious enough that the Justice Department opened a criminal investigation. Once again, it took several years to settle the case, this time with AIG agreeing to pay a fine of $80 million, with an additional $46 million in restitution. FP also signed a deferred prosecution agreement with the Justice Department—an extremely serious consequence.

The fine, however, would have been $20 million less but for the fact that at the last minute Greenberg reneged on the original settlement with the agency, vowing to fight the charges. AIG even issued a press release calling the government's actions "unwarranted." The SEC was furious, and the AIG board was shocked. It demanded that Greenberg settle. In addition to the extra $20 million and the deferred prosecution agreement, the government installed a full-time monitor inside AIG—in effect, a government compliance officer.

In late 2003, with the PNC investigation in full swirl, Cassano met with Greenberg, as he did every year, to show him how he planned to distribute the FP bonuses. As they were going through the numbers, Greenberg said, "Joe, if we're paying a fine on PNC, it is going to come out of your pocket"—meaning the FP bonus pool. Cassano was startled. "We're partners," he replied. "We split things down the middle, good or bad. That's our agreement." Greenberg said, "I don't go for people breaking the law. I'm telling you I'm not picking it up." Furious now, Cassano flashed Greenberg the temper that the FP traders knew so well. "Go fuck yourself," he said, pushing his finger in Greenberg's face. "Calm down, Joe," said Greenberg. "Don't get upset." Cassano did calm down—and Greenberg took the SEC fine out of FP's bonus pool. There wasn't a thing Cassano could do about it.

You would think that, by now, Greenberg would have learned at least one lesson—that a company accused of wrongdoing shouldn't give the government the back of its hand. All that did was cause the government to dig in its heels. Thanks to Enron in particular, the rules had changed. The kind of "earnings management" that had routinely gone on in corporate America was no longer okay. State insurance regulators, who had long looked the other way at some of AIG's accounting, were stiffening their spines. But Greenberg, stubborn to the end, expected the same kind of deference from government officials that he routinely received from the corporate world and from his employees. Which is why it was all the more unfortunate that the next government official to go after AIG was Eliot Spitzer, the attorney general of New York. Spitzer, who was preparing to run for governor, reveled in taking on tough guys like Greenberg.

By 2004, Spitzer had become the scourge of Wall Street. He had exposed conflicts of interest by Wall Street analysts and dug into sleazy behavior in the mutual fund industry. He had sued another tough guy, Richard Grasso, the former head of the New York Stock Exchange, attempting to claw back some of Grasso's $140 million pay package. Most recently, he had turned his attention to the insurance industry. His original target was Marsh & McLennan, the world's largest insurance broker, which, it so happened, was run by Greenberg's eldest son, Jeffrey. In October 2004, brandishing a raft of incriminating e-mails, Spitzer accused the company of conducting a long-running bid rigging scheme. He also said he wouldn't even begin to talk about a settlement until Jeffrey Greenberg resigned. The Marsh board quickly fired Greenberg. Four months after that, Marsh & McLennan agreed to pay $850 million restitution and apologized for its "shameful" conduct. Among the insurance companies accused of paying kickbacks to Marsh was AIG. Several AIG executives pleaded guilty for their role in the scheme.

Greenberg remained unrepentant. On February 9, 2005, just days after the Marsh & McLennan settlement was announced, AIG reported its $11 billion 2004 profits. During the earnings call with investors, Greenberg was asked about "the relatively hostile regulatory environment." He replied, "When you begin to look at foot faults and make them into a murder charge, then you have gone too far."

It would be hard to imagine a more poorly timed remark. On February 10, Spitzer got wind of a big reinsurance deal AIG had done with General Re, which was owned by Berkshire Hathaway. The information had come from Gen Re's lawyers, who had uncovered the deal in the course of another investigation. The purpose of the transaction, Spitzer was told, was to boost AIG's reserves by $500 million. Wall Street analysts had been calling for AIG to increase its reserve, and this, apparently, was the way the company had done it. Greenberg had reportedly instigated the deal himself, with a phone call to Gen Re's CEO. But, according to Spitzer and (later) the SEC, no real risk was transferred. The SEC would call the deal a "sham."

A few hours after Greenberg made his "foot fault" comment, Spitzer sent AIG a subpoena demanding documents relating to the Gen Re transaction. That evening, the New York attorney general happened to be the dinner speaker at a Goldman Sachs event. "Hank Greenberg should be very, very careful talking about foot faults," he said. "Too many foot faults and you can lose the match. But more important, those aren't foot faults."

Not surprisingly, the board was fast losing faith in Greenberg. Even before the Spitzer subpoena, the independent directors had hired Richard Beattie, a high-priced lawyer with Simpson Thacher & Bartlett, who was well known for advising boards faced with difficult situations. Beattie had several dinners with Greenberg, hoping to persuade him to retire. At one point, right around the time of the earnings announcement, Greenberg had agreed to step down. But the next day he told Beattie he had changed his mind.

Once the Spitzer subpoena arrived, a special committee of directors began an internal investigation. AIG's accounting firm, PricewaterhouseCoopers, was brought in to comb through the company's books. "They were finding problems everywhere," recalls a former AIG executive. It turned out that certain aspects of FP's derivatives accounting were incorrect. Some reinsurance transactions had to be unwound. Deals that walked right up to the line—which PWC had once okayed—were now ruled out of bounds. And there was another problem: the company had promised to cooperate with Spitzer, and he wanted to depose Greenberg. The board wanted to know whether Greenberg was going to plead the Fifth Amendment. Greenberg said he wasn't sure. How could the CEO take the Fifth and keep his job?

The climactic board meeting took place on March 13, 2005. It lasted all day, with the directors discussing among themselves whether to fire Greenberg and Greenberg, calling in from his boat and his airplane, arguing that he should keep his job. He had an odd way of going about it, though. "You people don't know what you're doing," he berated them. "You don't even know how to *spell* insurance."

Toward the end of the meeting, the accountants from PWC told the board that it would no longer vouch for the firm's books if Greenberg stayed as CEO. And that was that. Greenberg was allowed to stay on as chairman of the board, though that arrangement wouldn't last long, either. His replacement as CEO was a bland AIG lifer named Martin Sullivan, who had spent his entire career on the insurance side of AIG. Although Sullivan had a tremendous amount of insurance experience, because of the way Greenberg ran the company he knew very little about AIG-FP.*

Immediately after Greenberg's departure, the rating agencies dropped AIG's rating to double-A. Over the next few months, the intensity level inside the company was almost unbearable, as every subsidiary was turned inside out by swarms of accountants. "It was like a war zone," says a former executive. In July AIG announced its restatement: the company would reduce its earnings by $4 billion covering the previous five years. In those five years, AIG had reported around $40 billion in profits; the new numbers lowered AIG's profits by 10 percent. In other words, AIG didn't really have to play games—$36 billion in profits would still have earned it plenty of respect. It's just that Greenberg would have been seen as a mere mortal, instead of the great god of insurance.

Alain Karaoglan, a Wall Street analyst who had followed AIG for years, wrote several searing reports in the wake of Greenberg's resignation. One in particular stands out. After taking a close look at the Foreign Life unit—the same subsidiary that was always said to be one of the crown jewels—he concluded that there were significant gaps ". . . between statutory earnings reported in the 10-K and our summation of statutory account principle (SAP) earnings for the operating entities." In other words, try as he might, he could not make the earnings that AIG had reported for Foreign Life add up.

He also pointed out something that nobody had bothered to pay much attention to before. The rating agencies had consistently said that none of AIG's operating subsidiaries would have merited triple-A ratings if they had been stand-alone companies. Only the guarantee from the parent company made them triple-A credits. Yet, he noted, "AIG, the parent, is just a holding company and its strength and only source of cash flow to bondholders and shareholders comes from its subsidiaries." AIG's vaunted triple-A, in other words, was a product of circular logic that broke down upon close inspection. As Karaoglan continued his analysis, he openly wondered whether the operating units deserved even a double-A rating.

Then he wrote this: "[W]e were all to some degree complacent, and looked

---

* It should be noted that although both Spitzer and the SEC would soon bring charges against Greenberg, he has never gone to trial for any alleged wrongdoing. Although five people were convicted in the Gen Re case, including an AIG executive, Greenberg was not a part of that case, even though he was an unindicted coconspirator. And although Greenberg eventually settled with the SEC, neither admitting nor denying guilt, as of this writing he has yet to settle with the New York attorney general's office. Throughout, Greenberg has consistently denied any wrongdoing.

to some degree at the financials in a silo fashion and took comfort in the overall AIG whenever the silo could not stand on its own. In our view, we were all over-relying on Mr. Greenberg to sustain the company's tremendous track record and ensure it was real. Now, with significant financial improprieties revealed by the company, we can no longer do that."

⸺⧼⧽⸺

Not long before Hank Greenberg was ousted, an FP executive named Gene Park got a call from an old high school friend who was trying to buy his first house. The price of the house was $250,000. The friend didn't make a lot of money. Yet two mortgage originators had lined up to give him loans—one for the first mortgage, and the second for a loan to cover the down payment. The friend wanted to know if Park would lend him $5,000 to cover the closing costs, which he also didn't have. Though a little startled by what he'd heard, Park loaned him the money.

Shortly before the closing, the man lost his job. He called Park again, worried that the deal would fall through. But it didn't; when the friend told his mortgage broker that he was now out of work, the broker simply told him not to mention it. Sure enough, he closed on the house. Now Park was *really* startled.

A few months later, Park read an article in the *Wall Street Journal* touting the high dividend being paid by a hot mortgage company, New Century. He decided to take a closer look at the stock—and realized that New Century was a subprime lender that specialized in no-doc loans. He quickly dropped the idea of investing in it. Then a third data point popped up on his radar screen: in a trade publication somewhere, he read that multisector CDOs had very large concentrations of subprime mortgages.

By the spring of 2005, Al Frost was marketing a veritable assembly line of multisector CDO deals—FP had ten or fifteen in the pipeline at any given time. "It was almost mechanical," says someone who was there. They were so routine, they got very little scrutiny from the risk managers or anyone else at AIG-FP. Every firm on Wall Street was going to AIG to buy credit default swaps on their super-senior tranches. Though the spreads remained small, the sheer volume of business made it a big profit center for FP.

Nor did the credit default swap deals slow down after Greenberg left. Although the business had its best quarter ever in late 2004, its second biggest quarter was in the spring of 2005, after Greenberg's departure. From

$50 billion in 2004, the business ballooned to $110 billion by the end of 2005, according to the Congressional Oversight Panel. (By September 2008, when AIG was bailed out by the government, the exposure had been reduced to $60 billion.) Though it was still a small portion of AIG's $2.7 trillion derivatives book (in notional value), the run-up was startling nonetheless. And Frost wasn't the only one putting the pedal to the metal now that Greenberg was gone. The securities lending program also went into overdrive, and the mortgage insurance unit threw caution to the wind. The whole company, it sometimes seemed, was doubling down on subprime mortgages.

At both FP's and AIG's headquarters, the increasing number of multisector CDO deals was not viewed with alarm. On the contrary, Frost was seen as a hero. The downgrade to double-A had hit AIG-FP hard—it had to unwind billions of dollars worth of complicated transactions that had been dependent on the triple-A rating. A large part of the FP staff spent 2005 either unwinding deals or dealing with the restatements. Neither activity put money in the till. Frost's multisector CDO business was something everyone else at FP could be happy about.

Which is also why Cassano decided in the fall of 2005 that the time had come to give Al Frost a promotion. At the same time, he decided to put Gene Park in charge of the multisector wrap business.

Park, however, wanted nothing to do with multisector CDOs. By then, he had done a little experiment. He had asked some people involved in the FP business to guess the percentage of subprime mortgage-backed securities in some of the recent CDOs that FP had wrapped. Most of them had guessed it was around 10 percent. Then he asked one of them to look up a few recent deals. What he found was stunning. The percentage of subprime securities in the CDOs wasn't 10 percent—*it was 85 percent!* Without anybody at FP noticing, the multisector CDOs had become almost entirely made up of risky subprime securities.

Seriously worried, Park took his concerns to Andrew Forster, one of Cassano's chief deputies in London, who had begun to have thoughts along the same lines. The two men then made the rounds of the Wall Street underwriters to better understand the collateral. What they heard was not comforting. The firms all acknowledged that the credit histories were not very good—but they all insisted it was okay because historically, housing prices only went in one direction: up. As long as that was the case, homeowners would be able to refinance and repay the debt.

Park and Forster both knew this was a terrible rationale. The collateral, clearly, was unsound. The supposed diversification benefits of having a variety of credits in a multisector CDO had disappeared. They knew they needed to get out of the business.

And yet, how to break this news to Cassano without having him blow his stack? How to explain that this seemingly great business was exposing the firm to enormous risks that no one had been aware of? They couldn't. Park himself never spoke to Cassano, but Forster decided that the best way to approach him was to say that the business had changed and the underwriting standards were deteriorating. "We're comfortable with the portfolio today, but we're not comfortable going forward," Forster told Cassano, according to several former FP executives. "They were afraid to say they had made a mistake," adds one of them. "They couldn't admit to that." After listening to Forster's argument, Cassano agreed that, yes, they should stop writing new CDO business. But because nobody had been willing to tell Cassano how dire the situation really was, he—and AIG-FP—remained far too sanguine about the risks that remained on its books.

Park had wanted AIG not only to stop writing new business, but to begin hedging its exposure—and even to begin shorting securitized subprime mortgages. But that never happened. Most people at FP still couldn't envision the possibility that their deals might ever go sour. At one point, Park spent about a month trying to work out a deal where FP would buy credit default swaps from one of its clients for some of its super-senior exposure. But the cost—20 basis points, or two-tenths of a percent—was considered too high for so unlikely an event. So Cassano and Forster vetoed the deal, according to several FP executives. (Cassano, through his lawyers, denies that he vetoed a hedging deal. Rather, he says, FP executives concluded that hedges were generally ineffective.)

In February 2006, Frost and Park went to the big annual asset-backed securities convention in Las Vegas. There were thousands of people in attendance; everyone who was anyone in the securitization business was there. They had meetings with all the firms they did business with. Frost introduced them to Park, and explained that AIG-FP "would be taking another look at the business." Everyone knew what that meant. "During that period, he was not happy," recalls someone who worked with Frost. "He thought Park was trying to undermine his business to make him look bad. He thought he was turning over the crown jewels. He personally took offense."*

---

* Through his attorney, Frost denies being upset, and says that he was "part of the process."

After the crisis, it would be revealed that FP did not completely turn off the spigot at the end of 2005, even though that is what the company later told the world. By the time 2005 had come to a close, the firm had a number of deals still in the pipeline. Not wanting to anger its clients, AIG-FP decided to close those deals, which meant it was continuing to insure multisector CDOs well into 2006. What's more, under the terms of the swap contracts it wrote, CDO managers had the right to switch collateral to help maintain the yield—without having to inform AIG. As borrowers prepaid mortgages, for instance, the CDO managers would replace those earlier mortgages with mortgages that had been written in 2006 and 2007. Those latter mortgages, written as the housing bubble was reaching its peak, were far worse than even the mortgages written in 2005. And with Greenberg now gone, there was literally not a single executive at AIG's headquarters who knew that a decline in the market value of the tranches AIG wrapped could trigger a collateral call.

But that would only emerge much later. Over the course of the next year, as the subprime bubble peaked and then began to crack, Cassano, Forster, and Park all truly believed they had dodged a bullet.

14

Mr. Ambassador

From the early days of subprime lending, there was a small, lonely group who sided with the consumer advocates fighting the subprime companies: the attorneys general in a handful of states like Iowa, Minnesota, Washington, and Illinois. They, too, had heard borrowers' complaints firsthand, and saw the havoc that subprime lending was wreaking on communities. Some of them also understood that this wasn't just about the borrowers. "It's not in anyone's long-term interest for consumers to get loans they can't pay back," says Prentiss Cox, the former attorney with the Minnesota attorney general's office. "It's only in the short-term interest of those who are raking in fees." On a conference call with several other AGs in 2005, he said bluntly, "This whole thing is going to collapse."

This alliance of attorneys general had investigated First Alliance (aka FAMCO) and then struck a landmark $484 million settlement with House-hold Finance in 2002. "I first heard about FAMCO when someone walked into my office with a complaint from a consumer that he had paid 20 percent of the loan amount in fees," says Cox. "I said, 'That's a typo. Call 'em back.'" It wasn't a typo. Cox's second big wake-up call came after the Household settlement. "We thought we had done a big thing," he says. "We thought we had solved the problem of predatory lending. Stupid us. Immediately after we did this, the industry tripled."

By 2004, the AGs were targeting another lender, one that Cox called the "prototype" of the new breed of subprime lenders. Its loan volume was enor-mous. "We had these spreadsheets showing all the loans," Cox says. He recalls thinking to himself, "Oh my God. The scope of their lending is unbeliev-able." The company was Roland Arnall's Ameriquest.

That summer, Cox first started hearing complaints from consumers that

Ameriquest had inflated the value of their homes, qualifying them for loans they couldn't afford. In fact, all over the country, complaints were flooding in that Ameriquest had not only inflated appraisals, but had encouraged customers to lie about their income or their employment and had misled borrowers about the fees embedded in their loans. They had promised people they'd be able to refinance out of expensive loans without disclosing that Ameriquest had stuck on hefty prepayment penalties if they did so. And on and on.

By then, Cox knew not to expect help from federal regulators. He started calling the OCC the "Office of Corporate Counsel" for the banking industry. The Fed, he says, viewed the AGs as "mosquitoes." After all, those smart bankers on Wall Street wouldn't securitize subprime loans if they were that terrible—would they? "Who do you trust?" Cox says. "A bunch of stupid public service lawyers who mostly aren't even making six figures, or the people on Wall Street who are making eight or nine figures? It was an easy answer for the Fed." He adds, "The regulators were totally uninterested in looking on the ground at what was happening to actual human beings. We were the only cops on the beat. And we were the people with the smallest hammer."

In August of 2004, a group of Ameriquest executives, including general counsel Tom Noto, flew to Iowa to meet with Iowa attorney general Tom Miller and several others. The Ameriquest executives were cooperative. Their response to the complaints was consistent: "We don't do that"; "That's not the kind of company we are." When faced with a particularly ugly loan, they'd say, "That's an outlier." How could that be, the AGs wondered, when the horror stories were so uniform—and came from all over the country? "I think they were clever," says one participant. "This was a clever company led by an exceedingly clever man. I mean clever in the sense of shrewd, street smart."

In early 2005, as the negotiations were getting under way, the *Los Angeles Times* published a scathing exposé of Ameriquest. The headline read "Workers Say Lender Ran 'Boiler Rooms.'" Among other things, the story noted that lawsuits filed by consumers in California and at least twenty other states "allege a pattern of fraud." One person who read the article was Robert Gnaizda, the general counsel of the Greenlining Institute. Over the years, Gnaizda had become friendly with Arnall, seduced by his charm and his seemingly sincere commitment to good lending practices. "He said they were trying to be the best subprime lender in the country, and I thought, 'This guy could do it,'" Gnaizda recalls. His nonprofit had taken grants from Arnall for affordable housing and was in discussions with Arnall about an additional $1.5 million grant.

When the *Times*'s expose was published, Gnaizda called Arnall. One of Arnall's executives called him back and told him the story was all wrong. "I said, 'This is too disturbing,'" says Gnaizda. "I need a written refutation, or I'm out." He also insisted that Arnall call for an independent investigation of the allegations. Arnall refused. Gnaizda sent back a $100,000 check that Greenlining had received from Ameriquest. "I was told that Roland was infuriated." He adds, "I got to know Arnall very well, I got to like him, and then I was very disappointed by him, to put it mildly."

As the negotiations with the AGs heated up, several state attorneys general and their aides flew out to Orange County for a meeting at Ameriquest's headquarters. Arnall, who was not part of the negotiating team, asked Iowa's Tom Miller and Arizona attorney general Terry Goddard to come to his office. "We've got a few bad apples, and we didn't deal with it quickly enough," Arnall told them. Miller quickly disagreed. "The problems are pervasive," he said. Later that night, about a dozen people from both sides— "It was like the Arab-Israeli peace accords!" jokes Cox—went out to dinner at a restaurant in Anaheim. During the dinner, Arnall stood up and said, "I'm embarrassed that you all had to come out here. I'm ashamed."

"I started thinking, well, just a few hours ago you were saying this was just a few bad apples," recalls Miller. "When that didn't work, you changed direction."

Cox, for his part, was seething. After the dinner, he sent $50 to Ameriquest to reimburse them for his meal. Ameriquest told him that the cost was actually $98 per person. He forked over the remaining $48 with a note that said, next time, his treat—at a fast-food restaurant.

On January 23, 2006, the AGs announced that Ameriquest had agreed to pay $325 million to settle allegations from forty-nine states that it had engaged in extensive consumer abuse. (Ameriquest didn't operate in Virginia because the state requires detailed financial disclosure by the main shareholder of any company doing business there, which Arnall refused to provide.) Ameriquest denied all the allegations but agreed to make major changes in its business, including changing how appraisals were handled, eliminating incentives to sales personnel to include prepayment penalties or any other fees, and charging the same interest rates and discount points to customers with similar credit profiles. It also set up a fund to make restitution to customers who could show they had been ripped off by the company. Most of the AGs were happy; they felt this established a model that the rest of the industry would have to follow. Indeed, after the settlement, New Century wrote in its annual report that if it had to follow the guidelines Ameriquest had agreed to, "some of our practices could be called into question and our revenues, business, results of operations and profitability could be harmed." Which, in effect, was an admission that the entire industry had been built on a foundation of fraud.

As if to prove the point, Ameriquest never really recovered from the settlement. "Corporate is making a big push now to clean up its dirty image because of the heat coming down (they even took the Red Bull machines out of the offices)," wrote one employee on the consumer Web site Ripoff Report in the spring of 2005. (This employee added, "Good luck to everyone who is fighting this devil of a company. You will need it.") A few months later, on the same site, someone who called himself Eric and said he was an Ameriquest executive wrote, "We will not come out stronger, the company will be better, cleaner, and less profitable. . . . The glory days are over in this company, so pack up your glory and head elsewhere."

In May, less than five months after the settlement was struck, Ameriquest announced that it was closing all 229 retail branches and eliminating 3,800 jobs, and would henceforth operate through four large regional call centers. "It seemed kind of heartless because they made such a big deal out of team, family, and then, all of a sudden—boom," says one employee who was laid off. "The way it was done was especially impersonal." Each department was called into a conference room to hear the news via a conference call—which wasn't even live, but rather a tape loop that played over and over again. At headquarters, the mood was bleak. "Once the AGs really starting digging around, and more information became available to employees, that's when people really began to question who we were and what we were doing as an organization," says a former executive.

Aseem Mital, a veteran of Ameriquest's parent company, ACC, became CEO in June. Mital insisted that Ameriquest could still succeed with its new model, and that growth would be steady. But it turned out "Eric" was right, either because Ameriquest couldn't operate profitably under its agreement with the AGs or because it couldn't operate at all. For instance, an appraiser Ameriquest hired to help clean up its practices discovered that in New York the company's loan officers were paying huge sums to a group of appraisers—all of whom worked for the same outside firm—and these appraisers were consistently valuing the homes at 100 percent of the value that the loan officers had assigned the properties. (Inflated appraisals were one of the most common forms of fraud during the housing bubble.) Upon further digging, he discovered that the owner of the outside firm was the wife of one of Ameriquest's employees. And while Ameriquest was supposed to install a new system that ferreted out appraisal fraud in its four new call centers, this person says that the company made a decision not to install it in its Sacramento office.

By late 2006 Ameriquest was searching for a buyer, and by early 2007 ACC was running low on cash. Then came a revealing moment, one that gave a glimpse into just how clever Roland Arnall could be. In 2004, he had invited Deval Patrick—the same Deval Patrick who had led that early Justice Department investigation into the lending practices at Long Beach—to join ACC's board. Patrick was paid $360,000 a year. He resigned from the board two years later to run for governor of Massachusetts, and he won. In March 2007, as ACC was flailing, Governor Patrick made a call on behalf of Arnall. According to the *Boston Globe*, he phoned Robert Rubin, who was then the vice chairman of Citigroup and someone Patrick knew from the Clinton administration. A week after the call, Citigroup agreed to put fresh working capital into ACC. Arnall also contributed some of his personal wealth to keep the company going.

By the fall of 2008, Ameriquest had been shut down; Citigroup took over the $45 billion portfolio of loans that needed to be serviced from ACC's Argent division. Patrick later apologized for making the call, acknowledging that "financial exploitation of the poor, elderly, and minorities [was] pervasive at Ameriquest." But that call, as it turned out, wasn't the only favor he did for Arnall.

In 2008, the OCC put together a document called "Worst Ten in the Worst Ten." It listed the ten worst lenders in the ten metropolitan areas with the highest rates of foreclosure. The document vividly displayed the havoc that Arnall's companies were wreaking on the American landscape. There were a total of twenty-one companies on the ten lists. Arnall's Argent made the top ten in all ten cities, and was number one in Cleveland and Detroit. Long Beach made nine of the ten lists, landing the top spot in Sacramento, Stockton, Memphis, and Denver. And Ameriquest made seven of the ten lists, despite having slowed down its lending significantly since the settlement with the state attorneys general. (ACC says that it is "unfair and inaccurate to tie" Long Beach to Arnall's other companies, given that ACC had severed its links to Long Beach more than a decade before the OCC's report.)

And yet, at the time, it was as if the Ameriquest investigation and settlement had happened in a parallel universe. In the spring of 2005, after the *Los Angeles Times* exposé had been published but before the big AG settlement, President Bush nominated Arnall to be the U.S. ambassador to the Netherlands. Maybe this shouldn't have been a surprise—according to the *Los Angeles Times*, between 2004 and 2008 Arnall and his wife, Dawn, raised and gave more than $12 million to GOP causes and candidates. The donations included $5 million from Dawn to the Progress for America Voter Fund, which shared some donors with the Swift Boat ads that helped bring down the 2004 Democratic presidential candidate, John Kerry. Shortly after winning reelection, Bush announced the appointment of the Arnalls as honorary cochairs of the inaugural fund-raising committee. That wasn't really a surprise either: As *USA Today* wrote, "Inaugural fundraisers Dawn and Roland Arnall found a creative way to pump more than the $250,000 limit into the event. Their mortgage firm, Ameriquest Capital, contributed the maximum, as did three subsidiaries, for a total of $1 million." Arnall said that he supported Bush's stance on Israel, but few believed that was the only explanation. "Many of his philanthropic pursuits and major marketing campaigns were designed to generate the greatest political influence," says a former executive.

Arnall's confirmation hearing took place in November 2005. His wife and his brother Claude sat proudly in the audience. Tom Lantos, a Holocaust survivor and a Democratic congressman from California who Arnall had long supported, introduced him. "I strongly believe, Mr. Chairman, that Roland is one of the great anonymous philanthropists of our time," said Lantos. Norm Coleman, the Republican senator from Minnesota, called Arnall a "friend," and said, "I'm particularly proud of Mr. Arnall's achievements." Senator George Allen, the Republican from Virginia, noted that the governor of Mississippi, Haley Barbour, had sent a thank-you note for Arnall's generosity in the wake of Hurricane Katrina, and he pointed out that letters supporting Arnall had arrived from the speaker of the California State Assembly, the governor of Pennsylvania, and the mayor of Los Angeles. Not surprisingly, Ameriquest—or Dawn Arnall personally—had given generous political contributions to all three.

When it was Arnall's turn to speak, he began by saying, "I have made 'Do the right thing' my motto." He added, "I would consider our company the antipredatory company. In the late eighties when we founded the company, we provided credit to folks who did not have the opportunity because of their credit history to borrow directly from the institutional banks." And so it went.

There were only two senators that day who seriously challenged Arnall. One was Paul Sarbanes, who pointed to the still ongoing Ameriquest investigation and asked whether Arnall had truly lived up to his motto. Arnall responded with his "few bad apples" line: "Some of our employees did not do the right thing. When we found out, they were let go and action was taken so that it wouldn't happen again."

The other senator was Barack Obama. "I mean, if you go through the record of the allegations that were made, they were allegations that I think most of us would consider to be very problematic," said Obama. "And I'm wondering whether it is appropriate for us to send someone to represent our country with these issues still looming on the horizon."

"Thank you, Senator," Arnall responded. "I've read up on your background and I'm very impressed with your life history, and I can appreciate your concerns. I can assure you, Senator, that I have absolutely nothing to do, nor does my wife, in terms of these negotiations."

Then Obama said, "I've gotten a couple of letters here from people who were previously antagonistic to Ameriquest's activities that are now writing letters of support, which I think is a testament to you and your capacity to win over and work with people who may not have been on the same side initially. I've got a letter from Deval Patrick, who actually is a good personal friend of mine. . . ."

"As you know," Arnall replied, "he's a man of high integrity, and would not sit on my—on our board unless he felt that it was worthy of who he is and what he represents."

"Absolutely," said Obama.

Says one person who was fighting Arnall's nomination: "We were absolutely devastated. Here was a prominent African-American Democrat saying that this guy was giving opportunities to minorities, and providing cover for Democrats." On February 8, 2006, Arnall was confirmed by the Senate. The vote took place one month after the announcement of the $325 million settlement with the state attorneys. Press reports said that the payment "cleared the way" for Arnall's confirmation. One last time, Arnall's willingness to pay to make problems go away had served him well.

Prentiss Cox had not been among the state officials pleased by the Ameriquest settlement. Yes, it was likely to put an end to the worst of Ameriquest's lending abuses, but Cox didn't believe for a second that the settlement was going to slow down the seamy practices that permeated the subprime mortgage industry. These tactics were the only way these companies knew how to do business.

He was right. It was in almost exactly the same time frame as the Ameriquest settlement—early 2006—that the subprime mortgage business went truly mad. Or as Lisa Madigan, the Illinois attorney general, later told Congress, it was "the moment when we began to see the underwriting practices of mortgage lenders erode at a disturbingly accelerated pace."

According to an SEC report, those 2/28 mortgages, whose rate shot higher after two years, made up 31 percent of subprime mortgages in 1999, and almost 69 percent in 2006. Loans with a combination of incomplete documentation—so-called liar loans—*and* low or no down payment rose from almost nothing in 2001 to almost 20 percent of subprime originations by the end of 2006, according to a working paper by the Federal Reserve Bank of Atlanta. Overall, nontraditional mortgages like pay option ARMS and other subprime mortgages grew from almost nothing to almost half the total volume of mortgage originations in 2006, according to Susan Wachter, a professor of financial management at the Wharton School.

One former subprime executive says that his "aha" moment came in late 2005, when an underwriter at his company said, "We need to have a policy for no-doc loans when there's a doc in the file." What the underwriter meant was that the broker had been stupid enough to include a W-2 showing that a borrower whose income was supposed to be, say, $90,000 only made $40,000. "The decision," this executive says, "was to send the file back to the broker and tell them to 'clean it up.' We knew if we declined the loan, the broker would just take it to the guy down the street."

Robert Simpson, a mortgage industry veteran whose company, IMARC, investigates the reasons that loans fail, remembers reviewing a stated-income loan where the woman's occupation was "ferret farmer." Her stated income: $15,000 a month. In reality, she made $1,500 a month and worked in retail. "The loan officer decided to see if he could get away with it," Simpson says. "You see loans like that, and it tells you two things: the loans are going to go bad, and any system that makes these loans is broken."

For brokers who believed in old-fashioned underwriting, it was a deeply disconcerting time—a little like trying to remain a disciplined value investor at the height of the Internet bubble. You felt as if you were stuck in mud while the world was passing you by. Eventually, you rationalize that it all must be okay because, after all, it wasn't the brokers who approved the loans. Surely, the originators know what they're doing.

One such person was Debbie Killian. A mortgage broker in Danbury, Connecticut, she had housing in her blood: her parents had owned a real estate company, and it was what she had done most of her career. In 1996, she and her husband founded a small local company, Charter Oak Lending Group. She watched the growing madness with distaste, but she also put a handful of her clients into subprime loans. Subprimes were the loans originators were peddling. And they were the loans that many borrowers wanted. Her business grew during the bubble.

"At one time I had fifty-seven lenders all competing for our business," she recalled in an e-mail, describing the bubble years from her perspective:

> Every one of them would ask the same thing: "*Lemme take a look at whatcha working on? Anything I can close?*" Imagine all the small broker offices like mine, with all these account executives coming in every day looking for business. They would bring cookies, sandwich platters, candy, all kinds of little chotskies.
>
> Many account executives were good, honest, ethical people who were truly just trying to do their job. But there were also AEs who sold only by price. They would lead off with "We're offering an extra point for this or a ½ point for that" or "Hey, get two on the front and two on the back." And it wasn't just subprime lenders. It was all the big banks, too. They all had Alt-A and subprime products.
>
> It wasn't subprime products alone that put us where we are. Option ARMs can be an appropriate product for a certain kind of borrower. We never thought of them as subprime. It was the behavior, the mind-set that took hold. The gun didn't kill the market—the shooter did.
>
> Twenty-six-year-old college grads, with their navy blue suits and cuff links and slicked-back hair, would come in to broker shops acting all full of themselves because they were pulling down $150K a year. They didn't know anything about the business, but they were inviting us to parties and conventions and the music played, and the booze flowed.

I had an originator that made $31,200 on *one loan* that I referred to her at a 40 percent split, yet she had the audacity to tell me that it should have been a 50/50 split. That one loan paid her more money than her salary for an entire year at her previous job. That exchange was eye opening to me about a dark mind-set that had taken over.

There were commission incentives for prepayment penalties. Lenders enticed originators offering bigger YSP* on specific products they wanted to sell and would charge hard discounts on those they didn't. The entire industry was driven by yield. Lenders were simply driving volume, any way they could. The fight for loans and market share was fierce. All that marketing power slowly evolved into a way of life. We were hammered every day.

I ran an accounting business before I got into the mortgage business. My perspective was one of how to be creative and stay within the guidelines. At one time, there was a clearly delineated line of who qualified and who didn't. With each new day came a new product that moved that line ever so slowly away from prudent risk management into the world of high fees. There were those in the business who couldn't get it done within the lines—they just moved the lines. It was known as "structuring" the loan. That meant if it didn't qualify one way, *make it qualify another way.*

I remember giving a Realtor seminar one day and not only saying, but actually believing, "The lenders are offering these products. . . . They have lots of brain power in their risk, legal, compliance, and secondary market departments. They know the risk they are taking and they price for it. Who was I to question them?" So much for that! I remember a woman who worked for me making incredulous statements like, "Hey, they just dropped the FICO requirement to 580!"

"It is clear to me," Killian concluded, "that a *slow creep* took over . . . a slow moving slime that ultimately permeated the industry. I have this picture of lava . . . just creeping along until every business was covered with it, eventually getting smothered."

---

* YSP stands for yield spread premium. Ostensibly it means a deal in which the borrower agrees to a higher interest rate in return for lower up-front costs. But during the bubble, YSPs were horribly abused, and the phrase YSP came to refer to the rebate that brokers got for putting borrowers into higher-interest loans. Elizabeth Warren, the Harvard law professor and well-known financial consumer advocate, calls them "hidden kickbacks."

What infuriated Prentiss Cox more than anything was the realization that no one cared. "The war was lost," he says.

Even as the subprime business descended into true madness, the national banking regulators remained hopeless. In late 2005, the bank supervisors asked for comment from the industry on proposed "guidance" for "nontraditional" mortgages. The industry pushed back. The American Financial Services Association argued that it was "unnecessarily stringent" to require lenders to assess whether a borrower would be able to pay the full cost of a loan. The American Bankers Association said that the guidance "overstates the risks of these mortgage products." It was "incorrect," said the ABA, that they were riskier: "[R]ather, they simply present different types of risks that may be well-managed by prudent lenders." The AFSA also asked the regulators to make it clear that "guidance" was "not intended to be statements of absolute rules."

Consumer groups pleaded for stricter rules. The California Reinvestment Coalition argued that regulators shouldn't allow certain kinds of risk layering, such as stated-income option ARMs, calling such loans a "deadly combination for unsuspecting and uneducated consumers." Wrote Kevin Stein, the CRC's associate director: "Underwriting practices that misrepresent a subprime borrower's ability to repay a loan benefit neither consumers nor the economic stability of financial institutions." He added, "Borrowers are increasingly stuck with loans they cannot afford . . . all the ingredients for a financial disaster are in place."

When the regulators finally issued the guidance in the fall of 2006, it required lenders to include "consideration of a borrower's repayment capacity." But the guidance applied only to the category of mortgages that allowed borrowers to defer the payment of principal or interest. And, most important, it was just guidance. It didn't carry the force of law. Subprime companies could ignore it.

To see what that meant in practice, you needn't look any further than the Office of Thrift Supervision, which supervised Washington Mutual. After a meeting with the OTS in the fall of 2006, a WaMu executive wrote an e-mail in which he summarized the regulator's position: "Their initial response was that they view the guidance as flexible. They specifically pointed out that the language in the guidance say [sic] 'should' vs. 'must' in most cases and they are looking to WaMu to establish our position on how the guidance impacts our business practices."

A Senate investigation later concluded that during the drafting of the guidance, the OTS had argued for less stringent standards. It was very much in keeping with the turn the agency had taken. Under James Gilleran, the agency's director from late 2001 to the spring of 2005, the OTS had shrunk disastrously: Gilleran chopped 20 percent of its staff in 2002. The OTS's new goal, it said, was to "place emphasis on institutions, not the regulator, to ensure compliance with all existing laws, including consumer protection statutes."

What's more, the OTS was funded from fees paid by the thrifts themselves, based on their size. When Gilleran had taken the job, the OTS had been, as he later put it, "in a deficit financial position." WaMu's rapid growth, thanks to its exploding subprime business, meant that it was becoming an ever more important source of funds for its regulator. Between 2003 and 2008, for instance, WaMu's fees represented 12 to 15 percent of the agency's revenue, according to the Senate Permanent Subcommittee on Investigations. Perhaps that explains why John Reich, Gilleran's replacement at OTS, once described Kerry Killinger, WaMu's CEO, as "my largest constituent asset-wise."

When Washington Mutual executives analyzed the consequences of implementing the regulators' guidance, they concluded that it would reduce volume by 33 percent. So they didn't do it. As late as June 2008, an FDIC examiner found that WaMu was "not in compliance with Interagency Guidance on Nontraditional Mortgages."

That it took regulators until so late in the subprime madness to announce the guidance can't be blamed only on the OTS. There was another culprit: the Federal Reserve. The Fed's mind-set was on display in a late 2004 piece, published by the New York Fed, entitled, "Are Home Prices the Next 'Bubble'?" The answer: "As for the likelihood of a severe drop in home prices, our examination of historical national home prices finds no basis for concerns." Even after Ben Bernanke had replaced Greenspan as chairman in February 2006, it remained, in spirit, Greenspan's Fed. The market still knew best. The market knew better than career bureaucrats how to properly price risk. Market discipline would prevent truly bad things from happening. The most important task of the banking regulators was to get out of the market's way.

The president of the New York Fed by then was one of Rubin's protégés from the Clinton Treasury: Tim Geithner, who had risen to be undersecretary for international affairs while still in his thirties. When he was named to head the New York Federal Reserve in 2003, he was all of forty-two. Having studied at the feet of Rubin, Summers, and Greenspan, it was perhaps inevitable that he would share their mind-set about the virtues of the market. As the guidance was being discussed within the government, there were bank supervisors who were arguing that the Fed needed to clamp down on both mortgage lending and commercial real estate practices, especially given the rapid growth of both asset classes since 2000. But there were, shall we say, alternate concerns, which were expressed by Geithner and others who shared his views. What would the effect be on the mortgage and housing market if the Fed were heavy-handed? What would the effect be on the bottom lines of banks? "The Fed slowed down the guidance," says one person. "It was slowed down by internal debates about how far the regulators should go since most of the mortgages were sold into the market—and this guidance would replace investor risk appetites with regulatory standards."

⌘

As the mania reached its peak, an odd problem loomed: who was left to borrow money? Historically, the subprime lending business had leaned heavily toward refinancings. Sometimes that meant persuading people who had a thirty-year fixed loan—or had paid off their old mortgage entirely—to remortgage their home. Other times the homeowner was already a subprime borrower who needed to refinance after a few years, when the interest rate on his loan ratcheted up beyond his means to pay. But by 2006, 40 percent of actual home purchases in the United States were made with a subprime or Alt-A loan, according to Deutsche Bank. Why? Because soaring real estate values had priced legitimate buyers out of the market, and because brokers were seeking out borrowers who had never even thought about owning a home and who, under normal circumstances, would have no hope of doing so. Loans were being made to people who couldn't even afford the teaser rate, much less the reset rate. Borrowers would sign the papers, get the loan, move into the house—and stop paying within the first few months.

At the same time, the rapid rise in home values finally began to slow. That meant that homeowners who had known from day one that they would need to refinance before the loan reset didn't get the appreciation they needed to make a refinancing possible. "Whoever made that last loan, they were the lender of last resort," says an industry veteran. In other words, both the borrower and the lender were stuck with the bad loan.

In loan offices around the country, the tension grew, particularly for those lonely souls whose job it was to prevent bad loans from being made. Such as veteran appraiser John Ferguson, who had gotten his start at the Money Store ("the sleazy edge of subprime," he says) and then moved to BankUnited, a Florida-based bank whose exposure to subprime mortgages would eventually help bankrupt it. Ferguson had started rejecting more and more deals as he saw the quality declining. In the spring of 2006, he wrote to his boss at BankUnited's Walnut Creek, California, office: "When everything is going great guns and you kill a couple of deals then so what. But when it gets to be crunch time . . . every time you become an obstacle to someone getting their pay check things get ugly. It becomes sales vs. the review department. In this office in CA everyone knows that when I cut/kill a deal then that hurts the production numbers."

By the following spring, the panic was evident in the office-wide e-mails sent by the sales manager of the office Ferguson worked in. On April 2, 2007, he wrote, "We almost broke 36 million for 92 units, which is lower than February's numbers, which is the lowest we have been since we opened, almost. . . . I never thought we would get to this low number . . . but we did and hopefully we can learn from what we have done and do better. . . . WE JUST HAVE TO. . . . We are moving in the wrong direction folks and something has got to change."

The subprime companies were like rats racing on a wheel, going faster and faster, knowing that if they stopped, the jig was up. They *had* to keep their volume up; their very survival depended on it. They needed a constant influx of cash—either from the sale of loans to Wall Street or from selling equity and debt—to keep going. Slowing volume would be a sign that the party was coming to an end. Investors and lenders would bolt.

By comparison, the fact that the loans were getting worse and worse was a nonissue. *Who cared?* Regulators and executives alike assumed they had kicked the can to someone else—namely, the investors who purchased the mortgage-backed securities where most of these loans wound up. In a 2005 memo about Washington Mutual, the FDIC summed up the prevailing sentiment: "Management believes, however, that the impact on WMB [of a housing downturn] would be manageable, since the riskiest segments of production are sold to investors, and that these investors will bear the brunt of a bursting housing bubble."

And what did Wall Street think about the way the subprime business had gone mad? Wall Street didn't care, either. If anything, Wall Street was *encouraging* the subprime companies in their race to the bottom. Lousier loans meant higher yields. "A company would come to us and say, 'We can't believe your FICO doesn't go to 580,'" recalls a former Morgan Stanley executive. "'You're 620, but Lehman will go to 580.'"

Here was the ultimate consequence of the delinking of borrower and lender, which securitization had made possible: no one in the chain, from broker to subprime originator to Wall Street, cared that the loans they were making and selling were likely to go bad. In truth, they were all taking on huge risks in granting these terrible loans. But they were all making too much money to see it. Everyone assumed that someone else would be left holding the bag.

15

"When I Look a Homeowner in the Eye . . ."

By 2006, there was a distinct Dr. Jekyll and Mr. Hyde–like quality to Angelo Mozilo. The good Angelo had been warning for a surprisingly long time that his industry was heading into dangerous territory. "I'm deeply concerned about credit quality in the overall industry," he said in the spring of 2005. "I think that the amount of capacity that's been developed for subprime is much greater than the quality of subprime loans available." A year later, he said to a group of analysts, "I believe there's a lot of fraud" in stated-income loans. And he flatly told CNBC's Maria Bartiromo that a housing recession was on the way. "I would expect a general decline of 5 percent to 10 percent [in housing prices] throughout the country, some areas 20 percent. And in areas where you have had heavy speculation, you could have 30 percent," he said.

The bad Angelo insisted that none of this would be a problem for Countrywide. Countrywide wasn't just some fly-by-night subprime lender; it was "America's Number One Home Loan Lender!" Mozilo and other executives repeatedly stressed the high standards that Countrywide used to make its mortgages. Countrywide's "proprietary technology" would help it "avoid any foreclosure," Mozilo told investors, according to the *Los Angeles Times*.

Inside Countrywide, however, Mozilo was not so sanguine. In the spring of 2006, he wrote an e-mail describing Countrywide's 80/20 subprime loan as "the most dangerous product in existence and there can be nothing more toxic." Around the same time, Mozilo sent another e-mail saying that he had "personally observed a serious lack of compliance within our origination system as it relates to documentation and generally a deterioration in the quality of loans originated versus the pricing of those loan[s]." He clearly seemed worried.

The discrepancy between private worry and public proclamation would later cause the SEC to charge Mozilo and several of his top aides with fraud for not disclosing Countrywide's growing risks to investors. In Mozilo's case, the government also charged him with insider trading: from November 2006 through August 2007, he got total proceeds of almost $140 million from cashing in stock options. A judge overseeing a class action lawsuit filed against Countrywide wrote in one ruling that it was "extraordinary" how the "company's essential operations were so at odds with the company's public statements."*

There is little question that the money, and the accolades, had come to matter too much to Mozilo. And yet it's unclear whether Mozilo was, in fact, trying to deceive Countrywide's investors, or whether he was so desperate to win the market share battle that he simply couldn't see the ultimate cost of the bad loans Countrywide was making. He remained, quite simply, the truest of true believers, both in his company and in the transcendent virtue of subprime loans Countrywide made. He used to say that if 10 percent of subprime borrowers defaulted, that meant 90 percent were paying their mortgages on time, every last one of them a borrower who wouldn't have otherwise had a shot at the American Dream. "Angelo, he totally believed," says a former executive. "He'd say, 'When I look a homeowner in the eye, I can tell if they'll pay.' We'd say, 'Angelo, we don't even do a personal interview anymore—would you stop saying you can see it in their eyes?'"

As for Countrywide, Mozilo was convinced that it had become so big and so strong that it was impregnable. By 2006, it ranked 122 on the Fortune 500, with $18.5 billion in 2005 revenue, $2.4 billion in profits, and a mortgage origination engine that had generated a staggering $490 billion in loans. Surely, a company with that kind of financial might could weather even a severe housing downturn. It might even help Countrywide in the long run, by putting some of its subprime-only competitors out of business. During an investor presentation in 2006, Mozilo read the names of some of the companies that had exited the business: Great Western, Home Savings, Glen-Fed, American Residential, and others. "These are the very ones that equity analysts told me that I should be fearing . . . all gone," he said. "And ten years

---

* Countrywide later paid $600 million to settle the suit, while denying the allegations.

from now when we read this list, you'll see that most of the players today will be gone. Except for Countrywide."

Yes, Mozilo saw that Countrywide was making some risky loans, but what he didn't see—what he couldn't see—was that these loans could make his company every bit as vulnerable as the competitors he disparaged. "If you're a true believer, you can ignore things you shouldn't ignore!" says one former Countrywide executive. "That was Angelo Mozilo's problem." Another puts it a little differently: "He's a great salesman, and great salesmen are often the guys who get sold."

<hr />

Mozilo had long planned to retire from Countrywide at the end of 2006. He was approaching seventy years old, and he had been in the mortgage business, in one way or another, for over fifty years. Although he still held the title of CEO, he was no longer involved in the day-to-day realities of running the business, thanks in part to his undisclosed health problems. His trusted lieutenants, with whom he'd built the company, were taking charge, starting with Stan Kurland, who was his designated successor. A transition had been set in motion.

But in 2005, Mozilo began to feel better. As he regained his health, he became less sure he wanted to leave the company he often called his "baby." Another executive recalls a conversation he had with Kurland around then. "You realize I run this company," Kurland said to this person. "Angelo doesn't know any of the details." A few weeks later, this same executive was with Mozilo, who said abruptly, "All Stan is interested in is the hedging reports," referring to the ways in which Countrywide hedged its interest rate risk. "All he does is the daily hedge. He really doesn't want to run this company."

Executives at Countrywide noticed another change, too. Decisions had always come from Angelo and Stan; now they came from Angelo, Stan, and Dave—Dave Sambol.

At the same time, Sambol and Kurland were increasingly disagreeing about key aspects of Countrywide's strategy. With the Fed tightening interest rates, Kurland, fearing its effect on the housing market, wanted to pull in the horns a little, say several former executives. Sambol wanted to keep gunning for growth. And more and more Mozilo was siding with Sambol. Those in the Kurland camp felt increasingly marginalized: "2005 was tough," says one of them. "You were always trying to say no." One former executive recalls hearing Kurland's voice, raised and angry, coming from his office during an apparent argument with Sambol. The culture, which had been tough to begin with, became "a culture of intimidation," says another ex-executive. A turning point for this executive came when he saw Drew Gissinger, the six-foot-five former San Diego Chargers offensive lineman who served as Sambol's number two, standing over John McMurray, Countrywide's chief risk officer, browbeating him, or so it appeared to this person. "Your chief risk guy should be the most respected person in the organization," another former executive says, recalling the incident.*

In the fall of 2005, Countrywide's board asked Kurland for guidance on how he envisioned dividing responsibilities with Mozilo once he became CEO. What ensued became a topic of much discussion and speculation in Countrywide's top ranks. As other former executives recount the story, Kurland was furious. He didn't want *any* division: either he was going to be CEO or he wasn't. He didn't want the title if he wasn't going to truly be in charge, especially given that Mozilo could be a loose cannon and that Sambol, in his view, needed reining in. Kurland sent Mozilo an e-mail that became infamous in Countrywide's upper ranks, outlining his expectations for the role Mozilo would have when he stepped down. Essentially, Kurland outlined a structure in which he would be running the company and Mozilo would assume the classic role of the ex-founder: "non-executive chairman of the board," an honorific with no power. Kurland, says one person, was even reluctant to have Mozilo continue as the company's spokesperson on CNBC.

The memo led to a bitter—and childish—feud between the two men, one that consumed inordinate amounts of everyone's energy. Mozilo was deeply offended and, as the story goes, when Kurland tried to apologize, Mozilo refused to accept it. "There's no way I deserve this after a thirty-year relationship," Kurland told one person.

Increasingly, Kurland felt like he was fighting a losing battle on two fronts, according to someone he confided in. "A period of torture" is how this person says he described Kurland's time at Countrywide after the feud began. As the Fed continued to increase interest rates—it did so seventeen times in a row between June 2004 and June 2006—Kurland became increasingly worried about the housing market. But within the company, he and others who felt that way were the Chicken Littles. Kurland, according to another

---

* A Gissinger defender says that this is inaccurate, and that Gissinger and McMurray had a professional working relationship.

person, also agreed with Countrywide's supervisors at the Federal Reserve, which oversaw the holding company (while the OCC regulated Countrywide's bank), about the importance of both the proposed industry-wide guidance on nontraditional mortgages as well as uniform standards for appraisal practices. Both Mozilo and Sambol pushed back. Kurland told a confidant that he didn't think he could win a battle for control with Mozilo, because the board was in the founder's pocket. He felt that he could have gotten the executive ranks to line up behind him. But doing so would have required cutting a deal with Dave Sambol and giving him more control than Kurland wanted him to have. "Maybe I'm not cutthroat enough," Kurland said at one point.

Finally, Kurland reached his limit, according to executives who watched the feud play out. The entire company had become obsessed with what some called "the battle at the top." It was distracting. The company needed to be focusing its energies on the housing market, not its internal soap opera. Kurland told Mozilo that if their standoff didn't end, it would destroy the company. Although no one on the outside knew it, by the spring of 2006 Kurland was essentially out of Countrywide's management.

By the summer, people who paid attention to Countrywide were starting to realize that something was up. "I was in Denver with Angelo," recalls one analyst. "We were riding in the car, and Mozilo said something to me about how unique Sambol was, that he had technical knowledge, plus he was an excellent salesman. The comment came out of the blue. I wasn't asking about Sambol, and I began to wonder why he was telling me this. Was Sambol in the running?"

He was. In September 2006, just after the *American Banker* gave Mozilo its Lifetime Achievement Award, Countrywide announced that Stan Kurland was leaving the company and Sambol would replace him as president and COO. Mozilo would stay on as CEO until 2009, by which time he would be seventy-one. Kurland's departure was the culmination of the estrangement that had developed between the two men, who had worked together for three decades. Kurland left without so much as a good-bye e-mail to the staff. Hurt and embittered, he told a friend that he didn't see the point in pretending otherwise.

One former Countrywide executive recalls explaining to Mozilo why Sambol was the wrong choice: "I tried to get Angelo to appreciate where Sambol was coming from. I'd say, 'He's not strategic and he's not long term.' Angelo would just stare blankly back at me."

But to anyone who thought about it, there wasn't really a big mystery as to why Mozilo had fallen so hard for Sambol. Sambol was a salesman, just like Mozilo. Sambol craved market share, just like Mozilo. He was passionate about Countrywide. He was a believer. With Sambol as president, he didn't have to turn over the reins of his company to anyone else, not just yet. What's more, with Sambol as his number two, Mozilo could avoid having to face the hard choices that needed to be made. Sambol didn't seem to want to play defense, even if that's what the company needed, as subprime madness spread and interest rates continued their ascent. In the spring of 2006, he told investors, "We're extremely competitive in terms of our desire to win and we have a particular focus on offense."

A few months before Kurland officially left, Mozilo had sent an e-mail to Sambol, CFO Eric Sieracki, and other executives. It could have been written by two different people. (Kurland was only CC'd.) He began the e-mail with what amounted to an acknowledgment of reality: "As we are all aware Stan has begun a major undertaking to assure that we reduce midline expenses as rapidly as possible and to be reduced at least in concert with expected revenue reductions from our production divisions." He continued, "I want you to examine our risk profile."

But then, as he wound it up, he displayed where his heart really was: "By the way," he wrote, "we must continue to grow our sales force and all other businesses that keep the top line increasing particularly in the origination channels."

In late 2006, another meeting of mortgage executives was taking place, this one in Kauai, Hawaii. This was a gathering of Washington Mutual's top producers. As part of the festivities, a handful of WaMu employees did a skit about a funeral for one of its competitors. At the podium, one employee solemnly read a note. "For this day, we have lost one of the true legends in our industry." As he spoke, a coffin imprinted with a logo was carried out onto the stage by four pallbearers dressed in black, wearing black sunglasses. The logo read: COUNTRYWIDE.

"So many of us warned the dearly departed about the risky—some may say reckless—behavior they engaged in," he continued. "Throwing money around like Paris Hilton and selling products they don't really know or understand." As the sounds of "Na Na, Na, Na, Hey Hey, Goodbye" filled the room, he added that there was a bright side to the passing of WaMu's biggest rival: "[S]ome really scary and dangerous people won't be on the street anymore."

This was fiction, of course. At the time it took place, Countrywide was the biggest mortgage lender in the country. But the point was this: within the industry, it wasn't any secret that Countrywide was out on the edge of the mortgage market, even if Mozilo himself didn't want to believe it. Even WaMu, which was doing plenty of its own risky lending—enough to eventually bring it down—could see the excesses taking place at Countrywide.

It's hard to know when the turning point took place at Countrywide. Risky loans were undoubtedly made on Kurland's watch: he too pushed Countrywide's market share ambitions. A shareholder lawsuit would later charge that Mozilo, Sambol, and Kurland were "principally responsible for [Countrywide's] 'culture change' and concerted foray into leveraged and high risk lending practices." According to this lawsuit, Kurland sold $192 million of stock from March 2004 to March 2008. But there were a few signals that lending wasn't completely out of control. Eliot Spitzer had launched an investigation into whether Countrywide's 2004 loans reflected racial bias. This was around the same time that Ameriquest was being investigated. In the end, Countrywide agreed to commit $3 million to consumer education—a far cry from the $325 million Ameriquest paid to settle the charges against it. One former executive says that Spitzer's staff was crawling all over Countrywide; surely if they had discovered deeper problems, Spitzer would have come down harder on the company. (Countrywide cooperated with Spitzer, unlike J.P. Morgan, HSBC, and Wells Fargo, which took refuge in preemption.)

And at Countrywide, as with other mortgage originators, there had been a brief moment of sanity right before the Ameriquest settlement was announced. According to the *Wall Street Journal*, Countrywide was going to make it "tougher for borrowers to qualify for a 1 percent teaser rate on its option ARMs." Internally, Kurland was pushing for that, according to a former executive; the company also issued a "no exceptions" policy in early 2006, meaning that there would be no more exceptions to underwriting policies. Besides, the government was going to issue that guidance on nontraditional loans, and Countrywide wanted to be on the right side of that. But as it became clear that any new guidance would have no teeth—and perhaps as Kurland lost power—the moment passed.

Once Kurland was officially out the door, Sambol began taking control of Countrywide. One of the first things he did was sideline some of the company's governance structures, such as its executive risk committee, according to a former executive. Under Kurland, the protocol had always been to meet roughly a half dozen times a year. Under Sambol, it met once. Every meeting after that was canceled. "They devalued operational excellence and overvalued their own intellect," says another former executive.

What's more, no sooner had Kurland left than Sambol and Mozilo decided to switch regulators, shedding the OCC and the Fed for the OTS. "This move is one of the places where they made a terrible mistake," says a former executive. Having the Fed and the OCC regulate the company gave it a bit of a halo effect that disappeared when it moved to the OTS. And really, insulting the Fed by cutting the regulatory cord was hardly a smart move.

By the end of 2006, Countrywide's underwriting guidelines were "wider and more aggressive than they had ever been," the SEC later charged. In a memo Mozilo sent to the board and all the top executives on December 7, 2006, he wrote that "subprime has evolved from a sector largely comprised of borrowers with impaired credit . . . to a sector offering very high leverage and reduced documentation." And he noted the following shocking facts: In 2001, Countrywide's maximum loan size in subprime was $400,000, with a maximum loan-to-value ratio of 90 percent (meaning a 10 percent down payment). You could do a stated-documentation loan only if you were self-employed. Countrywide did not have either interest-only loans or 80/20 loans in its product line. By 2006, however, subprime borrowers could get a loan up to $1 million. The maximum loan-to-value ratio was by then 100 percent. The only qualification for doing a stated-income loan was that you were a "wage earner." Countrywide now offered interest-only loans to borrowers whose FICO scores were as low as 560, and 80/20 loans to borrowers with 580 FICO scores. As a result, 36 percent of Countrywide's subprime originations in 2006 were done on a stated-documentation basis, versus just 13 percent in 2001. Twenty-three percent were interest-only, and 24 percent were 80/20 loans.*

To put it another way, it was hard to imagine *anyone* who wouldn't qualify for a Countrywide subprime loan during the final throes of the housing bubble. In a lawsuit that would later be filed by the Mortgage Guaranty

---

* In that same memo, Mozilo noted that while purchase loans—loans used to actually purchase a house—had increased from 19 percent of Countrywide's subprime business in 2001 to 33 percent in 2006, the other two-thirds of its subprime loans were refinancings. In other words, even at Countrywide, this wasn't really about putting people in homes.

Insurance Corporation, which had insured many Countrywide loans, investigators went back and dug up details of some of the loans Countrywide had made during the subprime bubble. One loan Mortgage Guaranty investigated was for $360,000 made to a woman in Chicago who was supposedly earning $6,833 per month as an employee of an auto body shop. According to her loan application, the house she was purchasing was intended to be her primary residence. In truth, the woman was a part-time housekeeper who earned about $1,300 a month. She "posed as a front buyer to help her sister . . . and brother-in-law . . . acquire the home." A few months after closing on the house, "[she] returned to her home in Poland because she was unable to find steady work in Chicago."

Was this an example of a borrower pulling the wool over the eyes of the loan officer? Not exactly. "[The borrower] reported to MGIC that she disclosed her true employment, her actual income, and her intention to help her family purchase the property to the loan officer." The loan officer told her she could "pose as a front buyer, obtain mortgage financing for her sister and brother-in-law, and avoid personal responsibility for the loan." When the loan officer learned that she was a friend of the son of a man who owned an auto body shop, she "helped prepare a document" for the man to sign stating her employment and monthly income. Then she forged the man's signature.

Another borrower was supposed to be a dairy foreman making $10,500 a month; he was really a milker at the dairy earning one-tenth that amount, and buying the house for his son rather than himself. The loan officer, according to the lawsuit, told him that he would be "lending your son your credit" and would not be responsible for the monthly payments. The borrower, who didn't speak English, simply signed where the loan officer told him to. He got a $350,000 loan.

A "sales executive for Bay Area Sales and Marketing earning $8,700 a month" had actually been unemployed since 1989 and had no income. (And there was no such business as Bay Area Sales and Marketing.) She got a $398,050 refinancing. A house in Atlanta that had been appraised for $395,000 was worth no more than $277,000. A borrower's tax return, claiming earnings of $17,661, was fraudulent, and his bank account was nonexistent. A borrower who claimed to be an account executive for "GNG Investments in Santa Clara, California"—another nonexistent firm—turned out to be a janitor making $3,901.58 a month. She never made the $30,000 down payment Countrywide was claiming. She got a $600,000 house.

According to the Mortgage Guaranty lawsuit, "by about 2006, Country-wide's internal risk assessors knew that in a substantial number of its stated-income loans—fully a third—borrowers overstated income by more than 50 percent. Countrywide also knew that many appraisers were overstating property values to drive originations by making loans appear less risky . . . Countrywide deliberately disregarded these and other signs of fraud in order to increase its market share."

But those subprime loans weren't the only thing that increased the risk drastically at Countrywide. In that schizophrenic e-mail Mozilo had sent back in May, he also wrote that "we must pay special attention to helocs [home equity loans] and pay options. With interest rates continuing to rise unabated helocs will become increasingly toxic. . . . As for pay options the Bank faces potential unexpected losses because higher rates will cause these loans to reset much earlier than anticipated and as a result causing mortgag-ors to default due to the substantial increase in their payments."

In fact, Countrywide was originating huge numbers of pay option ARMs. In 2005 and 2006, Countrywide originated more than $160 billion worth of pay option ARMs—between 17 percent and 21 percent of its *total* loan orig-inations, prime and subprime combined, according to a lawsuit later filed against the company. In 2007, with the market on the verge of collapse, Countrywide originated another $160 billion of these loans, according to *Inside Mortgage Finance.* The *Los Angeles Times* reported that Countrywide made one-quarter of all the option ARM loans in the country in 2007.

Although a high percentage of Countrywide's pay option ARMs went to borrowers with high FICO scores—something Countrywide bragged about to its investors—that was a misleading statistic. The majority of the loans went to borrowers on a low- or no-documentation basis. And according to the Center for Responsible Lending, more than 80 percent of the option ARMs Countrywide originated in 2005 and 2006, totaling $138 billion, did not meet the new voluntary guidelines regulators had published in late 2006. In a letter to regulators, which was leaked to the *Los Angeles Times,* Coun-trywide admitted that it often judged whether borrowers could qualify for a loan based on the teaser rate, not the full rate, and that in the fourth quarter of 2006 about 60 percent of Countrywide's adjustable-rate borrowers would not have qualified at the higher rate. (This appeared to contradict claims by Mozilo that the company's policies required that borrowers be able to pay the higher rate.)

On July 10, Mozilo sent another e-mail to his top executives. "If I am reading these numbers correctly," he wrote, "it appears to me that the loans (pay options) with neg am have a higher delinquency than our standard book of business. If this is the case, this is quite alarming, because of the very low payment requirements of a neg am loan." He added in another e-mail, "I would like Gissinger and Hale to make certain that a letter, in BOLD TYPE, is included in every new pay option loan that clearly indicates the consequences of negative amort and encourage them to make full payment. . . ."

And then there were home equity lines of credit, a product that was growing geometrically at Countrywide. As early as April 2005, John McMurray reported that the risk that home equity loans would default had doubled over the past year, mainly due to lack of documentation. That warning did nothing to slow the growth, nor tame the risk. Countrywide would later admit that a big chunk of its home equity lines resulted in the homeowner having debt that was close to 100 percent of the value of the property.

Back in the fall of 2006, with Sambol in charge and Countrywide's market share hovering at just above 15 percent, the company put on a conference for investors. On the surface, at least, it was a high moment for the company. It would soon report 2006 revenues of $24.4 billion, up nearly $6 billion from 2005. Profits hit an all-time high of nearly $2.7 billion. Its ranking on the Fortune 500 rose from 122 to 91. So seemingly confident was the company in its financial strength that instead of conserving capital it announced a $2.5 billion stock buyback. In February 2007, Countrywide's stock hit an all-time high of over $45 a share. What few at Countrywide seemed to understand was that it wasn't just Countrywide's customers who were assuming a great deal of risk. So was the company itself.

Like other mortgage originators, Countrywide kept the riskiest piece of a securitization, the residuals, on its own balance sheet. Kurland's policy had been to presell subprime loans, the argument being that if you couldn't sell the whole thing, then you shouldn't make the loan. But a former executive says that changed. Another former executive recalls arguing to Drew Gissinger that these assets were risky and that the value at which Countrywide was booking them was inflated. Gissinger disagreed; these were high-quality assets, he said. "But that's if everyone pays!" this executive responded. By the end of 2006, Countrywide had $2.8 billion worth of residuals on its balance sheet, representing about 15 percent of Countrywide's equity. The company's internal enterprise risk assessment map—a key risk report—was flashing orange.

Then, starting in 2005, Countrywide began to keep both pay option ARMs and a chunk of home equity loans—both the loans themselves and the residuals from home equity securitizations—on its balance sheet as well. In theory this made sense. Countrywide wasn't just a mortgage shop, dependent on the vicissitudes of the mortgage market—it was a financial institution that could thrive in all markets. The rationale, once again, was that while there would be some delinquencies, the income stream from these loans would provide stability during tougher times. But, of course, that depended on the quality of the loans.

In the spring of 2005, Kurland argued that Countrywide was taking on too much balance sheet risk in home equity loans, according to the SEC. But the numbers just went higher. By the end of 2006, Countrywide had more than $20 billion worth of home equity loans on its books, almost double 2004's level. And while Kurland had entered into hedges with Wall Street firms, offsetting the risk if the value of the residuals declined, those hedges were removed once he was pushed aside, according to one former executive. After all, by early 2007 they were in the money, and you could book a gain! "It wasn't supposed to be about the *gain*," says one former executive. "It was a *hedge*."

Finally, Countrywide was putting pay option ARMs on its own balance sheet instead of selling them to Wall Street. By the end of 2006, Countrywide had $32.7 billion worth of pay option ARMs on its balance sheet, up from just $4.7 billion at the end of 2004. As Mozilo later wrote in an e-mail to Sambol and Sieracki, "We have no way, with any reasonable certainty, to assess the real risk of holding these loans on our balance sheet. . . . The bottom line is that we are flying blind on how these loans will perform in a stressed environment." He began urging Sambol to sell the portfolio of option ARMs. But by that time, it was way too late.

There were some inside Countrywide who worried that the risks weren't being adequately disclosed to investors. The SEC would later charge that, throughout 2006, McMurray "unsuccessfully lobbied to the financial reporting department that Countrywide disclose more information about its increasing credit risk, but these disclosures were not made." In early 2007, McMurray provided Sambol and others with an outline of where it was likely to suffer losses. He asked that a version of the outline be included in the company's year-end financial report. It wasn't, according to the SEC. Later that year, he again argued that the company should disclose its widened underwriting guidelines to investors.

According to the SEC, Sieracki and Sambol made the decision not to include McMurray's concerns about the underwriting guidelines in the company's financial report. But it doesn't seem like McMurray exactly laid his body across the tracks, either. He later said in a deposition that he was "comfortable" after discussing his issues with Anne McCallion, Countrywide's deputy CFO. McCallion, for her part, said that "there were disclosures that were contained in the document that addressed the substance of his comments."

But whether Countrywide was under a legal obligation to disclose more is almost beside the point. It was particularly important for a company like Countrywide that the market not get any nasty surprises, because Countrywide lived and died on the market's confidence in it. Like all nonbank mortgage originators, Countrywide relied on cash from sales of its loans, and from selling equity and debt, to fund itself. Countrywide also relied on its ability to pledge its mortgages as collateral for loans in the overnight repo market. In fact, Countrywide was even more reliant on these funding sources because it also kept the rights to service the mortgages that it made, which it valued at $16.2 billion at the end of 2006. (Many other companies sold these rights.) Kurland had planned on this as a way to ensure that Countrywide could survive a market downturn caused by rising interest rates: the ongoing payments from servicing mortgages were supposed to provide a cushion in years when the company couldn't make as many mortgages. But it meant that Countrywide got less cash in the door up front.

The risk of Countrywide's dependence on the market could be mitigated if it were tightly managed, which explains why Kurland worried so incessantly about the operational aspects of the business. But the more loans and residuals that were put on Countrywide's balance sheet, the harder the risk was to manage.

In other words, if the market ever got spooked about Countrywide's health—if, say, investors began to question the value of the residuals or the loans on Countrywide's balance sheet—and shut off the supply of cash, Countrywide could be in jeopardy.

Says another analyst: "I told Angelo that his Achilles' heel was funding. In his typical way, Angelo said, 'You're all wrong.'"

16

Hank Paulson Takes the Plunge

The head of investment banking at Merrill Lynch for much of the Stan O'Neal era was a charming, gregarious, politically shrewd executive named Greg Fleming. He was only thirty-nine years old when he took charge of Merrill's investment banking arm—a job he got in the summer of 2003 after O'Neal fired Tom Patrick and then pushed out Arshad Zakaria, who had overseen investment banking. Fleming had a knack for getting powerful men to warm up to him; it was one of the reasons he was a good investment banker. After the 9/11 attacks damaged Merrill's headquarters, he and about a hundred of his employees camped out on an empty floor provided by BlackRock, according to the *Wall Street Journal*. BlackRock was the big money management firm Larry Fink had founded in 1989 after leaving First Boston. A friendship soon developed between the two men, which, four and a half years later, helped bring about a $9.8 billion deal in which Merrill took a 49.8 percent stake in BlackRock, while Fink's firm took control of Merrill's money management unit.

Fleming had befriended O'Neal in similar fashion. They had known each other since the mid-1990s, when Fleming was a wet-behind-the-ears investment banker and O'Neal was a man on the make. After O'Neal was named president—with the top job all but guaranteed—Fleming made a point of getting together with him. "We'd talk about what was going on, who was doing what. He actually became an adviser," O'Neal told the *Journal*. "He helped educate me very quickly."

Fleming had been a believer in O'Neal early on, agreeing with his assessment that Merrill culture needed toughening up. Over time, however, his relationship with O'Neal got testier, especially as O'Neal became more isolated. After the BlackRock deal, the *Journal* wrote an article highlighting

Fleming's role; although O'Neal was quoted in it, Fleming got the strong sense that O'Neal resented the fact that he had gotten the publicity. Also, unlike most of the executives O'Neal surrounded himself with after *l'affaire* Patrick, Fleming was willing to speak his mind. Although Fleming had perfect pitch when it came to knowing just how far he could push O'Neal, unlike his peers in the executive suite, he did push. For instance, O'Neal desperately wanted to buy a mortgage originator, which many of Merrill's competitors used to supply them with the raw material for mortgage-backed securities and CDOs. Fleming had successfully prevented Merrill from buying New Century, a company that would turn out to be one of the worst of the subprime lenders—and which Merrill had come "within a hair" of buying, according to one former executive. Fleming was the executive O'Neal said he could no longer have dinner with, because it was "too painful" to hear Fleming disagree with him.

And one other thing: Fleming had a close relationship with Jeff Kronthal. As one of O'Neal's top deputies, Fleming had gotten early word of the firing. He couldn't believe it. Kronthal wasn't just a good trader; he was probably the best trader Merrill had. He had been around mortgage-backed securities his whole career, going back to Salomon Brothers and Lew Ranieri. He was deeply loyal to Merrill, where he had worked for seventeen years. Though he didn't have the title, he was clearly the head of trading at Merrill Lynch.

Fleming's first instinct was to try to get the decision reversed. He asked O'Neal to move Kronthal and his team to Fleming's jurisdiction and let them continue to run the credit desks. After thinking it over, O'Neal said no; Fleming recalls an early morning phone call from O'Neal in which he told Fleming he needed "to play ball." When Fleming asked O'Neal why Kronthal had to be fired, O'Neal replied, "You don't understand. Dysfunction is good on Wall Street." Dow Kim told Fleming that under no circumstances was he to give Kronthal advance word that he was being let go. That was Kim's job, and he would be doing it soon enough.

It was the middle of July 2006. Fleming and his wife were in London. When they were out shopping one day, Fleming's cell phone began ringing and ringing. It was Kronthal. At first, Fleming ignored the calls, but as they kept coming his wife asked him what was going on. When he told her, she urged him to stop ducking the calls and talk to his friend. Kronthal told Fleming he was hearing rumors that he and many of Merrill's veteran traders were all going to be fired. Fleming hemmed and hawed, but by the end of their long, anguished, teary conversation, Kronthal knew that the rumors were true.

Fleming didn't speak to O'Neal for a month and a half. The ice was broken only when O'Neal pleaded with Fleming not to leave the firm, something he had been contemplating. Fleming did stay—in fact, he stayed right through the financial crisis, becoming Merrill's president along the way and brokering the deal Merrill cut with Bank of America on the infamous "Lehman weekend" in mid-September 2008. But the Kronthal firing was something he never stopped thinking about. Not only because it betrayed "a lack of basic human dignity," as Fleming would later put it. And not only because it was so unnecessary. To Fleming, that July day in 2006 when Kronthal and his team were fired was the day Merrill Lynch's fate was sealed. Yes, Fleming knew he was biased, but given what later happened, it seemed irrefutable. Prior to that day, Merrill may well have avoided the subprime problems that would soon bring Wall Street to its knees. After that date, Merrill was doomed to make the same mistakes as most of its competitors.

"It was one of the dumbest, most vindictive decisions I have ever seen," Fleming would later say. And he was right.

The reason Jeff Kronthal had to be fired was that, several months earlier, O'Neal had been persuaded to bring in a fast-rising bond salesman named Osman Semerci and give him a title—global head of fixed income, currencies, and commodities—that effectively made him Kronthal's boss. Semerci, a thirty-nine-year-old British citizen of Turkish descent, had a reputation for being extremely driven and extremely aggressive—exactly the traits O'Neal wanted on the trading desks. Semerci wouldn't be afraid to take big risks to generate big profits. He wouldn't be excessively cautious the way Kronthal sometimes was.

Semerci also had a reputation for being a mean boss, which O'Neal didn't mind at all. "He was in your face," says a former Merrill executive. "He had a reputation internally that if you got on his bad side, he would write your name down and look for a chance to get you." Merrill traders used to call it the blacklist; Semerci would actually walk the floors with a pen and clipboard in hand, writing down things he didn't like.

Semerci was also someone who couldn't tolerate anyone who might be a threat to him. Kronthal, the most respected trader at Merrill Lynch, certainly fit the bill. So as a condition of taking the promotion, he insisted that he be able to fire Kronthal and those close to him, and assemble his own team of executives and traders. O'Neal assented. He also insisted that he never have to report to Greg Fleming, whom he loathed. O'Neal assented to that as well.

Dow Kim had been one of the men who convinced O'Neal to promote Semerci. The other was Merrill's chief administrative officer, Ahmass Fakahany. Although Fakahany had spent his career on the administrative side of Merrill, overseeing such functions as human resources and computer systems, he wielded outsized power because he was indisputably the one executive who was close to O'Neal. "Fakahany was the one guy who could go into Stan's office, close the door, and say, '*Can you believe . . . ?*'" says a former executive. He had worked in the Merrill finance office when O'Neal had been CFO, and had essentially hitched his wagon to O'Neal's pony.

By general consensus, Fakahany was deeply in over his head. He knew virtually nothing about trading—or about the complications of managing a balance sheet the size of Merrill's. He was also in charge of Merrill's risk management function, another subject about which he knew next to nothing. He was backing Semerci more because he knew Semerci would appeal to O'Neal than because Semerci knew how to run a mortgage desk. In fact, Semerci knew very little about the credit markets. "He didn't understand U.S.-based risk," says a former Merrill executive.

O'Neal would later tell friends that nobody had recommended Kronthal for a promotion, while Semerci had been recommended by two of his top guys, Fakahany and Kim. But that remark just serves to illustrate how out of touch O'Neal had become. O'Neal had never been the kind of CEO who walked the trading floor. The intricacies of the firm's trading positions held no interest for him, except to the extent they showed profits or losses. His constant demand that his trading executives take more risk was based mainly on his annoyance that Goldman Sachs and Lehman Brothers had more profitable trading desks, rather than on a deep understanding of what those risks entailed. His feel for the firm's risk positions came primarily from reading the daily VaR reports. Whenever he went to Washington or attended conferences, he would hear about the riskiness of, say, leveraged loans, so he kept close tabs on that part of the business. But nobody ever mentioned possible problems with mortgage bonds—so he didn't worry about them. By 2006, O'Neal was so divorced from his own firm that he failed to appreciate the utter lunacy of Semerci's desire to clean house. Did he really think Semerci could get rid of the firm's most experienced mortgage traders and not harm the mortgage desk? Sadly, it seems that O'Neal didn't think about it at all.

The arrival of Semerci should have put Dow Kim on high alert, if only because he had no way of knowing whether Semerci was up to the job. Semerci was coming into his new position with a lot of pressure on him.

Though Chris Ricciardi was gone, Merrill desperately wanted to maintain its position as the number one CDO underwriter. And, says a former Merrill colleague, Semerci felt another kind of Wall Street pressure: "Osman wanted to make a lot of money in a short period of time."

The CDO business was changing. AIG had stopped insuring super-senior tranches. The banks that had always bought the super-seniors weren't buying them anymore. CDOs were becoming harder to sell to investors. Yet from the summer of 2006, when Kronthal and the other veteran traders were ousted, to the summer of 2007, Merrill Lynch continued to churn out CDOs. It retained its position as the number one underwriter. The mortgage desk reaped fees and posted profits. The traders themselves made big bonuses. Whenever anyone asked, Semerci would tell Merrill executives that the firm had very little exposure to subprime mortgage risk; he had made all this money for the firm, he said, while derisking the portfolio. But he told no one how, exactly, he was accomplishing this. Incredibly, no one thought to ask. Instead, from the boardroom to the trading floor, everyone simply assumed that all was well—that the business was being run the same way it had always been run. But it wasn't.

There was one person at Merrill Lynch who might well have asked the right questions, had he been in a position to do so. His name was John Breit, and he was a risk manager who specialized in evaluating derivatives risk. A calm, soft-spoken ex-physicist, Breit had joined the long march from academia to Wall Street, landing at Merrill Lynch in 1990. He was hardly antiderivatives; like most quants, he believed that derivatives were a useful tool. Nor was he the kind of risk manager who feared all risk. On the contrary, he was one of the people who believed that Merrill had shot itself in the foot by being too risk averse in years gone by.

The problem with O'Neal's Merrill, Breit believed, was that even as the CEO was pushing the desks to take more risk, the institution still recoiled at a $50 million loss. Merrill's schizophrenia about risk caused traders to seek out risks that wouldn't show up in the risk models, Breit believed. "If the VaR is small," he liked to say, "it means we are taking risk in things we can't measure." Breit used to tell Merrill management that VaR didn't measure black swans—the rare but real risks that could destroy a firm. That was its fatal flaw.

Breit had also learned over the years that by the standards of a physicist, Wall Street was quantitatively illiterate. Executives learned terms like "stan-

Lewis Ranieri, the Salomon Brothers bond trader who helped invent the mortgage-backed security in the 1980s. "I wasn't out to invent the biggest floating craps game of all time," he once said. "But that's what happened." (© Phil McCarten/Reuters)

As CEO of Fannie Mae, David Maxwell (right, with future Fannie CEO Jim Johnson) formed an uneasy alliance with Ranieri and transformed his organization into the most powerful player in housing finance. (© Doug Mills/AP Photo)

After creating some of the first mortgage-backed securities for First Boston in the 1980s, Larry Fink later served as a key government adviser during the financial crisis. (© Mat Szwajkos/Getty Images)

Blythe Masters helped invent the credit default swap for J.P. Morgan. (© Bloomberg/Getty Images)

Dennis Weatherstone, J.P. Morgan's CEO in the early 1990s, wanted an all-purpose risk model that could measure risk across the entire bank. The result was Value at Risk, or VaR, which became the de facto standard on Wall Street. Unlike other Wall Street executives, Weatherstone understood VaR's limitations as well as its uses. (© JPMorgan & Co. Incorporated)

Hank Greenberg built AIG into the largest insurance company in the world and appeared to have his finger on the pulse of every one of the company's hundreds of subsidiaries. But when he was forced to resign in 2005, he left AIG without a viable successor. (© Bloomberg/Getty Images)

Joe Cassano was known for his raging temper and his modest lifestyle. He pushed AIG-FP to begin selling credit default swaps on CDOs. The AIG-FP swap contracts had "collateral triggers" that would eventually help bring the company down. (© Parsons/Bauer-Griffin)

Jim Johnson (above left) and Franklin Raines (above right) followed David Maxwell as CEOs of Fannie Mae, driving up profits, bullying its regulator, and pushing the company further from its original mission. (Johnson: © Manuel Balce Ceneta/AP Photo; Raines: © Bloomberg/Getty Images)

As the head of the OFHEO, Fannie Mae and Freddie Mac's regulator, Armando Falcon Jr. went to war with the companies he was charged with regulating. (© Bloomberg/Getty Images)

Daniel Mudd, who ran Fannie Mae from 2005 to 2008, described the many problems he faced as "a choice between poking my eye out and cutting off a finger." (© Bloomberg/Getty Images)

John Reich (above left) and James Gilleran (above right), directors of the Office of Thrift Supervision under George W. Bush, pushed to get rid of what they saw as the red tape of regulation. (Reich: © Jonathan Ernst/Reuters; Gilleran: © Paul J. Richards/Getty Images)

As comptroller of the currency from 1998 to 2004, John Hawke exempted banks from state and local regulations intended to curb subprime lending. (© Scott J. Ferrell/ Getty Images)

Robert Rubin, who spent twenty-six years at Goldman Sachs before becoming the secretary of the Treasury in 1995, knew firsthand the problems derivatives could cause. But he refused to do anything about them. (© Bloomberg/Getty Images)

Larry Summers served as Robert Rubin's deputy before succeeding him as Treasury secretary. On his watch, Treasury backed a law that exempted derivatives from regulation. (© Reuters Photographer/Reuters)

As chairman of the Federal Reserve, Alan Greenspan was seen as a heroic figure. Highly skeptical of regulation while in office, he later admitted that "market discipline" failed to curb the market's excesses. (© Kevin Lamarque/Reuters)

A tenacious lawyer, Brooksley Born attempted to increase oversight of derivative dealers as chair of the CFTC, but was thwarted by her fellow regulators. (© Larry Downing/ Reuters)

Edward "Ned" Gramlich was one of the leading critics of subprime mortgages, but as a governor of Greenspan's Federal Reserve, he was a minority of one. (© Bloomberg/Getty Images)

Ralph Cioffi (above left) and Matthew Tannin (above right), who ran two hedge funds with $20 billion in investments for Bear Stearns. The collapse of the fund in the summer of 2007 marked the onset of the financial crisis. (Both photographs: © Chip East/Reuters)

Roland Arnall was a respected philanthropist and diplomat, but he made his fortune building Ameriquest, a subprime lending empire that relied on blatantly deceptive lending practices. Other lenders adopted similar tactics in an effort to compete with Ameriquest. (© Bas Czerwinski/AP Photo)

Angelo Mozilo, the CEO of Countrywide Financial, dreamed of spreading home-ownership to the masses and became a billionaire in the process. But he couldn't resist pressure to enter the subprime mortgage business. (© Mark Wilson/Getty Images)

Gus Levy, Rubin's mentor, was a tough trader who rose to run Goldman Sachs from 1969 to until his death in 1976. (© Bettmann/CORBIS)

Henry "Hank" Paulson Jr., Steve Friedman, and Jon Corzine (left to right). After Friedman departed as senior partner in 1994, Corzine persuaded the partnership to turn Goldman Sachs into a public company. Shortly before the IPO, he was ousted in a coup and replaced by Paulson. Goldman attempted to portray Corzine's departure as an amicable event. (© Ed Quinn/Corbis)

Robert Rubin's tenure at Goldman Sachs coincided with the firm's rise as a global powerhouse. But in the 1980s, "he was always the guy saying, 'I'm not sure how much principal risk we should be taking with the derivative book.'" (© John Marmaras/Woodfin Camp/Getty Images)

Goldman Sachs CEO Lloyd Blankfein helped engineer the shift at Goldman that critics say turned "customers" into "counterparties." (© Bloomberg/Getty Images)

Under Dan Sparks, Goldman Sachs's mortgage department moved aggressively to get subprime mortgage exposure off the company's books. (© Mark Wilson/Getty Images)

Goldman Sachs mortgage trader Fabrice Tourre at a Senate subcommittee hearing on April 27, 2010. Tourre was the only Goldman employee named in the SEC's suit when it charged the company with fraud. (© ASTRID RIECKEN/epa/Corbis)

Martin Sullivan spent his entire career at AIG, taking over as CEO after Greenberg's departure. Although he pulled AIG out of one crisis, he seemed increasingly lost as the financial crisis closed in on the company. (© Ramin Talaie/Corbis)

Robert Willumstad stepped in as the CEO of AIG in the summer of 2008 after Sullivan's dismissal. He planned to unveil his strategic plan in September. But by then the government had been forced to rescue the company. (© Bloomberg/Getty Images)

Stan O'Neal, the CEO of Merrill Lynch, ignored the risks of the subprime mortgage-backed securities that were building up on Merrill's balance sheet until it was far too late. When he tried to salvage the situation by selling Merrill Lynch to a big bank, the board fired him instead. (© Chip East/Reuters)

Jeff Kronthal was a veteran trader at Merrill Lynch. For years, he limited the company's exposure to CDOs backed by subprime mortgages. In 2006 he and his team were summarily fired—and their replacements loaded up on subprime securities. (© Dan Kronthal)

State attorneys general like Iowa's Tom Miller fought to defend borrowers from the abuses of subprime lenders like Ameriquest. (© Bloomberg/ Getty Images)

Andrew Forster, one of Joe Cassano's deputies at AIG-FP, grappled with the company's exposure to subprime default risk. (© Bloomberg/Getty Images)

As Treasury secretary, Hank Paulson claimed the government seizure of Fannie and Freddie was the single thing he had done during the crisis of which he was most proud. (© Win McNamee/ Getty Images)

dard deviation" and "normal distribution," but they didn't really understand the math, so they got lulled into thinking it was magic. Traders came to believe the formulas were not an approximation of reality but reality itself. Which is also why firms needed good risk management departments, he believed. The risk managers were the ones who imposed the reality checks that the traders preferred to ignore.

But ever since Fakahany had been put in charge of it, Merrill Lynch's risk department had been in steep decline. Historically, the top risk executives at Merrill reported directly to the chief financial officer. That was fine when Merrill had a strong CFO like Tom Patrick, who knew that part of the job was to adjudicate the inevitable disputes between the risk managers and the trading desks over what constituted too much risk. As head of Merrill's market risk, Breit had reported to Patrick.

Once Fakahany took over risk management, the risk officers' influence began to wane. Within a year, Breit lost his access to the board. Fakahany seemed to view the disputes between traders and risk managers as "squabbling among children," as a former risk manager put it. Slowly, risk management went from being primarily a front office function—meaning that risk managers sat on trading desks—to a back office function, where they looked at models and spreadsheets and had very little interaction with the traders. "And they started to make less money," a former risk manager explains. A number of good risk managers either left Merrill Lynch or became traders.

In early 2005, Fakahany decided to push the risk management function down a notch further. He promoted the executive who was head of credit risk to be a kind of risk czar, to whom all the other risk managers would now have to report, instead of to Fakahany directly. Furious at what he saw as the degradation of the risk function, Breit sent Merrill's CFO, Jeff Edwards, a letter of resignation and he left the firm.

He was away for only a few months, however. Late that spring, one of the fixed-income desks suffered a big loss. Kim tracked down Breit and asked him to return to Merrill, where he would have a desk on the trading floor and work for him personally. Although Breit rejoined the firm's risk oversight committee, he had no real authority within the firm. Because Kronthal and the other veteran traders knew him and trusted him, Breit was able to develop what he called his "spy network," to keep apprised of the risks the desks were taking. Once Semerci took over, everything changed. The spy network dried up. Dow Kim, who wanted to leave and start a hedge fund—O'Neal had asked him to stay after the Kronthal firing—was losing interest. (He would leave the following spring.) Breit got tossed off the risk committee. Semerci's traders wouldn't tell Breit anything. Eventually, he was moved off the trading floor entirely and given a small office elsewhere in the building.

Which also meant that, like virtually everyone else at Merrill Lynch, Breit had no idea what Semerci was doing with Merrill's CDO business. Though he was one of the few people left at Merrill with the knowledge and background to sniff out problem trades, he was shut out entirely.

Toward the end of 2006, Merrill Lynch took a final step in its ongoing quest to be the dominant Wall Street player in subprime mortgages. It finally bought that mortgage originator O'Neal had been hankering for. The company was First Franklin, a unit of National City Corporation that had made $29 billion in mortgage loans the year before, virtually all of them subprime.* The purchase price was $1.3 billion. Now Merrill would have its own source of mortgages that it could securitize to its heart's content. Or so the company hoped.

The Merrill executive who had been handed the job of landing a mortgage company for Merrill was Michael Blum. In truth, Blum was not a big fan of the First Franklin purchase, though he had dutifully completed it. In 2005, he and his staff held a meeting with O'Neal to lay out Merrill's possible options for getting into the mortgage origination business. O'Neal was eager to get going; Lehman Brothers already made four times what Merrill made in mortgages, in part because it owned BNC Mortgage, the eighth largest subprime company in the country. Blum thought the firm should start up its own originator rather than buy one. "Buying something will be painful because they are not well-managed companies and they are at the bottom of the food chain," he told O'Neal, according to people who were in the meeting.

O'Neal asked him how long it would take to build a subprime company from the ground up. Three or four years, replied Blum. O'Neal gave Blum a steely look. "I'm fifty-four fucking years old," he replied, "and I don't have three or four years."

Blum was also astounded by the price Merrill was willing to pay. (After the deal was announced, David Daberko, National City's CEO, told Dow Jones News Service that the deal "is exactly what we were hoping for.") But

---

* Ironically, First Franklin had been founded by Bill Dallas, who later started Ownit, the mortgage lender in which Merrill owned a 20 percent stake.

Merrill was so eager to get in the game that it would likely have paid even more; Blum could take comfort only in the fact that it wasn't New Century. First Franklin was supposed to be one of the better-run subprime companies.

Almost immediately after the deal was completed, First Franklin began taking losses. Like all the subprime originators, it had kept the residuals and posted gains that reflected an optimistic estimate of their value. Now, as delinquencies rose, those gains were being reversed. In a meeting in January 2007, as Blum was going through the losses in the residuals book, Dow Kim suddenly looked up from his BlackBerry with some news. "Lehman Brothers just had a record quarter in mortgages," he said, according to someone at the meeting. "I guess they're just smarter than we are," Blum replied.

And so it went. In a February meeting, Blum and his team argued that delinquencies were likely to get worse. He wanted Merrill to start hedging its exposure. Dale Lattanzio, whom Semerci had installed to run the CDO business after Ricciardi, brought out a series of charts, using the 1998 Long-Term Capital Management failure as his worst-case scenario. If something like that were to happen, he said, Merrill could lose as much as $70 million. Anything short of that scenario, the firm would be fine.

After the meeting, a risk manager told Kim that "there's no way" Lattanzio's estimate was right. Kim asked the risk manager to poke around and come up with a better estimate, according to a former Merrill executive. But the risk manager couldn't get any information out of Lattanzio and Semerci, and had to drop the effort.

Blum couldn't understand how the people running the CDO business could be so sanguine. They were using the same raw material he was: subprime mortgages. By early 2007, defaults were the highest they had been in six years, when subprime one had collapsed. HSBC, the big British bank, said in February that its bad debt charges would be 20 percent higher than previously anticipated, thanks to its deteriorating subprime business. And yet Merrill's mortgage desk continued to churn out CDOs and post profits. In the first quarter of 2007, the firm underwrote twenty-six CDOs, of which nineteen were made up primarily of subprime mortgages. First Franklin was taking $50 million to $100 million in quarterly write-downs, and top management at Merrill was all over Blum about its deteriorating financials. Yet somehow the CDO business remained untouched. How could this be?

In April, Blum gave a presentation to the board in which he put forth a downbeat and sober-minded assessment of the subprime business. Afterward, many of the board members sent him thank-you e-mails for his plainspoken presentation. What they had failed to notice, however, was that seated next to Blum at the board meeting was Osman Semerci. He never said a word about any problems he might be having with subprime mortgages. Nor did anyone think to ask him.

———∞———

All over Wall Street, an immense amount of risk was building up in the system. It wasn't just that firms were taking on risk when they bought subprime mortgages and bundled them into securities, or when they kept some of the leftover pieces themselves, or when they bought whole subprime mortgage originators. Over the course of a decade, subprime mortgages had managed to seep into Wall Street's bloodstream, as firms used products created out of them to increase leverage, reduce capital, generate profits, and, more generally, game the risk-based rules that were originally intended to give firms the flexibility to deal with the modern world. All of which also meant that the increasing risk was masked by layer upon layer of complexity, hidden where few on the outside could see it.

For instance, using a loophole in Basel I, banks set up off-balance-sheet entities that came to be known as SIVs, or structured investment vehicles. In a nutshell, banks didn't have to hold any capital—that's right, *no capital*—against these vehicles as long as their outstanding debt had a term of less than a year. (That's part of why Karen Shaw Petrou, the managing partner at Federal Financial Analytics, says: "Nothing about this crisis was in fact unforeseen. It was just unaddressed.") By the summer of 2007, there were twenty-nine SIVs with outstanding debt totaling $368 billion, of which nearly $100 billion belonged to Citigroup-sponsored SIVs. Because SIVs were looking for yield, just like every other buyer of triple-A securities, many of them began to buy more and more mortgage-backed securities. Ostensibly, SIVs were independent from the sponsoring bank. But if there was a crisis and the debt started to default, would an institution like Citigroup really be able to sit back and let the SIVs fail? Or would it have to rush in and put that debt on its own balance sheet, which would have a crippling effect on its capital?

Another source of hidden risk was in the plumbing of the market—plumbing that was utterly taken for granted. The big banks all had warehouse lines that the mortgage originators borrowed against to make their subprime loans. It was the primary funding mechanism for the industry. But the banks didn't just extend a big loan to the originators. Instead, they had discovered a more modern, efficient, capital-gaming way to do it. They would set up an off-balance-sheet vehicle that issued short-term commercial paper to fund itself. That commercial paper was backed by the mortgages. It was part of a market called ABCP, or asset-backed commercial paper. According to Fitch, by the spring of 2007 this market was shockingly big: $1.4 trillion in size. The commercial paper got a top rating from the rating agencies, making it possible for money market funds to buy it. However, in order to obtain that all-important top rating, the sponsoring bank, or another bank, invariably had to provide some kind of guarantee, in the event that the vehicle found itself unable to replace the commercial paper when it came due.

As the market got crazier, money market funds became more and more enamored of this paper; they, too, were competing for that extra little bit of yield. Although money market funds were serving the role of the old-fashioned bank—they were ultimately the real lender—they weren't regulated the way banks were. Since they were holding highly rated securities—as SEC rules required them to do—no one in the government was concerned with the quality of the collateral.

But what would happen if the money market funds all started questioning the quality of the assets backing their paper at the same time? What if they all stopped buying it? Either the sponsoring bank would have to provide liquidity—damaging its own balance sheet—or the vehicles would all have to start dumping assets to raise cash. Neither scenario was pleasant to contemplate.

Money market funds were also a core enabler of the deepest, darkest, least noticed part of the market's plumbing. This was the so-called repo market, which made it possible for firms to pledge assets in return for extremely short-term loans, often as short as overnight. Yale economist Gary Gorton—the game man who did risk modeling for AIG-FP—explains the repo market this way: Suppose Fidelity has $500 million in cash that it plans to use to eventually buy securities. It wants a safe place to earn interest on that cash while making sure the money will be available the instant it wants it back. Enter the repo market. Fidelity can deposit the $500 million with an investment bank—Bear Stearns, in Gorton's example—and be sure the money is safe, because Bear provides collateral to back up the loan. The difference between the money Fidelity gives Bear and the value of its collateral is called the "haircut," and before the crisis a 2 percent haircut—meaning Bear could get 98 cents in cash for every $1 in assets it pledged—was a normal number.

Secured lending, or lending against collateral, is almost always less risky than unsecured lending. On the Street, the repo market is called the last line of defense, because you can get money there when you can't get it anywhere else.

And yet, there were dangers in the repo market, too. It is a murky market, but a huge one: according to a report by the Bank for International Settlements, by 2007 the U.S. investment banks funded roughly half of their assets using the repo market. For firms that depended on this market, there could be a timing mismatch, because banks could pledge a long-term illiquid asset in return for short-term funding. If the short-term funds went away, they still had the asset—which needed financing. Another danger was that repo transactions are exempt from the normal bankruptcy process. Lenders didn't have to worry about their money getting tied up—they could simply grab their collateral at the first sign of weakness. And whichever lender grabbed first did best: no bankruptcy court judge was going to come along and decide what was and wasn't fair.

As the bubble grew, Street firms began using riskier and riskier assets—including mortgage-backed securities—as repo collateral. They did it for the usual reason: the lender could get a bigger return by accepting mortgage-backed securities as collateral than it could by accepting Treasuries.

But once again, what would happen if the lenders began to question the true value of the collateral? The lender might demand a bigger haircut—meaning that the loan the bank would get would shrink, and it would have to rapidly sell assets, or face a shortage of funds. Or what if the lender didn't want any collateral from a particular firm at all? Suddenly a routine repo transaction would be transformed into something far more ominous: a vote on whether an investment bank should survive.

Thanks to deposit insurance, the days were long gone when bank customers stood in line to pull their money out of a shaky bank, creating a run on the bank that usually ended in its collapse. But as Gorton and fellow Yale economist Andrew Metrick would later argue in a paper, the repo market created the conditions for the modern version of the bank run. You never saw this kind of bank run in photographs, but it was every bit as devastating.

Where were the regulators as this buildup of risk was taking place? They were nowhere to be found. Just as the banking regulators had averted their eyes from the predatory lending on Main Street, so did they now ignore the ferocious accumulation of risk, much of it tied to subprime mortgages, on Wall Street.

No regulator had the authority—or the ability—to systematically look across institutions and identify potential system-wide problems. That role just didn't exist in America's regulatory scheme. The Fed, for one, had little insight into the packaging and endless repackaging of mortgages. In part, this was because the Gramm-Leach-Bliley Act prevented it from conducting detailed examinations of the nonbank subsidiaries of the big banks. In other words, even though it was responsible for regulating the big bank holding companies, it had to rely on the SEC to oversee, for example, a bank's trading operation.

In any case, the Fed wasn't all that eager to look too deeply. Like all the regulators, the Fed believed that the risk was off the banks' books and distributed into the all-knowing market. The attitude was: "Not our role to tell the market what it should and should not buy," in the words of a former Fed official. This was true even after Alan Greenspan retired in early 2006 and was replaced by Princeton economist Ben Bernanke.

The Fed also had enormous—and unwarranted—faith in bank management. A GAO report would later find that all the regulators "acknowledged that they had relied heavily on management representation of risks." In 2006, the Fed had conducted reviews of stress-testing practices at "several large, complex banking institutions," according to the GAO. It found that none tested for scenarios that would render them insolvent and that senior managers "questioned the need for additional stress testing, particularly for worst-case scenarios that they thought were implausible." From 2005 through the summer of 2007, the Fed issued internal reports called "Large Financial Institutions' Perspectives on Risk." The report for the second half of 2006, issued in April 2007, stated, "There are no substantial issues of supervisory concern for these large financial institutions" and that "Asset quality across the systemically important institutions remains strong."

In at least one notable case, regulators reached for responsibilities that they weren't capable of handling. It took place in 2004 and involved the Securities and Exchange Commission, whose chairman at the time was William Donaldson.

Historically, the SEC oversaw everything that had to do with the buying and selling of stocks. The five big American investment banks—Bear Stearns, Goldman Sachs, Morgan Stanley, Merrill Lynch, and Lehman Brothers—all came under the regulatory purview of the SEC. But they had all formed holding companies and had affiliates engaged in all kinds of activities—such as derivatives trading—that had nothing to do with selling stocks. Astonishingly, no government agency regulated the holding companies.

In 2002, the European Union ruled that these holding companies had to be supervised by a U.S. regulator, or the EU would do the job itself for the subsidiaries that fell under their jurisdiction. This was *not* something the American investment banks wanted to have happen, so they asked the SEC to set up a program called Consolidated Supervised Entities, or CSE. It created a voluntary supervisory regime, thus getting around the SEC's lack of statutory authority to regulate the holding companies.

It would become part of the lore of the financial crisis that the CSE somehow abolished a previously held limit of 12 to 1 leverage at the broker-dealer level and allowed the banks to use their internal models to determine the capital they should hold. But the first part of that wasn't really true. The 12 to 1 limit hadn't been in place since 1975. At the end of 2006—that is, well after the implementation of the CSE—the investment banks' leverage was no higher than it had been at the end of 1998, when LTCM went down. In fact, according to the GAO, three firms had more leverage at the end of 1998 than they did at the end of 2006.

No, the SEC's real failure was something else. By setting up CSE, the SEC gave the impression that it had the manpower, the skill, and the savvy to see risks developing at the holding company level. It did not—something even its own commissioners seemed to understand at the time. In a recording of the fifty-five-minute meeting in which the five members of the SEC signed off on the CSE, commissioners can be heard saying things like, "This is going to require a much more complicated compliance, inspection, and understanding of risk than we've ever had to do. . . . You think we can do this?" and "What if someone doesn't give us adequate information? How will we enforce it?" The greatest note of caution came from Harvey Goldschmid, a Democratic commissioner. "We've said these are the big guys and clearly that's true," he said. "But that means if anything goes wrong, it's going to be an awfully big mess."*

"I equate the CSE regime to the USDA putting its imprimatur on rancid

---

* According to a former government official, one of the biggest cheerleaders for the CSE program was SEC commissioner Annette Nazareth. In fact, the CSE program was based on something called Basel II, an update of the original Basel rules, which was being widely implemented in Europe and which allowed banks to lower their capital requirements significantly, resulting in a

meat," says a former Bush administration official. "Bad regulation is much worse than no regulation because you create conditional expectations of safety. It helped feed the fiction that these risks could be quantified or even understood."

This, then, was the situation in May 2006: risk was building up everywhere in the system; the housing bubble was reaching its frenzied finale; Wall Street firms were madly churning out CDOs; subprime originators were making loans to anyone with a pulse; everything was interconnected in ways that were dangerous for the financial system; and the regulatory apparatus, charged with protecting the safety and soundness of the banking system, was in complete denial. This was what Henry Paulson Jr. was going to have to deal with, as his nomination to be secretary of the Treasury was announced late that month.

To the outside world, the news that Paulson was leaving Goldman Sachs to become Treasury secretary could not have been less surprising. Didn't every senior Goldman Sachs executive eventually join the government? By that point, the list included John Whitehead (deputy secretary of state in the Reagan administration), Steve Friedman (National Economic Council), Joshua Bolten (OMB director and George W. Bush's chief of staff), Jon Corzine (senator and later governor of New Jersey), Robert Rubin (of course), and many others.

Yet to Goldman insiders, Paulson's departure was startling. He had never expressed the slightest interest in the job. He didn't make lavish campaign contributions, or serve as finance chairman for ambitious politicians, or even hang around politicians. He told everyone, whether they were close confidants or passing acquaintances, that he was staying put at Goldman. Head fakes had never been his style. As he later related in his memoir, when he first got the call from the White House in the spring of 2006, he agreed to a meeting with the president, but then quickly canceled when John Rogers,

---

much higher leverage ratio. But Basel II never went into effect in this country, despite the urging of the big banks and the Federal Reserve, largely because of resistance from the FDIC. According to this same former official, the "chief proselytizer for Basel II" at the Fed was Federal Reserve vice chairman Roger Ferguson. As it happens, Ferguson and Nazareth are married.

the firm's veteran Washington hand, told him that going to the meeting was tantamount to accepting the offer.

Having been through several ineffectual Treasury secretaries, Bush wanted Paulson badly, largely because his Goldman Sachs credential gave him a stature his predecessors had lacked. Paulson was initially deterred by "fear of failure, fear of the unknown," he later wrote. But he finally said yes. "I didn't want to look back and have been asked to serve my country and declined," he later explained. "So I just took the plunge." He did so after getting an unprecedented agreement from Bush that he would have real power: regular access to the president, on a par with the secretaries of State and Defense, and the ability to bring in his own people.

For Paulson, one of the toughest parts of his decision was telling his mother. His entire family, including his wife, Wendy, and his mom, Marianna, was deeply opposed to the Bush administration. In his book, Paulson recalls standing in the kitchen of his house in Barrington, Illinois, announcing the news. "You started with Nixon and you're going to end with Bush?" his mother replied. "Why would you do such a thing?"

In some ways, Paulson was an odd choice for Bush. As an ardent environmentalist, Paulson believed that climate change was real, a view not embraced by the White House. More important, he was neither a partisan Republican nor a free-market ideologue. He would later cite the pressure on him to get rid of Sarbanes-Oxley, the law passed in the wake of the Enron scandal, which Republicans in Congress hated. Paulson refused. "I don't find a single provision bad," he said.

He also worried about the widening gap between rich and poor—also not a subject often discussed in the Bush White House. In a speech at Columbia on August 1, 2006, he said that "amid this country's strong economic expansion, many Americans simply aren't feeling the benefits." The comments sent Republicans into a tizzy.

Like all captains of industry who join the Treasury, Paulson was in for a bit of a shock after his nomination was approved by the Senate in July 2006. He hadn't understood how outdated Treasury's systems were—there was no real-time access to market information, and the voice mail system was antiquated. (Voice mail has long been Paulson's primary method of communication.) As he recounts in his book, he was shocked to discover that "an extraordinary civil servant named Fred Adams had been calculating the interest rates on trillions of dollars in Treasury debt by hand nearly every day for thirty years, including holidays." Nor had Paulson fully appreciated how limited Treasury's tools were: Treasury was not a bank regulator. It had moral suasion, but no supervisory levers, and it couldn't spend money unless it had been appropriated. "At Goldman, he had the responsibility, but also unbridled command over thousands," says one Treasury employee. "Here, he had the responsibility times a thousand, but no ability to command."

The new Treasury secretary gave longtime department aides a bit of a shock as well. "People were taken aback by Hank's aggressiveness," says one staffer. "He's a force of nature. He gets people to do stuff they'd never do." They weren't used to a boss as relentless or as blunt as he was. Paulson also made decisions by talking, and frequently repeating himself. "If you're in a meeting with experts, you usually let the experts talk," says one staffer. "But when it's Hank, then the first ten minutes are Hank talking!" Like many, this staffer grew to respect and admire Paulson. But for people who didn't know him well, it was his "let's get this done yesterday" demeanor that stuck in their minds. Staffers quickly spread stories of Paulson's impatience and his odd mannerisms. "He'd just appear in people's offices and start talking while you had your back to him typing," marveled one person, who also remarked that Paulson gave Treasury an energy and sense of purpose that it had lacked. Later, during the crisis, Paulson would come in, eat oatmeal, and then, by seven a.m., start making the rounds. His longtime assistant, Christal West, would send out a heads-up: "Be prepared! He's roaming!"

Like everyone both on Wall Street and in Washington, Paulson didn't see—and wouldn't see for a long time—just how bad things were and where they were headed. He would later argue that even if he had seen it coming, he still couldn't have done anything, given the inadequate tools at his disposal and the difficulty he faced in getting Congress to take action even after the situation had become dire. "If I had been omniscient, there's not a single additional thing I could have done that would have made a difference," he'd later say.

What is surprising, in retrospect, is that Paulson did try to do something. He is anxious by nature, and you could see that anxiety at work—that fear of what might be lurking around the corner—in the actions he took when he got to the Treasury. He was convinced that the country was headed toward another financial disruption. His reasoning was simple: in recent history, financial crises seemed to occur every four to eight years. The country was due. He and Ben Bernanke ran scenarios so they could prepare for different kinds of crisis: a spike in energy prices, say, or the failure of a big hedge fund. War games, the staff called them. Treasury's conclusion, after researching all of the agency's past statements about financial crises, was, as one former staffer puts it, "Treasury equals confidence. The Fed equals liquidity. Specifics are for the rest of the agencies."

That August, in Paulson's first visit to Camp David, he gave the president a presentation on the growth in over-the-counter derivatives, focusing in particular on credit derivatives. Paulson had long seen that the market was rife with problems. When he was at Goldman Sachs, industry players were complaining that others were assigning trades without consulting the original counterparty, and there were processing and payment errors galore. Even before he left Goldman, Paulson, along with Rubin's old protégé Tim Geithner, by now president of the New York Fed, had begun pushing to fix such "back office" problems. But at Camp David, Paulson went beyond the back office issues, showing that while credit derivatives could be legitimately used to hedge an existing position, they also created risk and leverage that wasn't readily apparent. Finally, he told the group that no one knew the total number of credit default swaps outstanding. "There was incredulity at the table," Paulson recounts. "The reaction was 'How can you have a market this big and this opaque? You mean you can tell us the dollar value of the bonds GM has outstanding, but you can't tell us the CDSs outstanding?'"

Paulson also embarked on a hugely ambitious project to revamp the regulatory system. In the spring of 2008, when he rolled out a 228-page blueprint, observers said it would be the most radical overhaul of the laws in eighty years. Among other things, he advocated merging the SEC and the CFTC, getting rid of the OTS, imposing stricter rules on the leverage that investment banks could employ, setting up a federal Mortgage Origination Commission—which would finally institute rules for subprime originators—and giving the Fed the power to serve as a systemic regulator that could "go wherever in the system it thinks it needs to go for a deeper look," as Paulson explained at the time.

Yet the blueprint did not make much mention of the issue that was causing Paulson such deep concern: regulation of over-the-counter derivatives. Some would see this as evidence that Paulson—Goldman's former CEO, after all, who had never worried about the dangers of derivatives while running the firm—was as reluctant to force the industry to change as his predecessors had been. But Paulson would later insist that wasn't true, and that he wanted changes in the regulation of derivatives. He and Geithner had gotten the industry to document its existing trades and to agree on a set of operational rules. These fixes would prove critical in the crisis that was coming.

But Paulson didn't feel they were sufficient. In fact, derivatives were a deeply frustrating issue for him, because he felt more oversight was necessary, but he also knew he wasn't going to get a legislative solution in the waning years of the Bush administration. Besides, other regulators worried that if they took on more oversight of derivatives, their agencies, already stretched on budgets, staff, and capability, would be blamed if something went wrong.

Instead, Paulson began using the President's Working Group—the same group that Rubin had used to keep Brooksley Born away from derivatives regulation—as a way of "persuading, jawboning, and sometimes pressuring industry participants to take actions they were reluctant to take," as he later put it. Paulson and Geithner quietly began pushing other regulators to agree on language calling for an industry cooperative to clear derivatives trades. They pushed the industry to agree as well. The new clearinghouse would set capital requirements, and it would also serve as a buffer that would insulate others should a big counterparty fail. After the crisis, Paulson would insist that the Treasury and the New York Fed had done everything that was possible to deal with what he called "a messy legacy derivative situation."

There was one big problem Paulson missed, however. When he made his Camp David presentation, he didn't mention any potential problems in housing or mortgages. That's because Paulson didn't suspect that housing or mortgages could be the catalyst for a crisis.

This was Paulson's blind spot—though not because he was a free-market ideologue. Perhaps because he had spent his entire career on Wall Street, he thought the way others on Wall Street did and the way economists did: Housing prices hadn't declined on a nationwide basis since the Great Depression! People always paid their mortgages! He didn't see the boarded-up homes that were blackening neighborhoods like rotten teeth in places like Cleveland. His was a bloodless view, the world as seen from the perch of high finance.

Besides, why would Paulson suspect that Wall Street's securitization process was deeply flawed? After all, Goldman Sachs had moved into this business on Paulson's watch. Paulson was part of the machine, not outside it. That also meant, for all of Paulson's worries about derivates, he didn't understand the dangerous potential of credit default swaps on mortgages. (Though he'd later say, "If I had known some of the things that were happening, I wouldn't have been able to sleep at night.")

Paulson certainly wasn't alone. Everyone else on Wall Street and in Washington shared his views. In late 2005, Bernanke said that home prices, rather than being in bubble territory, "reflect strong economic fundamentals." In 2006, he said that he expected the housing market to "cool but not to change very sharply." He went on to tell CNBC, "We've never had a decline in house prices on a nationwide basis. So what I think more likely is that house prices will slow, maybe stabilize." As late as the spring of 2007, he said, "[W]e believe the effect of the troubles in the subprime sector on the broader housing market will likely be limited, and we do not expect significant spillovers from the subprime market to the rest of the economy or the financial system."

Another reason for Paulson's blind spot, say people who worked with him, was that he had too much faith in regulators. "He thought the regulators were more capable than they were," says a staffer. Paulson today concedes he'd put too much faith in regulation itself. During his time in office, Paulson would change his tune. "The system was so outdated and screwed up, you just couldn't have imagined it," he'd later say. A big part of the problem, of course, was that both the regulators and Paulson assumed that financial institutions were more competent than they were. Paulson spent his career at Goldman, which at least didn't need anyone else to tell it how to protect its own bottom line. He had no idea that other firms weren't as capable of looking out for their own interests. "No financial institution wants to blow itself up," he'd later explain. "So I've always taken some confidence in the fact that their survival instinct would help protect the system. But I was shocked by how bad risk management was in some institutions. And many banks thought they were smarter than they were."

By 2006, John Dugan, the comptroller of the currency, was fretting to other regulators about the growth in nontraditional—i.e., subprime—mortgages, according to several former Treasury officials. But here was a "disconnect," says one official. "The people in the Treasury building who spent most of their time on housing were the economists. The people on the market side were the ones dealing with leverage. Even in this building, with a small senior staff, people were not talking every day. Looking back, you can see how one thing would lead to another—how mortgages were used to create instruments that were used to create leverage." But no one made the connection at the time.

There was another component to the thinking, too. The leverage in the system had built up slowly. "It was a gradual process that got us to where we were," says a former Treasury official. "So you'd think it would be a gradual process that got us out."

In this assumption, however, they could not have been more wrong.

17

"I'm Short Your House"

Scene 1: Summer 2006. Seemingly out of nowhere, New Century Financial, the country's second largest subprime-only originator, has a pressing need for cash. Having made $51.6 billion worth of subprime loans in 2005, it is discovering that too many of its loans are going sour way too fast. Particularly troubling: early payment defaults are spiking. Those are loans where the borrowers are in default practically from the moment they agree to the loan. Early payment defaults can often trigger repurchase requests from investors, requiring the lender to buy them back. That is happening to New Century. In 2004, it repurchased $136.7 million worth of bad loans. In 2005, that number rose to $332.1 million. By June of 2006, it has been forced to repurchase an additional $315.7 million in defaulted loans.

Worse, one of New Century's tried-and-true techniques for recirculating its repurchased loans is no longer working. In previous years, after buying defaulted mortgages out of securitizations, it would simply stick them into a new sale, according to one close observer. This worked because New Century's loan volume was growing so rapidly that the bad mortgages could be buried as a small part of a big new sale. But by 2006, volume is starting to slow. New Century's perpetual motion machine is grinding to a halt.

Meanwhile, New Century is running low on cash. On August 17, CFO Patti Dodge sends an e-mail to Brad Morrice, the CEO: "We started the quarter with $400mm in liquidity and we are down to less than $50mm today," she writes. In explaining the problem to the company's board, Morrice cites "continued difficult secondary market conditions leading to warehouse line margin calls, higher investors kick outs [meaning that wary investors are refusing to purchase loans] and loan repurchases." Internally, top management begins receiving a weekly report monitoring its problems. It is entitled "Storm Watch."

Does Wall Street know about New Century's problems? Of course it does! One Wall Street banker tells New Century that its problems aren't all that unusual, according to a report done later by a bankruptcy examiner. There are, the examiner will write, "dramatic industry-wide increases in early payment defaults and lower origination volumes."

Amazingly, Wall Street is still willing to extend a lifeline to New Century: the company raises $142.5 million in the second half of 2006. Yet investors are largely left in the dark. New Century doesn't disclose either the big increase in early payment defaults or the staggering $545 million backlog of repurchase claims—i.e., claims that the company has received but hasn't yet paid. Instead, New Century tells investors that it believes that repurchase requests "will stabilize, then decline."*

❦

Scene 2: Fall 2006. Larry Litton is a mortgage servicer. In 1988, he and his father, Larry Litton Sr., founded Litton Loan Servicing, building it into one of the nation's largest mortgage servicers. Inevitably, they service a lot of mortgages for subprime originators, including Bill Dallas's Ownit and WMC, which was founded by Amy Brandt and which GE Capital bought in 2004. The two combined are cranking out more than $40 billion worth of loans a year.

Litton also notices that early payment defaults are soaring. The mortgage originators are freaking out and blaming him. "The WMC guys are saying, 'You suck,'" Litton recalls. He remembers thinking, "Maybe we're doing something wrong." So Litton comes up with what he calls an "ultra-aggressive move": hand delivering welcome packages to new homeowners, so there will be no confusion over where the mortgage checks should be mailed. But when the Litton employees arrive at the newly purchased homes, they discover something truly startling. "My people came back and said, 'Thirty percent of the houses are vacant,'" Litton recalls. In other words, borrowers who closed on mortgages had so little means to make even the first payment that they never bothered to move in. Litton calls Amy Brandt at WMC. "It's

---

* Three New Century executives later settled with the SEC, neither admitting nor denying guilt, over charges that they failed to disclose important negative information.

kinda hard to collect payment when someone ain't there! You might want to take a look at it," he tells her.

———— ❧ ————

Scene 3: December 11, 2006. Midmorning. An auditorium at the Office of Thrift Management. Lew Ranieri—yes, *that* Lew Ranieri—is giving a speech. His tone of voice may be mild, but his words convey something else entirely: anger, dismay, worry.

The occasion is an all-day housing symposium the OTS is putting on. The room is filled with bank regulators, housing lobbyists, economists, community activists, and members of the subprime mortgage establishment. Sheila Bair, the new chairman of the FDIC, is there. So is David Berson, the chief economist at Fannie Mae, and John Taylor, the longtime subprime critic from the National Community Reinvestment Coalition. Hank Paulson makes the welcoming remarks. Congressman Barney Frank gives the luncheon speech.

The main topic is the subprime business, which now accounts for around a quarter of the nation's mortgages but which is clearly slumping. Ranieri is on a panel with Berson from Fannie Mae, a banker representing the Mortgage Bankers Association, and the deputy comptroller of the currency. Their presentations are full of on-the-one-hand, on-the-other-hand equivocations. There is general agreement that subprime mortgages are here to stay. A panel devoted to subprime fraud focuses entirely on *borrower* fraud; incredibly, not a single word is mentioned about the widespread fraud being perpetrated by the companies themselves.

Ranieri, however, has a much dimmer view of the state of the subprime mortgage industry than most others speaking today. Over the past few years, he has become horrified by what has happened to the mortgage-backed securities business he helped invent in a more innocent time. The lack of proper underwriting, Wall Street's unending desire for poor-quality loans, the way triple-B tranches are being repackaged into new triple-A securities: this is not what Ranieri envisioned when he and Larry Fink and others were starting up the market. He had always just assumed that the vast majority of loans in securitizations would be good loans, not bad ones. Why would investors want to buy *bad* loans? The fact that no one seems to care anymore is shocking to him.

And that's what he tells this roomful of subprime experts, bluntly and

forcefully. The man who spent much of the 1980s trying—unsuccessfully—
to minimize Fannie and Freddie's role in the securitization business now
laments the way they have been rendered irrelevant by the subprime securitizers. He can see now what an important and useful role they played: they
were, he says, the "gatekeepers," forcing mortgage companies to adhere to
their underwriting standards. "If a mortgage originator didn't follow Fannie
and Freddie's underwriting standards, nobody would buy them," says Ranieri.
"That standard has completely gotten pushed aside."

Who now can keep the market in check? The rating agencies? Hardly.
Government regulators? A joke. The private mortgage-backed securities market, says Ranieri, "is unchecked by today's regulatory framework."

He bemoans the layering of risk in subprime mortgages ("One of my
favorites is a negative amortization ARM, combined with a simultaneous
second lien and a stated-income loan"). He sneers at the phrase "affordability products," the industry's euphemism for subprime mortgages. He dwells
at length on the rise of CDOs as a "major distribution mechanism" and
laments their bewildering complexity. It is nearly impossible, he says, for
investors to understand what they are buying. And he makes a crucial point
that Wall Street itself has largely missed: the CDO business has become a
kind of daisy chain. "Who is buying the subordinated tranches?" he asks.
"Who is taking all that risk? The answer in many cases is nobody. No person.
It is a thing—another CDO. Imagine taking the support tranches of the
CDO and putting it in another CDO, further diluting the information flow.
Does the buyer really understand the risks entailed? They buy senior
tranches—I know, I buy senior tranches. But I like senior tranches to remain
senior tranches. I like triple-A to remain triple-A."

The poor level of disclosure in CDO prospectuses, Ranieri says, "makes
the risk levels neither readily apparent nor easily quantifiable." You can hear
the anger in his voice. "This. Is. A. Private. Securities. Market," he says evenly.
"It gets sold to the public. It gets sold to foreign investors who, I will tell
you, don't have a clue. It is supposed to be equal information that is available
to all."

When Ranieri finishes, an audience member asks a simple question:
"What do you see as the less than rosy scenario when the mortgage market
goes into the toilet?"

"I don't understand what the ripple effects would be," he replies. "All sorts
of people are holding risks that would be hard to track down. And in some
cases they wouldn't even know they are holding the risk."

Scene 4: Same place, same morning. "Finally," Josh Rosner thinks to himself as he listens to Ranieri. "Someone is calling it as it is."

Rosner is the skeptical analyst who back in 2001 wrote the prescient paper "A Home without Equity Is Just a Rental with Debt." In mid-2005, his sources at the Fed start telling him that rates are going to rise significantly, in no small part to "cure" the excess speculation in housing. He is soon warning clients that the housing market has peaked.

In recent years, Rosner has continued to dig into the numbers underlying the housing boom. It is apparent, he says, that "we've bumped up against the law of large numbers in homeownership." At the end of 2000, the official homeownership figure stood at 67.4 percent. Four years later, with the subprime bubble well under way, the homeownership rate hits 69 percent. That is as high as it will ever go. All of that craziness—not just the bad loans themselves, but the devastated neighborhoods, the people thrown out of their homes, the huge buildup of debt on both Main Street and Wall Street—for a gain of 1.6 percent? Is it really worth it?

To Rosner, the answer is clear: no. His data shows that most of the frenzy hasn't even been about purchasing a place to live. Rosner's eureka moment comes when he sees data showing that about 35 percent of the mortgages used to purchase homes in 2004 and 2005 are not for primary residences, but for second homes and investment properties. And as he has been saying for years, the number of people borrowing to buy an actual home is dwarfed by the number of people borrowing to refinance. The refis, in turn, are made possible by rising home values—which may not even be real, given all the inflated appraisals. (In fact, Alan Greenspan himself noted in a study he co-authored in 2007 that about four-fifths of the rise in mortgage debt from 1990 to 2006 was due to the "discretionary extraction of home equity.")

Like Ranieri, Rosner has become worried about the CDO market. Around the same time as Ranieri's speech, Rosner approaches a finance professor at Drexel University, Joseph Mason, to co-author a paper with him. They deliver it in February 2007 at the Hudson Institute. The title is a mouthful: "How Resilient Are Mortgage Backed Securities to Collateralized Debt Obligation Market Disruptions?" Their conclusions, however, are straightforward. The issuance of CDOs, which have mushroomed to more than $500 billion in 2006, is propping up the housing market by buying almost all of the riskier tranches of mortgage-backed securities. Investors—real investors, who are not part of the daisy chain—no longer want them. Even investment-grade CDOs will lose money if home prices begin to fall substantially, Rosner and Mason write. If that happens, it could set off a contagion of fear, as investors rush to unload their CDO positions. A vicious circle would then start that would have terrible ramifications, not just for the housing market but for the economy.

Rosner and Mason have also pondered some larger questions. If housing is such an important component of U.S. social policy, and the funding mechanism for housing has become this shaky pyramid of debt, does it really make sense to have the housing market at the mercy of this hugely unstable funding? And inasmuch as investors around the world have sunk their money into U.S. mortgage-backed securities, what are the implications if that market starts to crack? "Perhaps of greater concern is the reputational risk posed to the U.S. capital markets," they write.

Scene 5: February 7, 2007. New Century files what's called an 8-K, a document that conveys important news that can't wait until the next quarter's results. The headline is stark: "New Century Financial Corporation to Restate Financial Statements for the Quarters Ended March 31, June 30 and September 30, 2006." Part of the reason for the restatement, the company says, is to "correct errors" in the way it has accounted for its many repurchase requests. The stock, which had hit its high of $51.22 just a few months earlier, plunges 36 percent in one day. By March, the company admits that it is unable to file any financial reports. By then, its repurchase claims have risen to a staggering $8.4 billion. The stock falls to about a dollar. By April, New Century is bankrupt. Never once, during the entire housing bubble, did the company report a quarterly loss before filing for bankruptcy.

By the end of 2006, anyone could have found his or her own data points to know that the subprime market was in trouble. The clues were everywhere. The staggering rise in home appreciation, which in some parts of the country had averaged 10 to 15 percent a year, was slowing down. In places like Arizona, California, Florida—the states where the housing bubble had been most pronounced—housing prices were already declining. Subprime borrowers with option ARMs, the ones who were counting on an increase in their home equity to refinance, were suddenly out of luck. With their homes no longer increasing in value, they had no way to refinance. Foreclosures were nearly double what they had been three years earlier. Delinquencies: up. Stated-income loan defaults: up. And of course those early payment defaults—the ones that signaled just how reckless the subprime originators had become—were *way* up. Subprime originators had created the conditions for "the perfect storm," said John Taylor at that OTS housing symposium.

Sheila Bair, who had been sworn in as the new chair of the FDIC that summer, was shocked to discover how far underwriting standards had fallen in the four years since she left the government. Back in 2002, when she had been assistant secretary of the Treasury for financial institutions, there had been problems with predatory lending, for sure, but nothing like this. Nothing even close. One of the first things Bair did upon taking office was order up a database that included every securitized subprime mortgage. It was immediately obvious when she looked at it that there was going to be a massive problem when the ARMs reset.

Meanwhile, a risk manager at one of the big Wall Street firms started noticing something unprecedented: people were walking away from their homes. "Historically," this risk manager said, "people stopped paying their credit cards first, then their cars, and only then their homes. This time, people with $50,000 cars and $300,000 mortgages would get in their cars and drive away from their homes."

The newspapers offered further evidence of the looming problems. All through the fall, the business press wrote article after article about the rise in foreclosures and the troubles suddenly hitting the subprime companies. "Payments on Adjustable Loans Hit Overstretched Borrowers," declared the *Wall Street Journal* in August of 2006. "Foreclosure Figures Suggest Homeowners in for Rocky Ride," the *Journal* said a month later. A month after that, Washington Mutual reported that its home loan unit had lost $33 million in the third quarter. HSBC, which had been a major buyer of second-lien mortgages, announced huge losses and shut down its purchases. And on and on.

On Main Street, the subprime bubble was grinding to a halt. There was going to be a great deal of pain, for both the borrowers and the subprime companies. But Wall Street had one more trick up its sleeve. This was a mechanism created by Wall Street to allow investors to short the housing market similar to the way investors can bet against stocks. It was a natural development—at least from Wall Street's point of view—but it evolved into one of the most unnatural and destructive financial products that the world has ever seen: the synthetic CDO.

The key ingredient in a synthetic CDO was our old friend the credit default swap. For that matter, the key to shorting the mortgage market was the credit default swap. By 2005, credit default swaps on corporate bonds were ubiquitous, with a notional value of more than $25 trillion. (The notional value of credit default swaps peaked in 2007 at $62 trillion.) They were used by companies to protect against the possibility that another entity it did business with might default. They were used by banks to measure the riskiness of a loan portfolio, because their price reflected the market's view of risk. And they were used in the mortgage-backed securities area by CDO underwriters to wrap the super-senior tranches. The AIG wrap, you'll recall, was the key to allowing banks with triple-A tranches on their books to reduce their capital.

In the corporate bond market, traders were using credit default swaps not just as protection against the possibility that a bond they owned might default. They were also using them to make a bet—a bet that a company might default, even when the trader didn't own the underlying bonds. These credit default swaps had become standardized, meaning that the conditions under which the buyers and sellers got paid were always the same. That's the way markets tend to evolve: first comes hedging, and then comes speculation. To Wall Street, this is all good, because the more players in the market—whatever their reasons—the more trading there is.

In the mortgage-backed securities market, the credit default swaps that people were using to insure those super-seniors *were* a kind of short, since the buyer of the protection would be paid off if the super-senior tranches defaulted. But no one thought of them this way—they were focused on the regulatory capital advantages. And they were a customized agreement between two parties, which made them hard to trade, because any buyer would have to understand all the complex terms of the deal.

But why couldn't you create a standardized credit default swap on mortgage-backed securities? That way, anyone could play. Instead of having to painstakingly scratch out terms with the party on the other side, you could trade these instruments the way people do stocks. That would dramatically expand the market—and all the more so if you also published an index of the prices of mortgage-backed securities. Wall Street likes to say that indices are good because they offer transparency—everyone can see what the prices are—and liquidity, meaning it's easier to get in and out of trades that are based on a public index. That's probably true. But it's also true that indices reduce complexity to the simplicity of a published number, allow investors to think they understand a market when they really don't, and create a frenzy of trading activity that mainly benefits Wall Street.

Developing a big market of tradable credit default swaps on mortgage-backed securities would have several consequences. It would encourage Wall Street firms that were nervous about having mortgage risk on their own books to stay in the business, because now they could hedge their exposure. It would encourage people who had no economic interest in the underlying mortgage-backed securities to simply place bets on whether or not they could decline, because now it was relatively easy to do so. And it would also mean that someone had to take the other side of those bets, because that is, by definition, the way a credit default swap works.

Three firms—Deutsche Bank, Goldman Sachs, and Bear Stearns—led the drive to turn credit default swaps on mortgage-backed securities into easily tradable, standardized instruments. The group, which included Deutsche Bank trader Greg Lippman, Goldman trader Rajiv Kamilla, and Bear trader Todd Kushman, began meeting in February 2005 to figure out what the holders of a short interest should receive, and when they should receive it. Should the protection buyer—as Wall Street called the counterparty on the short side—get his or her money when the mortgage defaulted? When it was ninety days delinquent? The traders decided that the protection buyer should get paid as the mortgage lost value—which would be determined by the Street firm that sold the instrument—in sums that made up for the lost value. They called their concept Pay As You Go, or PAUG. (The correct pronunciation rhymes with "hog," says one person who was involved.) "To tell the truth, it's not very glamorous," Lippman later told Bloomberg reporter Mark Pittman.

In January 2006, an index based on subprime mortgages began trading for the first time. ("THE market event of 1H '06," proclaimed a Goldman analyst.) Just as an index like the S&P 500 has five hundred big company stocks, this new index, called the ABX, would list specific tranches of mortgage-backed securities. Once the ABX was up and running, investors could buy or sell contracts linked to the price of mortgage-backed securities, sorted by rating and by year. So, for instance, an investor could short the ABX 06-1 triple-A, meaning a triple-A slice that was originated in the first half of 2006. "Before that, no one ever thought about whether to be long or short mortgages, because everyone was always long and it always worked," says one trader who was involved.

That wasn't quite true. The ABX made shorting the mortgage market much easier than it had been before. But even before its creation, a handful of investors—skeptical hedge fund managers, primarily—had sought a way to make a bearish bet on the mortgage market. They had pushed Wall Street firms to sell them customized credit default swaps on specific tranches of mortgage-backed securities. The most famous of these hedge fund managers was John Paulson, who would wind up making $4 billion in 2007 betting against subprime mortgages. He was hardly the only one, though. Michael Burry, a hedge fund manager in California, had become convinced after digging through mountains of paper and actually looking at the underlying loans that the housing market was going to crack. As early as the spring of 2005, he began to enter into trades with Wall Street firms in which he took a short position.

Greg Lippman at Deutsche Bank was one of the few traders operating inside the CDO machine who openly turned against subprime mortgages; indeed, his growing negative view was part of his incentive for getting involved in creating tradable credit default swaps in the first place. Having been, he later said, "balls long in 2005," he did an about-face when he saw a chart showing that people whose homes had appreciated only slightly were far more likely to default than those whose homes had risen by double digits. Everyone had always thought that unemployment caused mortgage defaults. Lippman realized that the world had changed—now all you'd need was a slowdown in the rate in home appreciation. Lippman would later say that it "takes a certain kind of person to acknowledge that what they spent a lifetime toiling away at doesn't work anymore." In the classic fashion of the convert, Lippman became Wall Street's most enthusiastic salesman for shorting subprime mortgages, making presentations to anyone who would listen. An exuberant, crude man, he had T-shirts made up that read, "I'm short your house."

Another skeptic was Andrew Redleaf, who ran a big hedge fund in Minneapolis called Whitebox Advisors. His hedge fund traded primarily in what he liked to call "stressed" bonds. ("If a distressed bond has an 80 to 90 percent chance of default, a stressed bond has a 50 percent chance of default," he explained.) Shaky mortgage bonds were right in his wheelhouse.

A brilliant mathematics student at Yale, Redleaf became an options trader who searched for anomalies between the prices of two different but related securities. By taking advantage of those anomalies, he made money. From a standing start in 1999, Redleaf built Whitebox into a $4 billion hedge fund.

An advocate of the new field of behavioral economics, Redleaf believed that markets were not always rational, that models were not always right, and that Wall Street's blind adherence to both gave him plenty of opportunity to make money. To him, the mortgage market was as good an example of Wall Street's shortsightedness as anything you could possibly find. After the crisis, he wrote a book with a Whitebox colleague, Richard Vigilante, entitled *Panic*, in which he spelled out his philosophy:

> This ideology of modern finance replaces the capitalist's appreciation for free markets as a context for human creativity with the worship of efficient markets as substitutes for that creativity. The capitalist understands free markets as an arena for the contending judgments of free men. The ideologues of modern finance dreamed of efficient markets as a replacement for that judgment and almost as a replacement for the men. The most gloriously efficient of all, supposedly, were modern public securities markets in all their ethereal electronic glory. To these most perfect markets the priesthood of finance attributed powers of calculation and control far exceeding not only the abilities of any human participant in them but the fondest dreams of any Communist commissar pecking away at the next Five Year Plan.

To Redleaf, the cause of the crisis was simple: Wall Street had "substituted elaborate, statistically based insurance schemes that, with the aid of efficient financial markets, were assumed to make old-fashioned credit analysis and human judgment irrelevant."

Redleaf's subprime epiphany had come years before, when he listened to a presentation by a New Century executive at an investment conference. He was struck by the fact that 85 percent of New Century's mortgages were cash-out refinancings. He asked the New Century executive about the default rate for the refinancings as opposed to mortgages that were used to purchase a new home. The man said he didn't know, but speculated that they probably weren't any different. This didn't ring true to Redleaf, whose experience with corporate bonds suggested that defaults were much higher when the debt went to pay off insiders than when it went for general corporate purposes. Cash-out refis struck him as the homeowner's version of paying off insiders.

Redleaf had another insight. Even back then, he could see that the business model so long touted by the subprime originators made no sense. The companies were saying that they could grow market share, on the one hand, while still using underwriting standards that weeded out borrowers likely to default. "I've seen this movie before," he said. "You can't have tighter standards *and* grow share. You can't even have *different* standards. In the end, you wind up lending money to people who can't pay it back, and that isn't a good business model for a public company."

Still, Redleaf didn't immediately act on his insight. "Seeing the New Century guys in 2002 just put the thought in the back of my head," he said later. He knew it was early in the cycle, and "being early is often the same as being wrong." Besides, there was no way to short the subprime market except by shorting the mortgage originators themselves, an unappealing prospect given how fast their stocks were climbing.

By 2006, though, the combination of the ABX index and the new credit default swap market made it possible to short subprime securitizations. Redleaf was ready to take the plunge. "We had negative feelings about New Century, about Ameriquest, about a few other lenders. We looked for securities with those mortgages." He also looked for mortgage bonds that were heavily weighted toward cash-out refis. In the spring of 2006, he began "massively" buying credit default swaps on hundreds of millions of dollars worth of securitized subprime mortgages.

Redleaf and Vigilante would later write that their biggest fear was that the trade would quickly disappear. "The mortgage market was so obviously headed for trouble that by early 2006, when we started shorting mortgage-backed securities, we feared the fun would be over before we were fully invested," they wrote in *Panic*. "We needn't have worried," they continued. "Rather than the trade vanishing too quickly, we repeatedly found ourselves scratching our heads in disbelief that we could short still more mortgage securities that were obviously going to blow up." All year long, as the headlines blared about subprime originators running into trouble and with foreclosures rising, Redleaf added to his short position. Every time there was a big piece of news—like the New Century restatement—he expected Wall Street to come to its senses. It didn't happen. On the contrary: the swaps were so cheap, it was clear Wall Street still didn't understand the risks it was insuring. The big Wall Street firms continued to view the triple-A tranches as utterly safe; the new ABX index would show them trading at par—that is, 100 percent of their stated value—for at least another year.

After the crisis hit, and writers and journalists began to look back at what had happened in those critical years of 2006 and 2007, a conventional wisdom sprang up according to which only a tiny handful of people had had the insight to realize that subprime mortgages were kegs of dynamite ready to blow. But Redleaf believes that his insight was not nearly as unique as it's been portrayed in such books as Michael Lewis's *The Big Short* or Gregory Zuckerman's *The Greatest Trade Ever*, which chronicles John Paulson's massive bet against the housing market. By Redleaf's count, there were maybe fifty or so hedge funds that would likely have considered this kind of trade. At least twenty of them, maybe more, were heavily short subprime bonds. "If you look at the disinterested smart players," he says, "a lot got it."

Indeed, the market took off. Credit default swaps "grew faster than even we predicted with more than $150B of structured product CDS outstanding at year end '05 vs. $2B at year end '04," Goldman Sachs reported in a presentation in early 2006. But it didn't take off because Wall Street firms wanted to be on the other side of the bets their smart hedge fund clients were taking. The reason it exploded had to do with one last little wrinkle Wall Street had dreamed up—the one that turned that keg of dynamite into the financial equivalent of a nuclear bomb: the synthetic CDO.

Long before anybody thought to use credit default swaps to short mortgage bonds, Street firms had taken to combining credit default swaps on a variety of corporate bonds and creating CDOs out of them. They were called synthetic CDOs because the CDOs didn't contain "real" collateral; rather they were based on the performance of existing bonds held by someone else. In Street parlance, they "referenced" the real bonds. The gains and losses would be real enough, but the underlying collateral was at one remove. Unlike a cash CDO that held collateral, and in which all the investors were long and got their payments from the underlying corporate bonds, a synthetic CDO could work only if there were investors on both the long side and the short side of every tranche. To put it another way, each position required two counterparties. Those who were long got cash flows that mimicked those of the underlying bonds, while those who were short paid a fee for the swap protection (which created the cash flows), but got the right to a big payoff should enough companies default on their debt. As ever, the cash flows were carved into tranches that were rated all the way from triple-A to junk.

By 2005, the hot new thing in the market was "correlation trading": going long one tranche, maybe triple-A, while shorting another tranche, the triple-B, say. It was all driven by demand by investors for a particular slice of risk and models that purported to show what the spread, or the difference in price, between various tranches "should" be. It also allowed firms to make these correlation trades with immense leverage, because their models told them that the trades balanced out and therefore carried little risk. Remember 2004, when the SEC allowed Wall Street firms to use their own models to calculate the amount of capital they had to hold? Here was the consequence of that decision: because the models for correlation trading said they were near riskless trades, the firms didn't have to put much capital against those trades. It was like Long-Term Capital Management on steroids.

In the spring of 2005, a warning shot was fired about the dangers of this brave new world when the credit rating agencies unexpectedly downgraded the debt of General Motors and Ford. All the models went haywire; press reports speculated that some hedge funds—and some Wall Street banks—had lost huge sums. That May, *Investment Dealers' Digest* ran an article entitled "The Synthetic CDO Shell Game: Could the Hottest Market in All of Fixed Income Be a Disaster in the Making?" It noted ominously that many players in the market weren't capable of assessing the risks. Michael Gibson, the Federal Reserve's chief of trading risk analysis, told the magazine, "What we are hearing from market participants is that there is a minority of CDO investors—perhaps 10 percent—who do not really understand what they are getting into." Said an unnamed market participant: "I imagine the number is higher. It's mind-boggling how much data you have to get a handle on to measure your exposure." Risk expert Leslie Rahl explained, "[T]here could be a substantial difference between what a theoretical model tells you something is worth and where a buyer and seller are willing to transact."

As usual, what should have been a wake-up call was ignored. Quickly, the synthetic CDO market in corporate bonds rebounded. And Wall Street took the next step: it began repackaging credit default swaps on mortgage-backed securities into synthetic CDOs. (Some of these synthetic CDOs only referenced mortgage-backed securities; others also included some actual mortgage-backed securities, or even other asset-backed securities, such as commercial mortgages, credit card debt, student loans, and so on.) Not only did this up the ante in complexity, but it also upped the amount of leverage at work. A corporate credit default swap had its share of leverage, but at least the underlying instrument was an obligation of a real company. More often than not, the underlying instrument being referenced in these new synthetic CDOs was a 100 percent loan-to-value mortgage made to a homeowner who probably couldn't pay.

And yet the appeal was overpowering. There was so much demand for these securities that no matter how fast the originators made mortgages, it wasn't fast enough. In 2005, Lars Norell, who worked with Chris Ricciardi at Merrill Lynch, told U.S. Credit, "In ABS [asset-backed securities], the availability of assets has been a sticking point. There's a finite amount of them issued." He pointed out that after subprime mortgages were crafted into residential mortgage-backed securities, there was only about $10 billion to $12 billion in the lowest-rated triple-B tranches. Since those were the tranches with the best yield, and therefore were the most attractive raw material for CDOs, it had the effect of putting a "natural cap," as Norell put it, on CDO issuance. Plus, buying all the securities for a CDO could take up to six to nine months.

But with a synthetic CDO, it didn't matter anymore if the originators could make new mortgages—or even if they went out of business entirely. Because synthetic CDOs made of credit default swaps referenced mortgage bonds that already existed, you didn't need any more bonds. You could clone the same risky tranches again and again—five, ten, twenty times if you wanted. And you could do this quickly, without waiting around to buy real securities. Even if there wasn't a single new mortgage bond created, the supply of securities was now infinite and immediate, thanks to credit default swaps and synthetic CDOs. But that also meant that as subprime mortgages continued to default—and those losses eventually began to erode the value of the CDOs—those losses were going to be greatly amplified because so many side bets had been made so quickly through the purchase of synthetic CDOs.

The gains were amplified, too, because synthetic CDOs are a zero-sum game: someone has to lose and someone has to win. Even after all the damage had been done, some would make the argument that there was nothing wrong with this. In a free market, shouldn't all participants be able to "express their views"—a euphemism for placing a bet—on the direction of mortgage-backed securities? Maybe so. But if the ability to short a mortgage-backed security, and maybe even the construction of the index, brought a kind of transparency to the market, then the synthetic CDO took it away. That's because the synthetic CDO allowed Wall Street to take all of Mike Burry's and Andy Redleaf's bets, and instead of holding the other side of those bets—or finding investors who actually wanted to be long a tranche of triple-B-rated mortgage-backed securities backed by New Century loans—it could instead reassemble those bets into triple-A-rated securities. (And, yes, the rating agencies put those triple-A ratings on large chunks of synthetic CDOs.)

That way, the other side of the bet wasn't someone who had investigated the mortgage-backed security—like Burry and Redleaf did—and thought he was betting on its performance. It was someone who was buying a rating and thought he couldn't lose money.

"Negative news on housing nags the market," Burry wrote in an early 2006 letter to his investors. "Yet mortgage spreads in the cash market fell substantially." What he meant by that was that the market was acting as if there was less risk instead of more. This development, Burry wrote, is "indicative of ramping synthetic CDO activity."

18

The Smart Guys

"We're not trying to outsmart the smart guys. We're trying to sell bonds to the dumb guys."

So said a big time Kidder Peabody trader named Mike Vranos back in 1994, according to colleagues who talked about him to the *Wall Street Journal* on May 20, 1994

"This list [of potential buyers] may be a little skewed toward sophisticated hedge funds with which we should not expect to make too much money since (a) most of the time they will be on the same side of the trade as we will, and (b) they know exactly how things work . . . vs. buy-and-hold ratings buyers who we should be focused on a lot more to make incremental $$$ next year. . . ."

So wrote a young Goldman Sachs salesman named Fabrice Tourre in an internal e-mail on December 28, 2006

—◦◦◦—

On one level, the creation of synthetic CDOs was the apotheosis of the previous twenty-five years of modern finance. They were stuffed with risk, yet, thanks to the complex probabilistic risk models developed by Wall Street's quants, large chunks of them were considered as safe as Treasury bonds. They were Wall Street's version of a lab experiment gone mad. Unlike a corporate bond, backed by the assets of a corporation—or even a mortgage-backed security, backed by actual mortgages—they existed solely to make complex bets on securities that existed somewhere else in the system (which, as often as not, were themselves bets on securities that existed somewhere else in the system). They had the imprimatur of the rating agencies, whose profits depended on stamping these complex bets with triple-A ratings. They massively increased leverage in the system. They were made possible by the invention of the credit derivative, the most glittering innovation in finance. And their raw material—the debt upon which everything else was built—was mortgages, quite often poorly underwritten subprime mortgages. The stew was now complete.

On another level, synthetic CDOs were a classic example of how things never really changed on Wall Street. The sellers of synthetic CDOs had a huge informational advantage over the buyers, just as bond sellers have historically had an advantage over bond buyers. Buying a synthetic CDO was like playing poker with an opponent who knew every card in your hand. Conflicts abounded. Those "buy-and-hold ratings-based investors," as Tourre described them—or the "dumb guys," to use Mike Vranos's less polite words—weren't necessarily less intelligent; they were simply less plugged in, and either unwilling or unable to do the analysis necessary to compensate for that. Stretching to get the extra yield that synthetic CDOs seemed to offer, lacking a clear understanding of what they were buying, they were the perfect willing dupes.

What's remarkable, in hindsight, is that despite their many advantages, so many Wall Street firms, blinded by the rich fees and huge bonuses the CDO machine made possible, duped themselves as well. As one close observer says, "There was plenty of dumb smart money." There was also some smart money that was genuinely smart.

Chief among the smart guys was Goldman Sachs. In the aftermath of the crisis, Goldman Sachs would be excoriated by the press and the public—and investigated by Congress, the SEC, and the Justice Department—for the way it used synthetic mortgage-backed securities to advance its own interests, often at the expense of its clients. There was something a tad unfair about this focus on Goldman; its mercenary behavior wasn't all that unique. Goldman was simply more skilled than its peers in looking out for its own interests. The firm had no grand scheme to destroy Wall Street. Its executives had no idea how bad the destruction would be. Mainly, Goldman's traders were just doing what they had always been taught to do: *Protect the firm at all costs.*

Yet somehow it was inevitable that Goldman would land at the center of the storm. The modern Goldman attitude—that there was no conflict it couldn't manage, no complex product too complex, and few trades the firm should turn its back on—was bound to leave a bad taste in the mouths of people who were not part of Wall Street. Other members of the Wall Street tribe often resented Goldman for the way it ran roughshod over its clients and counterparties. But they accepted it. It was just "Goldman being Goldman."

But for large swatches of the American public, many of whom lost their homes or jobs because of the financial crisis, Goldman's behavior was deeply offensive. Taking advantage of clients to save its own skin—and then denying that that's what it had done—was not the way companies were supposed to act. People were also offended as they realized that Goldman had played as big a role as the rest of Wall Street in blowing the bubble bigger. Yet unlike millions of subprime borrowers, it largely escaped the damage it helped create.

It was the mortgage market that definitively put the lie to Goldman's famous, sanctimonious first business principle, the one John Whitehead had articulated three-plus decades earlier: *Our clients' interests always come first.* They didn't—and hadn't for quite some time. As a 2007 training guide for the Goldman Sachs mortgage department noted, "However, this [the first business principle] is not always straightforward, as we are a market maker to multiple clients," meaning that even when Goldman was servicing clients, it often had to choose which clients' interests would come first. The presentation could have added that one of those clients, as often as not, was Goldman Sachs itself.

What Goldman never lost sight of was Dick Pratt's old warning: the mortgage was the most dangerous financial product ever created. It's what Goldman forgot that caused all its problems. It wasn't just dealing with a financial product. It was dealing with people's homes.

The Goldman Sachs mortgage department, which at its peak had some four hundred people, was, by its nature, conflict central. It underwrote mortgage-backed securities, which it sold to clients. It built CDOs that included its own mortgage-backed securities and those of others. It created synthetic CDOs, allowing clients to take either the long or short side of the bet. Sometimes Goldman itself was on the other side of a client bet. Most of the time, the client had no knowledge of Goldman's position. It also actively traded all those instruments for its clients—and itself. Sometimes it bought or shorted mortgage-related securities because it couldn't get the deal done without committing its own capital. Other times, it did so because it had its own "view" about which way the securities were headed and it was trading for its own account. In any case, the line between client-related trading and proprietary trading was very blurry: if Goldman hedged a position that was a result of facilitating a client trade, did that count as a client trade or a proprietary trade?

Goldman's chief risk officer, Craig Broderick, would later say that "our client base is extremely aware and clear about what function we are performing." But contemporaneous e-mails—and complaints after the fact—would paint a messier picture.

The structured product group, which was part of the mortgage desk and which put together many of Goldman's most complex trades, was co-headed by Michael Swenson, a former Williams College hockey player in his late thirties, and David Lehman, a young star hired from Deutsche Bank around 2004, when he was just thirty. They made a decision early on that synthetic business could be big, so they staffed up accordingly. Or, as Swenson put it in his 2007 self-evaluation, "I can take credit for recognizing the enormous opportunity for the ABS synthetics business two years ago. I recognized the need to assemble an outstanding team of traders and was able to lead that group to build a number one franchise." And that he did. Among those he recruited was Josh Birnbaum, a star trader who traded the new ABX index.

Until synthetics came along, Goldman had been a middling player in both the mortgage-backed securities and the CDO markets. But it quickly became a force in this new market, which consisted of both synthetic CDOs and hybrid CDOs. (These contain both real mortgage-backed securities and credit default swaps.) Quickly, Goldman began to climb up the rankings; in both 2006 and 2007, it was the fourth largest underwriter of CDOs. Wrote Birnbaum in his 2007 self-review: "#1 market share in ABS CDS [ABX and single name] est 30–40%." Although mortgages were a relatively small piece of Goldman's overall business—the department's 2006 revenue barely topped $1 billion, compared to nearly $38 billion for the firm itself—almost half of the mortgage desk's 2006 revenue came from "structured products trading and CDOs."

One of the earliest Goldman synthetic CDOs, put together in 2004, was called Abacus. It came about when IKB, a German bank that had become an aggressive CDO investor, came to Goldman seeking exposure to a specific set of mortgage-backed securities. Goldman was happy to oblige, and built a synthetic CDO based on the securities IKB wanted to reference. The dollars IKB received would come from the customers who took the short side of the transaction. Over the next few years, Abacus became a kind of Goldman franchise, with about sixteen deals and $10 billion worth of securities sold, according to the Senate Permanent Subcommittee on Investigations.

Later, Goldman would insist that the synthetic CDO deals the firm put together were "often initiated by clients," to quote Goldman's 2010 letter to shareholders. In that original Abacus CDO, this was clearly true. "IKB craved this product," says a person familiar with the deal. He adds that, in the early years, the hard part was finding someone to take the short side of the trade, because no one wanted that risk.

But the firm's later insistence that it was merely a "market maker" in these transactions—implying that it had no stake in the economic performance of the securities it was selling to clients—became less true over time. And even those early deals made a mockery of the notion that most investors understood what they were buying. For one thing, the synthetic deals were stuffed full of multiple kinds of risks. Take Abacus 2005-3, another early deal. The reference obligations—that is, the securities the CDO referenced—consisted of 130 credits. Those credits included everything from tranches of mortgage-backed securities issued by Long Beach Mortgage, Countrywide, Ameriquest, and New Century, to commercial mortgage-backed securities, to trusts backed by Sallie Mae student loans, to credit card debt issued by MBNA and Chase. Who could possibly understand all the risks contained in these securities? Is it any wonder that investors were essentially buying ratings instead?

Nor was it possible for investors to know Goldman's own position. Was Goldman merely standing between two customers, the way a true market maker did? Or was Goldman using—and designing—the CDO in order to hedge an existing position or to "express" its own view about the referenced securities? For instance, Goldman could attempt to profit by having, say, a long position in triple-A-rated securities, and then use a synthetic CDO to establish a short position in triple-B-rated securities. Or, if Goldman was long in New Century mortgage-backed securities, the firm could hedge its position by constructing a synthetic CDO that referenced those securities, and take the short side of that trade. Buyers had no way of knowing whether Goldman was the dealer at the card table, a player, or both. Goldman supporters would later argue that buyers shouldn't have cared what Goldman's position was—they were responsible for doing their own analysis of the underlying securities. "The deal is the deal," Dan Sparks, the former head of the Goldman mortgage desk, later told the Senate Permanent Subcommittee.

But many buyers didn't do that analysis. And it would later become clear that at least some certainly did care what Goldman itself was doing.

Just as a cash CDO was the perfect mechanism for laundering risky mortgages, so was a synthetic CDO the perfect vehicle for laundering positions a firm wanted to get off its books. For instance, if you owned a bunch of New Century mortgage-backed securities, it might be hard to find someone who wanted to own the risk that New Century loans were going to go bad. But if you could establish a short position for yourself by selling your clients the long position in a synthetic CDO—thereby insulating yourself from your unwanted junk by creating new triple-A securities—well, *voilà*! Given that Goldman was a big warehouse lender to New Century—and far more likely than its clients to have early knowledge that New Century mortgages were doomed—the whole edifice begins to take on a very dark hue. As Janet Tavakoli, a structured finance expert who became a fierce, prescient critic of CDOs, later put it, "They had reason to know what they were hedging shouldn't have been created in the first place."

In addition, Goldman, says one person who has looked into these deals, "had a stranglehold on every aspect of the transaction." The fine print of one Abacus prospectus says that the "Protection Buyer"—i.e., Goldman—"may have information, including material, non-public information," which it did not provide to the buyers. Thus, if Goldman did have knowledge of New Century mortgage defaults, it was under no legal obligation to share that knowledge with a client who was about to buy a synthetic CDO that referenced New Century securities. In some of the Abacus deals, Goldman could unwind the trade after three years if it didn't like how it was going. (One blogger later called this "Heads I win, tails you lose.") Another prospectus notes that Goldman's many roles "may be in conflict with the interests of the investors in the transaction." In fairness to Goldman, these pitfalls were identified in writing. But the disclosure didn't make the conflicts go away.

The point is, investors were hardly buying an existing security from a neutral market maker. They were buying a security that had been constructed to enable someone to accomplish a specific goal. Quite often, that "someone" was the market maker itself. As Goldman's Tourre wrote in a June 2006 e-mail, "ABACUS enables us to create a levered short in significant size." (It was levered because Goldman didn't have to put up cash.)

And there were times when it appears Goldman wasn't a market maker at all, but rather a principal. Consider this exchange between David Lehman and Josh Birnbaum: "[We] need to decide if we want to do 1–3bb of these trades for our book or engage customers," wrote Lehman. Replied Birnbaum, "On baa3 [the lowest rung of investment grade], I'd say we definitely keep for ourselves. On baa2 [the second lowest rung], I'm open to some sharing to the extent that it keeps these customers engaged with us."

It is also clear from internal e-mails that by 2006 there were Goldman traders—not all of them, but some—who viewed some of their subprime holdings as junk. One trader described a Goldman mortgage-backed security this way: "It stinks. . . . I don't want it in our book." Swenson later wrote in a self-review that "during the early summer of 2006, it was clear that the market fundamentals in subprime and the highly levered nature of CDOs was going to have a very unhappy ending."

The year 2006 was when Dan Sparks became the head of the mortgage desk. Sparks, an intense Texan who had joined Goldman as an analyst in 1989 after graduating from Texas A&M, spent his early years at the firm helping the Resolution Trust Corporation dispose of assets from the S&L crisis. He made partner in 2002. Sparks was a classic trader: he didn't let a lot of hope, fear, or sympathy creep into the equation. The price was what the market said it was, and if you were willing to buy securities at that price, whatever happened after the sale was your responsibility. It wasn't Goldman's job to protect clients from their own mistakes, he believed; they were all big boys. Whatever the firm's purpose was in constructing a particular synthetic CDO—market maker, principal, whatever—was irrelevant. In protecting Goldman's interests, that would prove to be a useful attitude.

Consider, for instance, a November 2006 deal called Hudson Mezzanine, a synthetic CDO that referenced triple-B subprime securities. In terms of serving Goldman's interests—in a way that wouldn't be obvious to investors—it was a classic.

The CDO had been constructed, Goldman executives later told the Senate Permanent Subcommittee, while the company was trying to remove triple-B assets from its books. Among those assets was a long position in the ABX index that Goldman had gotten "stuck" with while putting together deals for hedge fund clients that wanted to go short. Unable to find counterparties to take the long position off its hands, Goldman used Hudson as a means by which it hedged its long position.

Goldman selected all the securities that Hudson would reference. These included $1.2 billion in ABX index contracts, offsetting the long ABX position Goldman wanted to hedge, and another $800 million in single-name

CDS, or credit default swaps that referenced specific mortgage-backed securities issued in 2005 and 2006.

None of which was clear from the Hudson prospectus. Instead, the disclosure merely said that the CDO's contents were "assets sourced from the Street," making it sound as though Goldman randomly selected the securities, instead of specifically creating a hedge for its own book. Page four of the pitch book also said, "Goldman Sachs has aligned incentives with the Hudson program by investing in a portion of the equity." Only on page thirteen does the pitch book make the standard disclosure that Goldman was providing the initial short position. But according to the Senate Permanent Subcommittee, Goldman didn't then sell that short position to a client, as a true market maker would. Instead, "Goldman was the sole buyer of protection on the entire $2 billion of assets," as an internal Goldman e-mail put it.

If the job of a market maker is to sit between two investors, each of which affirmatively wants to take a different view, the Hudson deal didn't come close to that definition. Nor is it possible to argue that Goldman was doing something its clients were clamoring for. Rather, it was a deal Goldman had to sell, and sell hard, to reluctant clients. Swenson would later write about such deals, "[W]e aggressively capitalized on the franchise to enter into efficient shorts. . . ."

Later, as Hudson and other deals went sour, Goldman's clients were furious at how they had been taken in. "Real bad feeling across European sales about some of the trades we did with clients," wrote Yusuf Aliredha, Goldman's head of European fixed-income sales, in an e-mail to Sparks. "The damage this has done to our franchise is very significant."

On December 5, 2006, just before noon, Dan Sparks sent an e-mail to his bosses, Tom Montag, head of sales and trading in the Americas, and Rich Ruzika, co-head of global equity trading. "Subprime market getting hit hard—hedge funds hitting street, wall street journal article." (He was referring to a *Wall Street Journal* story published that morning about how subprime borrowers were increasingly falling behind on their mortgages.) "At this point we are down $20 mm today. Structured exits are the way to reduce risk."

More and more traders on the mortgage desk were getting increasingly uncomfortable being on the long side of the mortgage markets—the Hudson deal had shown that. Individual traders were even shorting mortgage securities. Yet as a firm, Goldman still had a large overall long position. At the end of November, the firm had $7.8 billion in subprime mortgages on its balance sheet, and another $7.2 billion in subprime mortgage-backed securities. Goldman also had a big long position in the ABX index, as well as warehouse lines extended to New Century, among others. The gossip among traders at other firms was that Goldman Sachs was heavily exposed to the mortgage market—and they were right. But they couldn't see inside Goldman Sachs.

Roughly a week after Sparks's e-mail, CFO David Viniar convened a meeting in his office. Even though Goldman's internal risk measures, such as VaR, suggested that everything was okay, the mortgage desk had nonetheless suffered losses ten days running. Gary Cohn, as president, would later testify that the firm's internal risk models had "decoupled" from the actual results in December 2006. Goldman's top executives were sensitive to the losses because the firm was fanatical about using mark-to-market accounting, valuing the securities it held daily, based on the price they would get if they sold the securities in the market that day. They reflected any gains or losses on the firm's books, and reported this information to Viniar and Goldman's other top executives. Unlike every other firm on Wall Street, in other words, Goldman had no illusions about how its mortgage-related securities were performing.

The group that met that day included Viniar, Sparks, and various members of "the Federation," the back office risk managers and accounting people. They reviewed Goldman's exposures, including that ABX position, the securities, the warehouse lines—and the bad loans that Goldman was trying to get New Century and other originators to repurchase. Out of that meeting came a mandate from the top that the firm needed to "get smaller, reduce risks, and get closer to home," as Birnbaum later put it. It was agreed that Goldman would pull back from its long position so that the firm wouldn't get caught if the mortgage market continued to sink, as the firm now expected. In an e-mail, Sparks listed his follow-ups, which included "Reduce exposure, sell more ABX index outright," and "Distribute as much as possible on bonds created from new loan securitizations and clean previous positions." The next day, Viniar chimed in: "[L]et's be very aggressive distributing things because there will be very good opportunities as the markets [sic] goes into what is likely to be even greater distress."

In the coming months, the Goldman team would do all of the above and more. Birnbaum bought all the short positions he could in the ABX.

Goldman demanded collateral from hedge fund clients that had bought mortgage-backed securities on margin, earning it the enmity of many fund managers. It also followed Viniar's directive to be "aggressive" about "distributing things." And the firm was able to "amass large amounts of cheap single name protection," as Birnbaum later wrote in a self-review, because "CDO managers were in denial." Goldman, however, wasn't, which is why it was so anxious to reduce its risks as quickly as possible. As another Goldman trader wrote on February 11, "The cdo biz is dead we don't have a lot of time left."

Among Goldman's deals:

• Because it did business with New Century, Goldman was carrying New Century mortgages and securities on its balance sheet. But a CDO it sold in late February 2007 served to reduce that exposure. This was a CDO called Anderson Mezzanine Funding, which consisted of sixty-one credit default swaps totaling $305 million on mostly triple-B-rated securities backed by mortgages produced by New Century and other subprime lenders. Although 70 percent of the CDO was rated triple-A, buyers were so reluctant to invest that Sparks, at one point, suggested liquidating the transaction. To get the deal done, Goldman ended up with a chunk of the equity and the lower-rated securities. On the deal itself, Goldman contends it lost money, something the firm says it did on many such deals. But the Senate Permanent Subcommittee says that Goldman kept a large chunk of the short position for itself, which created a hedge against its New Century exposure.

The subcommittee would also allege that buyers weren't told that Goldman would profit if the securities tanked; some of the e-mails that were exchanged as Anderson was being marketed certainly suggest that was the case. One potential client asked, "How did you get comfortable with all the New Century collateral in particular the New Century serviced deals—considering you are holding the equity and their servicing may not be around . . . ?" And a Goldman salesperson asked for additional ammunition so that he could "position the trade as an opportunity to get exposure to a good pool of assets" and not "as a risk reduction/position cleanup trade." Which is exactly what it was. At the time the deal was done, the underlying mortgages in some of the securitizations were already close to double-digit default rates. Buyers of the triple-A-rated piece clearly believed that the rating meant that their investment was sufficiently insulated from those losses. They were wrong.

Within seven months, the deal was downgraded to junk.

• In May 2006, Goldman helped underwrite $495 million of bonds backed by second-lien mortgages made by Long Beach. It was a terrible deal. Although two-thirds of the tranches had been rated triple-A, the loans in the securitization were some of the worst subprime mortgages imaginable, and the default rate was very high. According to an analysis later done by a research firm called Amherst Holdings, only 32 percent of the loans had full documentation, and the weighted average loan to value was almost 100 percent. As early as 2007, Goldman was demanding that Long Beach buy back defaulted loans; within two years, the triple-A tranches had been downgraded to default status. Didn't Goldman have a responsibility to investigate the loans before selling them? Of course: as Goldman's general counsel later wrote in a letter to the Financial Crisis Inquiry Commission, "the federal securities laws effectively impose a 'gatekeeper' role on the underwriter." Goldman claimed that it did due diligence on both the mortgage originators it did business with and the loans themselves. But the quality of both has to make you wonder about how closely Goldman—or for that matter any of the Wall Street underwriters—looked. In any event, the advent of credit default swaps on mortgage-backed securities made it possible for Goldman to underwrite such a deal while mitigating any risk to its own bottom line: in this particular case, Goldman took care of itself by buying $10 million worth of protection on those securities. "Ultimately, in this transaction, Goldman Sachs profited from the decline of the very security it had earlier sold to clients," as Senator Carl Levin, the chairman of the Senate Permanent Subcommittee, later put it.

• In the spring of 2007, as the clock was ticking on the mortgage market, Goldman created a $1 billion CDO squared that was a mixture of cash and synthetic collateral called Timberwolf. Part of the collateral for that CDO included credit default swaps that referenced securities backed by Washington Mutual pay option ARMs. Timberwolf also included Abacus CDO securities in its collateral.

Once again, Goldman had to push hard to sell the deal. Finally, though, Goldman was able to sell about $300 million of Timberwolf securities to Bear Stearns Asset Management. The firm sold another $78 million—at a sizable discount—to an Australian fund called the Basis Yield Alpha Fund, which at the time had only $500 million under management. According to a $1 billion lawsuit Basis later filed—a suit whose central claim is that the Timberwolf purchase forced Basis into insolvency—Goldman told Basis that the market was stabilizing. And while the Timberwolf prospectus states that Goldman owned equity in Timberwolf, the Senate Permanent Subcommittee would later highlight that Goldman also had a substantial short position. "Goldman was pressuring investors to take the risk of toxic securities off its books with knowingly false sales pitches," said Basis's lawyer. Goldman called the lawsuit "a misguided attempt by Basis, a hedge fund that was one of the world's most experienced CDO investors, to shift its investment losses to Goldman Sachs." One fund manager who knows Basis has a different take: "Dumb money," he says.

Within a year, Timberwolf's triple-A securities had been downgraded to junk, as the WaMu option ARMs defaulted. The Goldman trader responsible for managing the deal later characterized the issuance of Timberwolf as "a day that will live in infamy." Tom Montag put it more bluntly. "Boy that timeberwof [sic] was one shi**y deal," he wrote on June 22, 2007. Once again, Goldman insists that it lost hundreds of millions of dollars on the Timberwolf deal, but to the extent that the deal provided a way for Goldman to exit or hedge existing positions, the firm lost less than it would have otherwise.*

• And then there was Abacus 2007-AC1, the most infamous of all the Goldman synthetic CDO deals. Nearly three years after the deal was completed, the SEC would charge Goldman with fraud, alleging that the firm made "materially misleading statements and omissions" in connection with the deal. Goldman heatedly disputed the SEC's charges at first, but ended up settling the case for the record sum of $550 million and conceding that the marketing materials were "incomplete." But in truth, the legal issues were far from the most disturbing thing about Abacus 2007-AC1.

---

* Washington Mutual executives also worried about Goldman Sachs. E-mails exchanged between WaMu CEO Kerry Killinger and other executives in late 2007, when the thrift was looking for an investment banker, offer a perfect snapshot of the modern Goldman Sachs. Todd Baker, WaMu's executive vice president, wanted to bring in Goldman.

"Hiring the best brains is always wise when the stakes are high," Miller wrote in an e-mail to Killinger. "Goldman also has the strongest balance sheet, market heft and risk appetite to do many things themselves for us that others couldn't as part of the solution. On the other hand . . . we always need to worry a little about Goldman because we need them more than they need us and the firm is run by traders." Killinger wrote back, "I don't trust Goldy on this. They are smart, but this is swimming with the sharks. They were shorting mortgages big time while they were giving CFC [Countrywide] advice."

In fact, Goldman's mortgage department had bought equity puts on WaMu's stock when it was around $40 a share, meaning that Goldman would make money if the stock fell. By the summer of 2007, the department was also seeking permission to short Countrywide, IndyMac, Bear Stearns, Merrill Lynch, Lehman Brothers, Morgan Stanley, and MBIA.

It began with John Paulson, then a little-known hedge fund manager, who along with Andrew Redleaf, Michael Burry, and a handful of others, had been painstakingly buying credit default swaps on subprime mortgage-backed securities. Paulson and his staff were convinced that the entire mortgage market was poised to collapse. Their analysis, in retrospect, was prescient. As a Paulson employee wrote in January 2007, "[T]he market is not pricing the subprime RMBS wipeout scenario. In my opinion this situation is due to the fact that rating agencies, CDO managers and underwriters have all the incentives to keep the game going, while 'real money' investors have neither the analytical tools nor the institutional framework." Anticipating that "wipeout scenario," Paulson was seeking to do something that would have a big potential payoff. He wanted to make an industrial-sized short by betting against all the triple-A tranches of a single synthetic CDO—a CDO, in fact, that he would secretly help construct. In other words, he would make money if homeowners couldn't pay their mortgages—and to improve his odds, he was going to, in effect, select which homeowners he thought were least likely to pay.

It was an astonishingly brazen idea—like "a bettor asking a football owner to bench a star quarterback to improve the odds of his wager against the team." That was the description Scott Eichel, a Bear Stearns trader, gave to Gregory Zuckerman, the *Wall Street Journal* reporter whose book *The Greatest Trade Ever* documented Paulson's audacious short. Eichel explained to Zuckerman that when Paulson broached his idea with Bear Stearns, it said no. "[I]t didn't pass the ethics standards," said Eichel. *It didn't pass Bear Stearns ethics standards?* The same Bear Stearns that had created some truly terrible subprime securities without batting an eyelash? Yet Goldman Sachs had no such qualms.

Paulson knocked on Goldman's door at a fortuitous moment. The firm had begun thinking about "ABACUS-rental strategies," as Tourre described it in an e-mail. By that, he meant that Goldman would "rent"—for a hefty fee—the Abacus brand to a hedge fund that wanted to make a massive short bet. Paulson's idea fit perfectly.

Paulson paid Goldman $15 million to rent the Abacus name. The buyers of the CDO—the longs on the other side of the Paulson short—assumed it was a deal instigated by Goldman, since Abacus was a Goldman platform. They had no idea that Paulson was helping to select the securities that would make up the deal. Indeed, as the deal was nearing completion, the Paulson team decided to throw out mortgages originated by Wells Fargo. Wells Fargo mortgages, after all, might actually perform. Goldman's failure to disclose Paulson's involvement in selecting the securities in its marketing material for the transaction became the heart of the SEC's case against the firm.

(According to one person familiar with the deal, Goldman even contemplated keeping the short position for itself instead of giving it to Paulson, who was not considered an important client. The irony is rich: had Goldman kept the short position for itself, it would have double-crossed Paulson, but the SEC would have had no case.)

There were no clean hands here. In renting the Abacus platform and helping to select the referenced securities, Paulson was doing something that may have been perfectly legal, but was awfully sleazy. He wound up shorting most of the $909 million super-senior tranche. The rating agencies were cooperative, as always, even though the Abacus deal was specifically stocked with securities that had been chosen in the expectation that they would fail. Eric Kolchinsky, the Moody's analyst who oversaw the rating process, later testified that he hadn't known about Paulson's involvement and that it was "something that I personally would have wanted to know." He added, "It just changes the whole dynamic of the structure, where the person who's putting it together, choosing it, wants it to blow up." But this was a lame excuse. If there was one party with a duty to do its own due diligence on the securities Abacus referenced, surely it was the rating agencies.

The CDO manager that was supposed to be choosing the securities, a firm called ACA Management, took its fees and appeared to look the other way— exactly what Goldman hoped it would do. E-mails show that one CDO manager had even turned the deal down "given their negative views on most of the credits that Paulson had selected," as Tourre wrote. (The SEC claimed that ACA didn't understand that Paulson was going to short the deal, which is a little hard to believe.) ACA also invested $42 million in the securities, and its insurance arm took the other side of the Paulson bet by guaranteeing the $909 million in super-senior tranches.

The final counterparty was an Abacus veteran: IKB. IKB was no lamb being led to slaughter. It had bragged incessantly about its expertise in the CDO market and, according to a lawsuit later filed against it by the French bank Calyon, was trying to off-load its own bad deals onto others. In June 2007, IKB also created a structured investment vehicle called Rhinebridge. Rhinebridge, like other SIVs, issued debt that it then used to buy mortgage-backed securities and CDOs like Abacus. The debt issued by Rhinebridge, which was rated triple-A, was bought by, among others, King County, Washington, which managed money on behalf of one hundred other public agencies. This was money used to run schools and fix potholes and fund municipal budgets. Rhinebridge was wound down in the fall of 2008, with its investors getting fifty cents on the dollar. In a lawsuit, King County alleged that IKB created Rhinebridge "for the purpose of moving investment losses off of its own balance sheet." For all of Goldman's later claims that it dealt only with the most sophisticated of investors, the fact remained that those investors could be fiduciaries, investing on behalf of school districts, fire departments, pensioners, and municipalities all across the country. It was their money, at least in part, that was funding the CDO games Wall Street was playing.

There was another problem with the "sophisticated investor" defense. These deals were so complicated that in many cases *nobody* understood the risks, not even the underwriter. Yet investors—even sophisticated investors like IKB—were buying deals like Abacus for a simple reason: they didn't want to lose money. Triple-A-rated securities were supposed to be the closest thing an investor could get to a risk-free investment. If Goldman knew that a triple-A rating no longer meant what it once had—and that these complex securities carried far more risk than their ratings implied—did it really have no responsibility to say anything? Shouldn't there have been a point at which Goldman just said no? If Paulson's bet paid off, it would happen because millions of Americans were losing their homes. Wasn't that worth thinking about before deciding to go through with the Abacus deal? In 2004, Scott Kapnick, who had headed Goldman's investment banking department, had said to *Fortune*, "The most powerful thing we can do is say no." But by 2007, Kapnick, like many other senior bankers, had left the firm.

On March 7, 2007, Tourre sent an e-mail to his girlfriend. "I will give you more details in person on what we spoke about but the summary of the US subprime business situation is that it is not too brilliant . . . According to Sparks, that business is totally dead, and the poor little subprime borrowers will not last so long!!! All this is giving me ideas for my medium term future, insomuch as I do not intend to wait for the complete explosion of the industry."

That same day, the Goldman Sachs Firmwide Risk Committee heard a presentation from the mortgage desk. According to a summary of the meeting, the first bullet point read, "Game Over—accelerating meltdown for subprime lenders such as Fremont and New Century." The second bullet point: "The Street is highly vulnerable, potentially large exposures at Merrill and Lehman."

On June 24, Gary Cohn, at the time Goldman's co–chief operating officer, sent an e-mail to Viniar and several others, noting both the big losses Goldman was taking on the mortgage securities it had been unable to "distribute" and the even bigger gains it was booking from its short position. Viniar's response: "Tells you what might be happening to people who don't have the big short."

Later, the Senate Permanent Subcommittee would charge Goldman with making a fortune—$3.7 billion—by betting against its customers when it knew the market was going to fall apart. But that's not really what happened. The huge gains Goldman made from its short position in 2007 were offset by substantial losses from the securities it couldn't get rid of. Indeed, the firm made less money than it might have, because at certain points during the meltdown, most notably in the spring of 2007, Goldman covered its short position. It didn't envision the "wipeout scenario," as Paulson had. Rather, it was trying to figure out what the market was doing and stay one step ahead of it. Overall, Goldman's mortgage department made $272 million in the first quarter of 2007, lost $174 million in the second quarter, made $741 million in the third quarter, and made $432 million in the fourth quarter. In total, Goldman's mortgage department made $1.27 billion in 2007, a big number, obviously, but not even close to the $4 billion John Paulson made. "Of course we didn't dodge the mortgage mess," Goldman CEO Lloyd Blankfein wrote in the fall of 2007. "We lost money, then made more than we lost because of shorts." True enough.

Other firms besides Goldman were also trying to dump their exposure onto buyers who hadn't figured out that the ratings had become degraded. Other firms also sold synthetic CDOs while keeping a short position. But Goldman was unquestionably better at it than its competitors. What Goldman Sachs really did in 2007 was protect its own bottom line, at the expense of clients it deemed disposable, in a conflict-ridden business that maybe—just maybe—the old Goldman Sachs would have been wise enough to stay away from.

—∞—

In all the subsequent frenzy over who did what to whom in the synthetic CDO market, a series of deeper, more troubling questions tended to get overlooked. One was this: What, exactly, was the point of a synthetic CDO? It didn't fund a home. It didn't make the mortgage market any better. It was a zero-sum game in which the dice were mortgages.

"Wall Street is friction," said Mark Adelson, the former Moody's analyst. "Every cent an investment bank earns is capital that doesn't go to a business. With an initial public offering, you get it. But with derivatives, you can't tie it back. You could argue that at least it's not hurting things, and that was a compelling rationale for a long time." He concluded, "We may have encouraged financial institutions to grow in ways that do not directly facilitate or enhance the reason for having a financial system in the first place."

If only that were the worst of it. But it wasn't. The invention of synthetics may well have both magnified the bubble and prolonged it. Take the former first. Synthetic CDOs made it possible to bet on the same bad mortgages five, ten, twenty times. Underwriters, wanting to please their short-selling clients, referenced a handful of tranches they favored over and over again. Merrill's risk manager, John Breit, would later estimate that some tranches of mortgage-backed securities were referenced seventy-five times. Thus could a $15 million tranche do $1 billion of damage. In a case uncovered by the *Wall Street Journal*, a $38 million subprime mortgage bond created in June 2006 ended up in more than thirty debt pools and ultimately caused roughly $280 million in losses.

As for prolonging the bubble, synthetics likely did it in two ways. Firms were much more willing to buy and bundle subprime securities from some of the worst originators knowing they could use a synthetic CDO to hedge any exposure they might be stuck with. Would Goldman have sold over $1 billion of Fremont mortgages to investors in early 2007 if it hadn't been able to enter into credit default swaps to hedge some of its own resulting exposure to Fremont? Without the means to off-load these exposures, investment firms would likely have been more cautious—and shut off the spigot sooner.

Secondly, selling the equity in the CDO, the riskiest piece, required finding buyers willing to take that risk. There weren't that many to begin with, and once they had enough equity risk on their books and stopped buying, the market for mortgages would have naturally wound down.

But around 2005, some smart hedge funds began to realize that there was a compelling trade to be made by buying the equity in a CDO while shorting the triple-As. If the mortgages performed, the return offered by the equity pieces, which could be upwards of 20 percent, more than covered the cost of the short. And if the mortgages didn't perform? Then the short position would make a fortune. It was a classic correlation trade. It was also practically foolproof.

The arrival of this trade may have been the final bit of juice that the market needed to keep from running out of gas. No longer did the underwriter have to find buyers willing to take on the equity risk. Instead, buyers of the equity slice could not have cared less about the risks in that portion of the CDO. If the equity made money, they made money. If the equity lost money, they made even more money. Suddenly, the equity portion was a very easy sell.

This trade gained popularity just when it looked on the ground like the subprime madness was grinding to its inevitable end. Instead, the business kicked into one last crazed frenzy, as subprime originators handed out mortgages to anyone and everyone.

"Equity is the holy grail of CDO placement," wrote Lang Gibson, the Merrill Lynch CDO researcher. "The compelling economics in the long ABS correlation trade [buying the equity while shorting more senior tranches] will propel the mezz CDO market forward, no matter the evolution of fundamentals in residential mortgage credit, in our view." Which is exactly what happened.

In January 2007, Tourre sent another e-mail to his girlfriend. "Work," he wrote, "is still as laborious, it's bizarre I have the sensation of coming each day to work and reliving the same agony—a little like a bad dream that repeats itself. . . . When I think that I had some input into the creation of this product (which by the way is a product of pure intellectual masturbation, the type of thing which you invent telling yourself: 'Well, what if we created a 'thing,' which has no purpose, which is absolutely conceptual and highly theoretical and which nobody knows the price?'). It sickens the heart to see it shot down in mid-flight. . . . It's a little like Frankenstein turning against his own inventor. . . ."

Of course, the one thing that was neither conceptual nor theoretical was the losses. They were all too real, and in 2007, as winter turned to spring, they were coming.

19

The Gathering Storm

Questions about who owns the risk—it's spread out all over the world in various formats including repackaging vehicles. Not that obvious to find out who is feeling the pain.

—Dan Sparks e-mail, March 1, 2007

❧

On Friday, March 2, 2007, a man named Ralph Cioffi, who ran two hedge funds at Bear Stearns that had some $20 billion invested in asset-backed securities, held a small, impromptu meeting in his office. Matt Tannin, who managed the two funds with him, was there, as was Steve Van Solkema, a young analyst who worked for the two men and another partner in the funds. They had gathered to discuss the deteriorating market conditions. The week had opened with a drop in the stock market of more than 400 points, the largest one-day decline since the aftermath of 9/11. Cioffi described February as "the most treacherous month ever in the market." They talked about the plunge in value of the riskier tranches of the ABX index. Even some of the triple-A—the *triple-A*—were showing a strange wobbliness. That wasn't supposed to happen—ever. The men were anxious.

On paper, their two hedge funds hadn't performed that badly: one fund was down a little; the other was up a little. But it had suddenly become difficult to obtain prices on the securities they owned, so they couldn't be sure what their funds were truly worth. Plus, they'd often told investors that the funds operated like a boring, old-fashioned bank—they were supposed to earn the difference between their cost of funds (a good chunk of which were provided through the repo market) and the yield on the super-safe, mostly triple- and double-A-rated securities that they owned. Investors expected fairly steady, low-risk returns. *Any* losses, no matter how small, could spook them. The Bear team had made money on short positions they had placed on the ABX, but the volatility was worrisome. Because the higher-rated securities were supposed to be nearly riskless, the Bear Stearns hedge funds were highly leveraged: only about $1.6 billion of the $20 billion was equity. The rest was borrowed. Earlier in February, they'd started to get margin calls, meaning that their lenders were demanding more collateral. They'd met the margin calls, but their fears had not abated.

Trying to calm the others, Cioffi told them about the time he and Warren Spector, Bear's co-president, with whom Cioffi had risen through the ranks, had been caught with a big bond position way back when. They didn't panic, and they ended up making a lot of money. Tannin commiserated with Van Solkema about how the stress made it hard to get any sleep. For Van Solkema, it was comforting to hear that even the "big senior guys," as he later called them, weren't sleeping, either. And then Cioffi opened a small fridge in his office and took out a very good bottle of vodka. They all did a shot out of paper cups, toasting to better times ahead.

Cioffi also suggested that they keep the discussion among themselves, which Van Solkema interpreted to mean that they should try to avoid worrying other employees.

At 6:32 a.m. the next morning, Cioffi sent a message to Tannin, trying to put their stress in perspective. He wrote: "1. We have our health and our families. 2. We are not a 19 year old Marine in Iraq. 3. We have each other and a great team."

Tannin responded: "We are not marines—in fact—we have all triple won a Powerball lottery a few times over."

Within six months, both funds were bankrupt. A terrible storm was gathering.

The Bear team was in many ways a paradigmatic example of how Wall Street had evolved. Both Cioffi and Tannin were self-described "securitization people." They believed in the models and the ratings and the notion that risk was being divvied up and tucked away. They bought supposedly safe securities that offered a little extra yield. To boost the yield and produce respectable returns, they took advantage of the cheap, short-term money available in the repo market. "The borrowing was the absolute lifeblood of the funds," Tannin's lawyer later said.

Their first fund, the High-Grade Structured Credit Fund, which was part of Bear Stearns Asset Management, was started by Cioffi in the fall of 2003. Like many Bear employees, Cioffi had been a scrappy, lower-middle-class kid; during his eighteen years at the firm, he had risen to become a highly successful fixed-income salesman. Fearing that he would bolt to another firm, Bear staked him with $10 million and allowed him to start a hedge fund, even though Cioffi had never before managed money. Cioffi was soon making hedge fund compensation: $17.5 million in 2006, up from around $4.5 million just two years earlier. He owned a multimillion-dollar house in the Hamptons and became the executive producer of the indie film *Just Like the Son*. His lack of experience, though, was an issue. "Ralph was not a trader," says one person who knew him. "He was an honest guy trying his hardest, sitting at his desk twenty-four/seven, but he was like a deer in the headlights."

In 2003, Cioffi recruited Tannin to help him run the fund. Tannin had even less experience than Cioffi. A philosophy major who'd graduated from the University of San Francisco law school in 1993, Tannin had joined Bear's capital markets group before moving to the derivatives desk. After a brief stint at a start-up, he returned in 2001 to work as a junior analyst in the structured finance division. Even in good times, he was full of angst, befitting a philosophy major. Working with Cioffi was a huge opportunity for him, and he knew it. As his pay rapidly climbed from meager (just $66,000 in 2000) to respectable, at least by Wall Street standards ($2.5 million in 2006), Tannin never forgot to whom he owed his good fortune. "I want to thank you again from the bottom of my heart for all you have done for me," he wrote to Cioffi in early 2007. "I will be eternally grateful."

The High Grade fund started small. Some of its investors were high-net-worth customers of Bear Stearns, one of whom would later say that he thought he was getting in on a special "club." In truth, though, High Grade wasn't all that selective. Eventually, the three biggest investors were so-called funds of hedge funds, meaning they pooled investors' money and doled it out to hedge funds. Such funds often had a reputation for being "hot money," meaning they had no loyalty to any hedge fund. They would yank their money at the first sign of trouble.

By the summer of 2006, the High Grade fund had become one of the biggest buyers of mortgage risk in the market. That was when Cioffi and

Tannin launched a second fund whose name could not have been more perfect for the times. The fund was called the Bear Stearns High-Grade Structured Credit Strategies Enhanced Leverage Limited Partnership (Enhanced Leverage, for short). Its point of differentiation was the enormous leverage it planned to use—as much as 27 to 1—to produce higher returns. Although High Grade had produced forty straight months of gains, spreads had continued to narrow and it had become increasingly difficult to earn more than Treasury bills. That also explains why, in 2006, Cioffi began focusing on the triple-A and double-A slices of CDOs, much of which was backed by subprime mortgages. Like IKB, he, too, was looking for that little bit of extra return. He bought $7 billion worth of highly rated tranches.

In addition to using the repo market, Cioffi developed a second source of funding, one that both was indicative of the market's growing insanity and would serve as a powerful transmitter of the subprime virus.

In essence, the Bear funds set up their own CDOs. They sold assets they owned to the CDOs, which they then managed. They retained the equity piece of the new CDO and used the fresh cash to buy yet more assets. Tannin referred to this as "internal leverage." For the Bear guys, this was indeed a savvy way to get low-cost, low-risk leverage; among other things, lenders couldn't simply yank cash from the funds, the way repo lenders could. But the risk was still there—in this case, it resided at the bank that underwrote the CDO. That's because instead of selling long-dated debt, the new CDOs sold very short-term, low-cost commercial paper. This paper, in turn, was bought by money market funds around the country. In order to make the commercial paper palatable for money market funds, the bank that underwrote the CDO—often Citigroup and, later, Bank of America—would issue what was called a liquidity put. That meant that if buyers for paper became scarce—in the event, say, of a disruption in the market—the banks would step in and buy it themselves. Cioffi raised as much as $10 billion this way, according to *BusinessWeek*, while Citigroup earned $22.3 million in fees for underwriting the CDOs and was paid another $40 million a year for providing the liquidity put. At the time, this appeared to be free money.

And yet, as early as the summer of 2006, the angst-ridden Tannin was worried. The Enhanced Leverage fund had been successfully launched and Tannin had been named a senior managing director. It should have been a happy time for him. But he would later note in his diary: "As I sat in John's office"—John Geissinger, the chief investment officer at Bear Stearns Asset Management—"I had a wave of fear set over me—that the fund couldn't be fun the way that I was 'hoping.' And that it was going to subject investors to 'blowup risk.'" He continued, "This all hit me like a ton of bricks—and the first result—almost immediately—was for me to lose my ability to sleep. Classic anxiety . . . Let me try and describe my mental state: I was incredibly stressed . . . why was I stressed? I became very worried very quickly . . . I was worried that this would all end badly. . . ."

"Fear." That was the subject line of an e-mail that Cioffi sent to the funds' chief economist, Ardavan Mobasheri, on March 15, 2007, at 11:22 p.m. It was two weeks after his vodka toast with his two colleagues. "I'm fearful of these markets," he wrote. "Matt said it's either a meltdown or the greatest buying opportunity ever, I'm leaning more towards the former . . . It may not be a meltdown for the general economy but in our world it will be. Wall Street will be hammered with lawsuits. Dealers will lose millions and the cdo business will not be the same for years."

The weeks since the toast had not brought better days for the Bear Stearns team as they had hoped. Both funds were now losing money. "Im sick to my stomach over our performance in march," wrote Cioffi in another e-mail to Mobasheri as March drew to a close.

Ironically, during this stretch the funds were losing money because of their short position in the riskier tranches of the ABX, which was in the midst of a three-month rally. (The index rose from about 63 in late February to a high of about 77 in mid-May.) When the index hit its low in February, many of those who were short—including Goldman—began covering their positions, which forced the index higher. As Cioffi also noted in an e-mail, another reason the ABX might have been going up was that there was, as he put it, "significant rhetoric around certain types of bailout programs and financing and refinancing facilities that various banks were implementing."

In fact, around this time there had been efforts by some of the big Wall Street firms to salvage their triple-A tranches by buying actual mortgages and preventing enough foreclosures to keep those tranches from eroding. Bear, which owned the mortgage originator EMC, announced the EMC "Mod Squad" in early April, which was supposed to help delinquent borrowers avoid foreclosure. Other firms, including Merrill Lynch and Morgan Stanley, were meeting to see if they could do something collectively to keep homeowners from defaulting. The simple act of buying up the mortgages and then forgiving the loans would not only save homeowners, but save Wall Street billions of dollars in potential losses.

But there were all kinds of problems. Regulators were deeply suspicious. The firms themselves were worried about antitrust concerns. And the servicers, as one person involved in the effort put it, "were largely controlled by people who might not want mortgages rescued." Still, this source adds, "it should have been possible to overcome."

It wasn't to be. In particular, a number of the big investors who were short the triple-A tranches were furious when they discovered what was going on. They were going to make money if enough homeowners were foreclosed on! They didn't want anyone helping out homeowners at the expense of their profits. Some of the controversy broke into public view in April, when the *Wall Street Journal* reported on an exchange between the Bear Stearns mortgage desk and John Paulson. Bear sent Paulson a copy of language it drafted to the basic ISDA swap contract. It unequivocally gave the underwriter of any mortgage-backed security the right to support failing home loans in a mortgage security. "We were shocked," Paulson lieutenant Michael Waldorf told the *Journal*. Deutsche Bank and others with big short positions rallied behind Paulson. They said that the Bear proposal was tantamount to market manipulation.

The plan to prevent foreclosures went nowhere.

Despite their worries, Cioffi and Tannin never let on to their investors that anything was amiss. Doing so would have turned their fears into a self-fulfilling prophecy, causing panicked investors to yank their funds. Nor did they go out of their way to detail the extent of their subprime exposure. Their written communication to investors showed that only 6 percent to 8 percent of the funds' assets were invested "directly" in subprime mortgages, when the actual exposure—including CDOs backed by subprime mortgages—was closer to 60 percent. Although they did give a fuller account whenever they were asked in conference calls about the subprime exposure, some investors would nevertheless feel that the Bear team had misled them.

And so would the government, which would later bring civil and criminal charges against Cioffi and Tannin, charging them with talking up the funds while entertaining deep private doubts. (Cioffi was also charged with insider trading for taking $2 million of his money out of the fund without telling investors.) But a jury found both men not guilty of the criminal charges, and when you read their e-mails in full, you can understand why. (As of the fall of 2010 the civil case was still open.) It wasn't so much that the men were lying as that they were scrambling for salvation, trying to find ways to make it all work, and grasping on to any small crumb of hope to help convince themselves that this market, upon which their fortunes depended, couldn't really be disintegrating before their eyes.

On April 19, for instance, Van Solkema did some preliminary analysis with a new credit model he was working on, in which he reverse engineered some mortgage-backed securities, drilling down to the individual mortgages. He wanted to be able to play around with default scenarios at the homeowner level, to see how different default rates would affect CDO tranches. It is both telling and stunning that a firm of the size and supposed sophistication of Bear Stearns didn't have the ability to do this before launching hedge funds whose prospects would be dependent on that very thing.

Van Solkema later told the jury that when he ran his model, "the bad [mortgages] looked even worse than what I thought they were." After getting the results, Tannin e-mailed Cioffi's wife, Phyllis, from his personal e-mail account: "[T]he subprime market looks pretty damn ugly . . . if we believe the runs Steve has been doing are anywhere close to accurate, I think we should close the funds now. The reason for this is that if [the runs] are correct then the entire subprime market is toast. . . . If AAA bonds are systematically downgraded then there is simply no way for us to make money—ever."

In mid-March, Cioffi sent an e-mail listing "problem positions," next to which he noted his stress level. Among them: $120 million worth of Abacus bonds, which he had bought from Goldman Sachs. Stress level: medium to high.

And yet at the same time, the two men simply couldn't bring themselves to believe that the picture was as dire as the model suggested. In that same e-mail to Cioffi's wife, Tannin stated that Andrew Lipton, the head of surveillance at Bear Stearns Asset Management—and a former Moody's executive—was still positive. "I sat him down on Friday and asked how serious he thought the situation was. He calmly told me that the situation wasn't going to be as bad as people are saying," Tannin wrote. Tannin also wrote that Bear's CDO analyst, Gyan Sinha, had issued an optimistic report about subprime mortgages in February.

Denial seemed to be rampant at Bear Stearns. On March 1, two Bear analysts *upgraded* New Century's stock. The stock of Bear itself hit an all-time high of $172.69 on January 17, 2007; a few months earlier, S&P had upgraded the firm's credit rating to A+ (one notch up from a single-A), partly due to the strength of its mortgage business. Thanks largely to Cioffi's friendship with Warren Spector, Bear itself put $25 million into the funds in late April 2007.

And even as Cioffi and Tannin began to recognize that a triple-A rating might not mean anything, they clung to the belief that *their* triple-As were different. Van Solkema testified that after running his model, he still thought the funds would survive. On an April 25 conference call, Tannin told investors, "[I]t is really a matter of whether one believes that careful credit analysis makes a difference, or whether you think that this is just one big disaster. And there's no basis for thinking this is one big disaster."

By then, though, big investors were warning that they were thinking about withdrawing their money, and the funds' repo counterparties were starting to demand yet more collateral. In fact, on March 11, Ray McGarrigal, who worked on the funds with Cioffi and Tannin, wrote to the others, "I would move as much away from Goldman as possible. I do not wish to trade them in any fashion at this point. I would highly recommend moving any and all positions away from them as soon as is feasible and only be a net seller to them going forward." The Goldman "get closer to home" meeting in David Viniar's office had taken place back in December, and the firm was aggressively reducing its marks, or prices, on securities that either contained or referenced mortgages. Which meant that Goldman was also getting more aggressive in demanding collateral to make itself whole. McGarrigal continued, "The only other group that makes me nervous is UBS. They are long a lot of super-senior."

And so, the Bear hedge fund managers made two final, desperate efforts to raise cash. In the fall of 2006, they had started working on a deal to sell off the equity—the riskiest part—of ten CDOs to a new company called Everquest. Now, in the spring of 2007, they tried one last push to have Everquest itself sell shares to retail investors in an IPO. "The deal appears to be an unprecedented attempt by a Wall Street house to dump its mortgage bets," wrote Matthew Goldstein in a May 11 article in *BusinessWeek*. The Everquest deal would have allowed Bear to raise cash and pay down a $200 million line of credit from Citigroup. But the deal seemed so obviously self-serving that a furor erupted, and it became impossible to complete.

The Bear Stearns team also began rushing to complete another deal that had been in the works: a CDO squared made out of the funds' holdings of CDOs. The idea was, as Cioffi put it in an e-mail, to "get as much of our assets off our books . . . as possible." He was hoping it would result in more stable financing for a lot of the funds' assets, instead of using increasingly fractious repo lenders. This deal did close, on May 24, 2007. Bank of America, the underwriter, wrote a liquidity put requiring the bank to buy the $3.2 billion of commercial paper that was issued by the new CDO in the event of problems. Money market funds bought most of the commercial paper.

Later, Bank of America sued Bear Stearns, Cioffi, Tannin, and McGarrigal for allegedly hiding the funds' true condition. As part of the lawsuit, the bank also claimed that it had gotten a verbal agreement from Cioffi that he wouldn't put certain "high-risk" assets into the new CDO, but that Cioffi ignored that agreement. There was one asset in particular that Bank of America singled out in its complaint, an asset that quickly lost all its value: Goldman's Timberwolf deal. (This lawsuit was also ongoing as of the fall of 2010.)

By the time the Bank of America deal closed, the funds were in serious trouble. Investors had demanded half their money back from Enhanced Leverage, leaving Cioffi and Tannin with little choice but to wind it down. Tannin, at least, seemed to finally recognize that the jig was up. In late May, a Bear salesman announced good news: Tokio Marine wanted to invest $10 million in the High Grade fund. When Tannin heard the news, he asked for a meeting with Greg Quental, who was the head of Bear Stearns Asset Management's hedge fund business. After the meeting, Quental announced that the Bear funds wouldn't be taking any new investments.

At the end of May, Cioffi e-mailed Spector, his longtime supporter at Bear. "Warren, I'm almost too embarrassed to call you," he wrote. "I feel especially badly because you have been a big supporter of mine for so long . . . I know apologies are meaningless at this stage but I am sorry . . . Emotionally, I am obviously keeping a business as usual persona at work and on the job 24–7. I assure you of that. But it is very stressful and strange when it looks like one's business is collapsing around him . . . we are running out of options."

More bad news was coming. A few weeks earlier, Bear had told investors in the Enhanced Leverage fund that it had lost 6.5 percent in April. But at a meeting on May 31, Bear Stearns's pricing committee, which determined the funds' returns by surveying how its counterparties were marking the securities, decided the fund had actually lost 18.97 percent in April. One key reason for the stunning change was Goldman's low marks.

According to the SEC, Cioffi tried to argue that his original marks were right. When he gave up, he wrote an e-mail to a member of the pricing committee: "There is no market . . . its [sic] all academic anyway –19 percent is doomsday."

Which, in fact, it was. While Bear could and did prevent its investors from taking their money out—a common tactic when hedge fund investors are all trying to exit at once—it was powerless to do anything about the repo lenders. "It's like borrowing from the devil times three," says one person who was there, speaking of the repo lenders. "They can come and say, 'You pay me,' and you can do nothing, nothing, nothing. There are no rules, and you have no ability to see where they've marked the same assets on their own books. It's a grab."

On June 11, Cioffi wrote to Tannin and George Buxton, who worked in Bear's private client services, "Right now we're fighting the Battle of the Bulge with our repo lenders. So far so good but it is very tough and stressful . . ." He was trying to convince the lenders that if they grabbed the collateral and tried to sell it into a shaky market, everyone would get hurt. After all, the Bear team argued, they all had the same positions, and panicked selling would turn theoretical declines in the market value of the securities into hard cash losses.

The men were also deeply frustrated. While Wall Street's repo desks were demanding money, the trading desks at the same firms were refusing to reflect the value of the Bear team's short positions. They were being squeezed from both sides. "The pressure was tremendous," says one person who was there. "And everyone was scared." On June 14, Bear held a meeting with the repo lenders to try to cut deals. At that meeting, according to *House of Cards*, William Cohan's book about the fall of Bear Stearns, the Bear executives gave a presentation showing the exposure the rest of the Street had to the firm's hedge funds. Overall, sixteen Wall Street firms had lent the funds $11.1 billion in the repo market. Among them were Citi, with nearly $1.9 billion outstanding, and Merrill Lynch, with $1.46 billion outstanding.

A few days later, one firm broke from the pack. Merrill Lynch seized $850 million in collateral, which it said it would sell on the open market. Any chance of an orderly wind-down of the funds was now gone. It was a classic run on a bank—except that those racing to pull their money out weren't depositors. They were bankers.

When Merrill tried to sell the assets, it discovered that Cioffi had been right: nobody wanted to buy the collateral, at least not at the price that Merrill was valuing the securities. The firm largely abandoned the effort. J.P. Morgan and Deutsche Bank, which had followed Merrill's lead, canceled their plans to sell assets, too. Here was the moment of truth: triple-A tranches of CDOs stuffed with subprime mortgages simply weren't salable, not at a hundred cents on the dollar, and maybe not at any price. In fact, mortgage-backed securities weren't salable, period. "All these guys grabbed for Bear's mortgage-backed securities thinking they'd be able to write them up, not realizing they'd have to write them down," says one person who was there. "All of a sudden, it became an internal witch hunt everywhere. How much of this do *we* own?"

As Goldman's Josh Birnbaum later wrote, "The BSAM situation changed everything. I felt that this mark-to-market event for CDO risk would begin a further unraveling in mortgage credit." Goldman, which had covered its short position, quickly began to rebuild it.

Although Bear itself did eventually put up $1.6 billion to try to save the High Grade fund, it wasn't enough. On July 31, 2007, both funds filed for bankruptcy.

But Wall Street was still too blind to see that the line between the Bear hedge funds—highly leveraged entities dependent on the repo market with big exposure to toxic subprime mortgages—and the firms themselves—highly leveraged entities dependent on the repo market with big exposure to toxic subprime mortgages—was a very thin one indeed. That lesson was yet to come.

As the prices on triple-A-rated notes plunged in the early summer of 2007, the rating agencies continued to insist to the outside world that everything was just fine. At the beginning of the year, S&P had predicted that 2007 would bring "fewer ratings changes overall, and more upgrades than downgrades." As the year went on and the skepticism about the validity of the ratings increased, the agencies claimed that they had run stress tests and scrubbed the numbers. Moody's told *Fortune*, for instance, that its investment-grade-rated products were "designed to withstand losses that are materially higher than expectations."

The rating agencies were in the midst of a spectacularly profitable run. "The first half of 2007 was the strongest we had in five years," Moody's CEO Ray McDaniel would later say; its revenues had hit $1.2 billion over that period. Why? Because the Wall Street firms could all see the handwriting on the wall. With the ABX declining and triple-A tranches faltering, the CDO business was soon going to shut down. So Wall Street raced to shove as many CDOs out the door as it could; firms like Goldman wanted to get the bad paper off their own books onto someone else's while there was still time. In that same six-month period, from January to June 2007, CDO issuance peaked at more than $180 billion. "[B]ankers are under enormous pressure to turn their warehouses into CDO notes," Eric Kolchinsky, the Moody's executive in charge of rating asset-backed CDOs, wrote in an August 2007 e-mail. Amazingly, the rating agencies continued to facilitate that effort by rating large chunks of these deals triple-A.

Had the agencies noticed the increasing early payment defaults that had started in 2006? Of course. S&P and Moody's had responded by increasing the amount of credit enhancement required to get investment-grade ratings on securities backed by subprime mortgages. But as the Senate Permanent Subcommittee on Investigations would later point out, neither agency went back to test old mortgage-backed securities or old CDOs using this new methodology. Thus, the old, flawed ratings continued to live on in portfolios all over Wall Street. Even worse, they were recycled into new synthetic CDOs, as old tranches were referenced in new securities. "Reevaluating existing RMBS securities with the revised model would likely have led to downgrades, angry issuers, and even angrier investors, so S&P didn't do it," said Senator Carl Levin, subcommittee chairman. Moody's didn't, either.

Despite the optimistic glow the rating agency put on things to the outside world, there were plenty of people internally who feared the worst. In an e-mail exchange in early September 2006 among S&P employees, Richard Koch, a director in S&P's structured products group, cited a *BusinessWeek* article on the bad lending practices in option ARMs. "This is frightening. It wreaks [sic] of greed, unregulated brokers, and 'not so prudent' lenders . . . Hope our friends with large portfolios of these mortgages are preparing for the inevitable." Six weeks later, Michael Gutierrez, another director in S&P's structured products group, forwarded a *Wall Street Journal* story to several colleagues about how ever looser lending standards were leading to higher defaults. He wrote, "Pretty grim news as we suspected—note also the 'mailing in the keys and walking away' epidemic has begun—I think things are going to get mighty ugly next year!"

"I smell class action!" responded a colleague.

By February, S&P was having internal discussions about how to respond to the deteriorating value of mortgage-backed securities. "I talked to Tommy yesterday and he thinks that the ratings are not going to hold through 2007," wrote Ernestine Warner, S&P's head of global surveillance, to Peter D'Erchia, an S&P managing director. "He asked me to begin discussing taking rating actions earlier on the poor performing deals." She continued, "I have been thinking about this for much of the night."

On March 18, one unnamed employee at S&P sent this in an e-mail: "To give you a confidential tidbit among friends the subprime brouhaha is reaching serious levels—tomorrow morning key members of the RMBS rating division are scheduled to make a presentation to Terry McGraw CEO of McGraw-Hill Companies and his executive committee on the entire subprime situation and how we rated the deals and are preparing to deal with the fallout (downgrades)."* At Moody's, the story was similar. The company's own subsidiary, Economy.com, issued a prescient report in October 2006 called "Housing at the Tipping Point," in which it reported, "Nearly twenty of the nation's metro areas will experience a crash in house prices: a double-digit peak-to-trough decline." A double-digit decline in housing prices is precisely what the rating agencies' models said could never happen. In addition, big investors had started complaining that the ratings were flawed. At one point, Josh Anderson, who managed asset-backed securities at PIMCO, the giant bond manager, confronted Moody's executive Mary Elizabeth Brennan. In an internal e-mail, Brennan reported, "PIMCO and others (he mentioned BlackRock and WAMCO) have previously been very vocal about their disagreements over Moody's rating methodology." She continued, "He cited several meetings they have had . . . questioning Moody's rating methodologies and assumptions. He found the Moody's analyst to be arrogant and gave the indication that 'We're smarter than you' . . ." Anderson went on to say, Brennan wrote, that "Moody's doesn't stand up to Wall Street . . . In the case of RMBS, its mistakes were 'so obvious.'"

And *still* the agencies continued to stamp their triple-As on mortgage-backed securities. The evidence didn't seem to matter. In late December 2006, Moody's analyst Debashish Chatterjee was shocked by his own graph of the number of mortgages at the top ten issuers that were more than sixty days delinquent. Fremont Investment & Loan, in particular, was drowning in

---

* In response to Levin's charge that S&P refused to reevaluate existing residential mortgage-backed securities, S&P said that previously issued securities were "already subject to surveillance based on an analysis that incorporates more applicable information regarding the actual performance of the collateral" than the new methodology would offer. In response to the Koch and Gutierrez e-mail, S&P said that it was publishing studies showing that even a more severe housing downturn would still result in triple-A securities maintaining their ratings, and that neither Koch nor Gutierrez had been involved in the rating process. When asked to comment about the meeting with Terry McGraw, S&P said that it "made changes to its surveillance practices multiple times in late 2006 and 2007."

them. "Holy cow—is this data correct? I just graphed it and Freemont [sic] is such an outlier!!" he wrote in an e-mail to colleagues. A month later, when S&P was rating a Goldman CDO that contained Fremont loans, the analyst on the deal asked a colleague, "Since Fremont collateral has been performing not so good, is there anything special I should be aware of." The response: "No, we don't treat their collateral any differently." Both Moody's and S&P rated five tranches of that offering triple-A; not surprisingly, two of the five were later downgraded to junk, according to analysis by the Senate Permanent Subcommittee on Investigations.

It wasn't until July 2007—the same month the Bear hedge funds collapsed— that the rating agencies made their first major move toward downgrading. E-mails imply that they had been considering such a move among themselves for months. It also appears that they were discussing it with at least some Wall Street firms as well. "It sounds like Moody's is trying to figure out when to start downgrading, and how much damage they're going to cause— they're meeting with various investment banks," a UBS banker had written back in May. A judge overseeing a lawsuit involving UBS would later find "probable cause to sustain the claim that UBS became privy to material non-public information regarding a pending change in Moody's rating methodology."

Yet even in July, the rating agencies still weren't ready to go all in and actually downgrade triple-A tranches. Instead, on July 10, 2007, S&P placed 612 tranches of securities backed by subprime mortgages on "review" for downgrade; almost immediately, Moody's followed, placing 399 tranches on review. Both agencies made a great point of saying that the downgrades affected only a sliver of the mortgage-backed securities they had rated.

Why had it taken so long? Sheer overwork played a part, as did paralysis. But it was also because the rating agencies feared the consequences of a widespread downgrade of mortgage-backed securities. With ratings so embedded in regulations, downgrades would force many buyers to sell. That forced selling, in turn, would put more pressure on prices, which would create a downward spiral that would be nearly impossible to reverse. With subprime mortgages, that situation was exacerbated a thousandfold, because the flawed ratings of residential mortgage-backed securities had been used to create countless CDOs—and synthetic CDOs. Downgrades of the underlying mortgage-backed securities could cause the CDOs to default even before any losses had shown themselves. The ripple effect was bound to be enormous.

Later that day, S&P held a conference call for investors to discuss the pending downgrades. Most people were fairly polite. But one man on that conference call, a hedge fund manager named Steve Eisman, who had taken a big short position in mortgage-backed securities, was not.

"Yeah, hi, I'd like to know why now?" Eisman began. "I mean, the news has been out on subprime now for many, many months. The delinquencies have been a disaster now for many, many months. Your ratings have been called into question for many, many months. I'd like to know why you're making this move today when you— And why didn't you do this many, many months ago?" S&P's Tom Warrack, a managing director in the RMBS group, tried to break in. "We took action as soon as possible given the information at hand . . ." But Eisman wouldn't be stopped. "I mean, I track this market every single day. The performance has been a disaster now for several months. I mean, it can't be that all of a sudden, the performance has reached a level where you've woken up. I'd like to understand why now, when you could've made this move many, many months ago. I mean, the paper just deteriorates every single month like clockwork. I mean, you need to have a better answer than the one you just gave."

The next day, Mabel Yu, an analyst at Vanguard, told Mary Elizabeth Brennan at Moody's that when Eisman started talking, "my phone was on mute but I jumped up and down and clapped my hands and screamed. He was the only one to say it, but all the investors were all feeling the same way." Yu went on to tell Brennan that Vanguard had stopped buying mortgage-backed securities in early 2006 because they were less and less comfortable with the ratings.

Although S&P and Moody's wouldn't actually begin downgrading CDOs until October, the party effectively ended that day in July. "[P]ut today in your calendar," wrote Robert Morelli, who was in charge of the CDO business at UBS, to colleagues. When he was later asked what he meant by that, he explained, "to the day was essentially the beginning of the end of the CDO business."

A few weeks later, Moody's Eric Kolchinsky forwarded some UBS research to colleagues. It showed that in a sample of 111 mezzanine asset-backed securities CDOs, the triple-B tranches could expect losses of 65 percent and that the losses would extend into the triple-A tranches. Kolchinsky quoted the UBS report to his colleagues: "This is horrible from a ratings and risk management point of view; perhaps the biggest credit risk management failure ever," it said.

On July 24, 2007, two weeks after the rating agencies made their first big downgrade move and one week before the bankruptcy of the Bear Stearns hedge funds, Countrywide announced its results for the first half of the year. In a last, desperate grab for market share, Countrywide had waited until March 2007 to stop offering "piggyback" loans that allowed borrowers to purchase a home with no money down. As other, weaker correspondent lenders—those that made loans themselves but then sold their loans to bigger lenders—began to go under, Countrywide ramped up its business of buying loans. Since Countrywide was no longer entering into agreements to sell its loans before they were made or purchased, the company was bearing all the risk that the market would crack on its own books.

The rot Mozilo had long insisted wouldn't infect Countrywide had started to spread. Although the company announced a profitable quarter, investors were shocked to hear that its earnings had declined for the third quarter in a row on a year over year basis—and that delinquency rates on Countrywide's subprime mortgages had more than doubled, to 23.7 percent, from less than 10 percent at the end of March. Delinquencies in prime mortgages—*prime* mortgages—also spiked. And the company revealed that it was taking several other hits, including $417 million worth of impairments, mostly due to declines in the value of home equity residuals, and another $293 million in losses in loans held on its balance sheet.

"We are experiencing home price depreciation almost like never before, with the exception of the Great Depression," said Mozilo on the company's conference call that day.

Morgan Stanley analyst Ken Posner was startled by the news. "That is just not a charge-off ratio one would expect for a—at least for an old-fashioned prime portfolio," he said on the conference call.

"Countrywide is a mortgage supermarket," responded chief risk officer John McMurray. "So it is my belief that the portfolio that we have for the most part is going to be a good reference for what exists on a broader basis."

At another point during the conference call, McMurray noted, "So the way I think about prime is that it covers a very vast spectrum. . . ." The implication was clear. Countrywide was acknowledging that prime and subprime weren't as clearly delineated as most had believed. While investors who dug through the prospectuses for Countrywide's mortgage-backed securities might have known that, it came as a shock to many.

McMurray also had two messages that were contrary to everything Mozilo had preached over the years. "Leverage at origination matters," he said. "More leverage means more serious delinquencies." That is, the more debt the customer borrowed, the more likely he was going to default. And he said, "Documentation matters. The less documentation, the higher the serious delinquency, all else equal."

That day Countrywide's stock fell more than 10 percent, to close at $30.50. Research analysts at Stifel Nicolaus, which had turned bearish on Countrywide earlier in the year, wrote in a report to clients, "[G]iven the magnitude of credit problems in the bank, we think mgmt made serious miscalculations (and possibly misrepresentations) about the quality of the loans added to the bank." They found that Countrywide's supposedly prime home equity securitizations were performing in line with a competitor's subprime deals.

Soon after that conference call, McMurray resigned. Later that fall, Walter Smiechewicz, the senior executive in charge of enterprise risk assessment, met with Countrywide's audit committee. Smiechewicz had been warning since 2005 that the residuals and the loans Countrywide had retained on its balance sheet posed a much bigger risk than was being acknowledged. According to several former executives, he said that if nothing was going to change, then he had no choice but to resign. He, too, left the company.

IKB—the German bank that was on the other side of John Paulson's Goldman-arranged Abacus trade—was beginning to spook the market. Over the weekend of July 28 and 29, state-owned German banks brokered a bailout of the bank that would eventually rise to $13.5 billion. It was the first bank to be rescued because of the securitized mortgages on its books. It would not be the last.

Then came August. On August 8, BNP Paribas, France's largest bank, suspended redemptions from three of its investment funds because it couldn't value some of its subprime mortgage-backed securities. Australia's Basis Yield Fund, which had bought into Goldman's Timberwolf deal, suffered severe losses. It would soon go into liquidation because of its exposure to subprime assets.

August home prices fell 4.4 percent from the previous year, the largest decline in six years. Youyi Chen, the head of mortgage portfolio management at Washington Mutual, sent an e-mail to a group of colleagues entitled

"Scenarios." He wrote, "A 20 percent down in HPA. From today's meeting, I understand that we don't have the courage to evaluate this scenario."

On August 9, five central banks around the world coordinated to increase liquidity for the first time since 9/11. Within a week, the Federal Reserve would begin cutting interest rates in an attempt to prop up the market.

It didn't work. The securitization market for mortgage loans shut down. First Magnus, a lender of mostly Alt-A mortgages, collapsed seemingly overnight. It had funded $17.1 billion worth of loans in the first half of the year, according to *Inside Mortgage Finance*.

And the entire market for asset-backed commercial paper—a market of more than $1 trillion worth of securities, and the primary means by which originators financed mortgage lending—began to seize up. Goldman Sachs chief risk officer Craig Broderick later explained in a presentation to the firm's tax department that between August and October 2007, the "unprecedented loss of investor confidence" had quickly shrunk the asset-backed commercial paper market by more than 30 percent. "For someone who has seen this market grow on a stable, steady basis for as long as I've been in the business, this is really remarkable," Broderick said.

Suddenly, no one wanted anything to do with securitization, or any form of asset-backed commercial paper, or anything that depended on credit ratings. In the all-important repo market, the "haircuts" on asset-backed securities began to increase, from between 3 and 5 percent in April 2007 to 50 and 60 percent by August 2008, according to an IMF report. "The market began searching for anything that smelled like something it didn't like," said one banker.

Most companies file their official quarterly documents with the SEC several weeks after announcing their results to Wall Street. Thus it was that on August 9, several weeks after its disastrous conference call, Countrywide filed its quarterly report with the SEC. In it Countrywide cited "unprecedented market conditions" and wrote that while "we believe we have adequate funding liquidity . . . the situation is rapidly evolving and the impact on the Company is unknown." The next day, Countrywide held a special board meeting, the board members participating by phone. Countrywide had always assumed that in desperate times it would be able to pledge its prime mortgages as collateral for a loan. But they couldn't. Street firms "in almost every case had a very large exposure to mortgages," as Countrywide treasurer Jennifer Sandefur later put it, and they didn't want more. Plus *everyone* was suddenly asking Wall Street for money. "It was an Armageddon . . . scenario," Sandefur said. "It was—you know, a worst-case scenario of kind of epic proportions."

As soon as he read Countrywide's filing, Kenneth Bruce, the Merrill Lynch analyst who followed the company, knew that it was at risk. "Liquidity Is the Achilles Heel," read the headline of his report to his clients. "We cannot understate the importance of liquidity for a specialty finance company like CFC," wrote Bruce. "If enough financial pressure is placed on CFC"—Countrywide's ticker—"or if the market loses confidence in its ability to function properly, then the model can break." His shocking conclusion: "[I]t is possible for CFC to go bankrupt."

Within days, Countrywide drew down its entire $11.5 billion credit facility—an obvious sign of desperation. It also tried to get the Fed to use its emergency lending authority, but the Fed refused. Maybe things would have been different if Countrywide were still regulated by the Fed. But it wasn't. "They burned their bridges," says one person who is familiar with the events.

On August 23, 2007, shortly before the market opened, Countrywide announced that Bank of America would invest $2 billion, giving the market the confidence that Countrywide had access to the deep pockets it needed to keep running. (Ironically, the bank had loaned Mozilo $75,000 in 1969, allowing him to start up Countrywide.) In an interview with CNBC's Maria Bartiromo, Mozilo blasted Bruce's report: "[T]o yell fire in a very crowded theater where you had, you know, panic was already setting in . . . was totally irresponsible and baseless." He added, "At the end of the day, we're the only game left in town."

After watching Mozilo, Kerry Killinger sent an e-mail to Steve Rotella, Washington Mutual's chief operating officer. "By the way," he wrote, "that great orange skinned prophet from Calabasas was in fine form today on CNBC. He went after the analyst at Merrill, predicted housing would lead us into a recession, said the chance of CFC bankruptcy was no greater than when the stock was at 40 and said 'what doesn't kill us makes us stronger.' He continues to give the class action lawyers good fodder for their stock drop lawsuits."

In his inimitable way, Mozilo tried to fend off the inevitable. In the fall of 2007, Countrywide hired a public relations firm to help launch a "game plan to regain control of the agenda," according to a memo obtained by the

Wall Street Journal. Although the memo was meant to serve as talking points for another top Countrywide executive—Drew Gissinger—the pugnacious tone had all the earmarks of Angelo Mozilo.

"Our position in the industry makes us a huge and very visible target," the memo read. "[W]e're being attacked from all sides today in large part because we're #1. Not just #1 overall, but for the first time in mortgage banking history, we're #1 in each of the 4 major divisions—Wholesale, Retail, Correspondence, and Consumer Direct. This is what makes us such a huge threat to our competitors."

"[I]t's gotten to the point where our integrity is being attacked," the memo continued. "NOW IT'S PERSONAL! . . . WE'RE NOT GOING TO TAKE IT."

It ended by asking Countrywide's employees to sign a pledge that they would "protect our house"—that is, defend the company from the growing storm of accusations about its lending practices. The stock continued to fall.

In January 2008, Countrywide hired Sandler O'Neill, a boutique investment bank, to explore its options. According to one person who was there, Countrywide CFO Eric Sieracki presented a "base-case scenario," a "stress scenario," and a "severe scenario." Jimmy Dunne, Sandler's blunt CEO, dismissed the base-case scenario out of hand. What was coming was likely to be even worse than Countrywide's severe scenario, he said. Countrywide needed to sell. And the best—maybe the only—buyer was Bank of America. "Ken Lewis, when he covets a target, cannot say no," Dunne said. (Lewis, the CEO of Bank of America, would become infamous for buying Merrill Lynch during the height of the crisis in a deal that was surrounded by controversy and criticism. Ultimately, that acquisition would cost him his job.)

Says one person who was there: "Mozilo and all these guys, they thought they were making widgets. They got too far away from understanding the real risk in the balance sheet. Even at the end, they were saying that things were okay. They believed it. They were crazy."

In January 2008, Bank of America acquired Countrywide for $4 billion; less than a year earlier its market capitalization had been more than six times that amount, at nearly $25 billion. During the second half of 2007, Countrywide took $5.2 billion in write-downs and increases to loan loss reserves, according to a shareholder lawsuit later filed against the company. The write-downs essentially wiped out Countrywide's earnings for 2005 and 2006.

Just before the acquisition, Mozilo told investors, "I believe very strongly that no entity in this nation has done more to help American homeowners achieve and maintain the dream of homeownership than Countrywide."

Wouldn't you know it? Moody's and S&P downgraded Countrywide on August 16—a week *after* the company filed its quarterly documents with the SEC. The day before, S&P had announced that structured investment vehicles—which had hundreds of billions of dollars in triple-A-rated debt among the $400 billion outstanding at the peak—were weathering the market disruption well. (A month earlier Moody's called SIVs "an oasis of calm in the subprime maelstrom," according to a lawsuit that was later filed by CalPERS, the giant California pension fund.) But just a week and a half later, on August 28, Cheyne Capital Management, a $7 billion SIV, sent both rating agencies a letter notifying them that it had breached one of its requirements, and would have to wind down as a result. S&P abruptly downgraded Cheyne's debt, including its triple-A paper. According to the CalPERS lawsuit, Moody's didn't react until September 5, which was the day that Cheyne was forced into receivership. "If the rating agencies have to downgrade six notches in a single day, it undermines investor confidence," wrote a J.P. Morgan analyst. "It . . . makes investors wonder whether the rating agencies were paying attention to what was going on in the portfolio."

In addition to owning mortgage-backed securities, SIVs had 30 percent of their assets in financial corporate debt, according to a report done by the congressional Joint Economic Committee. In other words, banks were setting up off-balance-sheet vehicles that they could then use to buy not just slices of CDOs but possibly also their own debt—all without incurring any capital charges. It was a free fee machine and a self-funding mechanism—until it wasn't. In the wake of Cheyne's collapse, the SIV market cratered; Citi eventually absorbed $58 billion in troubled, but supposedly off-balance-sheet, SIV debt onto its own balance sheet at the worst moment imaginable. In addition, Citi, Bank of America, and other banks that had written liquidity puts ended up taking those assets back onto their own balance sheets. "Thus the sponsoring banks implicitly acknowledged that these . . . SIVs should never have been considered as separate entities from either an accounting or a regulatory perspective," wrote the Joint Economic Committee in its report to Congress. Thus did another source of funding disappear from the market.

As the world would soon discover in spectacular fashion, the rating agencies weren't wrong just about RMBS, CDOs, and asset-backed commercial paper.* They were also wrong about the entire global financial system. In July 2007, Moody's issued a special comment entitled "Another False Alarm in Terms of Banking Systemic Risk but a Reality Check." "There is no easy way to predict whether a financial shock is systemic by nature," Moody's wrote. "The best way remains to look at the main financial institutions, i.e., the pillars of the system. In our view, their ability to withstand shocks is very high, perhaps higher than ever." Although Moody's conceded that "model risk has inexorably mushroomed," it said that most global financial institutions had a "rather high degree of risk awareness."

A few weeks later, in an "update," Moody's said that "there are currently no negative rating implications . . . as a result of [the banks'] involvement in the subprime sector." The truly shocking thing is that Moody's was willing to make this pronouncement even while acknowledging, *in the very same paper*, that there was no way the agency, or anyone else, could really know anything about the risks these institutions were holding. ("Public disclosures and position transparency make it virtually impossible for investors to accurately quantify each firm's credit, market and liquidity exposure.")

That was precisely the problem. The issue wasn't actual cash losses. It was uncertainty. No one knew where the subprime problem would pop up next, no one could figure out what any of this stuff was worth, no one believed what anyone else said about what it was worth, and no one believed that anyone who was supposed to know something actually did. That included the nation's top regulators. "I'd like to know what those damn things are worth," Federal Reserve chairman Ben Bernanke said during an appearance at the Economic Club of New York in October 2007.

Bernanke's comment infuriated an outspoken, deeply skeptical Georgia mutual fund manager named Michael Orkin. Not long after the Fed chairman's speech, Orkin wrote in his monthly letter to investors, "Since the first shot was fired across the credit bow in February 2007, investors have been force-fed a constant diet of half-truths and whole lies regarding the nature and status of the mammoth mortgage-based derivative machine and the housing market bubble it inflated . . . The fact that the credit crisis has now

---

* A chart later prepared by the Senate Permanent Subcommittee on Investigations showed that 91 percent of the triple-A-rated subprime residential mortgage-backed securities issued in 2007, and 93 percent of those issued in 2006, were subsequently downgraded to junk status.

turned into a confidence crisis should serve as a wake-up call to Wall Street, the Treasury and the Fed."

In late November 2007, a senior vice president in structured finance at Lehman Brothers, Deepali Advani, who had previously worked at Moody's, forwarded an e-mail from one of the firm's traders to a handful of her contacts. "The wheels on the bus are falling off, falling off, falling off . . . The wheels on the bus are falling off, all over Wall Street." William May, a managing director at Moody's, wrote back, "I think he's too optimistic."

"Bill, who ever thought CDOs would be WMD?" Advani wrote back. "Though have to say—every day more bad news—would be much too bad for the world to end—but that's sure how it feels."

20

The Dumb Guys

The collapse of the Bear Stearns hedge funds in June 2007 should have been a terrifying moment for Stan O'Neal. Merrill Lynch had been the first to make a grab for Bear's triple-A subprime collateral, which began the run on the bank that brought down the two funds. Yet it had been unable to sell that collateral because nobody wanted it. Nobody could say anymore what it was worth.

Dale Lattanzio, who ran Merrill's CDO business, and his boss, Osman Semerci, responded in exactly the way you would expect of two people whose multimillion-dollar bonuses were completely dependent on their ability to continue manufacturing CDOs. They told their superiors that the market was in the middle of a little rough patch, but there was nothing to worry about. Despite their obvious vested interest, O'Neal appeared to accept their analysis. According to *The New Yorker* magazine, the two men told O'Neal that "the CDO market would eventually stabilize, allowing Merrill to sell its holdings." The magazine added, "O'Neal seemed reassured." He did, however, ask them to try to hedge the position, which they insisted they were already doing. Indeed, in late 2006—around the same time Goldman Sachs concluded that it needed to get closer to home—Dow Kim was telling Semerci and Lattanzio the same thing. At a board meeting in July, the two men claimed the risk on the firm's books amounted to no more than $83 million—a claim that other Merrill executives viewed as implausible. Yet O'Neal didn't question them. When others tried to warn O'Neal that Semerci's loss estimates were too low, they were met with a steely glare, according to several former Merrill executives.

Shortly after that board meeting, Merrill announced its second-quarter earnings. On the surface, the numbers were terrific: $2.1 billion in profits on $9.7 billon in revenues; the profit number was 31 percent higher than

Merrill's second-quarter profits in 2006. In the accompanying press release, Merrill specifically pointed to the success of its "credit products." During the conference call with investors, CFO Jeff Edwards put it even more explicitly: the growth in fixed income was due in large part to "a substantial increase from structured finance and investment, which primarily reflects a better performance from our U.S. subprime mortgage activities." Acknowledging that the market for CDOs "has yet to fully stabilize" after the collapse of the Bear Stearns hedge funds, Edwards added that "[r]isk management, hedging, and cost controls in this business are especially critical during such periods of difficulty, and ours have proven to be effective in mitigating the impact of our results." Within three months, every one of these claims would prove to be delusional.

It seems inconceivable now that O'Neal himself had so little understanding of what lay ahead. He was a very smart man, a tough, seasoned Wall Street executive. One of the formative experiences of his career had been the Long-Term Capital Management disaster. He had been Merrill's CFO during that crisis, and it remained seared in his memory. He knew how a series of events could spiral into catastrophe. He remembered that awful feeling of realizing that Merrill couldn't put a value on the collateral it held. He saw how, in a crisis, "everything is correlated"—meaning that securities that were supposed to act as hedges suddenly started falling in tandem, exacerbating the losses. Panics have their own momentum, their own rhythms. It didn't matter how much cash you said you had; if your counterparties lost faith in you, you were finished. "You couldn't rely on anything," he liked to say.

O'Neal had worked fifteen hours a day for months during the LTCM crisis. He had gone home, night after night, worried about whether the firm would have enough liquidity to fund itself the next day. And, he liked to say, he never forgot those lessons. Yet now it appeared as if he *had* forgotten those lessons.

O'Neal had discovered another fact as a result of the Bear fiasco that should have shaken him to his core. He had learned the size of Merrill Lynch's subprime exposure. It was enormous. When Kronthal had left in July 2006, the firm had somewhere between $5 billion and $8 billion in subprime risk on its books. Most of it was either subprime mortgages waiting to be securitized, tranches of mortgage-backed securities waiting to be put into CDOs, or triple-B CDO tranches waiting to be repackaged into new CDOs as triple-As. This was hardly an insignificant exposure; if those subprime securities had to be written down in large numbers, Merrill was going to feel a good deal of pain. People would undoubtedly get fired. But it was not an amount that could bring the firm down.

A year later, Merrill Lynch held an astonishing $55 billion in subprime exposure on its balance sheet. In the space of one year, Semerci and Lattanzio had added somewhere between $45 billion and $50 billion in additional exposure. Some of it was the same kind of collateral that had been on the books when Kronthal had been running the show: mortgage-backed securities of one sort or another waiting to be resecuritized. But the vast majority of it was triple-A tranches of subprime CDOs.

Anyone who looked closely at this triple-A exposure would realize in an instant what Lattanzio and Semerci had done. With AIG no longer around to write protection—leading to a lack of buyers for the super-senior tranches—the only way Merrill could continue churning out new CDOs was to keep the triple-A risk itself. So that's what Semerci and Lattanzio had done. In the case of CDOs with subprime mortgage-backed securities, Merrill simply bought the triple-A tranches and put them on its books. In the case of synthetic CDOs—a business Merrill was also deep into—the firm would find a hedge fund to take the short position and take the long position itself. In most cases, Merrill bought protection from a monoline insurer like MBIA (which, under the rules, also enabled the firm to book the income on the triple-A tranches up front), but in the event of disaster, that wasn't likely to help much. The monolines had insured so much triple-A risk that any market event that hurt Merrill Lynch would destroy them.

The result of Semerci and Lattanzio's strategy was that Merrill Lynch would remain the number one underwriter of CDOs and the two men would get their big bonuses. But in the process, they had put Merrill Lynch itself at grave risk.

Did the two men understand that? At a certain point, late in the game, Semerci in particular seems to have understood the gravity of the situation. According to several former top Merrill executives, he appears to have managed his risk assumptions in such a way as to keep the estimated losses that he presented to management and the board artificially low. They also believed his marks were too high. These same executives are convinced, for instance, that Semerci knew full well when he made that board presentation in July 2007 that Merrill losses were going to be far higher than $83 million.

But until it was far too late, it appears that Semerci and Lattanzio did not fully understand the import of their strategy. Why? Because just like Ralph Cioffi and Mike Tannin at Bear Stearns, Semerci and Lattanzio still believed that a triple-A rating meant something. As the market had gotten shaky, they had begun shorting the ABX triple-Bs, but it never occurred to them that they were on the wrong side of the triple-A bets. Their belief in the value of the triple-A was why Semerci could tell Kim, with a straight face, that Merrill had very little exposure to subprime risk: he still thought the triple-As were close to riskless. That's why he could tell O'Neal he was reducing the risk in the portfolio. And that's why Semerci and Lattanzio could estimate Merrill's worst-case scenario losses in the tens of millions, rather than the billions. The two men were no different than the "real-money" investors who had been lured into the game by Wall Street, convinced they were getting the high-finance equivalent of a free lunch: an ultrasafe security that also generated higher yields than Treasury bonds. Even many of these investors, though, had become leery of a triple-A rating by the summer of 2007, especially as the spread between Treasuries and super-senior tranches narrowed to a smidgen. As Merrill Lynch had loaded up on triple-A mortgage-backed securities, the firm had become, without knowing it, one of the dumb guys. That was the real difference between Goldman Sachs and Merrill Lynch. "We fell for our own scam," John Breit, the Merrill risk manager, would later say.

⌘

For some time now, the synthetic CDO business resembled nothing so much as a daisy chain. It was just the way Lew Ranieri had described it in that speech he gave at the OTS. The buyers of the lowest-rated equity tranches weren't investors who were eager to take that risk in return for the promise of a high yield. Many of those investors were gone. Mostly, the buyers were hedge funds interested in doing that correlation trade, the one where they bought the equity and then shorted the triple-A, so they won no matter what the housing market did. The riskiness of the equity slice was meaningless to them. The buyers of the mezzanine, or triple-B, slices were other CDOs, which would then launder them into new triple-A slices. And the buyers of the triple-A were quite often the underwriters themselves, taking the long side against the same hedge fund that had also taken the short side of the triple-As. With no need for actual collateral—since everything was referenced—such deals could be done ad infinitum. If you were working feverishly to churn out CDOs and keep your number one ranking, this was an important component of your strategy—because these were the easiest deals to do. So in addition to underwriting cash CDOs, using mortgage-backed securities, Semerci and Lattanzio also dove into the synthetic game.

It was not a pretty thing to watch. Chicago-based hedge fund Magnetar would come to be the face of the correlation trade. According to the nonprofit investigative news service ProPublica, which conducted a six-month investigation into Magnetar's trades, some $30 billion worth of CDOs in which Magnetar owned the equity were issued between mid-2006 and mid-2007; by J.P. Morgan's estimate, Magnetar's CDOs accounted for between 35 and 60 percent of the mezzanine CDOs that were issued in that period. Merrill did a number of these deals with Magnetar. The performance of these CDOs can be summed up in one word: horrible.

The essence of the ProPublica allegation is that Magnetar, like Paulson, was betting that "its" CDOs would implode. Magnetar denies that this was its intent and claims that its strategy was based on a "mathematical statistical model." The firm says it would have done well regardless of the direction of the market. It almost doesn't matter. The triple-As did blow up. You didn't have to be John Paulson, picking out the securities you were then going to short, to make a fortune in this trade. Given that the CDOs referenced poorly underwritten subprime mortgages, they *had* to blow up, almost by definition. That's what subprime mortgages were poised to do in 2007.

Take a deal called Norma, a $1.5 billion synthetic CDO that Merrill Lynch put together in March of 2007, and which would later be dissected by the *Wall Street Journal*. The CDO manager Merrill chose to manage the deal was NIR. It was a former penny stock operator that Merrill had found and put into the CDO management business. Merrill had a number of similar captive CDO managers who knew without being told what kind of collateral the CDO was supposed to reference. Norma included a handful of subprime mortgage-backed securities—about $90 million worth, or 6 percent of the overall holdings, according to the *Journal*. It also included pieces of other CDOs, primarily triple-B mezzanine tranches, some of which Merrill had warehoused in order to launder them into new triple-A tranches at a later date, and some of which were being managed by CDO managers Merrill had hired—including Ricciardi himself, who had joined Cohen & Company, a big CDO manager. The rest of Norma consisted of credit default swaps that referenced tranches of other CDOs that contained subprime securities. In early 2007, all three rating agencies gave 75 percent of Norma's tranches a triple-A rating.

Magnetar bought the equity portion, of course. At the same time, it shorted the triple-A tranches of Norma, just as John Paulson had done in his Abacus deal. Merrill Lynch prepared a seventy-eight-page pitch book to help convince investors to buy pieces of the CDO. The *Journal* would later note that the pitch book stressed that mortgage-backed securities "have historically exhibited lower default rates, higher recovery upon default and better rating stability than comparably rated corporate bonds." Merrill's fee was in the neighborhood of $20 million.

Ultimately, Merrill was able to sell $525 million worth of tranches, most of them lower-rated ones, which Merrill Lynch was promising at 5.5 percent interest above Libor, a very high yield. (Libor is the interest rate that banks charge when they lend to each other.) This was so even though, according to a lawsuit later filed against Merrill for its role in underwriting Norma, the securities had declined by 20 percent even before the deal closed. By December 2007—just nine months after Norma had been created—most of the deal had been downgraded to junk by the rating agencies.

"It was a tangled hairball of risk," Janet Tavakoli, the CDO critic, told the *Journal.* "In March of 2007, any savvy investors would have thrown this . . . in the trash bin."

But wait. If it was a $1.5 billion CDO, and Merrill could sell only $525 million of it, what happened to the other $975 million of Norma—all of which was triple-A? That's what went onto Merrill's books; it took the long position on the triple-As. This was the exposure that Semerci was claiming was nearly riskless.

A lawsuit would later claim that Merrill was actively seeking to move its worst securities off its books and into the hands of unsuspecting clients. Without question, Merrill Lynch was doing that, especially with the triple-Bs. In one of the seamier examples of Merrill's efforts to unload some of the junk on its balance sheet, it actually securitized subprime loans from Ownit— Bill Dallas's subprime originator, which it partially owned—*after* Ownit filed for bankruptcy. Then again, every other big CDO underwriter on Wall Street—Citibank, UBS, Morgan Stanley, you name it—was doing the exact same thing. "People on the outside thought the market was going gangbusters because of all the deals getting done," CDO expert Gene Phillips told Bloomberg. "People on the inside knew it was a last-gasp effort to clear out the warehouses."

In the aftermath of the crisis, Goldman Sachs would be the firm that was by far the most criticized for selling its clients down the river in its efforts to get risk off its own books. In truth, Goldman was just better at it than Merrill and the others. It was tougher and smarter in the way it went about it. And there was an even bigger difference between the way Merrill and Goldman went about attempting to reduce risk. Goldman as an institution never believed that the tiny bit of extra return offered by triple-A subprime-backed securities was worth the risk. As it began marking down its securities—and pushing them off its books—it treated triple-As just as ruthlessly as it treated all the other subprime securities it was marking.

———— ∞ ————

On May 16, 2007, Dow Kim announced that he was leaving Merrill Lynch to start a hedge fund; finally O'Neal said he could go.* During the previous three years, the firm's trading revenues had doubled; in 2006, his last full year with the firm, Kim was Merrill's second highest-paid executive, after only O'Neal, taking home a paycheck of $37 million. Along with Fakahany, O'Neal had always viewed Kim as part of his inner circle and was gracious about his departure. It was only after the crisis that O'Neal would reflect back on Kim's sudden departure, wondering why his head of fixed income hadn't seen the problem coming. Or, worse, O'Neal would think in his darkest moments, maybe he *had* seen it coming. Maybe that's why Kim had left.

This seems unlikely. Semerci would later insist that he had shown Kim his risk positions, according to several former executives. But people who have seen the e-mail traffic say that that doesn't appear to be the case. One day, several months after he had left the firm, Kim returned to Merrill's headquarters, trying to rustle up a Merrill Lynch investment for his hedge fund. He ran into John Breit in the hallway. "It's a debacle," Breit told him, relating the enormous subprime exposure. Kim was stunned. "We don't have all that stuff!" he replied. Truly, he hadn't known.

For that *New Yorker* article, O'Neal's predecessor, David Komansky, told the writer John Cassidy that he simply didn't believe O'Neal was unaware of the firm's CDO exposure. Hard though it may be to believe, that does appear to be the case. "Stan was no longer dug in," says a former executive. At the same time Goldman executives were canceling vacations to deal with the burgeoning subprime crisis, O'Neal was often on the golf course, playing

---

* Although Kim hired a staff, his hedge fund never got off the ground because he was unable to raise any money. According to a lawsuit filed by Michael Pasternak, who claims to have turned down a $2 million yearly salary at Morgan Stanley to work for him, Kim told prospective hires that he had investors lined up to sink more than $2 billion into the fund. Indeed, Kim walked out of Merrill believing he had a $4 billion commitment from his old firm and several billion from other prospective investors. But as the market worsened, all of Kim's investors decided against investing. In August 2008, just a month before Lehman weekend, Kim shut down the fund, which he had been funding out of his own pocket.

round after round by himself. He had little or no direct contact with any of the firm's operations—he had delegated that to Fleming, Fakahany, and others. Always a loner, he had become isolated from his own firm. He had no idea that key risk managers had been pushed aside, or that the people he had put in important positions were out of their depths. Amazing as it sounds, the CEO of Merrill Lynch really didn't have a clue.

In August, O'Neal went to Martha's Vineyard for vacation. By then, the market was signaling that the end was near; on the ABX, even the triple As were starting to drop in value. In late July, the Dow had its worst week in more than four years. The CDO market continued to contract. Day after day, the decline continued. Somehow, the combination of the ongoing turmoil in the market and his ability to step back and see things more clearly while he was far away from Wall Street had the effect of finally rousing O'Neal. By the time he returned to work at the beginning of September, he was no longer in denial. O'Neal finally understood that the triple-A securities on Merrill's book posed a huge threat to the firm. At a minimum, the securities were going to have to be marked down, and there would have to be write-downs that would damage Merrill's earnings. The firm's third-quarter earnings report was due in October; he had a month to come to terms with the problem. As he thought about it, O'Neal wasn't just worried. The memory of the LTCM disaster was flooding back. He was scared.

John Breit understood the problem by then as well. In July, Lattanzio had commandeered two junior quants and told them to sign off on a new valuation method the mortgage desk wanted to use for CDOs squared. The quants, feeling they were being asked to ratify something that had not been vetted through proper channels, complained to their manager. The manager happened to tell Breit the story. Breit's curiosity was sparked. Calling in a favor from someone in the finance department, he got ahold of a spreadsheet with the collateral in the CDOs squared. He quickly saw how bad it was. He keep digging, quietly; before long he had discovered the $55 billion exposure.

But Breit was still persona non grata on the trading floor. He had no access to top management. He had long since been tossed off the risk management committee. Thus he resorted to the only action he could think to take: he began buttonholing people he bumped into at Merrill, telling them the losses on the mortgage desk were going to be in the billions, not the millions. In early August, Breit went on vacation in the Hamptons. One day he received a phone call from Semerci, who had heard through the grapevine what Breit was saying. Semerci was enraged, and insisted that the losses were only going to amount to a couple of hundred million dollars. By the end of August, the mortgage desk had upped its loss esimate to $600 million—a number Breit still thought was absurdly low.

By mid-September, Semerci and Lattanzio were conceded $1.3 billion in triple-A losses. Seeing the problems grow, Greg Fleming reached out to his old friend Jeff Kronthal. O'Neal had named Fleming co-president of Merrill Lynch—along with Fakahany—shortly after Dow Kim left. Although he was still under strict orders to stay away from fixed income, the problems on the mortgage desk seemed too deep to just look the other way. Kronthal explained to Fleming how CDOs work and began tapping into his own sources at Merrill Lynch to see if he could find out what was going on. One of those sources was Breit. Breit told Kronthal that he thought the write-downs were going to be much bigger than anyone on the mortgage desk was admitting, which by then was around $3 billion. Kronthal conveyed this to Fleming, who conveyed it to O'Neal. O'Neal asked to see Breit.

The two men had known each other for more than a dozen years; they had even worked together on occasion. O'Neal knew that Breit understood risk as well as anyone at Merrill. "I hear you have a model of the CDOs that disagrees with the valuations being put out there by Semerci," O'Neal began. No, Breit replied, he didn't have a model; just a back-of-the-envelope calculation. Then he gave O'Neal his number: $6 billion in losses. And he added, "It could be a lot worse. I haven't even looked at the high-grade CDOs, just the CDOs squared and the mezzanines."

O'Neal looked like he was going to throw up. "What about all the protection we bought?" he asked. Breit explained that with AIG no longer in the business, Merrill had been buying protection from the monolines, which had taken on so much risk they would be insolvent long before they could pay off Merrill. O'Neal kept probing. What about the risk models? he asked. Worthless, replied Breit matter-of-factly. The risk wasn't captured by VaR, and the VaR analysis of the underlying credit quality was wrong. Other risk models didn't do any better. As O'Neal listened in silence, Breit explained how an important Merrill risk measure had been changed in such a way as to disguise the increasing amount of triple-A risk on the firm's books. Breit today says he does not believe this was purposely changed to hide the ball— he thinks it might have even been a regulatory change—but it had that effect. "It distorted the true nature of the risk," he told O'Neal. After talking for a few more minutes, Breit shook O'Neal's hand and wished him luck. "I hope we talk again," he said.

That's when O'Neal told him he wasn't sure how much longer he would be Merrill's CEO.

For Breit, it was a sobering conversation; he could see how shattered O'Neal was at the news. For O'Neal, it was an infuriating conversation. How could Breit convey this information so calmly? Wasn't he supposed to be managing risk? Didn't he bear at least some responsibility for what the mortgage desk had done? O'Neal still had no idea that Breit had been pushed aside. He thought Breit was still a risk manager on the front lines of the mortgage desk. The fact that he himself had put in place the dynamic that allowed good risk managers like Breit to be cast aside eluded him entirely.

And yet, having belatedly woken up to the magnitude of the problem, O'Neal absolutely understood what had to be done. Very simply, the firm needed to be sold—as quickly as possible. One thing he understood clearly is that when you face a black hole of write-downs, there is no way to know how deep the hole really is. The knee-jerk solution would be to raise capital—which, in fact, firms all over Wall Street were scrambling to do. O'Neal thought that was foolish. What would happen if it turned out not to be enough? You would never be able to raise additional capital; investors would be too fearful that the next round might be washed away, too. It would cause even greater panic. "I couldn't look employees straight in the eye and say that everything is going to be okay," he later told friends. "Just selling equity and waiting for the crisis to unfold just didn't seem to be a winning formula."

O'Neal would later tell *Fortune* magazine that Merrill was like "a fighter in the middle of the ring with your hands tied behind you and an opponent, whenever he chose, could just whale away on you, punch you right in the face. And there was no referee, so he could kick you in the balls, give you an elbow to the chin, and you could do nothing except stand there until he decided he was tired or finished or beneficent or whatever it was and turned away and walked out of the ring." He added, "That seemed to me to be unbearable. We had to have alternatives." The only alternative that made sense to him was a merger.

By the middle of September, O'Neal was talking to Merrill's board members about the firm's exposure to subprime risk. The directors were startled. Previously, they had always been told that Merrill's subprime risks were minimal. Now they were hearing, for the first time, that the firm's estimated loss was more than $1 billion. The board hired its own outside lawyer to advise it. A number of directors asked for tutorials on CDOs.

Even more startling to the directors was O'Neal's demeanor. Almost overnight, he had gone from appearing unworried about Merrill's subprime exposure to being deeply and openly pessimistic. People who saw him in the office said he appeared to be depressed. It was such a startling about-face that the Merrill directors had a difficult time taking him completely seriously. It was not that they didn't think Merrill had a problem; it was that they thought O'Neal was panicking. But he wasn't. This time, O'Neal was dead right.

In September, O'Neal arranged a secret meeting with Ken Lewis, the CEO of Bank of America, at the Time Warner Center in midtown Manhattan. O'Neal knew that Lewis had long lusted after Merrill Lynch—and, as his earlier purchase of Countrywide had shown, Lewis couldn't say no to an acquisition he wanted. Ever since O'Neal had realized the depths of Merrill's problems, he had been holding private conversations with Lewis about a possible deal. He had done so without informing any of his lieutenants or the Merrill Lynch board—O'Neal wanted to be able to go to them with a deal in hand. Lewis had even thrown out a number: $90 a share. At the secret meeting, O'Neal suggested bumping the price to $100. Lewis didn't object.

It was after this meeting that O'Neal finally decided to sound out a board member about a possible merger with Bank of America. The director he spoke with was an old friend, financier Alberto Cribiore, whom O'Neal had put on the board in 2003. His response was extremely negative. "But Stan, Ken Lewis is an asshole," replied Cribiore, according to the account O'Neal gave to *Fortune*. (Cribiore would later say he didn't recall this conversation, but other Merrill executives back up O'Neal's version.) Cribiore didn't like the idea of Merrill Lynch losing its brand and identity to a bank based in Charlotte, and he still didn't think it was necessary. He thought Merrill should raise capital and take a big write-down—exactly what O'Neal felt the company shouldn't do. Strangely—and perhaps this had to do with O'Neal's mental state—O'Neal concluded that if he couldn't bring Cribiore around, he wouldn't be able to bring any of the directors around. So instead of taking the deal to the full board, he dropped the idea. As the other directors found out he had approached Ken Lewis but never informed them, they were furious.

In early October, O'Neal finally did something he should have done much earlier. He fired Semerci and Lattanzio. The week before he was let go, Semerci received an e-mail from Fakahany praising him for his risk management efforts. Yet Semerci, at least, seems to have sensed that his firing was near. The loss estimates were growing. Too many other executives were complaining—and trying to show O'Neal that the situation was worse than he was portraying it. A group of them, fairly high up in the company, had come to call his estimates of triple-A losses "The Fantastic Lie."

During August and September, Semerci methodically downloaded all his e-mail correspondence to O'Neal, Fakahany, Kim, and other top executives. Then, for reasons that people at Merrill Lynch still don't understand, he withdrew from the bank almost $10,000 in sequential hundred-dollar bills, and taped the money into one of his desk drawers. He did the same with a Turkish passport—a passport he had never registered with the firm, as executives are supposed to do. (When he traveled for the company, he used a UK passport.)

Semerci's office was on the seventh floor. He was brought to the thirty-second floor to be fired. After the deed was done, and he was being escorted out of the building and into a waiting car, he told the HR personnel who were guiding him out of the building about the money. He asked that he be allowed to leave with it. Someone went to find the bills and gave them to him when they got outside. He also called his secretary, told her about the passport, and had her slip it into his jacket, which he had left in his office. She met him by the car and handed the jacket to him. With his money and his passport, Semerci flew to London, where he now operates a hedge fund.

Fleming, meanwhile, brought Breit and another risk manager back from exile and gave them the task of sorting out Merrill's CDO business. Incredibly, it was the first time anyone at Merrill Lynch, independent of the traders themselves, had attempted to put a value on the firm's massive CDO exposure.

Two days after Semerci and Lattanzio were fired, Merrill Lynch "preannounced" its earnings, telling investors, in advance of its third-quarter earnings call, that it would be taking a large write-down in its subprime mortgage book, which it estimated at around $5 billion. It was going to be the largest trading loss in Merrill's history. This was the first investors would hear about Merrill's subprime exposure—indeed, it directly contradicted everything Merrill had said previously about its CDO portfolio and its risk management capabilities. The stock plunged.

A few weeks later, O'Neal met with the board to go over the third-quarter numbers. In the intervening weeks, new executives who had been installed in the mortgage departments had concluded that the firm should use more pessimistic assumptions in coming up with its CDO valuations. They recommended a write-down of $8 billion instead of $5 billion.

In the days prior to the meeting—and despite the earlier, negative reaction from Cribiore about his having approached Ken Lewis—O'Neal had sounded out a second CEO about a possible merger: Ken Thompson of Wachovia. Like Lewis, Thompson was receptive. O'Neal thought a Wachovia merger would be more palatable to the board; Merrill was the bigger name, unlikely to be subsumed the way it would be in a Bank of America deal. O'Neal decided he would use a dinner with board members to make the case for a merger.

On their way to the board dinner, Fleming counseled O'Neal on how to approach the board. "You have to walk them through this," he said. "You can't just tell them we need to sell the company. They aren't going to buy it. The company was performing tremendously until this quarter. That's how they are viewing it."

Shooting him a suspicious look, O'Neal responded, "Why are you saying that? Who are you talking to?"

"I haven't talked to anybody," replied Fleming. "I'm an investment banker. This is what I've done my whole career."

But that kind of gentle persuasion just wasn't in O'Neal's toolkit. The dinner itself was "frosty," according to one participant. The directors were angry. "There was no small talk, no humor." The board members were served their food, and practically before they could take a bite O'Neal said, "I think we should sell to Wachovia."

The board members were stunned. Their anger turned to fury. Some began grilling O'Neal on Merrill's exposure; others complained that his approaching Wachovia was a terrible breach of corporate etiquette—a CEO is supposed to get a board's permission before approaching another company. "Their reaction was vitriolic," recalls one participant. "I've never seen that kind of interplay between a CEO and a board of directors." The board had zero interest in pursuing a merger with Wachovia.

"I'm on the board of a public company now," Komansky told *The New Yorker*. "If I thought the CEO was out trying to sell the company, I'd have a hard time having confidence in that fellow." Well, maybe. But while O'Neal's bedside manner may have been lacking, he was doing exactly the right thing in trying to sell Merrill Lynch. This time, it was the board that was in denial.

The board meeting took place Sunday and Monday, October 21 and 22, 2007. It wasn't a lot of fun; the board had lost confidence in O'Neal and he was smart enough to see it. And the numbers Merrill was about to unveil were truly ugly. On Wednesday, October 24, the earnings were released. Merrill Lynch announced a net loss of $2.3 billion, which included a write-down of $7.9 billion in subprime mortgage securities.* "The bottom line is, we got it wrong by being overexposed to subprime, and we suffered as a result of an unprecedented liquidity squeeze and deterioration in that market." O'Neal accepted the blame.

The following evening, Jenny Anderson of the *New York Times* began calling and e-mailing various board members and executives, trying to confirm a rumor she had heard. She got Fleming on his cell phone around seven thirty. After a few pleasantries, she said one word to him: "Wachovia." He gave her a quick "No comment" and got off the phone. But another source, later that evening, confirmed O'Neal's approach to Wachovia, and she had the story in the paper the next day. O'Neal was already hanging by a thread; that story finished him off.

On October 29, four days after the *Times* broke the news of his approach to Wachovia, Stan O'Neal was gone. He took with him $161 million in retirement benefits and Merrill Lynch stock, feeling at once embittered, embarrassed, and frustrated. "I should have known better," he told Fleming bitterly, shortly before he resigned. After he was gone, though, it wasn't his mistakes he dwelled on, but the mistakes of the men he had surrounded himself with: Fakahany, Semerci, and Kim. He had trusted them and they had let him down. He never seemed to understand that he himself had planted the seeds of destruction by placing his trust in the wrong people. "The fixed income guys got us in '98, and I swore they would never do it again," O'Neal used to say, referring to the Long-Term Capital crisis. "But they did it again." For this, he had only himself to blame.

Eleven months after his ouster, though, O'Neal got a small measure of satisfaction when Merrill was sold to Bank of America, for $29 a share, during the most traumatic weekend of the financial crisis. O'Neal sent Cribiore an e-mail, according to *Fortune*. "My former friend," it read, "you should have helped me sell this business when we had the chance."

A final coda: Not long after O'Neal was safely out the door, Greg Fleming brought Kronthal back to Merrill Lynch to help clean up the mess. The first day he walked out onto the trading floor, all the traders stood as one and cheered.

---

* Three months later, Merrill wrote down an additional $11 billion in subprime securities. In all, of the approximately $45 billion or so that Semerci and Lattanzio had added to Merrill's books in the year after Kronthal left, a staggering $42 billion would wind up being written off.

21

Collateral Damage

On July 11, 2007, two executives at AIG-FP had a private phone conversation to discuss their company's subprime exposure. One of the executives was Andrew Forster, the Cassano deputy who had helped persuade his boss to stop writing new credit default swaps on triple-A tranches of multisector CDOs at the end of 2005. He was in AIG's London office. The other man was Al Frost, who had helped lead AIG-FP into the business and who had marketed dozens of credit default swap deals until the spigot was turned off, at which point AIG was on the hook for some $60 billion worth of subprime exposure. He was calling Forster from AIG-FP's office in Wilton, Connecticut.

"What are you focused on?" Frost asked nervously.

"What are we focused on?" replied Forster, seeming incredulous at the question. "I'm focused on CDOs and subprime."

"Yeah, obviously."

"Nothing else," Forster continued. "And spending most of my time answering questions of . . . AIG, you know, Sullivan, Lewis, all the rest of it." Sullivan was Martin Sullivan, AIG's CEO. Lewis referred to Bob Lewis, the company's chief risk officer.

What Frost and Forster knew—and Sullivan and Lewis didn't—was that embedded in AIG-FP's swap contracts were those collateral triggers. AIG-FP's counterparties, who had been paying it millions of dollars over the years to insure their triple-A tranches, had the right to demand what amounted to cash margin calls if one of three things happened: if AIG's rating dropped to single-A or below; if the ratings on the super-senior tranches AIG was insuring were lowered by the rating agencies; or if the value of the tranches fell—even without a ratings downgrade. In all the time FP had been writing credit protection on multisector CDOs, no one could ever imagine any of these things ever happening. AIG was just too strong financially, and besides, the super-senior tranches FP insured had plenty of subordination; the default rate on the underlying mortgages would have to be almost unimaginably high to ever reach the tranches that FP insured.

Even after FP stopped writing the business in 2005—indeed, even after the parent company's rating was dropped to double-A after Greenberg's departure—the division executives remained convinced they had nothing to worry about. FP executives took solace in the fact that the 2006 and 2007 "vintages" of subprime mortgages were far worse than the 2005 vintage that FP had wrapped. Tranches with those later mortgages, they believed, would be hit long before any of the tranches that AIG insured. A government official who began poking around FP's swap business in 2005, not long after Greenberg left, recalls looking at the collateral triggers and thinking, "This is a company with 9 percent tangible capital and an earnings stream to die for. It would truly take an Armageddon scenario. You're thinking, 'This is never going to happen.' There's risk, sure, but there's also risk I could walk out the door and a brick could fall on my head."

By the middle of 2007, however, Armageddon looked a lot closer than it had in 2005. And Forster was clearly worried that downgrades—and collateral calls—were coming. All he had to do was look at what had happened to the Bear Stearns hedge funds to know that the unimaginable was now a very real possibility.

"Every fucking one, every rating agency we've spoke to . . . every time they come out with more downgrades we have to go and . . . analyze all the exposures we've got in the rest of it. So, you know, it's fairly time consuming," Forster said. "The problem we're going to face is that we're going to have just enormous downgrades on the stuff that we've got. So you know, we sort of sit there with a $60 billion CDO book, and now we're sort of sitting and saying, it's super-senior. It isn't going to be too much longer before we're saying, we've got, you know, $20 billion of single-A risk. And that's going to happen. There's no doubt about it."

"Do you think it's going down that far, single-A?" asked Frost.

"Oh, yeah," said Forster. "It's going to get very, very, very ugly."

The conversation turned to another potential problem: given what the market was doing, the value of the super-senior tranches was getting hit even without a ratings downgrade. How was AIG going to avoid marking down the value of the securities it insured—which would also result in collateral calls?

"Is there an event that could cause us to [lower our marks]?" asked Frost.

Forster replied that the rumbling of downgrades by the rating agencies would inevitably cause counterparties to focus on AIG's marks, which were still at par. "I mean, we have to mark it," he told Frost.

"We're fucked basically," he concluded.

It took only two weeks after that conversation for Frost and Forster's worst nightmare to come true. On July 26, a junior AIG-FP official sent Frost a short e-mail with the heading "Sorry to bother you." (Frost had left for vacation.) It read, "Margin call coming your way. Wanted to give you a heads-up."

"On what?" asked Frost.

"20bb of super-senior," replied the official.

The next day the demand for cash officially arrived. It sought $1.8 billion, meaning that the counterparty was claiming that $20 billion in super-seniors that AIG had wrapped had declined by that amount, and FP had a contractual obligation to make up the difference. FP executives were stunned at the size of the demand. It "hit out of the blue, and a fucking number that's well bigger than we ever planned for," Forster complained in another phone call a few days later. Nor was this your run-of-the-mill counterparty that was making this demand. It was Goldman Sachs.

Faced with its first collateral call, AIG-FP pushed back hard. For the next few days FP and Goldman Sachs argued ferociously about how much collateral AIG needed to put up. FP insisted that because the actual underlying collateral remained sound, it was not required to mark the securities to market and could keep it at par. Which meant it didn't have to put up any cash. It also argued that Goldman was unfairly lowballing the marks to squeeze more cash out of AIG than was justified.

For its part, Goldman argued that under the terms of the contract, it didn't matter how sound the underlying collateral was. All that mattered was how the market was valuing it at any given moment. At *this* given moment, the market was saying that the value of the super-seniors had declined. Therefore FP's marks had to be lowered—and it had to put up cash. Those were the rules of the game.

On August 1, FP executive Tom Athan e-mailed Forster; he had just gotten off what he described as a "tough conf call with Goldman." The firm, he said, was "not budging and acting irrationally." "I played almost every card I had," he wrote. "Legal wording, market practice, intent of the language . . . and also stressed the potential damage to the relationship. . . ." Goldman was unmoved. Meanwhile, Goldman Sachs executives viewed AIG as the irrational party. Goldman was making similar demands to counterparties all over town. Nobody was happy about it, but nobody was fighting it like AIG. "These were head-butting conversations," says a former Goldman employee.

On August 2, Cassano got involved. Taking another look at its marks, Goldman lowered its collateral demand to $1.2 billion and sent a new spreadsheet with its marks for the disputed securities. An AIG accountant then put together a spreadsheet for Cassano showing how Merrill Lynch was valuing the same securities. Goldman had one CDO valued at 85 cents on the dollar; Merrill had it at 98 cents. Goldman had another CDO at 85 cents that Merrill valued at 99 cents. AIG-FP had them both valued at par.

Finally, on August 10, after another week of wrangling, Cassano and the Goldman trader he was negotiating with agreed that FP would post $450 million in collateral. Why that amount? Not because the two sides had come to an agreement. (In fact, they signed a separate side letter acknowledging that the $450 million did not satisfy the collateral agreement.) The real reason, recalls a former AIG executive, was that "they were both going on vacation and didn't want it lingering." For Goldman, the fact that it had gotten money out of AIG was viewed as a victory. For the FP executives, the fact that the amount was less than half of what Goldman had demanded caused them to mistake Goldman's seriousness of purpose in getting the collateral it felt it was owed. "We thought, 'This can't be real,'" recalls a former AIG executive. "If they had been serious about the $1.2 billion, they would have been in here with an ax."

A few days later Frost e-mailed Forster again. The posting of $450 million, he wrote, was an effort "to get everyone to chill out." But, he added, "this is not the last margin call we are going to debate." Forster agreed. "I have heard several rumors now that gs is aggressively marking down asset types that they don't own so as to cause maximum pain to their competitors," he e-mailed back. "It may be rubbish, but it's the sort of thing gs would do."*

Unbeknownst to AIG, Goldman Sachs did something else to protect itself. Concluding that it could no longer trust AIG to pay off its swap contracts in full if the triple-A tranches started to default, Goldman began buying

---

* Around this same time, according to *Institutional Investor* magazine, Goldman's insurance analyst, Tom Cholnoky, issued an unusually tough-minded report entitled "Don't Buy AIG." Cholnoky's rationale, the magazine reported, was the likelihood of "further rating agency downgrades and capital-raising activities that would dilute shareholders."

protection on AIG itself. Goldman would later claim that this was standard practice: it always bought protection on a counterparty if that counterparty was fighting margin calls. But it's also true that Goldman, having done so many deals with AIG over the years and having served as AIG's longtime investment banker, had a deeper understanding of AIG and all its foibles than anybody else. If anyone knew in advance that AIG was headed for trouble, it was going to be Goldman. Whatever the reason, between August 1 and August 10 Goldman bought $575 million worth of credit default swaps on AIG—swaps that would pay off in the event of an AIG bankruptcy.

From all outward appearances, AIG seemed to have done remarkably well in the two-plus years since Hank Greenberg's departure. Having gotten through the trauma of Greenberg's abrupt leave-taking, and then the earnings restatements, the company still wound up making enormous sums in both 2005 and 2006—more than $10 billion in 2005, followed by a record year in 2006, with profits that exceeded $14 billion and revenue that topped $113 billion. Its total assets were around $1 trillion, while its stock, which had dropped into the low fifties after Greenberg's resignation, rose back up to the seventies. Sullivan was amply rewarded: his pay package in 2006 was $26.7 million.

In the view of the AIG board, Sullivan had earned those millions. When Greenberg left—with all of AIG's secrets in his head—Sullivan had been running AIG's sprawling insurance unit and had a seat on the AIG board. Though he was often described as Greenberg's handpicked successor, that was a wild overstatement. There was no one at AIG Greenberg viewed as a worthy successor; Sullivan was picked because the board knew him and because he headed the company's biggest division. Greenberg, who for a brief time remained chairman of the board, signed off on Sullivan's promotion because there was no better option. Succession planning wasn't exactly his strong suit.

Sullivan knew insurance as well as anyone at AIG, but despite being a director, he knew very little about the other parts of the company—which of course was the way Greenberg had always wanted things. Nor was Sullivan a natural leader. A diffident man, he had joined the company at the age of seventeen, had never gone to college, and had spent his life deferring to Hank Greenberg while he rose through the ranks. When Sullivan was preparing for the press conference that would introduce him as AIG's new CEO, he kept referring to his predecessor as Mr. Greenberg. Someone finally asked him, "Why are you calling him Mr. Greenberg?" Replied Sullivan: "I've always called him Mr. Greenberg."

And yet for a brief, shining moment, Sullivan rose to the occasion. The combination of Greenberg's departure, the restatements, and the various probes by the New York attorney general, the SEC, and the Justice Department were "life-threatening events for AIG," says someone who was there. "It was like having a heart attack and a stroke at the same time." This person adds, "Sullivan saved the company." He had to deal with the rating agencies, the investment community, government investigators, and his fellow executives. He had to mollify the accountants from PricewaterhouseCoopers, who were crawling all over the company, and AIG's employees, many of whom felt lost without Greenberg. "He did a great job of holding on to talent," says this same person. He was a calming influence at a time when AIG needed exactly that.

He also tried to bring AIG into the modern age, spending millions to upgrade the systems that Greenberg had always ignored. But in truth, these were mainly cosmetic changes. What Sullivan didn't do—what he lacked the capacity to do—was change AIG at its core. The silos that Greenberg had erected still existed. The sharing of information, especially bad news, was almost nonexistent. Division heads told headquarters only what they wanted headquarters to hear; there were still no systematic processes that cut across all divisions, the way there are at most big companies. Division managers could reach for extra profits however they saw fit—even if it entailed taking undue risk. Because executives didn't fear Sullivan the way they'd feared Greenberg, they often took liberties they would never have taken under Greenberg. Sullivan lacked the force of personality to curb their excesses.

Risk management, in particular, was a glaring weakness under Sullivan. Whatever Greenberg's other shortcomings, he did have a keen sense for when to take a risk and when to pull back—and of course he had all the information he needed at his fingertips, because when Hank Greenberg demanded it, he got it. Regular meetings that Greenberg had conducted about risk were canceled by Sullivan, who bumped most risk decisions to underlings. Under Sullivan, the risk managers were almost entirely dependent on the division heads for information. They often didn't have enough information to push back in areas where excessive risk might be building up. And they treated each division's risks as individual issues, never looking across the entire corporation to see if there were company-wide risks that needed to be addressed.

AIG's securities lending program, which was run out of the investment division, was a classic example of the company's risk management failings. That was the program in which, for a fee, AIG would lend out its securities to short sellers, who put up cash collateral. Then it would invest the proceeds in short-term securities that could be sold quickly when the short seller wanted his cash back. At the end of Greenberg's last full year, 2004, AIG had already begun the dangerous practice of investing some of the cash in mortgage-backed securities, which generated a higher return for AIG but were hardly the kind of short-term, liquid securities that could easily be sold.

In late 2005, the executive in charge of the securities lending program went to Bob Lewis, requesting that the company raise the limit on the securities he was allowed to purchase in the mortgage market. He also wanted to rev up the program itself, which at the end of 2004 had a balance of $53 billion. He made this request at the very same time that AIG-FP had decided to stop insuring the super-senior tranches because the subprime underwriting standards had deteriorated so badly. A well-run risk department would have immediately realized that one AIG division was asking to take more risk in the exact area where another division, far better versed in these kinds of securities, was cutting back. A good risk manager would have said no.

But Lewis did not say no. Instead, he cut a deal. As he later testified before the Financial Crisis Inquiry Commission, he agreed to raise the limit, but insisted that the securities lending program only invest in the "highest-quality" residential mortgage-backed securities. "No CDOs," he added. But while the securities the investment division bought weren't CDOs, they were still securitized subprime mortgages that had the same underwriting problems that FP was worried about. By the end of 2006, the balance on the securities lending program had risen by $20 billion, to $73 billion. And by the end of 2007, it had risen to $83 billion—by which time clients were rushing to return the securities they had borrowed and get their cash back. Because the mortgage-backed securities AIG owned were impossible to sell, the securities lending program began to have cash shortfalls—$6.3 billion by the end of 2007, and a staggering $13.5 billion one quarter later. The inability to return cash to clients in the securities lending program was one of the things that would eventually bring AIG down. Not long after AIG was bailed out by the federal government, Larry Fink, who had been brought in to help the company sort through its problems, was shown the details of AIG's securities lending program. "In all my years," he exclaimed, "I have never seen such disregard for managing money."

And then there was the relationship between AIG and AIG-FP—and between Sullivan and Cassano. If other divisions told headquarters as little as they could get away with, FP told headquarters even less. Cassano used to meet with Greenberg regularly; Cassano and Sullivan rarely met. (One former FP executive says that in three years, he saw Sullivan in the Wilton, Connecticut, office only once.) As little as Sullivan knew about, say, AIG's airline leasing business, he knew even less about its derivatives business. Cassano did little to enlighten him. For the most part, Cassano dealt with an AIG executive named Bill Dooley, who, as head of AIG's financial services division, which included AIG-FP, was nominally Cassano's boss. Mostly, they fought.

On the other hand, Sullivan had so many other fish to fry that it was easy to leave Joe Cassano alone. By all the obvious measures, he seemed to be running a shop that was at the top of its game. In 2006, the division made nearly $950 million in profits, meaning it was not only helping AIG's income statement but also minting millionaires, since the division still kept around a third of its profits as bonuses. (Cassano later acknowledged that he made around $300 million during his time at AIG-FP, although his lawyers claim that $70 million of that was deferred compensation that he lost when the AIG was bailed out by the government.)

As for the risks it was taking, no one could really see any significant problems on the horizon. The total notional value of AIG-FP's derivatives business was $2.66 trillion. Of that, some $527 billion was in the credit default swap book. Of that, FP insured a "mere" $60 billion in multisector CDO tranches. FP's subprime exposure, in other words, seemed like a relatively small piece of the business, around 3 percent of its total derivatives exposure. And no one at headquarters knew about the existence of the collateral triggers—including Dooley. When the risk managers at AIG headquarters ran FP's various derivatives business through their risk models and stress scenarios, it got a clean bill of health. After the big 2005 restatement—which included significant changes in the way FP accounted for some of its hedges—the board told Sullivan that he should take tighter control of FP. He agreed. But it never happened, in part because Cassano wouldn't let it happen. Sullivan kept telling the board he was moving in that direction, but there were always more immediate issues that took up his attention instead. And since FP was doing so well, nobody pressed the point.

By early 2007, the board of directors was beginning to get antsy about Sullivan's management. It wasn't just his unwillingness to get his arms around FP; there were lots of similar issues that the board wanted him to tackle but which he seemed to be avoiding. Sullivan was still resistant to the cultural changes that were so clearly necessary. With the 2005 crisis now well in the past, the board wanted Sullivan to begin accelerating the pace of change.

"By the summer of 2007," says a former AIG executive, "we were getting to the point where members of the board were saying, 'We need to start setting some harder milestones.'"

Which, of course, was exactly when the collateral calls began.

September 11: With everyone back from vacation, Goldman once again begins demanding collateral—$1.5 billion this time, in addition to the $450 million AIG has already posted. Société Générale, the big French bank, also demands collateral—$40 million—which AIG-FP executives immediately suspect has been instigated by Goldman, since Société Générale is a big Goldman client and its trades mirror Goldman's trades. AIG-FP disputes the marks submitted by the two firms. Société Générale backs down. Goldman doesn't.

September 13: Goldman buys an additional $700 million worth of protection on AIG, bringing the total to $1.5 billion.

September 20: Goldman announces its third-quarter results: profits of $2.9 billion, despite marking down its own subprime holdings. "Significant losses on nonprime loans and securities were more than offset by gains on short mortgage positions," says the firm.

October 1: AIG-FP accountant Joseph St. Denis, who had joined FP in June 2006, resigns. In a letter he would later write to congressional investigators, St. Denis says he became "gravely concerned" when he learned in September of the Goldman collateral calls—"as the mantra at AIG-FP had always been (in my experience) that there could *never* be losses" on the super-seniors. Cassano, he says, deliberately excluded him from meetings to discuss the valuation issue because, Cassano told him, "I was concerned that you would pollute the process." On the morning he resigns, St. Denis tells AIG-FP's general counsel that "I have lost faith in the senior-most management of AIG-FP."

November 2: Goldman ups its collateral demands to $2.8 billion. Yet again, AIG-FP disputes Goldman's marks.

November 7: AIG announces its third-quarter results: $3 billion in profits. But it also discloses that it has taken a $352 million write-down on "unrealized market valuation loss" in the quarter, which ended in September. It adds that, in October, its portfolio took on an additional $550 million in losses, which could get better or worse, depending on what happens in the rest of the fourth quarter. During the ensuing conference call, the only thing the analysts want to talk about is AIG's super-senior exposure.

November 8: Goldman's David Lehman e-mails Forster: "We believe the next step should include a line by line comparison of GS vs. AIG-FP prices. . . . Can we set aside 30 minutes to discuss live today or tomorrow?"

November 16: Société Générale demands $1.7 billion on a portfolio of $13.6 billion. Merrill Lynch demands $610 million on a portfolio of $7.8 billion. "Their average price is 84.20 [cents on the dollar]," Forster tells Cassano in an e-mail. Goldman's prices are much lower—in the high sixties.

November 18: Goldman ups its credit default swap protection on AIG to $1.9 billion.

November 23: AIG posts $1.5 billion in collateral, bringing its total to nearly $2 billion. Goldman's demands rise to $3 billion.

November 27: Cassano sends an e-mail to Bill Dooley at headquarters laying out, seemingly for the first time, all of AIG-FP's counterparty exposures as well as the collateral calls that have come in so far. It is a sobering document. Merrill Lynch has bought protection on $9.92 billion worth of triple-A tranches from FP and is demanding $610 million. Bank of Montreal wants $41 million on its $1.6 billion portfolio. Calyon, the investment banking division of the French bank Crédit Agricole, is demanding $345 million on its $4.5 billion portfolio. UBS has a $6.3 billion portfolio; it wants $40 million from AIG. A half dozen other big banks have billions of dollars worth of super-seniors insured by AIG and haven't yet made a collateral call—but obviously they could any day. And of course there's Goldman Sachs, which has a total of $23 billion in super-senior exposure insured by AIG-FP. It is demanding not millions like everyone else, but billions.

November 29: Eight thirty a.m. A week after Thanksgiving and four months after Goldman's first collateral call, AIG's top executives—among them Sullivan, Lewis, Dooley, and Steve Bensinger, the company's chief financial officer—finally meet to talk, via a conference call, about the mounting problem. Cassano, Forster, and a third AIG-FP executive join them on the phone. Three auditors from PricewaterhouseCoopers, including Tim Ryan, the lead auditor of the AIG account, also participate in the meeting. Someone takes notes, which are later obtained by the investigators.

By the time that late November meeting took place, AIG's top executives were well aware of the collateral calls. Prying the information out of Cassano, however, hadn't been easy.* In early August, about a week after the first one, AIG's auditors had scheduled a meeting with Cassano and several other FP executives on another topic. One of the auditors mentioned, more or less in passing, that he had heard a rumor that FP had been hit with collateral calls. Cassano acknowledged that FP had received a collateral call from Goldman but pooh-poohed its significance, arguing that the market would come back once traders returned from vacation. The auditors accepted the rationale and moved on to their main topic.

Toward the end of August, AIG CFO Steve Bensinger also began picking up rumors that FP was getting collateral calls. He asked one of his deputies, Elias Habayeb, CFO for the AIG's financial services division, to call Cassano and find out. Again, Cassano acknowledged the calls but dismissed their significance. Habayeb, having crossed swords with Cassano in the past, was not so quick to accept his say-so. Over the ensuing weeks—especially as the end of the quarter approached—Habayeb lobbed e-mail after e-mail into Cassano and his top deputies, trying to find out how the securities were being valued and to what extent the problems were. Cassano, annoyed by the e-mails, would assign one of his minions to respond.

At four thirty on October 8, for instance, Habayeb sent a lengthy e-mail to Cassano with a series of "follow-up questions" about valuing the super-senior portfolio, which FP needed to do quickly since the quarter had ended eight days earlier. "When should I expect to receive the valuation of the SS CDS (portfolios D & E) using the BET as of September 30, 2007?" was one question. (BET stood for binomial expansion technique, a methodology also

---

* Cassano's lawyers deny that he did anything wrong in his handling of the collateral calls. "Mr. Cassano followed appropriate procedures in a timely manner to report to his boss and outside auditors on the first collateral call by Goldman Sachs in early August 2007," they wrote in an e-mail. "Indeed, the information provided by Mr. Cassano was circulated through appropriate channels to AIG's CFO by mid-August." In addition, they deny that Mr. Cassano "had not prepared his company for the collateral calls—indeed, during Mr. Cassano's tenure, he had the tools to resist and reduce the collateral calls based on fundamental analysis and contractual defenses. This is why, during Mr. Cassano's tenure, the company had more than sufficient liquidity to meet collateral demands." They point out that after a lengthy investigation the Justice Department decided not to bring charges against Mr. Cassano.

used by the rating agencies, which FP was trying to quickly adopt.) "With respect to the valuations using BET, how are the effects of hedges reflected or not reflected in these estimates?" was another question. Habayeb concluded gently, "I understand that everyone is working hard . . . I further appreciate that this is not an easy exercise. However, as you can imagine, this has become the hottest subject at 70 Pine" (70 Pine was the Wall Street location of AIG's headquarters).

Three hours later, Cassano forwarded Habayeb's e-mail to his lieutenants. "More love notes from Elias," he wrote. "Please go through the same drill of drafting answers. . . ."

Meanwhile, AIG's auditors at PricewaterhouseCoopers had begun viewing the collateral calls as far more serious business than they had a few weeks earlier. Goldman Sachs, which was also a client of PWC, helped push it in this direction. At Goldman the collateral dispute was important enough that it was being discussed at the board level; its auditors sat in on those discussions. "It was a constant focus inside Goldman Sachs," says a former partner. As the ongoing dispute with AIG worsened, several Goldman Sachs executives began asking their auditors how it could be that "you have one set of numbers for one firm and a totally different set of valuations for another firm?" The lead partner on the Goldman account—who had nothing to do with AIG—told the executives he would take it up with HQ. Which he did. It wasn't long before PWC was bearing down on FP and AIG as well.

The essential problem FP faced as it grappled with how to value the superseniors was that it had never really thought about liquidity risk. Its models had always measured one thing: credit risk. That is, what was the likelihood of a triple-A tranche defaulting, which would cause FP to have to pay off the bonds in their entirety? Cassano had always been fixated on that question because that is where he saw the risk. And since AIG's risk models consistently showed there was virtually no credit risk, it always valued the securities at par.

But now, with the market in "a state of panic," as Cassano described it, the only question that mattered was what they were worth *today*. What could they be sold for in the marketplace? If it was less than 100 percent on the dollar—as it clearly was—then AIG-FP had a contractual obligation to put up collateral. That was the liquidity risk: the risk that the continuing drip, drip, drip of collateral calls would drain AIG-FP of cash and ultimately create a run on the firm that would destroy it—in much the same way that the Bear hedge funds had been destroyed.

Incredibly, this was a form of risk that Cassano had apparently never considered, and therefore had never modeled for. It was also a risk that AIG executives like Habayeb had never accounted for, in large part because they hadn't even known it existed. (That is why, too late, the company was now trying to adopt the BET methodology.)

In the short term, the problem was that the market for triple-A tranches of multisector CDOs was frozen. There was no way to use trading data to establish values for the securities because no one was trading the securities. Nobody knew what a CDO was worth anymore, nobody trusted anybody else's marks, and nobody dared to make an actual trade to find out. It was as if everybody in the mortgage market, having enjoyed a long, drunken revelry, was finally sobering up. Looking in the mirror was not a pleasant experience.

Thus everyone on Wall Street had to rely on models to come up with new marks. There was no other way to do it. This is also why everyone's marks varied so widely. Everyone had different inputs; the imperfections of quant-style modeling had never been so clear. Merrill Lynch was also marking down its securities. Its marks, however, were much higher than Goldman's; as Cassano liked to point out, Merrill's marks were around ninety cents on the dollar, while Goldman's were in the sixties and low seventies. Because Goldman's marks were so low, AIG-FP viewed them mainly as an example of "Goldman being Goldman," taking undue advantage of the situation to inflict pain on AIG.* But the fact that FP didn't have its own valuation model made it difficult to refute Goldman's marks.

Goldman would later insist that it was not trying to gouge AIG—that it alone was being realistic about its marks. One of its tried-and-true techniques, when counterparties objected to its marks, was to offer to sell at the low price to the counterparty. Not once did a counterparty accept the offer, which, to Goldman, was proof that its marks weren't low *enough*. Goldman would also later point out that because it had used AIG to hedge trades, it did not pocket the cash it got from AIG, but handed it over to the counterparties on the

---

* This view would gain great currency during the various investigations that took place in the wake of the financial crisis. Phil Angelides, the chairman of the Financial Crisis Inquiry Commission, would later question whether Goldman was acting like a "cheetah chasing down a weak member of the herd."

other side of the trade. In other words, it had no motive for putting the screws to AIG because the money wasn't going into its own pocket.

At that November 29 meeting, the one in which the top brass for FP and AIG finally met to hash out the situation, Cassano told the others that FP was already in the process of "going to ground" to create a new model that would allow it to value the super-seniors as quickly as possible. Yet at the same time, he once again downplayed the importance of the collateral calls. "Collateral calls are part of the business," he shrugged, adding that he "does not see this as a material issue with GS or any of the other counterparties," according to the notes of the meeting.

Then he was asked how the dispute might affect AIG's profits for the upcoming quarter. "JC noted if we agreed to GS values could be an impact of $5bn for the quarter," the notes read. "MS"—Martin Sullivan—"noted this would eliminate the quarter's profits. . . . JC noted that this was not what he was proposing but illustrative of a worse [sic] case scenario." Forster would later tell the Financial Crisis Inquiry Commission that, upon hearing the $5 billion figure, Sullivan said the number would give him a heart attack. (Sullivan later testified that he didn't remember saying that.) And with that, the meeting ended.

Or so Cassano thought. In fact, after the FP executives got off the phone, the accountants stayed in the room with Sullivan and Bensinger to discuss what they had just heard. If the first part of the meeting had been troubling for Sullivan, this latter part was even worse.

One gets the sense, reading the notes of the meeting, that the Cassano conversation was the last straw for the accountants. PWC lead Tim Ryan was not nearly as calm about the collateral calls as Cassano had been; on the contrary, he was quite agitated. He could see, in a way the AIG executives themselves could not, how their poor risk management practices were creating problems. He listed some of the things that bothered him: The fact that FP had posted $2 billion in collateral without bothering to inform headquarters. The way FP was "managing" the valuation process of the super-seniors. The growing exposure at the securities lending program. And the fact that the risk managers had inexplicably allowed the securities lending program to increase its exposure to subprime securities at the same time that FP was reducing its exposure.

"While no conclusions have been reached," Ryan told Sullivan and Bensinger, according to the notes, "we believe that these items together raise control concerns around risk management that could be a material weakness."

For Sullivan, there were no two scarier words than "material weakness." If that wound up being the accountants' conclusion, it would have to be disclosed to investors—and that would be devastating. He promised to do whatever he had to do to avoid such a declaration. And on that sobering note, the meeting finally ended.

AIG had a long-scheduled investors' meeting set for Wednesday, December 5, 2007. The planned topic was the company's life insurance and retirement services businesses. But as the rumors continued to swirl about AIG's subprime exposure, Sullivan decided to change the focus. The company would talk instead about its credit default swap business, along with the rest of its exposure to the mortgage market.

It was a very long meeting. Sullivan began by noting AIG's profitability over the past few years, its strong capital position and cash flow ($30 billion in the first nine months of 2007), and its lack of debt. "We have the ability to hold devalued investments to recovery," he told investors. "That's very important. . . . AIG-FP has very large notional amounts of exposure related to its super-senior credit derivative portfolio. But because this business is carefully underwritten and structured . . . we believe the probability that it will sustain an economic loss is close to zero."

Over the course of the day (with a break for lunch), fourteen AIG executives made presentations—including Cassano, Forster, model expert Gary Gorton, and Bob Lewis. Every one of them said essentially the same thing: there was little or no chance that the tranches AIG had either insured (in the case of FP) or bought (in the case of other AIG divisions) could ever lose money. Of the fourteen, nobody said this more fervently, or more often, than Cassano. "[W]e have an extremely low loss rate in these portfolios and the underlying reference obligations have a relatively low downgrade migration from the rating agencies," he said in a typical remark. "It is very difficult to see how there can be any losses in these portfolios." (Four months earlier, during an earnings call, Cassano had made a similar remark: "It is hard for us, without being flippant, to even see a scenario . . . that would see us losing one dollar in any of these transactions." That line would come back to haunt Cassano, as it was quoted ad nauseam in the aftermath of the crisis.) At least half a dozen times he rolled out all the explanations he had been using to push back against Goldman: The due diligence that had gone into assembling the subprime tranches AIG insured. The fact that it had little or no exposure to 2006 and 2007 vintages. The amount of subordination in the CDOs AIG insured, meaning that hell would have to come close to freezing over before any of AIG's super-seniors defaulted. He acknowledged that FP was in disputes with counterparties over marks but described those disagreements as "parlor games."

"There is a major disconnect in the market," he claimed, "between what the market is doing versus the economic realities of our portfolio." In other words, in Cassano's view, the market was simply wrong. And since the market didn't understand the strength of AIG's underlying collateral, he was damned if he was going to begin marking it down in any meaningful way. (He did tell the gathering that AIG was writing down another $500 million in November, but that was a pittance in the grand scheme of things.) "If you ask me how I manage the business," he said, "it's the fundamental underwriting that is the first line of defense, the first line of protection, the first thing that gets you comfortable in this business." Even now, months after the collateral calls began, Cassano still seemed unable to comprehend that the issue he was facing had nothing to do with the "fundamental underwriting" of the CDOs AIG insured. The issue was that the collateral triggers were putting the entire corporation at risk. AIG may have had plenty of capital, as Sullivan had suggested, but because it was an insurance company, that capital was strictly regulated and very little of it could be used to shore up AIG-FP as it faced the growing onslaught of collateral calls. The notion that FP was invulnerable because of its parent's financial strength—a notion the market had accepted for years—was suddenly exposed as a giant illusion. It was just the opposite: FP's sudden vulnerability to liquidity risk was endangering the larger company. That's what Cassano didn't understand.

When the time came for questions, most analysts seemed to accept Cassano's version of reality. Several, however, did not. One investor— unidentified in the transcript of the meeting—while acknowledging to Cassano that "you've clearly demonstrated no economic loss," asked what should have been an obvious question: "[W]hat if you did use the ABX index and the counterparties? What would your marks be?"

"It's nonsensical," Cassano replied curtly.

"But what would the nonsensical number—?"

"I don't know," Cassano cut him off. "It's nonsensical."

"Could it be north of $5 billion?" the investor pressed.

"You know I have no— Do you have any idea? I don't know. Look, we're in the business of going to the core of the fundamentals. The ABX is just not representative of the pool of business that we have." And that was that.

A few minutes later, Josh Smith, an analyst at TIAA-CREF, the financial services giant, posed another important question. "I noticed that some of the underlying collateral has been replaced with '06/'07," he began. "I think people take a lot of comfort that you stopped writing the '06/'07. Can you quantify the risk that the underlying collateral from the earlier vintages gets replaced with this '06/'07 stuff, which isn't as good?"

Here was something else almost no one had noticed before—either inside or outside of AIG. For all of FP's pride in having ended its multisector CDO business in 2005, it simply was not true that the referenced securities didn't include those terrible 2006 and 2007 vintages. A number of the CDOs that AIG insured allowed for the CDO manager to replace older subprime bonds with newer ones—bonds that would invariably generate higher yields precisely because they were riskier. AIG didn't even have to be informed that the collateral was being swapped out.

Take, for example, the $1.5 billion CDO known as Davis Square III, which Goldman Sachs underwrote in 2004. The CDO manager, Lou Lucido, worked for the Los Angeles investment firm TCW Group. During much of 2006 and 2007, Lucido was busy boosting the yield on Davis Square III by putting in subprime bonds from later vintages and kicking out many of the bonds that had been in the CDO when AIG agreed to insure it. Bloomberg estimated that, by 2008, "Lucido's team, following criteria set by Goldman Sachs, changed almost one-third of the collateral in Davis Square III." By May 2008, Davis Square III had been downgraded to junk, costing AIG $616 million in additional collateral calls—which came, of course, from Goldman Sachs.

At the investor meeting, however, none of this was divulged. When asked point-blank what percentage of AIG's collateral was 2006 and 2007 subprime vintages, Forster—whom Cassano had kicked the question to—said he didn't know.

Still, in the immediate aftermath of the meeting, the market seemed pleased. AIG's stock had been around $58 a share in the week preceding the investor meeting; after the meeting, it got a nice little pop, to $61 a share. And the meeting seemed to have energized Cassano as well. Two days after the meeting, on December 7, FP sent Goldman a letter demanding the return of $1.5 billion in collateral. Goldman, of course, refused. Several of the new marks that AIG-FP provided showed FP valuing the securities at par. David Lehman would later tell the Financial Crisis Inquiry Commission that AIG-FP's valuation was "not credible." He was right.

Though he didn't realize it, Cassano's biggest problem wasn't Goldman Sachs. It was Tim Ryan at PricewaterhouseCoopers. All through November and December, in meetings with management, with the audit committee, and with the full board of directors, Ryan continued to raise concerns about the way FP was valuing the super-seniors, about the way it was managing the process, and about the inability or unwillingness of AIG management to get involved. While Cassano was focused on fending off more collateral calls— by the end of the year counterparties were demanding $2.7 billion, of which $2.1 billion were demands from Goldman—Ryan was making the case that AIG could not continue to allow Cassano and his FP team to manage the situation themselves.

It wasn't until the beginning of 2008 that headquarters finally got involved, but by then it was too late. In a mid-January meeting with the audit committee, according to the notes of the meeting, "Mr. Habayeb believes that he is limited in his ability to influence change, and the super-senior valuation process is not going as smoothly as it could." Ryan responded, essentially, that this was not acceptable.

Meanwhile, Cassano was scrambling to come up with a value for the portfolio in time to report year-end results in early February. It was clear that there were going to have to be more write-downs. Using a theory he called a "negative basis adjustment," Cassano estimated the write-down would be $1.2 billion. (Essentially, he was claiming that this adjustment reflected the difference between the way the swaps were priced and the way the underlying securities were priced.) Without this adjustment, the write-down would be $5 billion. The board—and the accountants—first learned about Cassano's theory in a January board meeting. The auditors were not pleased, and they would have the final say. Over the next few weeks, Cassano attempted to convince the auditors that the negative basis adjustment was a legitimate valuation method. But Ryan wasn't biting. It had no basis in accounting rules, he said.

In late January, Ryan dropped the hammer, declaring that AIG had "a material weakness in its internal control over financial reporting and oversight relating to the fair value of the AIG-FP super-senior credit default swap portfolio." On February 5, AIG released the news of the material weakness in an SEC filing. The stock sank. Counterparties that had previously sat on the sidelines began demanding collateral. Cassano was furious. The "material weakness" announcement had "weakened our negotiation position as to collateral calls," he wrote in an e-mail.

But it was over for Cassano. The board no longer trusted him and insisted that Sullivan fire him, something Sullivan was still reluctant to do, according to a former AIG executive. Cassano made it easy for him.

"Joe, we have these issues," Sullivan said.

"Should I retire?" Cassano replied.

"Yes."

"Joe was just worn out," explains a former executive. A few weeks later, when the news was made public, Cassano was at AIG headquarters. Someone asked him if he had told his mother, who was in her eighties. "No," he replied. "She doesn't know what I do." A few minutes later, the phone rang. It was his mother, who had just heard the news. "No, Mom," Cassano could be heard saying on the phone. "I'm all right." He left with $34 million in unvested bonuses and a consulting contract worth $1 million a month.

When the year-end results were finally announced, on February 28, 2008, the super-senior write-down wasn't $1.2 billion, or even $5 billion. It was $11.47 billion. The following week, Goldman Sachs raised its collateral demands to $4.2 billion.

By June 2008, Martin Sullivan was gone as well. In May, the board forced Sullivan to remove Bensinger as CFO. At the same time, AIG managed to raise some $20 billion, which Sullivan—and everyone else—felt would be enough to carry the company through a possible crisis. But the collateral calls kept coming; by the end of the second quarter of 2008, AIG had posted $20 billion in cash to meet them. The securities lending problems continued to get worse. The PWC auditors continued to put pressure on management and the board to improve their internal controls. The value of the subprime securities FP insured continued to deteriorate. The Office of Thrift Supervision, which regulated AIG, got into the act, too. (AIG had purchased a small thrift in the 1990s, and when AIG, like the investment banks, needed a holding company supervisor because of requirements by the European Union, the OTS took on that role.) After the material weakness announcement, it began demanding that AIG improve the risk management on its credit default swap portfolio. "There was a sense that we were drifting," says a former executive. "I wouldn't say it was a crisis. But it wasn't normal."

However heroically he had performed during AIG's 2005 crisis, Sullivan seemed increasingly lost as the situation worsened. When it became clear that the additional $20 billion in capital hadn't restored confidence in AIG, the board finally—and belatedly—made its move. Several directors went to the chairman of the AIG board, Robert Willumstad, a former top Citigroup official, and asked him to step in as chief executive. Willumstad had only joined the board in 2006 and had recently started a private equity firm, which he would have to leave to take the AIG job. Reluctantly, he agreed to become the CEO. On June 15, Martin Sullivan left the company where he had spent his entire adult life.

Three days later, AIG-FP agreed to post $5.4 billion to Goldman Sachs—including cash to cover losses in five of the Abacus deals.

On his fourth day as CEO, Willumstad met with Larry Fink of BlackRock and asked him to evaluate the subprime exposure. He wanted to write down as much as he possibly could, as quickly as he could, and be done with it. He also thought a BlackRock imprimatur would finally give AIG the ability to fight back against the collateral calls. In August, he announced AIG's second-quarter results—a $5.5 billion loss. He also announced that he was conducting a strategic review of the entire company, and would soon unveil his plan. He hoped the market would give him time to get through the review. He promised to present his new strategic plan to investors on September 26.

But by then, AIG had been rescued by its new majority owner, the United States government.

22

The Volcano Erupts

And what was Fannie Mae doing during that awful summer of 2007, as the mortgage market descended into utter chaos and decades of wrongheaded policies, craven behavior, foolish mistakes, and misguided beliefs had come together to create a financial volcano that was beginning to stir? Panicking, perhaps?

No, Fannie was plotting its comeback.

Fannie at that point held or guaranteed almost $2.7 trillion in mortgages; Freddie another $2 trillion. Unlike John Paulson or Andrew Redleaf, they had no ability to short the housing market. Their singular role, set out in the charter that had long given them their advantages over their market competitors, was to support the housing market and help the country's citizens achieve the American Dream. Yet the fact that the housing market was in decline—instead of scaring the GSEs, as it should have—was a source of tremendous optimism. Subprime lenders were shutting down. Wall Street was afraid to securitize mortgages. Banks were reluctant to make new housing loans, since they could no longer sell them to Wall Street. Only mortgages guaranteed by the GSEs were viewed as safe enough to be sold and securitized. At long last, they were back in the driver's seat. The country needed Fannie and Freddie—truly needed them—in a way it hadn't in years. "I thought this was an opportunity for the GSEs to demonstrate their value to the world," Fannie CEO Dan Mudd would later say.

Politicians, housing advocates, Washington think tank types—they were all suddenly rallying around Fannie Mae and Freddie Mac. Democrats like senators Charles Schumer of New York and Chris Dodd of Connecticut, both high-ranking members of the Senate banking committee, were pushing hard to expand the GSEs' powers. Republicans weren't far behind. "This is what you're here for," Mudd recalls legislators of both parties telling him. Even the

Bush White House was backing away from its long-standing hostility toward the GSEs; no matter how much you might be ideologically opposed to Fannie and Freddie, it was hard to go after them when they were the only thing propping up the housing market. "The political environment was 'We're inviting you in! Come be part of the solution,'" Mudd later recalled.

By the end of August 2007, Fannie's stock, which had dropped to a low of $48 in the spring of 2005, was almost back to its 2004 peak of $70. "Politics seems increasingly a plus for GSEs," wrote Morgan Stanley analyst Ken Posner that fall. "Housing market stability is in the process of trumping the anti-GSE ideology that has held sway in recent years."

That summer, Mudd drafted the company's strategic plan for the next four years. He had stars in his eyes. He pointed out that over the last ten years, Fannie Mae's credit losses had amounted to $3.1 billion—compared to profits of $44.2 billion. "We have a great opportunity by taking more credit risk on the balance sheet." He called on the company to go "deeper into segments where we only have scratched the surface"—meaning, of course, subprime mortgages.

Over the years, whenever Alan Greenspan and others had criticized the GSEs, it was the interest rate risk they worried about. Fannie and Freddie were so huge, they believed, that it would take only one big hedging mistake—and a sudden shift in interest rates—to bring about catastrophe. But they had never focused on credit risk—the risk that the mortgages Fannie and Freddie guaranteed or held would default. Maybe it was because they had been so blind over the years to *all* the credit risk in the system, from subprime originators to AIG, that they never saw it coming with Fannie and Freddie, either.

Thus it was that in 2007 Fannie and Freddie would add $600 billion in net new mortgage debt to their books, debt that would wind up being highly destructive. They would continue to buy and guarantee mortgages well into 2008. And thus it was that the GSEs would lumber, slowly but inevitably, toward a cliff they didn't see. The financial crisis came on in fits and starts, and all the while Fannie Mae and Freddie Mac were accumulating the very mortgage risk that would cause the long-dormant volcano to finally erupt.

<hr>

With all the problems he was facing, Fannie and Freddie were hardly high on Hank Paulson's list of priorities. As Treasury secretary, he kept in close touch with all the Wall Street CEOs; he knew exactly what was going on. In his memoir, he describes a dinner in June 2007 with a handful of Wall Street chieftains, including Jamie Dimon of J.P. Morgan, Lloyd Blankfein of Goldman Sachs, and Chuck Prince, the CEO of Citigroup. "All were concerned with excessive risk taking in the markets and appalled by the erosion of underwriting standards," he writes. Prince, he added, "asked whether, given the competitive pressures, there wasn't a role for regulators to tamp down some of the riskier practices. Basically, he asked: 'Isn't there something you can do to order us not to take all of these risks?'"

Late July saw the German government bail out IKB. In early August, American Home Mortgage Investment Corporation, which was unable to sell its commercial paper, filed for bankruptcy. A few weeks later, Countrywide had to draw down that line of credit, signaling it was in trouble. On August 21, an auction of four-week Treasury bills nearly failed because the demand was so massive it overwhelmed the dealers. In mid-September, the British bank Northern Rock had to be rescued by the Bank of England.

The banks were all announcing huge write-downs while frantically trying to raise additional capital—something Paulson was pushing them to do. But the new capital was quickly overwhelmed by yet more losses. The SIVs that some banks had all used to off-load debt and lower their capital requirements were foundering as the money market funds began dumping their commercial paper. Treasury came up with a plan to create a "super SIV," which the banks would fund, that would buy the assets from the individual SIVs. The plan fell through. Citi—which had been the most promiscuous user of SIVs—had to put the SIV assets back on its balance sheet, at exactly the wrong time, and they eventually contributed to its many billions of dollars in write-downs. Paulson and his staff were frantically busy, trying to come up with solutions and stave off disaster. His restless energy went into overdrive. Today's idea wasn't necessarily consistent with yesterday's idea, but then, the problems were unprecedented. There was no manual for what to do when you're the Treasury secretary trying to prevent a financial crisis. As the year wore on, he and his small team at Treasury began to joke that they felt like Butch Cassidy and the Sundance Kid: they were being pursued and cornered, and even though they'd come out with guns blazing, they couldn't ever seem to get out in front of the problem.

Though he was a Bush appointee, Paulson had no patience for the White House's "holy war"—his words—against the GSEs. Yes, they were flawed institutions that were far too big and, quite possibly, posed systemic risk. But Paulson was a pragmatist. He dealt with things as they were. Fannie and Freddie weren't going away; they were a problem that needed to be managed. Besides, the GSEs were only partly to blame for the monsters they'd become. "This was created by Congress," he'd say.

When he did focus on Fannie and Freddie, he didn't gnash his teeth at the moral hazard they posed. Rather, he worked to reduce that moral hazard. One step was to get Fannie and Freddie a new regulator. It was no secret that OFHEO was outmatched; practically from the moment he was named Treasury secretary, Paulson had worked to push through legislation to create a new regulator that would have real authority to set capital requirements, conduct serious audits, and even—if it came to that—wind down the GSEs. To get such legislation, he had to compromise with Democrats. Paulson had no problem with that, but it was anathema to the White House staff. Paulson was perfectly willing to override them and go to President Bush directly, which he did. In 2006, he began working with the Democrats to get legislation that would create a better, tougher regulator. The effort ran into congressional roadblocks. Fannie's enemies—including its White House enemies—started speculating that Paulson was in the tank for Fannie because it was a big client of Goldman's. (Actually, it was a big client of every firm on Wall Street.) Goldman Sachs board member Jim Johnson, a typical charge went, had been the chair of the compensation committee when Paulson was CEO and had helped set his pay. And so on.

The second step Paulson took was to urge the GSEs to raise capital, the same way he was urging all the big firms to raise capital. He liked to say that he'd never seen a CEO of a financial institution get fired for having too much capital. And indeed, the GSEs did raise additional capital, selling a combined $13 billion in equity and preferred stock.

But $13 billion was a drop in the ocean for Fannie and Freddie. By 2008, the two companies held a total $84 billion in capital—less than 2 percent of what was, by that point, a combined $5.3 trillion in mortgages they owned or guaranteed. Even more than the banks, Fannie and Freddie could not afford major write-downs. There was absolutely no margin for error.

Yet Fannie and Freddie *were* taking write-downs. In February 2008, the GSEs announced their 2007 earnings: both lost money—$2.1 billion in the case of Fannie Mae, while Freddie Mac lost $3.1 billion, its first annual loss ever. The reason was deteriorating mortgages. Yet at the same time, they were taking on more and more risk—because nobody else could, or would. By early 2008, Fannie and Freddie were buying four out of every five U.S. mortgages, double their market share from two years earlier. In mid-February, President Bush signed a law that included a provision to raise the size of the jumbo mortgages Fannie and Freddie could buy, from $417,000 to $729,750 in high-cost areas—a stunning, unnecessary increase that was supported by both Democratic Speaker of the House Nancy Pelosi and Republican John Boehner, the House minority leader. (Paulson opposed the increase.)* It was insanity. Jim Lockhart, a Yale fraternity buddy of Bush's who had become the chairman of OFHEO, told Congress, "The GSEs have become the dominant funding mechanism for the entire mortgage system in these troubling times. In doing so, they have been reducing risks in the market, but concentrating mortgage risks on themselves."

It was Bear Stearns that went first, in March of 2008.

If the failure of the two Bear Stearns hedge funds in July 2007 served as a kind of prologue to the financial crisis—a taste of what was to come—then the collapse of Bear Stearns itself was a rousing act one. There wasn't much substantive difference between the two failures except in scale. Bear Stearns was awash in mortgage-backed securities of all sorts. It used them as collateral for its repo transactions. It had them on its balance sheet. It traded in CDOs and CDOs squared. Because it was both the smallest of the five major American investment banks and the most obviously exposed to mortgage risk, the market started asking questions about the value of its collateral. The answers didn't really matter; the questions were all it took to kill the firm.

"The interdependent relationships between banks and brokerages and institutional investors strike most laymen as impenetrably complex, but a simple ingredient lubricates the engine: trust," wrote Alan "Ace" Greenberg, former Bear Stearns chairman, in a memoir co-authored by Mark Singer. "Without reciprocal trust between the parties to any securities transaction, the money stops. Doubt fills the vacuum, and credit and liquidity are the chief casualties.

---

* Paulson fought the increase because he didn't see why the GSEs were needed to support the high-end housing market, and he told a group of Senate Republicans that he would hold firm. But it was a losing battle; raising the limits was popular with members of Congress on both sides of the aisle. In a meeting with Pelosi and Boehner, Pelosi told Paulson they were going to raise the limits. She said it in a way that suggested he would be unable to stop her. The she laughingly showed him a note that Boehner had slipped her. "Let's roll Hank," it said.

Bad news, whether it derives from false rumor or verifiable fact, then has an alarming capacity to become contagious and self-perpetuating."

Which is exactly what happened. On Monday, March 10—the beginning of its last week as an independent firm—Bear Stearns's stock stood at around $70 a share. It had bank financing of about $120 billion and $18 billion in cash. But, recalled Greenberg, "some of our counterparties were expressing skepticism about our liquidity and were wary of dealing with us." On Tuesday, Christopher Cox, the chairman of the SEC, told the press, "We have a good deal of comfort about the capital cushions at these firms." It didn't help. Bear's cash fell to $15 billion as hedge funds began pulling their money out. One hedge fund withdrew all the securities it kept at Bear—"tens of billions of dollars' worth," wrote Greenberg. "Before the trading day closed, the Dutch bank Rabobank Group had told us that they weren't renewing a $500 million loan due to mature at the end of the week and probably wouldn't renew a $2 billion line of credit the following week." On Wednesday, CEO Alan Schwartz went on CNBC, where he denied that Bear Stearns was having liquidity problems. If anything, that only made matters worse: going on TV to deny liquidity problems was likely to *create* liquidity problems, because it would spook lenders. Sure enough, repo lenders started refusing to roll over Bear's commercial paper. By Thursday night, Bear was down to $5 billion in cash—though, notes Greenberg, "in light of the obligations that came due Friday morning, for all intents and purposes the figure was zero." By Friday, the stock had dropped to around $30 a share. Bush was scheduled to give a speech at the Economic Club in New York that day. Already nervous at the beginning of the week, Paulson pressed Bush not to say there would be "no bailouts."

And by Monday morning, March 17, Bear Stearns had been sold to J.P. Morgan for $2 a share. Paulson, who had urged J.P. Morgan to make the deal so that Bear wouldn't go bankrupt—and wreak havoc on the financial system—had insisted on that punitive price. Later, facing a revolt by Bear shareholders, J.P. Morgan raised the price to $10 a share. In his book, Paulson describes the new price as "an unseemly precedent to reward the shareholders of a firm that had been bailed out by the government." And it had, because J.P. Morgan would not have done the deal if the Fed hadn't agreed to provide a $30 billion loan to a stand-alone entity that would buy a pool of Bear's mortgages that J.P. Morgan didn't want.

The banks' dirty little secret was now out in the open. It wasn't just Fannie and Freddie that had been creating moral hazard all these years. So had the nation's big banks. They had taken on terrible risks, built up immense leverage, and created such tight interconnections with their derivatives books that the failure of any one of them could bring down all the others. When things got bad, they assumed they had an "implicit government guarantee," just like Fannie and Freddie. In *On the Brink*, Paulson recalls a phone call he received from his former number two at Goldman, Lloyd Blankfein. It was the Saturday that Treasury and the Fed were negotiating with J.P. Morgan to take over Bear. "I could hear the fear in his voice," writes Paulson. The Goldman CEO told him that "the market expected a Bear rescue. If there wasn't one, all hell would break loose."

—⊶⊷—

At Fannie Mae and Freddie Mac, the losses continued to grow. Fannie was about to slide under OFHEO's capital requirements, which executives referred to as "the line of death." Even though they were convinced they could survive the losses, they worried that if they slid below even by a dollar, OFHEO would punish them in some way.

Some in the government were starting to freak out about the GSEs. In an e-mail on March 16 to others at Treasury, Bob Steel, the undersecretary for domestic finance and Paulson's point man on Fannie and Freddie, wrote, "I was leaned on very hard by Bill Dudley"—an executive vice president at the New York Fed—"to harden substantially the gty." That meant that the New York Fed wanted the U.S. government to explicitly stand behind the GSE's debt. It was an expression of the fear officials were starting to feel about the GSEs. And yet, on March 19, four days after Bear was rescued, OFHEO, backed by Treasury, issued a press release announcing that it had agreed to *reduce* Fannie and Freddie's capital cushion, which, claimed OFHEO, was "expected to provide up to $200 billion of immediate liquidity to the mortgage-backed securities market." A month earlier, OFHEO had loosened the portfolio caps the GSEs had agreed to after the accounting scandals. The two changes together "should allow the GSEs to purchase or guarantee about $2 trillion in mortgages this year," OFHEO reported. "These companies are safe and sound, and . . . they continue to be safe and sound," said Lockhart.

Lockhart should have known better. What OFHEO had really done was reduce Fannie and Freddie's protection against insolvency—even though the companies were edging closer to it every day. Because if it didn't, no one in America would be able to buy a house.

Later that day, Josh Rosner released a report entitled "OFHEO Got Rolled." "We view any reduction as a comment not on the current safety and soundness of the GSEs but on the burgeoning panic in Washington," he wrote. "While many are viewing these actions as a positive sign, we continue to believe that they highlight that the building is shaking from the top to bottom."

———∞———

"From March to September," says a former Treasury official, "the big question was, how would we attempt to deal with the next shoe dropping?" Nobody doubted another shoe was coming.

With his antennae so attuned to Wall Street, Paulson had long thought the next shoe could be Lehman Brothers, the second smallest of the big five. When Bear Stearns started its downward spiral, Paulson had called Lehman CEO Dick Fuld, who was on a business trip in India. "You better get back here," Paulson told him, according to *Too Big to Fail,* Andrew Ross Sorkin's book about Wall Street during the financial crisis.

Fuld was an aloof, stubborn executive who had run Lehman since 1994 and had seen his firm through crises before. He felt certain he could do it again. But he was playing a dangerous game. Instead of getting "closer to home," like Goldman Sachs, Lehman had decided to double down, in large part by financing and investing in big commercial real estate deals at the very height of the real estate bubble. Between the fourth quarter of 2006 and the first quarter of 2008, Lehman's assets had increased by almost 50 percent, to some $400 billion. Its leverage ratio was 30 to 1. "Pedal to the metal," is how David Goldfarb, Lehman's chief strategy officer, described the firm's growth, according to Lehman's bankruptcy examiner.

All that risk on its books was taking a toll, however. The market was starting to ask questions, just as it had with Bear. The stock was declining. And starting in 2007, according to one well-placed observer, Lehman had begun to lose access to unsecured funding, so it was increasingly dependent on the repo market. But repo lenders had begun to steadily increase the "haircut" they demanded from Lehman. On March 26, Eric Felder, Lehman's U.S. head of global credit products, sent an e-mail to Bart McDade, the head of Lehman's equity capital markets group. "I'm scared that our repo is going to pull away . . . We need to be set up for [commercial paper] going to zero and a meaningful portion of our secured repo fading (not because it makes sense but just because). . . . The reality of our problem lies in our dependence on repo and the scale of the real estate related positions. . . ."*

Ian Lowitt, who was then Lehman's co–chief administrative officer, wrote back, "People are on it. Agree there will be another run, but believe it will be industry wide not Lehman specific. You are not Cassandra, cursed by Apollo to be able to see the future but have no one believe you!!!"

That the government knew Lehman Brothers was playing with fire—and did nothing about it—would become clear in the aftermath of the crisis. The SEC, for instance, would later tell the Lehman bankruptcy examiner that it was well aware that the bank had repeatedly violated its own internal risk limits. But, the agency added, it "did not second-guess Lehman's business decisions so long as the limit excesses were properly escalated within Lehman's management."

The Federal Reserve developed rigorous stress tests for Lehman that were supposed to determine its ability to withstand a run on the bank. The Fed devised two scenarios, which they called Bear and Bear Stearns Lite. Lehman Brothers failed both. The Fed came up with an additional round of tests; Lehman failed those, too. Lehman did pass stress tests of its own devising. "It does not appear that any agency required any action of Lehman in response to the results of stress testing," the examiner later wrote.

And there was strong suspicion that Lehman's marks were inflated. Indeed, Tim Geithner would later tell the Lehman bankruptcy examiner that a fire sale of assets might have revealed that Lehman "had a lot of air in [its] marks."

What bothered Hank Paulson, though, was that Fuld just didn't seem to share his urgency. Although Fuld did raise $4 billion in additional capital in March, for which Paulson congratulated him, he was deeply resistant to Paulson's constant suggestion that Lehman Brothers was vulnerable and that Fuld needed to find a buyer. Fuld, Paulson would later tell the bankruptcy examiner, was "a person who heard only what he wanted to hear." What he wanted to hear, clearly, was that the government wouldn't let Lehman go under—a view that had become widespread inside the company, even though

---

* Lehman Brothers also used a quirk in the accounting rules to book repo transactions at the end of the quarter as real sales of assets, instead of as temporary financing. This strategy, called Repo 105—because the accounting rules required that the firm deliver assets worth $105 in order to get $100 of cash—enabled Lehman to reduce the leverage it reported. Then, once the new quarter started, Lehman would repurchase the assets. As the crisis deepened, Lehman upped its use of Repo 105, from $38.6 billion at the end of the fourth quarter of 2007 to $50.4 billion by the end of the second quarter of 2008. "Another drug we r on," as McDade later called it in an e-mail.

Paulson says he consistently told Fuld that help would not be forthcoming. "Hank was consistent in emphasizing to Dick, 'You've got to have a plan B and C. Hope isn't a strategy,'" Bob Steel told Vicky Ward, the author of *The Devil's Casino*, a book about the fall of Lehman.

Then again, maybe hope *was* a strategy. Ward also reports that around this time a former Lehman bond trader named Peregrine Moncreiffe bumped into a friend who was working for John Paulson. Fuld had recently visited Paulson's offices. "Fuld told us he's deliberately going to keep the balance sheet big," the friend told Moncreiffe. "He thinks that this way, the government will have no choice but to save him."

On June 9, Lehman preannounced its second-quarter earnings, saying it would lose $2.8 billion. That day, Skip McGee, Lehman's head of investment banking, forwarded a message to Fuld from another banker. "Fyi— representative email," McGee wrote. The message read, "Many, many bankers have been calling me in the last few days. The mood has become truly awfull [sic] and for the first time I am really worried that all of the hard work we have put in over the last 6/7 years could unravel very quickly. . . . Senior managers have to be much less arrogant and internally admit that some major mistakes have been made. Can't continue to say 'we are great and the market doesn't understand.'" Lehman's stock price fell below $30 a share, a 60 percent decline over the past year.

Three days later, Lehman announced that it was firing Erin Callan, its chief financial officer—who had become the face of the firm as she attempted to fight the rumors that it was in trouble—and its president, Joe Gregory. Somebody had to be sacrificed to the market gods, and they were chosen. The next day, Citigroup, which cleared trades for Lehman, asked the company to provide it with a "comfort deposit" of between $3 billion and $5 billion to help cover Citi's exposure to the firm. (The amount was later negotiated down to $2 billion.)

"Market is saying Lehman cannot make it alone," wrote Citigroup risk management officer Thomas Fontana to his colleagues. "Loss of confidence here is huge at the moment."

⚭

On July 10, 2008, a story appeared on the front page of the *Wall Street Journal* that began, "The Bush administration has held talks about what to do in the event mortgage giants Fannie Mae and Freddie Mac falter, according to three people familiar with the matter." The next morning, the *New York Times* chimed in. "[S]enior Bush administration officials are considering a plan to have the government take over one or both of the companies and place them in a conservatorship if their problems worsen," the paper said. Fannie's stock, which had slowly fallen to under $20 over the previous year, dropped 50 percent in two days. It was barely in double figures.

Mudd picked up the phone and called Paulson. "Jesus, Hank," he said. Paulson, says one person familiar with the conversation, told Mudd that he had "raised hell," telling the White House staff—who Mudd assumed were the source of the leaks—that they needed to keep out. (Paulson insists, "I can guarantee with 100 percent certainty that the White House knew nothing about a conservatorship strategy," because at that point, that wasn't part of Treasury's plan.)

Two days later, IndyMac, the Countrywide spinoff, was taken over by the FDIC. IndyMac's distinction had always been that it specialized in Alt-A loans, as opposed to subprime mortgages. The government takeover was a rude awakening for investors who believed that Alt-As were somehow safer than subprime loans. They weren't. And who had more Alt-A exposure—*way* more Alt-A exposure—than anybody else? Fannie and Freddie.

Debt investors around the world owned a staggering $1.7 trillion in either mortgage-backed securities guaranteed by the GSEs or GSE debt, according to the study by Jason Thomas. Suddenly, for the first time in memory, they were net sellers of that debt, unloading some $66 billion in Fannie and Freddie debt securities in July and August. Fannie and Freddie had literally billions of dollars in debt that they would need to roll over in the coming months.

Now Paulson was obsessively focused on Fannie and Freddie. He still didn't know the extent of the credit risk on their books. Indeed, their regulator was still saying they were in good shape, and Paulson had no way of judging for himself whether that assessment was right or wrong. And Fannie and Freddie were every bit as vulnerable to a run on the bank as Bear Stearns—maybe even more vulnerable, because their capital cushion was so small. It really wouldn't take much to put them over the edge.

If panicked investors around the globe started dumping Fannie and Freddie debt, the government would be helpless to do anything about it. That's the only thing Paulson really knew. "I had no power, and the regulator had no power, no responsibility, and no authority," Paulson later said. The would-be reformers had long clamored for a way to wind down a failing GSE. But

Paulson had already failed to push through legislation that might accomplish that.

Paulson's instinct—as it always was when faced with a problem—was to take control and do something. "Hank wanted to fire anyone who said the GSEs were OFHEO's problem," recalls a Treasury official. "He said, 'We own this problem. It's ours to solve.'" But how? The staff worked all weekend to come up with a plan: get Congress to give Treasury "emergency powers," to use Paulson's phrase, that would allow the government to put money into Fannie and Freddie. At the same time, the logjam surrounding the creation of a new regulator had finally broken. And so the bill that finally, at this desperate late date, passed Congress did a few things all at once. It created a new regulator for the GSEs (though it was really the old regulator with a new name). It gave the Federal Reserve power to look at the GSEs, so the Treasury staff didn't have to rely on OFHEO's judgment of their health. It made it easier for the government to take over the companies through conservatorship should they fail—it included, among other things, a provision that if their boards consented to a takeover, shareholders couldn't sue. And it gave Treasury the unlimited ability to use and increase those long-standing $2.25 billion lines of credit that Fannie and Freddie had. At that point, Paulson never intended to use it.

"If you've got a bazooka, and people know you've got it, you may not have to take it out," as Paulson explained it to Congress.

Less than two weeks later, Tim Geithner had a dinner party at the New York Fed, as he often did so the Treasury secretary could talk with Wall Street's chiefs. Paulson explained to the assembled CEOs why his actions on the GSEs should be reassuring to the market. Lloyd Blankfein raised his hand. "Hank, I don't mean to be disrespectful," he said. "But this is a strange market, one that's driven by fear. Stop and think." Blankfein paused before delivering his punch line. "Fannie and Freddie are the U.S. government's SIVs." He finished, "Hank, how long did it take before Citigroup had to step up to its SIVs and put them on its balance sheet?"

"I had to change the subject because the moment he said it, I knew he was right," Paulson later said.

The news of the bazooka did not turn the tide. The irony was powerful. For decades investors had bought Fannie's and Freddie's stocks, happy in the knowledge that the GSEs were backed by an implicit government guarantee. It had always been one of the most attractive things about owning the stock.

But now that the government was saying, quite explicitly, that it would back Fannie and Freddie, investors didn't like it at all. Why would they? The government might put in equity and become a preferred shareholder, putting itself ahead of the common shareholders. Or it might take over Fannie and Freddie and wipe the shareholders out entirely. Everyone saw that the animosity toward the GSEs that had existed for so long in Washington would make it practically impossible for the government to put money into them without punishing their shareholders.

But even if that hadn't been the case, the government's priority wasn't the shareholders. It was preventing the housing market from collapsing. For decades, Fannie and Freddie had worked to maximize profits at the expense of its government mission. Now that mission was paramount. The shareholders would have to fend for themselves. Fannie and Freddie's stocks continued to plummet.

Even after everything that had happened, getting the bill passed required Fannie and Freddie's support. Fannie got language inserted saying that the government could use its bazooka and inject equity only if Fannie approved. But Fannie executives didn't bother to fight the provision about consenting to conservatorship, because they thought that "consent" would require a negotiation. In which case Fannie thought it had a trump card: it could always threaten to shrink the company's balance sheet and stop supporting the mortgage market. And maybe there was a little hubris at work, too. "I used to say that if two accounting scandals, a Republican Congress and White House couldn't kill us, how could you kill us ever?" says a former executive.

The legislation was signed at the end of July. Immediately Paulson brought in bank examiners to comb through the GSEs' books. Just before heading off to Beijing for the summer Olympics—and just before Fannie and Freddie announced that they had lost a combined $3 billion in the first half of 2008—Paulson also hired Morgan Stanley to analyze the companies. He wanted to get an idea of how much money the GSEs could lose on mortgages they owned or guaranteed. He also wanted to get a feel for their ongoing liquidity—whether they would be able to continue to finance their operations. "Hank was very concerned with the overhang of this unraveling, and with $5 trillion, you don't wait for the razor's edge," says one person who was involved.

Three weeks later, on August 19, the Morgan Stanley team told Paulson it thought Fannie and Freddie could lose as much as $50 billion. It was a staggering number, far worse than Fannie's worst estimates. The examiners from the Fed were similarly horrified when they looked closely at the loans that made up the GSEs' Alt-A books. Fannie and Freddie may not have called them subprime, but they sure looked that way to the examiners.

At that moment, upon finally learning how deep Fannie and Freddie's problems were, Paulson decided the government had to take over the companies. "I started to race against the clock," Paulson later recounted. He knew that Lehman Brothers' third-quarter results were going to be disastrous. He was worried that Lehman's problems would spread to the GSEs and trigger a run. He met with Bernanke, who agreed. For the sake of the housing market, the government needed to step in and nationalize the companies. "We had no choice," Paulson would later say. Simply injecting capital—the original heart of the bazooka plan—would be a political disaster for the Treasury, given the Republicans' feelings. Nor, Paulson believed, would it bring back investor confidence. "Why would any sane investor put money into these companies without knowing what the ultimate disposition would be?" Paulson would ask.

On August 26, from the Situation Room on the ground floor of the West Wing, Paulson briefed President Bush, who was at his ranch in Crawford, Texas. He briefed the president a second time on September 4. "Do they know it's coming, Hank?" Bush asked.

"Mr. President," Paulson replied, according to his memoir, "we're going to move quickly and take them by surprise. The first sound they'll hear is their heads hitting the floor."

Even at this late date, Fannie and Freddie had powerful friends on Capitol Hill. Had they gotten advance word, they would surely have pulled every string they had to prevent what was coming. "We had to take them by surprise," Paulson later said. "We just did."

On the Thursday before Labor Day weekend, in a meeting with shareholders, Fannie gave reassurances that the government didn't have anything up its sleeve. The following Friday, September 5, Mudd was summoned to a meeting at the Federal Housing Finance Agency—formerly known as OFHEO—at three p.m. When the Fannie contingent arrived, nobody came to meet them, so they wandered around the lobby. They saw Bernanke come in the front door. They also spotted a *Wall Street Journal* reporter who had been given a heads-up about the meeting. It would have been "almost comical if it weren't tragic," Mudd later said.

In a conference room just off his office, Lockhart was seated between

Bernanke and Paulson. Lockhart read what appeared to be a script citing one regulatory infraction after another before he got to the real point. Although his team, admittedly, had given Fannie a clean bill of health recently, its capital was sorely deficient and the company couldn't fulfill its mission. The message, explains one person who was there, was "If you oppose us, we will fight publicly and fight hard, and do not think that your share price will do well with all of the forces of the government arrayed against you."

Then the government laid out its takeover terms. Existing shareholders of both common and preferred stock in both companies would be largely wiped out. The government would provide no up-front cash, but would put in preferred stock up to a combined $200 billion as equity fell below zero. Fannie and Freddie would be allowed to grow their portfolios through 2009 in order to support the mortgage market, but then they were supposed to begin shrinking them to $250 billion. Freddie, in a separate meeting, agreed immediately. The Fannie contingent at first objected, but eventually realized they had no choice. A government takeover was not easily resisted, not even by Fannie Mae—especially since the government had done one last thing to ensure it would get its way. The GSEs immediately had to fire all their lobbyists, so there could be no running to their friends on the Hill. "Cutting off the head of the snake," people involved called it.

When Paulson was asked on CNBC about how much money the GSEs would really require, he said, "[W]e didn't sit there and figure this out with a calculator."

Paulson would later say that putting Fannie and Freddie in conservatorship was the thing he was most proud of in the crisis. "I knew with great certainty that we were not going to get through this thing without them," he said.

Paulson had also hoped that the takeover of the GSEs would help calm the growing storm. "I hoped that we'd bring the hammer down and it would be the cathartic act that we needed to get through this," he later said.

But it didn't work out that way. If anything, the takeover of Fannie and Freddie only further damaged investor confidence. "The U.S. government, with access to information no private investor could summon, had lured investors into a trap," Redleaf later complained. "Had the CEO of a private company gone about telling investors that his company had 'more than adequate capital' and was in a 'sound situation' knowing that the company might be in bankruptcy within weeks, he would have gone to jail for securities fraud."

The real problem was a little different. The government's information hadn't been that much better than anyone else's, and the government's optimism was as naive as everyone else's. And the scale of the losses was simply beyond anything that Paulson had imagined. The takeover of the GSEs shredded some of the last lingering bits of delusion about how bad things really were.

It started all over again on Monday, September 8. Just as Paulson had sensed, Lehman Brothers was the domino. The market that day rose 2.6 percent, but Lehman Brothers dropped $2.05, to $14.15. On Tuesday, the news broke that a last-ditch deal Fuld had been negotiating with the Korea Development Bank had broken off. The stock dropped again. John Thain, Paulson's old colleague at Goldman who had replaced Stan O'Neal as the CEO of Merrill Lynch, called. "Hank," he said, "I hope you're watching Lehman. If they go down, it won't be good for anybody." On Wednesday, Lehman preannounced its third-quarter results. It lost $3.9 billion, thanks to a $5.6 billion write-down on its real estate holdings.

That Thursday, September 11, John Gapper, the financial columnist for the *Financial Times*, wrote a column, only half tongue in cheek, with the headline "Take This Weekend Off, Hank." Noting Lehman Brothers' mounting troubles, and the likelihood of another long weekend for the Treasury secretary, he wrote, "[W]hen he has worked on weekends recently, the taxpayers have paid dearly."

Paulson, of course, did work that weekend. Lehman, Merrill, WaMu, AIG—the vultures were circling all of them. Late Friday afternoon, Paulson flew to New York and spent the weekend at the New York Fed, in nonstop meetings with Fed officials and Wall Street CEOs, and they tried to stop what they all saw coming. By Monday morning, Lehman Brothers, unable to find a buyer—or to persuade the government to save it—was bankrupt. Merrill Lynch had been bought by Bank of America. Right behind them came AIG, which would be rescued by the government a few days later at an initial cost of $85 billion.

There was nothing the government, or anyone else, could do to hold it back any longer. Some thirty years in the making, the financial crisis had finally arrived. The volcano had erupted.

Epilogue: Rage at the Machine

On July 21, 2010, President Obama signed into law the Wall Street Reform and Consumer Protection Act, a 2,300-page, 383,000-word piece of legislation that marked, unquestionably, the biggest change in the regulation of the financial industry since the aftermath of the Great Depression. The law had been two years in the making, and most of it, in one way or another, was a reaction to the excesses that had led to the financial crisis.

The Federal Reserve would get new powers to look broadly across the financial system. A council of federal regulators led by the Treasury secretary would help ferret out systemic risk. A new consumer agency was created to help end the lending abuses and keep people from getting loans they could never hope to pay back. Under this new law, most derivatives will supposedly be traded on an exchange—meaning in the clear light of day, where prices and profits are transparent. The bill creates a process to liquidate failing companies, so that there is a reasonable alternative to bailouts. It outlaws proprietary trading at financial institutions that accept insured deposits—the so-called Volcker Rule. "Because of this law, the American people will never again be asked to foot the bill for Wall Street's mistakes," President Obama said. Well, maybe.

Footing the bill for Wall Street's mistakes was precisely what the American taxpayer had been doing since September of 2008, in a hundred different ways. And Americans were angry about it. It wasn't just the obvious examples—like the $182 billion in federal help that AIG required before it was over. The Federal Reserve guaranteed money market funds. It bought tens of billions of dollars of "toxic assets"—that was the culture's shorthand for securitized subprime mortgages after the crisis—to help the banks get back on their feet. The FDIC, meanwhile, guaranteed all new debt issued by bank holding companies, without which they could not have funded themselves in the debt markets. Let's face it: they were all now government-sponsored enterprises. And so they would remain, despite protestations to the contrary. Because as everyone learned with Fannie and Freddie, implicit government guarantees, whether they arise from a congressional charter or from the market's belief that the government will stand behind a failing company, are awfully hard to take away.

It took a while after Lehman weekend for the panic to quell. It is easy to forget now, but Morgan Stanley and Goldman Sachs both found themselves caught in the contagion, and could well have gone under. Morgan was saved only when it managed, at the last moment, to make a deal with Mitsubishi UFJ, a big Japanese bank. Goldman, along with Morgan Stanley, was allowed to become a bank holding company, thus receiving a government imprimatur that Dick Fuld could never get for Lehman Brothers. Washington Mutual was sold in a fire sale to J.P. Morgan. Wachovia was on the verge of collapse when Wells Fargo bought it in December 2008. Citigroup needed multiple infusions of federal cash.

So long as there was that deep uncertainty of how big the black hole was—that paralyzing fear that nobody knew anymore what anything was worth—the crisis didn't abate. "The way I think about the crisis is that it occurred because of the systemic abuse of trust in capital markets," says Australian financial analyst and historian John Hempton. "The blowups of subprime, then of Bear Stearns, and then of Fannie exposed massive lies. Then we went from a collective belief in soundness to a collective belief in insolvency."

It took the absolute certainty that the United States government would use its financial might to prevent that insolvency to stanch the bleeding. That was Paulson's most famous act during the crisis: along with Bernanke, he pleaded with Congress to give Treasury $700 billion that he could use to shore up the system. The money was called the Troubled Asset Relief Program, or TARP. On October 13, his $700 billion in hand, Paulson met the CEOs of the eight biggest banks in a Treasury conference room. He told them that they would all be taking money from the government, like it or not. Although several came to regret taking it, none had the nerve to say no to Hank Paulson.

The passage of the TARP marked the first outpouring of populist fury. Despite all the apocalyptic talk that the financial system was at stake, you had to feel that in your gut to believe it, because the only way anyone could prove it would have been to not pass the bill and see if the financial system went under. It was hard to make the connection between a big bank in New York that traded credit derivatives and a family in Ohio that couldn't get a loan if that faraway bank went under. All people could really know for sure was that taxpayers' money was going to prop up the very firms whose greed and mistakes helped cause the crisis.

The anger didn't subside after the danger had passed. If anything, it grew stronger. It would build in waves, crest, and then take aim at a different target.

People raged at the Bank of America–Merrill Lynch deal—at the way John Thain had accelerated the payment of $3.6 billion in bonuses to Merrill traders days before the deal was completed; at the way Ken Lewis had averted his eyes; at the way Bernanke and Paulson had pushed and prodded and bludgeoned Lewis into completing the deal when the CEO got cold feet at the last minute. The deal almost certainly averted Merrill's bankruptcy. It didn't matter; people wanted blood. Congress held three hearings on the Bank of America–Merrill Lynch deal, mainly so that members of Congress could vent on behalf of their constituents.

By March, the fury had found a new outlet: AIG. In March 2009, the news broke that AIG-FP was going to pay $165 million in bonuses to its traders and executives. Although most of them had had nothing to do with the destruction, the payments became a huge scandal. The House wasted no time in passing a bill taxing all bonuses—at 90 cents on the dollar—for any household that made more than $250,000. Republicans and Democrats vied to outdo each other. "This is absolutely appalling," said Senate Minority Leader Mitch McConnell. "It's like taking the American people's hard-earned tax dollars and slapping them in the face with it," said Elijah Cummings, a Democratic congressman from Maryland. "There are a lot of terrible things that have happened in the last eighteen months, but what's happened at AIG is the most outrageous," said Larry Summers, who had become one of Obama's top economic advisers. AIG executives received death threats. Some even had to have private security guards stationed in front of their homes. The Connecticut Working Families Party held a bus tour of AIG executives' homes.

Finally, there was Goldman Sachs. As part of the AIG bailout, the New York Fed made the decision to pay AIG's counterparties in its multisector CDO business 100 cents on the dollar. In mid-March, a day after the AIG bonus news broke, AIG disclosed that Goldman Sachs had received

$12.9 billion, more than any other firm. Goldman had claimed all along that its exposure to AIG was hedged.* Didn't this show that Goldman was lying? "This needless cover-up is one reason Americans are getting angrier as they wonder if Washington is lying to them about these bailouts," opined the *Wall Street Journal* editorial page. Wasn't this proof that Hank Paulson had protected his old firm by steering billions in cash Goldman's way? And what about all those ex-Goldman guys in positions of power everywhere?

By the middle of the summer, Goldman Sachs was producing blowout profits, had repaid its $10 billion in TARP funds, and had already set aside $11.4 billion—a record sum—with which to pay bonuses to employees. And Goldman executives began to say that maybe they'd never needed any help anyway. Although Lloyd Blankfein in particular was careful to express gratitude to taxpayers, the bonuses sent a signal that Goldman considered itself somehow divorced from the actions that had led to the crisis, when, in fact, Goldman had been right there in the thick of it. It was maddening. They may have been smarter than everyone else, but they weren't better. Not anymore.

By the following spring, Goldman's arrogance had landed it a solo hearing in front of the Senate Permanent Subcommittee on Investigations, in which the firm was lambasted for the way it had duped clients and furthered the crisis. Thus it was that Goldman Sachs, a firm whose Manhattan headquarters bears no name, which has no storefronts anywhere in the country, and which has never sold its financial products directly to run-of-the-mill consumers, became the public's favorite villain.

At the heart of the anger was a powerful sense that something terribly unfair had taken place. The government had bailed out companies—companies whose loans and capital raising are supposed to help the country grow—that had turned out to be making gargantuan side bets that served no purpose other than lining their own pockets. Homeowners, whose mortgages had served as the raw material for those side bets, got no such help. "I'm not even against a bailout," says Prentiss Cox. "We had to do it. But

---

* The argument that Goldman was hedged on its exposure to AIG was technically true. By the time AIG was rescued, Goldman had already collected more than $10 billion in cash from its collateral calls—along with cash collateral it had received from the counterparties that had sold it credit default swaps on AIG itself. That amount essentially covered the decline in the value of the securities Goldman had hedged with AIG to date. But if AIG had gone bankrupt and the value of those securities had declined further, Goldman would no longer have had its hedge, and it's debatable whether its counterparties on the AIG credit default swaps could have paid.

regulators are always concerned that we don't send a message to future home-owners that they can get away with this. They should have made it clear to lenders that there are consequences. Instead, it's all the money to the lenders and all the shame to the homeowners."

People also felt that a great crime had been committed, yet there was not going to be a great punishment. Ralph Cioffi and Matt Tannin, the only two people so far to have been indicted as a result of the financial crisis, were acquitted. The government decided not to bring charges against Joe Cassano. The SEC has charged Countrywide's Angelo Mozilo, David Sambol, and Eric Sieracki civilly; that case is set to go to trial in the fall of 2010. And the SEC got a $550 million settlement with Goldman Sachs that many people felt let the firm off easy. But as the case involving Cioffi and Tannin shows, it is very hard to find the line between delusion, venality, and outright cor-ruption. Much of what took place during the crisis was immoral, unjust, craven, delusional behavior—but it wasn't criminal. The most clear-cut cases of corruption—the brokers who tricked people into bad mortgages, the Wall Street bankers who knowingly packaged bad mortgages—are in the shadows, cogs inside the wheels of firms like Ameriquest, New Century, Merrill Lynch, and Goldman Sachs. We'll probably never even learn most of those people's names.

What was the point of it all? In spring of 2007, even before the crisis hit, the Center for Responsible Lending published numbers showing that between 1998 and 2006 only about 1.4 million first-time home buyers purchased their homes using subprime loans. That represented about 9 percent of all sub-prime lending. The rest were refinancings or second home purchases. The Center also estimated that more than 2.4 million borrowers who'd gotten subprime loans would lose or already had lost their homes to foreclosure. By the second quarter of 2010, the homeownership rate had fallen to 66.9 per-cent, right where it had been before the housing bubble. Ever so swiftly, the wave of foreclosures in the aftermath of the crisis wiped out the increase in homeownership that had occurred over the past decade. In other words, subprime lending was a net drain on homeownership. A lot of needless pain was created in the process.

Financial innovation? Collateralized debt obligations? Synthetic securities? What had been the point of *that*? "The financial industry is central to our nation's ability to grow, to prosper, to compete, and to innovate," President Obama said when he signed the new legislation. During the bubble it had been nothing of the sort. As Paul Volcker said at a *Wall Street Journal* conference in late 2009, "I have found very little evidence that vast amounts of innovation in financial markets in recent years have had a visible effect on the productivity of the economy."

The new law can't and won't fix the unfairness. Nor will it bestow on Wall Street a sense of moral purpose. It can't. The best it can do is protect against the worst of the abuses that took place during the bubble. It is difficult to know whether it will do even that. It is all well and good to have a systemic risk regulator, to cite one important example, but will that agency or person actually know how to look for systemic risk? It was often said in the aftermath of the crisis that agencies like the Fed and the SEC and the OCC had plenty of tools to curb the abuses that were taking place in the banking system. They just lacked the will. And that was true. These new regulations will also only be as good as the regulators themselves.

Perhaps the most glaring omission in the new law was any mention of Fannie Mae and Freddie Mac. With everything that happened in the two years since the crisis, neither the administration nor Congress has done anything to change the status of Fannie Mae and Freddie Mac. Right now, at least, they don't dare: by 2010, Fannie and Freddie (along with the Federal Housing Administration) were backing more than 95 percent of mortgages. Right now, you simply cannot buy a house in America without a government stamp of approval. Once upon a time, the private market wanted nothing so much as to marginalize the GSEs. Today, it's the private market that has been marginalized, afraid to make a loan that the government doesn't guarantee.

Fannie and Freddie have continued to lose money—the government has put $150 billion into them to keep them solvent on an accounting basis. (It is worth noting, though, that most of this doesn't yet represent actual cash losses on mortgages. The real number could be much bigger or smaller depending on where home prices go.) They have continued to be controversial. The same people who were GSE haters back when they were at the peak of their power now claim that Fannie and Freddie caused the crisis—by leading the charge into subprime mortgages to meet their housing goals. This is completely upside down; Fannie and Freddie raced to get into subprime mortgages because they feared being left behind by their nongovernment competitors. But never mind. They remain in a kind of limbo state, wards of the government, while underpinning a housing market that still can't function without them.

The reason that the legislation makes no mention of the GSEs is that nobody can figure out what to do. Can we ever have a truly private sector market for mortgage securitization, or will it always require the government? Can Fannie's and Freddie's roles eventually grow smaller as the financial system regains its confidence? Can they be privatized? Abolished? Turned into government agencies? None of these answers satisfy. In the spring, the Treasury Department requested public input on the reengineering of the mortgage system and the reform of the GSEs. In response, Treasury got more than 570 comment letters. There is no consensus.

All those years ago, Lew Ranieri captured the essence of today's debate when he asked, at the very dawn of mortgage-backed securities, "What should the government do? What should it be allowed to win at?" When the government held an invitation-only conference on the future of housing finance in the late summer of 2010, Lew Ranieri was asked to participate. He—and we—have had three decades to watch the mortgage market evolve in ways that turned out to be terribly destructive. Maybe, thirty-plus years after the creation of mortgage-backed securities, we can get it right this time.

AFTERWORD

It's easy to see, looking back, that the financial crisis was a bipartisan affair. Republicans pushed to keep derivatives unregulated—but so did Democrats like Larry Summers and Robert Rubin. Democrats gave Fannie Mae and Freddie Mac unwavering support—and, with rare exception, so did Republicans. And everyone, on both sides of the aisle, touted the unquestioned virtues of home ownership—the blind acceptance of which provided cover for the excesses and predations of the subprime lending industry, whose products were at the very heart of the crisis. This powerful political alignment helped shut out skeptical voices and pushed back against those who tried to stop the madness.

Not surprisingly, this consensus broke down in the aftermath of the crisis. After all, there was all that blame that needed to be apportioned! Democrats quickly blamed Republicans for the ethos of deregulation that helped bring about the crisis—and for supporting efforts by Wall Street and the banks to weaken what rules existed. Republicans blamed Democrats for, among other sins, failing to rein in Fannie and Freddie and supporting its "misguided" mission to help lower income people buy homes. (They seemed to have forgotten their own role in that regard.) In effect, the Democrats blamed business for the crisis; Republicans blamed government.

By January 2011, outright war had broken out. Having won a landslide victory in the November midterm elections, Republicans had taken control of the House, and, though still in the minority in the Senate, had gained seats there as well. With this shift in power, there were all kinds of new battlegrounds—over the budget, for instance, and the new health care that the Democrats had passed during President Obama's first two years in office. But the financial reform bill that had become law just six months earlier—the Dodd-Frank bill—was another key area where the battle between Democrats and Republicans was joined. In passing the bill originally, the Democrats had said that its provisions would prevent another financial crisis from ever happening again. Newly empowered, the Republicans said that it was simply another example of government overreach—and that most, if not all, of the bill was not only unnecessary but counterproductive. On the Web site of the of the House Financial Services Committee—which had been chaired by Barney Frank, coauthor of Dodd-Frank, before the midterm elections, and was now chaired by Spencer Baucus, a ten-term Republican from Alabama—the headline blared, COLLATERAL DAMAGE: THE REAL IMPACT OF THE DEMOCRATS' BAILOUT BILL. Subtle it was not.

As it turns out, the language of the new law was surprisingly vague; it was more a set of guidelines for regulators, who were then charged with filling in the details—details that would be critical in determining whether Dodd-Frank would have teeth. Yes, the Volcker Rule was supposed to prevent banks from trading for their own proprietary accounts. But it was left to the regulators to decide what constituted proprietary trading. Yes, Dodd-Frank called for plain vanilla derivatives to be traded on an open exchange, where all the market participants could finally see their prices. But the CFTC was given the task of defining which derivatives were plain vanilla and which were not. The bill called for mortgage originators to hold onto a sliver of all but the safest mortgages—in order to share in the risk of the mortgages it was securitizing—but the regulators were the ones who were supposed to come up with the definition of the so-called Qualified Residential Mortgages.

Dodd-Frank had a hundred different provisions like that. And it was precisely the vagueness of the law that gave the Republicans—and the banks themselves—their opening. Congressional committees threatened to withhold funding, for instance, to prevent the CFTC from carrying out its mandate to regulate derivatives, while Jamie Dimon, the CEO of JP Morgan—and the most vocal bank executive pushing back against the new regulations—complained that people simply didn't understand: derivatives, he said at one high-profile Chamber of Commerce event, hadn't really been one of the reasons for the crisis. Fierce battles were fought over what constituted a safe mortgage. (To its credit, the Treasury was insisting on 20 percent down payments, among other things.)

Even where the law wasn't vague, there were pitched battles. One of the fiercest was being fought over the new Consumer Financial Protection Bureau, which was set to go into business in the summer of 2011. Shortly after Dodd-Frank was signed into law, President Obama named Elizabeth Warren to an odd dual position—she became a special adviser to the White House as well as an official at the Treasury Department. Her real job, however, was to set up the new bureau, which she liked to describe as the kind of "cop on the beat" that might have prevented some of the abuses of the subprime lenders. A long-time Harvard Law professor, Warren specialized in consumer finance issues; she had invented the phrase "tricks and traps" to describe how credit card issuers gulled consumers into paying hidden fees and high interest rates. She had also come up with the idea for the bureau in the first place. But Obama had been unwilling to name her to become the bureau's first director. (As of the spring of 2011, he still hadn't named a director for the new bureau.) Loathed by the banking industry, Warren had become one of the chief targets of the Republicans, who vowed to block her nomination should the president pick her. None were more vehement than Senator Richard Shelby of Alabama, perhaps the most respected Republican on the Senate Banking Committee. Even without the actual nomination, however, as the person setting up the bureau, she had a bull's-eye on her back, and was regularly hauled before the House Financial Service Committee, where she was duly boxed about the ears.

Though the central argument against Dodd-Frank—that it unnecessarily burdened Wall Street with onerous regulations—was easy enough to shoot down, the bill was far from the panacea that the Democrats made it out to be. For starters, it reinforced one of the biggest problems leading to the crisis: Too Big to Fail. With the merger of Washington Mutual and Bear Stearns into JP Morgan, the merger of Wachovia into Wells Fargo, the merger of Merrill Lynch into Bank of America, and the failure of Lehman Brothers, the banks that remained were actually bigger—and their failure would be even more catastrophic than it would have been in 2008. Although Dodd-Frank had a new "liquidation authority," which was supposed to prevent future taxpayer-funded bailouts by giving the government the power to step in and wind down a failing firm, how that authority was used would involve political decisions. And once political calculus factors into what should be a purely market-based decision, all bets are off. Or as none other than Alan Greenspan put it in paper he authored in early 2011, "It will be exceedingly difficult to contain the range of possible [government]activism."

There were other aspects of the reforms that deserved legitimate debate—as opposed to partisan point-scoring. There is, after all, a trade-off to every new rule. If you protect consumers from getting credit that they can't afford, then some people who would have been able to get credit in the past won't be able to do so now. If you require banks to hold a great deal more capital, then banks will be safer, but less profitable than they were in the past. And some skepticism about the efficacy of rules and regulations is often justified. In the end, as was demonstrated by the Federal Reserve's failure to take action on subprime lending during the bubble, it's not the rules that matter, but the regulators' willingness to enforce those rules.

Still, it could seem almost surreal at times, a little like that infamous season of the old soap opera Dallas that turned out to be nothing but a dream by one of the lead characters. Didn't the financial crisis make it clear that we had to have a real debate about how best to regulate the financial system? But that wasn't what was happening. Instead, the banks and their political allies seemed to want to pretend that the crisis hadn't ever happened at all. When the Financial Crisis Inquiry Commission—charged with explaining to the country the reasons the crisis happened—finally released its report, the Republican members produced their own narrative that basically boiled down to, "shit happens." And hey, it was just a blip anyway. All the big banks had repaid the TARP money that Hank Paulson had forced them to take during that dramatic meeting in October 2008. Indeed, they'd returned it with interest, allowing Treasury to claim that the much-maligned program had turned a profit for taxpayers. Thanks in large part to continued support from the Federal Reserve—primarily extremely low interest rates that benefitted bank trading departments—the big banks had quickly returned to profitability. Even the two banks that had been the most badly hurt during the crisis, Bank of America and Citigroup, were making money again. Multimillion dollar bonuses were the norm again. Lloyd Blankfein got a pay package of nearly $10 million for 2010, after taking no bonuses the previous two years. Dimon, who was paid $20 million in 2010, began saying publicly that Americans needed to get over their anger at the banks. It was, he said, undeserved in any case.

And so in Basel, Switzerland, bank regulators attempted to come up with new, tougher capital requirements—the kind of capital requirements that would have prevented the banks from needing bailouts in 2008. The banks pushed back. The OCC had very quickly returned to its old ways, treating the banks it was supposed to supervise as clients to be coddled rather than as financial institutions to be overseen. (Only the FDIC remained skeptical of the banking industry, which resulted in its chairwoman, Sheila Bair, becoming an outcast among the other bank regulators and Treasury officials.) With the exception of AIG, which was still struggling to get out of the enormous hole it had dug for itself, there was no evidence that any of the institutions felt the slightest bit of remorse or any need for increased supervision or regulation. As for prosecutions, it was becoming increasingly clear that there weren't going to be any. On the eve of his civil trial, Angelo Mozilo settled with the SEC for $67.5 million, most of which was paid by Countrywide's owner, Bank of America. A few months later, the Justice Department decided not to prosecute him, concluding that he hadn't broken any laws. Rumor had it that the Justice Department wasn't going to prosecute Dick Fuld either. Same reason.

There were, of course, places where the reality of the financial crisis was still palpable—places where you knew instantly it hadn't all been a dream. But they weren't in the bank boardrooms or on Wall Street. As usual, they were on Main Street. Those same, mostly poor neighborhoods where the predatory practices of the subprime companies had been most prevalent: that's where you could see it. Just as homeowners in those neighborhoods had been the ones most taken advantage of during the bubble, they were now the ones paying the price in its aftermath. And a very heavy price it was. In places like Jamaica, New York, you could see boarded-up houses on every street, the result of the wave of foreclosures that had swept the neighborhood in the years after the bubble burst. "The rest of the country will come back in a decade or less," said a lawyer named Elizabeth Lynch, who worked to get banks to agree to mortgage modifications. "These neighborhoods won't come back for decades."

It was hard to disagree. As the banks realized that the Republicans and even the Obama administration weren't going to take a hard line, they became ever more unapologetic. The government efforts at persuading the servicing industry to extend mortgage modifications had been pitiful—an abject failure. Homeowners who tried to remain in their homes often got the runaround from the banks and the servicers (who were usually owned by the big banks), leading to months and sometimes years of frustration—and still ended up in foreclosure. Terrible, tragic mistakes were made. Eventually, the foreclosure mess blossomed into its own scandal, as it turned out the servicers were taking shortcuts that were—to put it bluntly—illegal. In what was almost a replay of the their efforts to crack down on predatory lending during the bubble, it was the states' attorneys general who undertook an investigation into the servicing industry that was far more aggressive than anything the federal government did. The only government official who got involved was Elizabeth Warren—for which of course she was castigated by the Republicans. As we went to press, it seemed possible that the investigation might at last lead to some overdue reform. But it was too early to know how strong they would be, and whether they would truly make a difference. Or whether they would happen at all.

Ironically enough, there was one place, just one, where Democrats and Republicans found an odd sort of unity, although neither party would ever put it that way. That was on the subject of Fannie Mae and Freddie Mac, the GSEs. Nearly four years after the crisis began in earnest, with the collapse of Bear Stearns hedge funds in the summer of 2007, there was no real reform of the GSEs on the table. True, Tim Geithner's Treasury Department and the Department of Housing and Urban Development put out a report in early 2011 that talked about shutting down the GSEs, which the Republicans had been agitating for ever since the crisis began. House Republicans, meanwhile, passed no fewer than eight bills that purportedly reformed the GSEs. But in truth, the most any of it did was tinker at the edges.

The problem was that in the wake of the crisis, Fannie Mae and Freddie Mac had become, almost unbelievably, even more important to the housing market than they had been in their heyday. Indeed, they *were* the housing market; it was nearly impossible to get a mortgage without a guarantee from Fannie, Freddie, or the FHA. The private label securitization market remained dormant. Investors were unwilling to buy even the most conservative of mortgage loans unless the government agreed to take on the credit risk. Fannie Mae and Freddie Mac remained in business in no small part because without them, there was a high likelihood that the housing market would collapse completely.

In truth, this should not have been all that surprising. Even before the crisis, the Fannie and Freddie imprimatur had been extremely important to investors; that is why they had been so dominant in the non-subprime market. It turns out that the kind of investors who bought conforming mortgages never wanted the credit risk. It's just that nobody had ever really seen that clearly until the crisis.

There was another reason it wasn't surprising. It was going to take just about every participant in the mortgage market—originators, lenders, and investors alike—a long time to regain any appetite for mortgage risk. In this one way, at least, they had not turned back the clock: they had been scarred by mistakes they had made and the losses they had taken. It was hard to know when they might be willing to take on some risk again, but it wasn't going to be anytime soon.

The biggest reason that it shouldn't have been surprising, though, is that in truth, no one knew how to envision a housing market without government support. The government had supported housing for decades. Government support had made possible things Americans viewed as their birthright, such as the thirty-year fixed rate mortgage. Creating a true private market was likely to mean higher interest rates, different kinds of mortgages that were less risky and more profitable to investors, perhaps even the end of the thirty-year mortgage. Nobody seemed to be talking about those potential consequences. What was missing is the same thing that had been missing during Fannie and Freddie's heyday: an honest discussion of what the country's housing policy should be, and how the purchase of a house—still the largest and most important purchase most Americans will ever make—should be financed.

No matter what reforms were ultimately enacted, or how stiffly they were enforced, there was no question that one day, a new bubble would arise, bringing with it, eventually, a new financial catastrophe. Bubbles were part of the human condition, a product of mass psychology. They have always been with us, and always will. In the 1970s, people believed that the price of oil could only go up—a belief that led to disastrous consequences that required a bailout of Continental Illinois, one of the biggest banks in the country. In the 1990s, they believed that Internet companies make investors rich, despite lacking profits and in many cases revenue. In that sense, perhaps, shit did happen.

The question facing the regulators and the legislators, though, was how long they could keep it from happening. That, at least, was in their control. In the aftermath of the Great Depression, the government established reforms, such as the creation of the SEC and the passage of the Glass-Steagall Act, that were so serious and far-reaching that they helped keep the next financial crisis at bay for many decades. It was, in retrospect, a regulatory triumph—about the best result anyone could hope for. At this moment, in the spring of 2011, it is simply impossible to know whether Dodd-Frank, with its multitude of unfinished regulations, will be as far-reaching or have as salutary an effect on the country.

One can only hope.

ACKNOWLEDGMENTS

First, a note on sourcing: In the course of researching this book, we spoke to several hundred people, including former and current Wall Street executives—from CEOs to risk managers in the trenches—as well as bankers, former and current employees of AIG, Fannie Mae and Freddie Mac, rating agency employees, executives at mortgage companies, loan officers, appraisers and fraud investigators, community activists, legislators, lobbyists, academics, and former and current officials at Treasury, the FDIC, the OCC, the OTS, and the Federal Reserve. Where possible, we have acknowledged our sources in the text of the book. But given the sensitivity, not to mention the ongoing investigations and lawsuits, the majority of people we spoke with did not want their names used. We are grateful for both their time and honesty, and for readers' understanding.

We were also fortunate to be able to draw on the mountains (literally) of fine newspaper stories, magazine articles, books, and academic papers on subjects related to the financial crisis. We owe a particular debt to reporters who wrote about the problems in the subprime world before they were revealed by the financial crisis; one article that stands out is the exposé of Ameriquest published in the *Los Angeles Times* in 2005. In the text, we've cited articles from which we drew specific facts and incidents. More broadly, in writing about the three decades of financial change documented in this book, we relied on the great contemporaneous work by the *New York Times*, the *Wall Street Journal*, the *Washington Post*, and the *American Banker*, which we found particularly helpful in its in-depth coverage of regulatory skirmishes over capital requirements, as well as the political infighting that affected the financial industry during years when most people weren't paying attention to such things.

There have been, of course, numerous books written about the financial crisis since the fall of Bear Stearns in the spring of 2008. We've cited a number of them in the text, but we would be remiss if we did not single out a handful that were particularly helpful to us. They include Gillian Tett's *Fool's*

Gold, an account of the creation of credit default swaps; *Liar's Poker*, Michael Lewis's rollicking tale of Lew Ranieri and the rise of mortgage-backed securities; *The Partnership*, Charles Ellis's history of Goldman Sachs; *The Greatest Trade Ever*, by Gregory Zuckerman, about John Paulson's audacious decision to short the housing market; *Panic*, by Andrew Redleaf and Richard Vigilante, which persuasively argues that efficient market theory was at the root of the crisis; and *Chain of Blame*, by Paul Muolo and Mathew Padilla, a great source of insight about the birth and inner workings of the subprime mortgage machine. Janet Tavakoli's *Dear Mr. Buffett* is a scathing exposé of the seamy underbelly of the derivatives and CDO businesses. Memoirs we relied on include *The Age of Turbulence*, by Alan Greenspan (and Peter Petre), *In an Uncertain World*, by Robert Rubin (and Jacob Weisberg), *The Rise and Fall of Bear Stearns*, by Alan "Ace" Greenberg (and Mark Singer), and most especially *On the Brink*, by Henry Paulson, a fount of insight about what key players were doing and thinking during key moments of 2007 and 2008.

We also drew heavily from the work that Congress has done in untangling the financial crisis. In particular, we relied on testimony that has been elicited, and documents unearthed, by the Senate Permanent Subcommittee on Investigations, the Financial Crisis Inquiry Commission, and the Congressional Oversight Panel.

There are a handful of people we returned to again and again for insight. In particular, we owe a debt to Jason Thomas, John Hempton, and Andrew Feldstein, who were too gracious to call our questions dumb, even when they were. There is a long list of other people who can't be named to whom we also owe our gratitude. They know who they are. Thank you.

We owe a huge debt to our good friend and agent Liz Darhansoff, who (once again!) talked us off the ledge more times than we can count. Ditto to our good friend and editor Adrian Zackheim, who, at several key points along the way, deftly pointed us in the right direction when we were getting lost in the thicket. At Portfolio we would also like to thank Will Weisser, Allison McLean, Jeff Miller, Alex Gigante, and especially Emily Angell and Courtney Young, who went above and beyond in getting us from sprawling manuscript to published book. In the early stages of our research, we were aided by our old friend Maggie Boitano. In the latter stages, we were ably assisted by two newer friends, Dan Slater and Zachery Kouwe, who chased down people, facts, and documents, often at the last minute.

Since there are two of us, we have two separate groups of friends and colleagues who helped us get through life as we were getting through this book. We would like to thank them now. Bethany first:

I'd like to thank *Vanity Fair*—in particular, Graydon Carter and Doug Stumpf—who have given me the freedom to explore the financial crisis and to take the time to write this book. I'd also like to thank *Fortune*, my longtime home, for teaching me the ropes of business journalism and allowing me to take months to write in-depth stories about, among other subjects, Fannie Mae. In addition, a special thanks to Ken Scigulinsky and Joe Ferrara, who served as unpaid research assistants and sources of ideas, debate, and inspiration.

On a personal note, I wouldn't have survived the process of reporting and writing this book without the love and support—and great sense of humor—of my wonderful husband, Sean Berkowitz. I also owe a big thanks to my circle of extended family and friends who have put up with my general grumpiness and lack of time during this project. In particular, my love and gratitude go to my mother-in-law, Naomi Berkowitz, who has made sure that Laine was fed, clothed, and diapered while I panicked at my computer, and to Lyle and Dana Berkowitz. Thanks also to Bob and Karen Ranquist, the team at Ranquist Development, and Jennifer Lissner for friendship, professionalism well beyond the ordinary, and a marvelous place to live and work. I'd also like to thank Karen Muirhead, Indira Jusic Zisko, and Sara Rodriguez for the loving care they've provided my daughter, and the peace of mind they've provided me. Of course, a thank-you to Laine for being as accommodating as an infant can be. My parents, Robert and Helaine McLean, and my sister, Claire McLean, have always helped me keep book writing in perspective. I would be lost without Steve Baerson's encyclopedic knowledge of history and extraordinary bookkeeping skills. And a final thank-you to my beloved Beast, who has now weathered two books and the corresponding loss of Frisbee time with as much grace as a bulldog can muster.

Joe's thank-you's:

The *New York Times* has been a wonderful home for me these last five years. Winnie O'Kelley took me aside not long before the crisis erupted in 2008 and told me in no uncertain terms that I would be well served to start focusing my column on the mounting problems on Wall Street. That was great advice, to say the least. Larry Ingrassia, my boss in the business section, involved me in several big projects in the immediate aftermath of the crisis that whetted my appetite for writing this book. He, along with executive editor Bill Keller and Gerry Marzorati, who until recently edited the *New York*

Times Magazine, were extremely generous in granting me the extended leave that allowed me to write this book. Gerry also assigned me a story on risk management for the magazine; that story became the basis for Chapter 4. Vera Titunik edited that story beautifully, as she always does. My colleagues Louise Story and Eric Dash helped me in numerous ways. Andrew Ross Sorkin was especially generous with insight and advice, especially once he'd finished *his* book about the financial crisis, *Too Big to Fail.*

Books consume writers; inevitably, that obsession winds up roping in their friends and families. Among the friends I'd like to thank are Steve Klein, Ken Auletta and Amanda Urban, Sam Waksal and Andrea Rabney, Bill Burd and Jane Noble, Charlie Borgognoni, Adam Bryant, Tim and Jennifer Smith, Paul and Jennifer Argenti, Greg Frank and Lauren Foster, Jimmy Smyth, Meg Rhodus, Roger and Claudine Parloff, Dan and Becky Okrent, and David and Lyn Grogan.

My three older children, Kate, Amato, and Nick, watched with bemusement and a touch of pride as I worked to complete the book; they've seen this act before. My future mother-in-law, Louise Schneider, arrived in the nick of time, just as Bethany and I were racing to the finish line, and offered a great deal of help and comfort.

As I was beginning to write this book, I acquired a puppy, a German shepherd named Lanka. I was always surprised and happy at the way he could lift my spirits, offering stretches of simple pleasure. About a month before this book was finished, a new member of the family arrived: Macklin Joseph. Baby Mack is a wonder, and a source of immense joy. I can't wait to dedicate my next book to him.

As for this book, it is dedicated to Dawn, the love of my life, who saw me through this project, as she has seen me through every part of our life together these past years. She makes it all worthwhile.

INDEX

Also by Bethany McLean

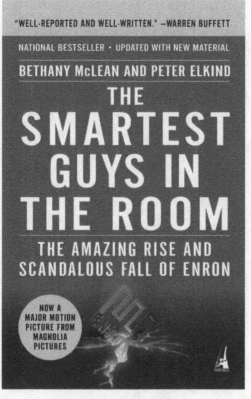

ISBN: 9781591840534
U.S. $16.00 / $17.50 CAN.

Portfolio / Penguin
A member of Penguin Group (USA) Inc.
www.penguin.com

Also by Joe Nocera

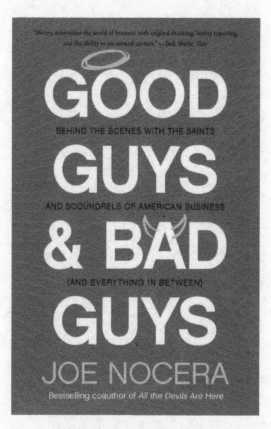

ISBN: 9781591844396
U.S. $16.00 / $18.50 CAN.

Portfolio / Penguin
A member of Penguin Group (USA) Inc.
www.penguin.com

HB 03.12.2024 0812